CW00434748

FOXPRO 2.5 FOR DOS
MADE EASY

FOXPRO 2.5 FOR DOS MADE EASY

Edward Jones

Osborne **McGraw-Hill**

Berkeley New York St. Louis San Francisco
Auckland Bogotá Hamburg London Madrid
Mexico City Milan Montreal New Delhi Panama City
Paris São Paulo Singapore Sydney
Tokyo Toronto

Osborne **McGraw-Hill**
2600 Tenth Street
Berkeley, California 94710
U.S.A.

For information on translations or book distributors outside of the
U.S.A., please write to Osborne **McGraw-Hill** at the above address.

FoxPro 2.5 for DOS Made Easy

Copyright © 1993 by McGraw-Hill. All rights reserved. Printed in the
United States of America. Except as permitted under the Copyright Act
of 1976, no part of this publication may be reproduced or distributed in
any form or by any means, or stored in a database or retrieval system,
without the prior written permission of the publisher, with the
exception that the program listings may be entered, stored, and
executed in a computer system, but they may not be reproduced for
publication.

1234567890 DOC 99876543

ISBN 0-07-881897-4

Acquisition Editor
Elizabeth Fisher

Associate Editor
Scott Rogers

Technical Editor
Denise Martineau

Project Editor
Edith Rex

Copy Editor
Jane Paulsen

Proofreaders
Jeff Barash
Kayla Sussell

Indexer
Phil Roberts
Peggy Bieber-Roberts

Computer Designer
Marcela Hancik

Illustrator
Susie C. Kim

Cover Designer
Compass Marketing

Information has been obtained by Osborne **McGraw-Hill** from sources believed to be reliable. However, because of the
possibility of human or mechanical error by our sources, Osborne **McGraw-Hill**, or others, Osborne **McGraw-Hill**
does not guarantee the accuracy, adequacy, or completeness of any information and is not responsible for any errors or
omissions or the results obtained from use of such information.

FOXPRO

CONTENTS AT A GLANCE

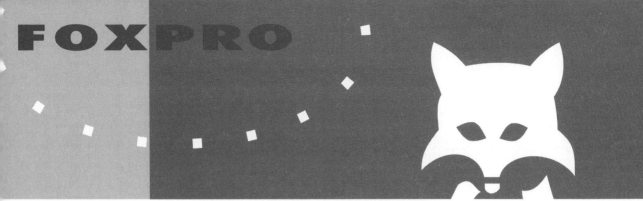

CONTENTS

FOXPRO

INTRODUCTION

FoxPro for DOS is, technically, a "relational database manager." However, that term doesn't tell the full story regarding what FoxPro has to offer. FoxPro provides speed, compatibility with dBASE IV and with FoxPro for Windows, and an outstanding environment for the development of business applications. Multiple windows, pull-down menus, mouse support, and more are all here within FoxPro for DOS.

NOTE: Throughout this book, the term "FoxPro" will be used as a shorthand for "FoxPro for DOS." It does not refer to the program's cousin, FoxPro for Windows.

About This Book

This book is designed to present the features of FoxPro in an easy-to-learn format. At the same time, "easy-to-learn" does not mean that you will be shortchanged in terms of depth; this book delves well into the more advanced uses of FoxPro, detailing programming techniques and concepts you'll need for effective development of your business applications. Most exercises throughout this book are presented in a step-by-step tutorial format, so you can follow along with your copy of FoxPro.

xix

How This Book Is Organized

This book is divided into 18 chapters. The first two-thirds of the book cover the use of FoxPro in building databases, performing queries and generating reports, and working with multiple files. The last third of the book primarily covers the topic of programming in FoxPro, providing skills that will be necessary in building complete applications.

Chapter 1 gets you started with the software. It explains the concepts of relational databases; illustrates how you will use FoxPro; and provides instructions for installing FoxPro, using the keyboard and (optional) mouse, choosing menu selections, and entering FoxPro commands. In Chapter 2, you begin creating databases, entering data, and using various FoxPro options and commands to get information from a database.

Chapter 3 provides details on changing databases. In this chapter, you'll learn how to edit records, how to make effective use of the Browse mode, how to delete unwanted records, and how to change the structure (or overall design) of a database. Chapter 4 provides details on how to sort or index a database to place records in any order you desire.

Chapter 5 covers the important area of performing queries. In a nutshell, you'll learn how to get the precise data you want out of a database. Chapter 6 shows how users of FoxPro can also use the RQBE window to quickly design sophisticated queries. And Chapter 7 introduces the topic of reports. You'll learn how to produce customized reports with the Report Generator built into FoxPro. And you will also learn to use various commands for creating quick listings of data with a minimum of hassle.

Chapter 8 covers file operations, such as copying, erasing, and renaming files. Here, you'll learn to use the Filer feature of FoxPro to easily perform file operations. In Chapter 9, you'll learn to use the macro features of FoxPro to automate often-used tasks.

Chapter 10 builds on the topics introduced in Chapter 7 by covering advanced reporting needs. In Chapter 10, you'll learn how the Report Generator can be used for more varied reporting tasks, such as form letters and invoices. You will also learn how to create and modify mailing labels and how various parts of commands (called expressions) can enhance the flexibility of the reports that you create. Chapter 11 provides coverage of the relational capabilities of FoxPro. Here, you'll learn to manage multiple files simultaneously and how to produce reports based on more than one database file at a time.

Chapter 12 details the use of FoxPro's ability to create complete applications, using the FoxPro Applications Generator. With the Applications Generator, you can create moderately complex applications to manage a database and produce reports without writing any program code.

Chapter 13 starts off the portion of the book on programming with FoxPro. In Chapter 13, you'll learn to create command files (or programs) to perform tasks in FoxPro. You will also learn how functions, variables, expressions, and operators can be used within a FoxPro program. Chapters 14 through 17 build on this programming knowledge by covering various aspects of programming in detail. In Chapter 14, you will become familiar with various commands that control the flow of execution inside a FoxPro program. Chapter 15 covers how programs can be written specifically for data entry and editing needs. Chapter 16 examines the specifics of programming for data retrieval, or the generation of reports. And Chapter 17 covers an assortment of advanced programming topics you will find useful when designing your own applications.

Chapter 18 provides tips on using FoxPro with other popular software packages, including Lotus 1-2-3 and WordPerfect. And the appendixes provide a detailed listing of FoxPro commands and functions and a list of dBASE IV commands that are not compatible with FoxPro.

Conventions Used In This Book

Throughout this book, you will be instructed to enter various commands. Each of these entries will either appear in boldface or be visually set apart from the text. Menu selections you should make will be detailed within the text in a step-by-step format.

CHAPTER

FOXPRO

1

GETTING STARTED WITH FOXPRO

Welcome to FoxPro, a high-powered relational database manager for the IBM PC and compatibles. You can use FoxPro to create database files that contain the necessary categories (fields) for your data. And you can display information in a format that best meets your needs with the custom form and report capabilities built into FoxPro. FoxPro displays information in a tabular format (known as Browse mode) or in a screen format (known as Edit or Change mode). The commonly used Browse mode is shown in the example in Figure 1-1.

NOTE: Throughout this book, the term "FoxPro" will be used as a shorthand for "FoxPro for DOS." It does not refer to the program's cousin, FoxPro for Windows.

Creating a database to store your data is a straightforward process. After choosing the New option from the File menu, you define the names and types of fields you will use. Seven different data types can be used in FoxPro: character (combinations of alpha and numeric characters), numeric, floating, date, logical (true or false), memo (which contain characters in varying lengths), and general, which can be used (under the control of a FoxPro program) to store other types of data, such as binary data files. Figure 1-2 shows the process of creating a database in FoxPro.

Once you have created a database, you can enter data by using on-screen forms that resemble the paper forms used in an office. You

System	File	Edit	Database	Record	Program	Window	Ru...	rowse

MEMBERS

Social	Lastname	Firstname	Address	City
123-44-8976	Miller	Karen	4260 Park Avenue	Chevy
121-33-9876	Martin	William	4807 East Avenue	Silve
232-55-1234	Robinson	Carol	4102 Valley Lane	Falls
901-77-3456	Kramer	Harry	617 North Oakland Street	Arlin
121-90-5432	Moore	Ellen	270 Browning Ave #2A	Takom
495-00-3456	Zachman	David	1617 Arlington Blvd.	Falls
343-55-9821	Robinson	Benjamin	1607 21st Street, NW	Washi
876-54-3210	Hart	Wendy	6200 Germantown Road	Fairf

browse last

FoxPro in use
(Browse mode)
Figure 1-1.

1

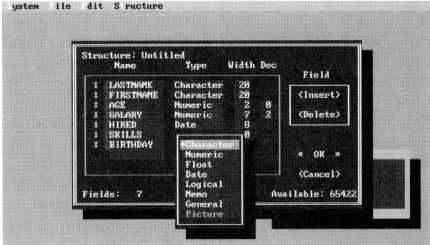

can also design custom forms with fields at locations you desire, along with borders or descriptive text.

To get more detailed information from your FoxPro databases, you will want to build detailed reports. For maximum flexibility in reporting, you can use the powerful Report Generator built into FoxPro to design custom reports in either a columnar or a freeform format. The Report Generator has a Quick Report option that lets you quickly design and produce a report.

If you are an advanced user, you will find that FoxPro has the power to match your complex database management needs. Using the relational capabilities of FoxPro, you can draw complex relationships between multiple database files. You can make use of macros, which are automated actions that FoxPro carries out as if individual commands had been entered at the keyboard. You can also write programs that perform complex tasks, using the command language that is an integral part of FoxPro. If you have existing programs written for dBASE III, dBASE III PLUS, or dBASE IV, you can use these programs with FoxPro. FoxPro is command compatible with dBASE IV.

What Is a Database?

Although *database management* is a computer term, it can also apply to the ways in which information is catalogued, stored, and used. At the center of any information management system is a database. Any collection of related information grouped together as a single item, as in Figure 1-3, is a *database*. Metal filing cabinets with customer records, a card file of names and phone numbers, and a notebook with a penciled listing of a store inventory are all databases. However, a file cabinet or a notebook does not make a database; the way information is organized makes it a database. Objects like cabinets and notebooks only aid in organizing information, and FoxPro is one such aid to organizing information.

Information in a database is usually organized and stored in the form of tables, with rows and columns in each table. As an example, in the mailing list shown in Figure 1-3, each row contains a name, an address, a phone number, and a customer number. Each row is related to the others because they all contain the same types of information. And because the mailing list is a collection of information arranged in a specific order—a column of names, a column of addresses, a column of customer numbers—it is a table. One or more tables containing information arranged in an organized manner is a database, as you saw in Figure 1-3. The multiple tables used to manage your data within FoxPro are also referred to as *database files*.

Rows in a table are called *records,* and columns are called *fields*. Figure 1-4 illustrates this idea with a comparison of a simple one-table database to an address filing system kept on 3x5 file cards. Each card in the box is a single record, and each category of information on a card is

Name	Address	City	State	Zip	Phone No.	Cust. No.
J. Billings	2323 State St.	Bertram	CA	91113	234-8980	0005
R. Foster	Rt. 1 Box 52	Frink	CA	93336	245-4312	0001
L. Miller	P.O. Box 345	Dagget	CA	94567	484-9966	0002
B. O'Neill	21 Way St. #C	Hotlum	CA	92346	555-1032	0004
C. Roberts	1914 19th St.	Bodie	CA	97665	525-4494	0006

A simple database

Figure 1-3.

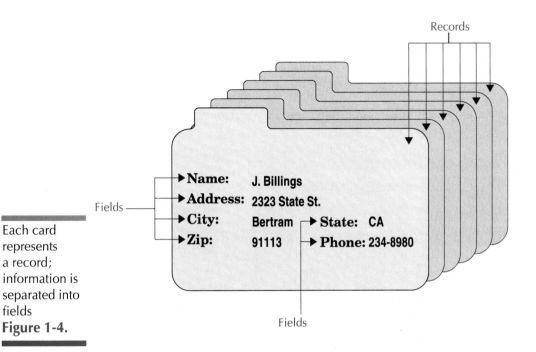

Records

Fields

Name: J. Billings
Address: 2323 State St.
City: Bertram → **State:** CA
Zip: 91113 → **Phone:** 234-8980

Fields

Each card
represents
a record;
information is
separated into
fields
Figure 1-4.

a field. Fields can contain any type of information that can be
categorized. In the card box, each record contains six fields: a name,
address, city, state, ZIP code, and phone number. Since every card in
the box has the same type of information, the card box is a database.
Figure 1-5 identifies a record and a field in the mailing list database.

Using a Database

In theory, any database is arranged in such a way that information
is easy to find. In Figure 1-5, for example, names are arranged
alphabetically. If you want to find the phone number of a customer,
you simply locate the name and read across to the corresponding
phone number.

You are already interested in how a computerized filing, or database,
system can make information storage and retrieval more efficient than
a traditional filing system, and you will find that FoxPro offers many
advantages. A telephone book, for example, is fine for finding of

Field ────┐
          ↓

	Name	Address	City	State	Zip	Phone No.	Cust. No.
	J. Billings	2323 State St.	Bertram	CA	91113	234-8980	0005
	R. Foster	Rt. 1 Box 52	Frink	CA	93336	245-4312	0001
	L. Miller	P.O. Box 345	Dagget	CA	94567	484-9966	0002
→	B. O'Neill	21 Way St. #C	Hotlum	CA	92346	555-1032	0004
	C. Roberts	1914 19th St.	Bodie	CA	97665	525-4494	0006
	A. Wilson	27 Haven Way	Weed	CA	90004	566-7823	0003

A record and a
field of a
database
Figure 1-5.

──── Record

telephone numbers, but if all you have is an address and not the name of the person who lives there, the telephone directory becomes useless for finding that person's telephone number. A similar problem plagues conventional office filing systems: if the information is organized by name and you want to find all the clients located in a particular area, you could be in for a tedious search. In addition, organizing massive amounts of information into written directories and filing cabinets can consume a great deal of space. A manual database can also be difficult to modify. For example, adding a new phone number to the list may mean rearranging the list. If the phone company were to assign a new area code, someone would have to search for all phone numbers having the old area code and replace it with the new one.

When a database is teamed with a computer, many of these problems are eliminated. A computerized database provides speed: finding a phone number from among a thousand entries or putting the file in alphabetical order takes just seconds with FoxPro. A computerized database is compact: a database with thousands of records can be stored on a single floppy disk. A computerized database is flexible: it has the ability to examine information from a number of angles, so you could search for a phone number by name or by address.

Tasks that would be time consuming to accomplish manually are more practical with the aid of a computer. In principle, a database in a computer is no different from a database recorded on paper and filed in cabinets. But the computer does the tedious work of maintaining and accessing a database, and it does it fast. A computerized database that can do all of this is known as a *database management system,* or *DBMS* for short.

Relational Databases

There are a number of ways to store information in a computer, but not all of these are relational database management systems. A word processing program can be used to organize data in the form of a list; however, it will offer only limited flexibility. You must still sort, rearrange, and access the information.

Move a level above word processors, and you get to the simple file managers and the spreadsheets with simple database management capabilities. Most file managers (and spreadsheets with data management capabilities) can also perform sorting and other data management tasks.

Relational database managers can also store information in database files. In addition to being more sophisticated than file managers, however, they can access two or more database files simultaneously. By comparison, file managers can access only one database file at a time, which can be a severe constraint. If the file manager is accessing information from one database file but needs three pieces of information from a second file, the file manager can't continue unless the second file is available. Only after the file manager is finished with the first file can it proceed to the second file. But what good is this when the file manager needs information from both files simultaneously? The only solution is to duplicate the three fields from the second file in the first file. Fortunately, this is not a problem with a relational database manager like FoxPro.

Let's look at an example. Suppose the mailing list stores customer information for a warehouse that distributes kitchen appliances. The warehouse would also have a separate table within the database for customer orders, which would include fields for customer number, merchandise number, price per unit, quantity ordered, and total cost. The mailing list and customer order tables make up a relational database because they have the customer number field in common (Figure 1-6). By searching for the customer number in the mailing list and matching it to the customer number in the order form, the database manager can determine who the purchaser is and where the purchaser is located from one table, and what the purchaser ordered and the total cost of the purchase from the other table. A database manager that draws information from different tables (or database files)

Mailing List

Name	Address	City	State	ZIP	Phone No.	Cust. No.
J. Billings	2323 State St.	Bertram	CA	91113	234-8980	0005
R. Foster	Rt. 1 Box 52	Frink	CA	93336	245-4312	0001
L. Miller	P.O. Box 345	Dagget	CA	94567	484-9966	0002
B. O'Neill	21 Way St. #C	Hotlum	CA	92346	555-1032	0004
C. Roberts	1914 19th St.	Bodie	CA	97665	525-4494	0006
A. Wilson	27 Haven Way	Weed	CA	90004	566-7823	0003

Customer Order

Cust. No.	Merchan- dise No.	Price per Unit	Quantity	Total Price
0001	15A	1500.00	5	7500.00
0001	15B	1750.00	10	17500.00
0002	311	500.00	3	1500.00
0003	555	1000.00	4	4000.00
0004	69	650.00	7	4550.00
0005	1111	300.00	2	600.00
0006	15A	1500.00	1	1500.00

Mailing list and customer order databases
Figure 1-6.

1

linked by a common field is known as a *relational database manager.*

To handle the same task with a file manager would be very difficult, since the file manager could not access the mailing list when it was time to find out where the merchandise should be shipped. The only alternative would be to combine the two tables, but this would result in a clumsy and inefficient database. For example, in order to represent both of R. Foster's purchases, you would have to duplicate his name, address, and phone number (Figure 1-7). If R. Foster had purchased 100 items instead, the extra typing would take far longer and use up valuable disk space.

How You Will Use FoxPro

Figure 1-8 shows the relationship between the database, the user, and the database software. At the core is the database from which you will retrieve, add, and delete information. The database must somehow be accessible to the user, and that is accomplished by the available menu options and commands provided within FoxPro. FoxPro lets you carry out operations in one of two ways: by choosing the options from a series of menus that appear at the top of the screen or by typing in a series of commands within the Command window. Whatever you want done to the database has to be communicated to the computer by means of the correct command or menu option.

FoxPro's commands and menu options offer you a host of ways to manage information. Among all these commands and menu options, however, you won't find a single command that creates a database, enters information into it, and prints the database on the printer. In any application, you probably won't be able to use only one command or make one menu choice that will perform the entire task. Instead, you have to divide the task into smaller chores that FoxPro will handle. For example, to create a mailing list, you need to perform the following steps:

1. Create the database structure.
2. Enter information into the database.
3. Print the contents of the database.

Even after breaking down the problem this far, you need to segment the process further, since, for example, there is no single command that

Name	Address	Phone No.	Merchan-dise No.	Price per Unit	Quan-tity	Total Price
J. Billings	2323 State St. Bertram CA 91113	234-8980	1111	0300.00	2	600.00
R. Foster	Rt. 1 Box 52 Frink CA 93336	245-4312	15A	1500.00	5	7500.00
R. Foster	Rt. 1 Box 52 Frink CA 93336	245-4312	15B	1750.00	10	17500.00
L. Miller	P.O. Box 345 Dagget CA 94567	484-9966	311	500.00	3	01500.00
B. O'Neill	21 Way St. #C Hotlum CA 92346	555-1032	69	0650.00	7	04550.00
C. Roberts	1914 19th St. Bodie CA 97665	525-4494	15A	1500.00	1	01500.00
A. Wilson	27 Haven Way Weed CA 90004	566-7823	555	1000.00	4	04000.00

Combined customer order invoice and mailing list database; unnecessary customer number field was eliminated **Figure 1-7.**

inputs information into the database. How does one know when the task is divided into sufficient steps for FoxPro to cope with it? Experience. You have to know the program, and you have to know what you can and can't get away with. This book is designed to provide that knowledge.

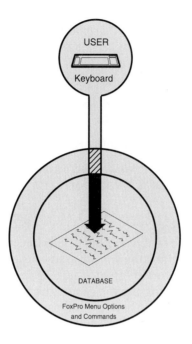

Simplified
layout of
database
manager
Figure 1-8.

System Requirements

To use FoxPro, you need an IBM XT or XT-compatible computer, such as the IBM XT, AT, or PS/2; the Compaq Portable, Plus, DeskPro, Portable II, Portable III, or Compaq 386; or any other 100%-compatible computer. Any personal computer that is software compatible with the IBM XT should be able to use FoxPro. Your computer must have a minimum of 512K of memory, and it must be equipped with one floppy disk drive and one hard disk drive. A mouse is not required but is recommended for ease of use. You must be using DOS 2.1 or a newer version, or OS/2 version 1.0 or above.

FoxPro can be used with either a monochrome or a color monitor and with any compatible printer. FoxPro is designed to take advantage of extra memory and can use the AST RAMPage, Intel Above Board, or any other memory board meeting the LIM (Lotus-Intel-Microsoft) specifications.

To use FoxPro on a local area network, you need work stations with a minimum of 640K of memory, any combination of disk drives (or no drives), and DOS 3.1 or above, or OS/2 version 1.0 or above. The operating system can be any of the following:

✦ Novell Advanced NetWare

✦ IBM PC network or Token Ring network with IBM PC Local Area Network program

✦ 3Com 3Plus network with 3Com 3Plus operating system

✦ Any other network configuration that is 100% NETBIOS compatible with DOS 3.1 or above, and with the networks just listed

Designing a Database

At this point, you may be anxious to load FoxPro into your computer and begin using the program. Resist the temptation to use FoxPro if you are new to the task of database design; there's an excellent reason for approaching the job of designing a database with patience. Planning is vital to effective database management. Many a buyer of database management software has gotten started with the software, created a database, and stored data within that database only to discover to his or her disappointment that the database does not provide all of the needed information. Although powerful databases like FoxPro let you make up for the mistakes you make during the design process, correcting such errors can nevertheless become a tedious job. To help you avoid such time-consuming mistakes, much of the remainder of this chapter focuses on database design. If you are experienced at database design but new to FoxPro, you may want to skip ahead to the "Installing FoxPro" section later in this chapter.

HINT: Creating a database without proper planning often results in a database with too few or too many fields.

Database design requires that you think about how the data should be stored and how you and others will ask for data from the database file. During this process, your problem (which FoxPro was purchased to

1

help solve) will be outlined on paper.

Just as you would not haphazardly toss a bunch of files into a filing cabinet without designing some type of filing system, you cannot place information into a database file without first designing the database. As you do so, you must define the kinds of information that should be stored in the database.

Data and Fields

Data and fields are two important terms in database design. *Data* is the information that goes into your database. An individual's last name (Smith, for example) is data. *Fields* are the types of data that make up the database. A field is another name for an attribute or category, so an entire category of data, such as a group of names, is considered to be a field. Names, phone numbers, customer numbers, descriptions, locations, and stock numbers are common fields that your database might contain.

Make sure to plan your database carefully before implementing it.

In addition to thinking about what kinds of information will go into the database, you must give careful consideration to the ways in which information will come out of the database. Information comes from a database in the form of *reports*. When you ask the computer for a list of all homes in the area priced between $100,000 and $150,000 or for a list of employees earning less than $15.00 per hour, you are asking for a report. When you ask for John Smith's address, you are also asking for a report. A report is a summary of information. Whether the computer displays a few lines on the screen or hundreds of lines on a stack of paper, it is providing a report based on the data contained within the database file.

To practice the techniques of database design, the example sessions in this text demonstrate how you can design and use a database with various hypothetical examples. Throughout much of this text, the database needs of a video rental store, Generic Videos, are used to illustrate many of the basics behind database management with FoxPro. From time to time, successive chapters of this text will show how the staff at Generic Videos successfully use FoxPro to manage information. By following along with these examples, you will learn how to put FoxPro to work within your particular application.

Three Phases of Database Design

Designing a database file, whether it is for Generic Videos or for your own purposes, involves three major steps:

1. Data definition (an analysis of existing data)
2. Data refinement (refining necessary data)
3. Establishing relationships between the attributes (fields)

Data Definition

During the first phase, data definition, you must make a list on a piece of paper of all the important attributes, or fields, involved in your application. To do this, you must examine your application in detail to determine exactly what kinds of information will be stored in the database.

In discussing the design for the database, the staff at Generic Videos determined that certain things must be known about each member: the name of the member, the member's address, date of birth, and the date the membership expires. The resulting list of fields is as follows:

Member name
Member address
Date of birth
Expiration date

An important point to remember is that during this database design phase, you should list all possible fields of your database. You may list more fields than are actually needed by your particular application, but this isn't a problem, because unnecessary fields are eliminated during the data refinement stage.

Data Refinement

During this phase, you refine the list of fields on your initial list so that the fields form an accurate description of the types of data that will be needed in the database. At this stage, it is vital to include suggestions from as many other users of the database as possible. The people who use the database are likely to know what kinds of information they want to get from the database.

Refinements are necessary with good database design.

When the staff of Generic Videos took a close look at their initial list of fields, they realized that most of the refinements were obvious. The address field, for example, should be divided into street address, city, state, and ZIP code. This will make it a simple matter to sort or select records based on a specific category, such as all persons living in a particular ZIP code. In your own case, some refinements may quickly become evident and others may not be as evident, but going over your written list of fields will help make any necessary refinements more obvious. For example, when the staff of Generic Videos further examined the initial field list, they realized that the index-card system of members contained multiple occurrences of members with the same last name. To avoid confusion, the "name" field was further divided into last name and first name. Also, the managers wanted a field indicating whether the member rented tapes in the older beta format, and a comments field for member preferences. The following shows the refined list of fields:

Member last name
Member first name
Street address
City
State
ZIP code
Date of birth
Expiration date
Beta?
Preferences

Establishing the Relationships

During the third phase, drawing relationships between the fields can help determine which fields are important and which are not so important. One way to determine such relationships is to ask yourself the same questions that you will ask your database. As an example, suppose that a personnel agency develops a database to track its employees and their work assignments. If the personnel manager of the agency wishes to know how many different employees worked on a particular job for Mammoth Telephone & Telegraph, the database must draw a relationship between a member identifier (such as the social security number) and the types of jobs that the employees worked.

Relationships will require multiple databases

Relationships can be more complex. A company vice president, using the same database, might want to know how many employees who are data entry operators worked for Mammoth Telephone between July and October. The database management system must compare fields for the type of job worked with fields for the time at which the job was performed. These types of questions can help reveal which fields are unimportant so that they can be eliminated from the database. During this phase, it is particularly important that you determine which, if any, relationships between data will call for the use of multiple databases, keeping in mind the fact that FoxPro is a relational database. In a nutshell, relational capability means that the data within one database can be linked, or related, to the data in another. When you are designing a database, it is important not to lose sight of that fact. Too many users take relational database management software and proceed to create bulky, nonrelational databases, an approach that drastically increases the amount of work involved.

As an example, the proposed staff database to be used by Generic Videos has fields that will be used to describe each member. A major goal of computerizing the records at the store is to support automated billing; by creating another database showing which tapes are checked out to a particular member, the store can quickly generate rental receipts and track needed inventory. If we take the nonrelational approach of adding another field for the name of a tape, we could store all of the information needed in each record. However, we would also have to fill in the name, address, and other information for each tape rental, every time a member rents tapes. The better solution is to create two databases, one containing the fields already described detailing each member, and the other containing a listing of rented tapes and a way of identifying the member.

When establishing the relationships, you may determine that an additional field is necessary. For Generic Videos, the method of member identification is by social security number, so this field was added to the proposed list of fields, resulting in the finalized list of fields shown here:

Member social security number
Member last name
Member first name
Street address
City
State
ZIP code
Date of birth
Expiration date
Beta?
Preferences

The sample database created in the next chapter is based on this list. A social security number is needed because in a relational database, the field you use to link the files must be unique in at least one of the files. Since under normal circumstances no two social security numbers are the same, the social security number serves as a unique method of identification. Using fields like last-name and first-name fields for linking files could provide problems later, because the data might not always be unique. If two persons with the same name joined the video club, confusion between records could result if a relational link were based on name only.

Be sure to get feed back from the database users during the design process.

During the design phases, it is important that potential users be consulted to determine what kinds of information they will expect the database to supply. Just what kinds of reports are wanted from the database? What kinds of queries will members make of the database? By continually asking these types of questions, you'll think in terms of your database, and this should help you determine what is important and what is unimportant. It often helps to consider examples of the data you will store while you design the database. For example, if your database contains many names that include salutations like "Dr." or "Honorable," you may need to create a separate title field to allow selections based on such information; you might, for example, want to provide a mailing to all doctors based on the contents of a sales database.

HINT: Look at examples of your data before finalizing your list of fields.

Keep in mind that even after the database design phases, the design of the database file is not set in stone. Changes to the design of a database file can be made later if necessary. But if you follow the systematic approach of database design for your specific application, the chances are better that you won't create a database that fails to provide much of the information you need and must then be extensively redesigned. FoxPro lets you change the design of a database at any time, although such changes are often inconvenient to make once the database is designed. Here is an example.

If you were to create a database file using FoxPro to handle a customer mailing list, you might include fields for names, addresses, cities, states, and ZIP codes. At first glance this might seem sufficient. You could then begin entering customer information into the database and gradually build a sizable mailing list. However, if your company later decides to begin telemarketing with the same mailing list, you may suddenly realize that you have not included a field for telephone numbers. Using FoxPro, you could easily change the design to include such a field, but you would still face the mammoth task of going back and adding a telephone number for every name currently in the mailing list. If this information had been added as you developed the mailing list, you would not face the inconvenience of having to enter the phone numbers as a separate operation. Careful planning and time spent during the database design process can help avoid such pitfalls.

Installing FoxPro

FoxPro comes in the form of assorted manuals and quick reference guides and assorted floppy disks. A label on the box indicates the disk size provided, and a packing sheet included with the documentation indicates how many disks you should have. If you are not sure whether all your disks are present, refer to your FoxPro documentation to be sure that you have the correct number of disks.

NOTE: If your computer is attached to a local area network, contact your network administrator for help in installing FoxPro on the network. Refer to the FoxPro documentation for specific directions regarding installation on different types of networks.

1

Hard Disk Installation

Installing FoxPro on a hard disk is a simple matter, thanks to the installation program contained on the Installation Disk and the detailed instructions contained in the "Getting Started" booklet packaged with your software. If you do not have the "Getting Started" booklet, you should locate it now. Because versions of FoxPro change and the instructions may change along with software updates, this text will provide only some general tips regarding installation. You should refer to your latest FoxPro documentation for detailed specifics on installing the program.

The installation program supplied as a part of FoxPro creates the necessary subdirectory on your hard disk and then copies the needed files into that subdirectory. Before installing FoxPro, you should make sure that you have at least eight megabytes (Mb) of free disk space remaining on your hard disk. (You can tell the amount of free space by using the DIR command; the description "*xxxxx* bytes free" that appears at the bottom of the directory listing indicates the amount of free space remaining.) The program itself requires roughly seven megabytes of disk space for installation; however, you will certainly need adequate space for storing your databases and sorting files.

NOTE: If you are using FoxPro for the first time, you should also be aware of the memory requirements of the program. FoxPro requires 512K (kilobytes) of installed memory. While your machine may be equipped with 512K or more, some memory is consumed by DOS, and memory-resident programs like SideKick or SuperKey also consume available memory. Also, although FoxPro may operate with some small memory-resident programs loaded, it will need to access the disk much more often when working with files of any size than when it has more memory to work with. For best performance, you should have at least 640K of memory in your machine, and you should avoid memory-resident programs while using FoxPro (unless those programs are designed to use other extended or expanded memory, which you may also have installed above 640K).

If your computer uses an 80386 processor or above and has two megabytes or more of memory, you can use FoxPro Extended. The FoxPro Extended version of the software provides enhanced performance, particularly with large databases. In appearance and operation, it is identical to the standard version of FoxPro, so the procedures demonstrated throughout this book will be the same, regardless of which version of FoxPro you are using. When you purchase FoxPro 2 or above, FoxPro Extended is provided in the package along with the standard version of FoxPro. Refer to your FoxPro documentation to be sure of the installation steps required for FoxPro Extended.

It's a good idea to store your data in a separate subdirectory.

To install FoxPro, turn on your computer and get to the DOS prompt in the usual manner. It is a good idea to create separate subdirectories in which to store the program and data files; this will keep your data separate from the variety of program files that come with FoxPro. For example, if your hard disk is C, you could use the following commands to create a program directory and a data directory:

```
CD\
MD\FOXPRO
MD\FOXPRO\DATA
CD\FOXPRO
```

The last line makes the FOXPRO subdirectory the current directory. You can then install FoxPro in that directory by performing the following steps:

1. Insert the Installation Disk into drive A.
2. Change the default drive to A by typing **A:** and then pressing the [Enter] key.
3. Enter the following command:

```
INSTALL C:
```

where C is the drive on which you want to install FoxPro. (If your hard disk uses a letter other than C, substitute that letter for your hard disk in this example.)

Refer to the "Getting Started" booklet supplied with your Foxpro documentation, and follow the instructions within to complete the installation process.

Creating a Batch File to Start the Program

You can create a batch file to make starting FoxPro and changing to the desired subdirectory an easier task. If you have installed FoxPro in a subdirectory named FOXPRO on drive C of your hard disk, the commands shown here can be used to accomplish this task. If your hard disk is not C, substitute your hard disk letter in the following commands. If you installed FoxPro in a subdirectory named something other than FOXPRO, refer to your DOS manual for specifics on creating batch files.

HINT: Batch files make starting FoxPro an easier process.

To create the batch file, first enter the following commands from the DOS prompt, pressing (Enter) at the end of each line:

```
CD\
COPY CON FOXPRO.BAT
```

When you complete the second command, the cursor moves down a line and waits for additional entries. Type the following lines, pressing (Enter) after each line:

```
PATH=C:\FOXPRO;C:\DOS
CD\FOXPRO\DATA
FOXPRO
```

Then press the F6 key followed by the Enter key. You should see the message "1 file(s) copied." From this point on, you can always start FoxPro and switch to the FOXPRO\DATA subdirectory simply by entering **FOXPRO** at the DOS prompt.

If you make a batch file like this one, keep this in mind: when you start FoxPro, the PATH command in the batch file changes the PATH that was established by your AUTOEXEC.BAT file, so you may not be able to run another program from any directory after running FoxPro (depending on how your AUTOEXEC.BAT file is set up). The solution to this dilemma is to instead add C:\FOXPRO in the path established by your AUTOEXEC.BAT file. See your DOS manual for details about AUTOEXEC.BAT files.

Starting FoxPro

Start your computer in the usual manner. OS/2 users should note that if you are using FoxPro for DOS, you need to run the program through the DOS Compatibility Box of OS/2; see your OS/2 documentation for details. If you created a batch file by following the directions in the previous paragraphs, you can enter **FOXPRO** and press Enter to switch to the proper directory and load the program.

If you are not an OS/2 user and have not set up the batch file, first set a path to the FOXPRO directory with the DOS PATH command. Next, switch to the subdirectory that will contain your data files and enter **FOXPRO** from the DOS prompt. For example, if your hard disk is drive C, the program is stored in a subdirectory named FOXPRO, and your data files will reside in a subdirectory named C:\FOXPRO\DATA, you could start the program by entering the following commands from the DOS prompt:

```
PATH=C:\FOXPRO
CD\FOXPRO\DATA
FOXPRO
```

Once the program starts, you briefly see an introductory screen and a copyright message. Within a moment, the FoxPro menus and Command window appear, as shown in Figure 1-9. The screen contains a menu bar with menu options, a Command window, and the working surface (the remainder of the screen). You can enter FoxPro commands, or you can select menu options that have the same results as entering

1

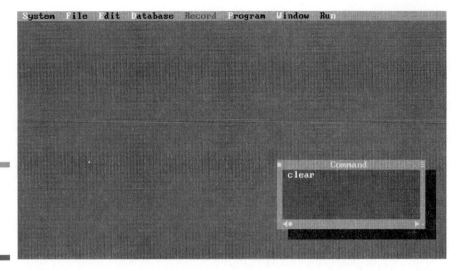

FoxPro menu
options and
Command
window
Figure 1-9.

FoxPro commands. Both methods for using FoxPro—through menus and
through the use of commands—are covered in detail throughout this text.

The top line of the screen shows the menu bar, which contains eight
choices. You can open any of the menus by pressing the [Alt] key and the
first letter of the menu name; for example, pressing [Alt]-[F] opens the
File menu. Such [Alt]-key combinations are known as hot keys. Mouse
users can point to any menu name and click the left mouse button to
open a menu. An alternative method of opening a menu is to press [F10],
use the [←] and [→] keys to highlight the desired menu, and then press
[Enter] to open the menu. When a menu is open, the appropriate menu
options appear in a rectangular box called a *pull-down menu.*

Selecting Menu Options

Once a menu has been opened, you can choose any option on that
menu by pressing the [↑] or [↓] key to highlight the option and then
pressing [Enter]. (An alternative is to press the highlighted letter in the
desired menu option; this is usually, but not always, the first letter of
the option.) As an example, if you open the System menu with [Alt]-[S],
you see the letter H highlighted within the Help option. Pressing [H] will
cause the Help window to appear (you can close the Help window by

pressing the [Esc] key). Note that not all of the menu options are available at all times. For example, you cannot access the Record menu until you open a database file.

Canceling a Menu

You can use the [Esc] key to close a menu without selecting any option. In a similar fashion, you can use the [Esc] key to exit from many options within FoxPro without performing the operation. However, you should be aware that some operations (like copying files) cannot be canceled once the process has actually begun.

HINT: [Esc] is your most useful key whenever you are somewhere you don't want to be. In most cases, repeatedly pressing [Esc] gets you out of an operation.

The Keyboard

NOTE: If you're already familiar with the PC keyboard, skip this section and begin reading at the next section.

FoxPro uses a number of special-purpose keys for various functions. In addition to the ordinary letter and number keys, you'll use the function keys often. On most IBM PCs and compatible computers, the function keys are the double row of gray keys at the left side of the PC keyboard, as shown in Figure 1-10. On newer IBM PCs and some compatibles, the function keys are placed in a horizontal row at the top of the keyboard, as shown in Figure 1-11. The function keys on the older PCs are labeled [F1] through [F10], for Function 1 through Function 10. The newer machines have 12 function keys. Usually grouped on the left side of the keyboard are four often-used keys: the [Esc] (Escape) key, the [Tab] key (it may have double arrows on it), the [Shift] key (it may have a hollow upwards-pointing arrow), and the [Alt] (Alternate) key. Some keyboards

The IBM PC
Keyboard
Figure 1-10.

have the [Esc] key in a different location. Find these keys before going
further; they will prove helpful for various operations.

You should locate the template supplied with your package of FoxPro
and place it where you can refer to it for the uses of the function keys.
The uses for the various function keys are detailed in later chapters as
pertinent operations are discussed.

Towards the right side of the keyboard is another [Shift] key. Located
below it on some keyboards is a key labeled [Caps Lock]; it is used to
change all typed letters to uppercase. Newer IBM PCs and many
compatible keyboards have the [Caps Lock] key above the left [Shift] key.
(The [Caps Lock] key does not change the format of the numbers in the top
row of the keyboard.) Just above the right [Shift] key is the [Enter], or [Return],
key; it performs a function that is similar to the Return key of a
typewriter. Above the [Enter] key is the [Backspace] key.

The enhanced
IBM PC
Keyboard
Figure 1-11.

On the right side of the keyboard, in the numeric key area, is a key labeled Del. The Del (Delete) key can be used to delete characters. Finally, the far right side of the keyboard has two gray keys with plus (+) and minus (–) labels. These keys produce the plus and minus symbols when pressed.

The far right side of the keyboard contains a numeric keypad. On some computers, this area serves a dual purpose. The keys in this area containing the up, down, left, and right arrows can be used to move the cursor in these directions. By pressing the Num Lock key, you can then use the same keys to enter numbers. Some keyboards have a separate area with arrow keys and a separate area with a numeric keypad.

REMEMBER: When Num Lock is pressed, the arrow keys on many keyboards create numbers instead of moving the cursor. If you press an arrow key and get an unwanted number, check the status of the Num Lock key.

The Mouse

Although FoxPro is designed to be operated without a mouse, you can make good use of a mouse if one is installed on your system. There are three basic operations you perform with the mouse: pointing, clicking, and selecting (also called dragging). The mouse controls the location of a special cursor called the *mouse pointer.* In FoxPro, the mouse pointer takes on the shape of a small, rectangular block.

To *point* at an object with the mouse, simply roll the mouse in the direction of the object. As you do so, the mouse pointer moves in the same direction on the screen. The term *clicking* refers to pressing the left mouse button. By pointing to different objects and clicking on them, you can select many of the objects while in FoxPro. The term *dragging* refers to pressing and holding down the left mouse button while moving the mouse. This is commonly done to choose menu options within FoxPro.

If you have just purchased your mouse for use along with FoxPro, a few hints are in order. Most mice require software drivers to be installed before they will work properly; refer to the instructions packed with your mouse for details on installing the mouse software. Obviously,

1

you'll need a clear surface on your desk to manipulate the mouse. What is not so obvious is that some desk surfaces work better than others. A surface with a small amount of friction seems to work better than a very smooth desk. Commercial pads are available if your desktop is too smooth to obtain good results. Also, the mouse will probably require cleaning from time to time. (Some mice do not require regular cleaning, so check your manual to be sure.) If you turn the mouse upside down, you will probably see instructions that indicate how the ball can be removed for cleaning. A cotton swab dipped in alcohol works well for cleaning the ball. If your mouse uses an optical sensor design instead of a large ball underneath, you should refer to the manual that accompanied the mouse for any cleaning instructions.

Using FoxPro Commands

The menus provide one way in which you can use FoxPro, but another method is to enter commands directly in the Command window. The options you can choose from a menu have equivalent commands that can be entered in this window. You get acceptable results from FoxPro regardless of which method you choose, but it does help to know a little about both methods of use.

If you do not use an Alt-key combination or F10 to open a menu, FoxPro assumes that any entry you type is a command, and it will appear within the Command window. FoxPro's basic command structure becomes obvious after you try a few commands. To print information on the screen, you use the question mark. As an example, type

```
? "Using FoxPro"
```

Once you press Enter, the response

```
Using FoxPro
```

appears on the screen, outside of the Command window. The ? command prints everything between the quotation marks. To clear the entire screen of information, enter

```
CLEAR
```

Note that you can go from Command mode back to the menus at any time simply by pressing the (Alt)-key combination for the desired menu.

FoxPro also accepts commands in abbreviated form. Only the first four letters of any command are necessary, so you could use CLEA instead of CLEAR to clear the screen. However, all commands in this book will be used in their complete form.

Conventions

Before you start working with FoxPro, you need to know some conventions that are used throughout the book.

All commands are printed in UPPERCASE, but you can type them in either uppercase or lowercase. Any part of a command surrounded by left ([ ) and right ( ]) brackets is optional, and any command followed by ellipses (...) can be repeated. Parameters in the command are in *italics*. Every command that you enter is terminated by pressing (Enter) (or (Return)). Pressing (Enter) indicates to FoxPro that you have finished typing the command and that you want it to execute. So whenever you are asked to enter a command, finish it by pressing (Enter) unless you are instructed otherwise.

Getting Help

Should you need help, FoxPro provides information on subjects ranging from basic database concepts to the use of programming commands and functions. This information is stored in a file that is always accessible to FoxPro, so you can get help at any time by pressing (F1). For example, let's suppose you are working with FoxPro from the command level and need information on the CLEAR command. Press (F1) now, and a menu of help topics appears. Since you want to know about the CLEAR command, type **CL** for CLEAR, and the CLEAR command appears in a highlighted list. Press (Enter), and a description of the CLEAR command, along with the command's variations, is displayed on the screen (Figure 1-12). If you already know the name of the command, you can circumvent the menus and go directly to the explanation by entering **HELP** followed by the command name within the Command window, such as **HELP CLEAR**.

1

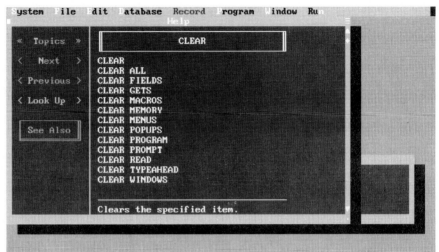

Help screen for
CLEAR
command
Figure 1-12.

The help file is quite extensive, so by all means take some time to
rummage through it, view the different options, and understand how it
is set up. Knowing where to locate information about a particular
operation or command can be a great aid when you work with some of
the more difficult operations in this book.

Windows

FoxPro makes extensive use of *windows*. In FoxPro, you can manipulate
windows with either the keyboard or the mouse. If the Help window is
not currently open, press F1 now to display it; you may want to take a
few moments to try various window operations using the Help and
Command windows.

With the Help window open, there are currently two windows on your
screen: the Help window and the Command window. Although FoxPro
can display as many windows as you can comfortably work with at the
same time, only one window can be *active*. Whichever window contains
the cursor is the active window; since the last window you opened was
the Help window, it is currently active. On most monitors, you can also

tell which window is active by noting that the top line of the window is highlighted.

If you press [Alt]-[W] now, the Window menu opens, as shown in Figure 1-13. This menu contains various commands that let you manipulate windows. The first option, Hide, hides the active window. The window remains open, but it is not visible. Once hidden, windows that contain databases appear by name in the Window menu; you can open the Window menu and choose the window by name to unhide or redisplay it.

Note that hiding a window and closing a window are two different things. If you hide a window, it is still open in memory. If you close a window, it is no longer active, and you have to reopen the window to redisplay it. Windows can be closed by opening the File menu with [Alt]-[F] and choosing Close, or by clicking the close box within the window. (The *close box* is the small rectangle in the upper-left corner of the window.)

Moving and Sizing Windows

Windows can be moved around the screen and resized at will. If you open the Window menu with [Alt]-[W], you will note two options for

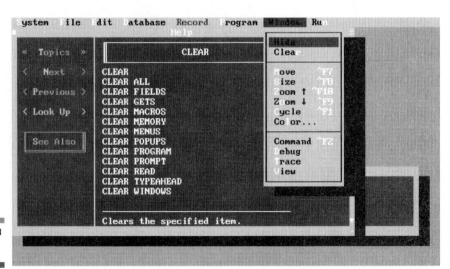

Window menu
Figure 1-13.

these tasks: the Move option and the Size option. Both of these options also have Ctrl-key equivalents; pressing Ctrl-F7 is the equivalent of choosing Move, and pressing Ctrl-F8 is the equivalent of choosing Size.

To move a window, choose Move, and the window frame starts flashing. Use the cursor keys to move the window to its desired location, and then press Enter or the Spacebar to complete the movement. You may want to try this technique now with the Help window. As you move the window around, note that you can move it anywhere on the screen, including over other windows such as the Command window.

To change a window's size, use the Size option of the Window menu. If you open the Window menu with Alt-W and select Size, the active window starts flashing. You can then use the cursor keys to change the window to its desired size and press Enter or the Spacebar to complete the resizing. You may want to try this technique now with the Help window.

Mouse users can quickly move and resize windows. To move a window, simply click anywhere on the title bar (the top bar of the window containing its name) and drag the window to the desired location. To resize a window, click the size control dot at the lower-right corner of the window, and drag the window frame to its desired size.

Ctrl-F10 can quickly expand a window.

The Zoom option can be used to expand a window so that it fills the entire screen. If you open the Window menu and choose Zoom (↑) (try it now with the Help window), you see the window expand to fill the screen. The Ctrl-F10 key combination can be used as a shortcut for the Zoom (↑) option. In this case, the key combination also serves as a *toggle;* that is, Ctrl-F10 expands the window, and Ctrl-F10 again contracts the window to its previous size. Once the window has been expanded, you can also contract it to its previous size by opening the Window menu and again choosing Zoom (↑). Mouse users can use the *zoom control,* which is the broken rectangle at the upper-right corner of the window frame. Clicking the zoom control alternately expands and contracts the window.

Changing Windows

When more than one window is displayed, you can switch between windows with the Cycle option of the Window menu. The Ctrl-key equivalent for this option is Ctrl-F1. If you open the Window menu now and choose Cycle, you see that the Command window becomes the active window. The Cycle option moves through all displayed windows currently on the screen; if you have more than two windows displayed, using Cycle causes each window to be activated in the sequence in which the windows were opened. Press Ctrl-F1 now until the Command window becomes the active window.

The Color option of the Window menu can be used to change the colors of the windows. The use of this option, as well as the dialog box that appears when you select it, is covered in detail in Chapter 15.

The Command Window

At any time, Ctrl-F2 brings up the command window.

As mentioned earlier, the Command window is where FoxPro commands normally appear when you enter them. If you open the Window menu and choose the Command option, the Command window is made the active window. (Ctrl-F2 is the shortcut key for this menu option.) The Command option and its Ctrl-F2 equivalent can also be used to display the Command window if it has been hidden.

All commands that you type appear in the Command window. By means of the Command window, you can control FoxPro operations when in the *interactive,* or Command, mode. Try entering the following commands now:

```
? 2 * 4

DIR *.*

HELP
```

When the Help window appears, press Ctrl-F2 to again make the Command window the active window. In response to each of your commands, FoxPro performs some sort of action: displaying the result of 2 times 4 on the screen, showing a directory of files in response to the DIR *.* command, or bringing forward the Help window. With the Command window now active, you can see that the commands you just entered are still displayed within the window.

You can scroll through the Command window by using the ↑ and ↓ keys. Mouse users can scroll by clicking the up or down arrows in the scroll bar at the right edge of the window. All the commands you see in the Command window are remembered by FoxPro, so you can repeat a command by moving the cursor up to that command and pressing [Enter]. For example, if you now move the cursor back up to the command ? 2 * 4 and press [Enter], the calculation is again performed and the result displayed at the left edge of the screen (it may be covered by the Help window).

This capability of remembering commands can be quite useful for correcting mistakes. If you make an error when entering a command, simply move the cursor back up to that line; then use [Backspace], [Del], and the cursor keys to correct the error. When done with the correction, press [Enter] to repeat the command.

Like all windows, you can resize the Command window. You may find this helpful, as many of the more complex commands that you enter will extend beyond the visible width of the default Command window size. Note that you are not restricted by the size of the Command window as to the length of the command you type; when you enter a long command, it simply scrolls to the left when you reach the right side of the window. Mouse users who make a mistake in entering a long command can go back to the incorrect line and use the left or right arrow in the scroll bar at the bottom edge of the window to scroll horizontally in the window. Keyboard users have to settle for the use of the cursor keys; however, you can use [Ctrl]-[←] and [Ctrl]-[→] to move left or right a word at a time.

If you hide the Command window (or close it by clicking on the close box or choosing Close from the File menu), you can still enter commands. However, you will in a sense be "flying blind," because you will not be able to see the commands you enter. The [Ctrl]-[F2] key combination can be used to quickly restore the Command window to view.

The remaining options available in the Window menu are Debug, Trace, and View. The Debug and Trace options are used for programming in FoxPro, and the View option lets you manipulate files and set many FoxPro options.

Dialog Boxes

FoxPro also makes extensive use of *dialog boxes,* which are boxes designed to accept various responses. Many menu options and some commands will result in the appearance of a dialog box. Although different dialog boxes contain different options, navigating through the dialog boxes is similar in all cases. If you now open the File menu with Alt-F and choose Open, you see the File Open dialog box, as shown in Figure 1-14. The use of this dialog box is detailed in the next chapter, but you should become familiar with the overall design of a dialog box.

A dialog box contains various objects, including buttons, menus, a check box, and a pick list. The rectangles next to the words "Drive," "Directory," and "Type" are menus. You can open a menu by clicking it or by tabbing to the item and pressing Enter. You can move in the reverse direction through the choices with Shift-Tab. For example, if you now tab over to the Drive menu and press Enter, a pull-down menu listing all available disk drives appears. Menu options can be selected by highlighting the desired one and pressing Enter or by clicking the desired one. For now, just press Esc to close the menu.

Check boxes can be selected by tabbing to them and pressing the Spacebar or by clicking in between the brackets. The line in the dialog box currently labeled

```
[] All Files
```

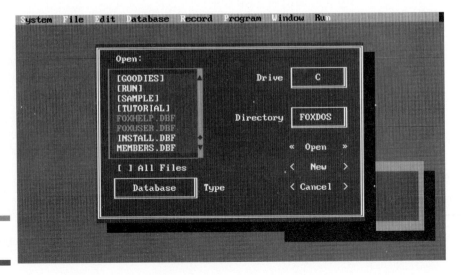

Figure 1-14.

1

is a check box. If you tab down to this entry and press the (Spacebar), an X appears in the brackets, and the list box (just above) changes to view all files in the current directory. You can again tab to the All Files check box and press the (Spacebar) (or just click the box) to change back to viewing only database files.

A *list box,* like that occupying most of the left side of this dialog box, contains a list of items that is sometimes called a *pick list.* In this example, a list of database files appears; if none have been created yet, the list will be empty. Depending on how you set up your directories, there may be database files like ARCHIVE.DBF, FOXHELP.DBF, and FOXUSER.DBF in your list that were created by FoxPro during the installation process. These are used by FoxPro, and you should not try to change the data in these files unless your documentation suggests it. You can use the (↑) and (↓) keys to scroll among items in the list box, and you can select an item by pressing (Enter). Mouse users can click an item in a list box to select it. If more items are in the list box than are visible at one time, mouse users can use the scroll bar, which then appears at the right edge of the window, to scroll in the list.

Buttons are used to perform a particular action, such as opening the selected file or canceling the use of the dialog box. In this dialog box, the available buttons are labeled Open, New, and Cancel. Keyboard users can select a button by tabbing to it and pressing (Enter). Mouse users can select a button by clicking it. For now, either tab over to the Cancel button and press (Enter), or click the button with the mouse, to cancel this operation and close the dialog box.

Desktop Accessories

FoxPro offers some desktop accessories, which are available from the System menu. Since most of these accessories don't deal specifically with database management, they aren't covered in detail in this book. However, you should be aware of their existence. The following paragraphs provide a brief description; you can learn more details on the accessories from the FoxPro documentation.

If you open the System menu with the mouse or with (Alt)-(S), you see options for a filer, a calculator, a calendar/diary, special characters, an ASCII chart, a capture, and a puzzle. The filer can be used for DOS file management, such as erasing and renaming files. Its operation is discussed further in Chapter 8.

The Calculator option, when selected, provides a desktop calculator. Modeled after a pocket calculator, its operation is fairly obvious. You can use the numeric pad (after pressing (Num Lock)) to enter numbers, or you can use the numbers on the top row of the keyboard. The (Enter) key can be used to complete the entry of numbers or math symbols.

The Calendar/ Diary option can be used for your "To-Do" list

The Calendar/Diary option, when chosen, displays the current month (based on the computer's clock) along with a Diary area in which you can type notes of your choosing. To enter a note, press (Tab) and begin typing. When you close the calendar (by clicking on the close box at the upper-right corner or by choosing Close from the File menu), the note is saved automatically. You can repeatedly press the (↑) or (↓) key to move from month to month, and you can press (T) (for Today) to return from anywhere to the current date.

The Special Characters option displays a chart of foreign characters and special graphics characters. The ASCII Chart option displays a chart of all ASCII characters in the ASCII character set. These options are of interest to programmers, who may need to refer to the list from time to time. If you do not know what an ASCII character set is, don't worry; you will not need it for performing database management tasks.

The Capture option lets you capture a block of information on the screen and paste it into the Editor. (Among other things, the Editor is used for writing and debugging FoxPro programs.) The use of Capture may come in handy for certain programming tasks, but it is not needed for any operations covered in this text.

The Puzzle option displays an entertaining puzzle on the screen resembling a child's number puzzle. You can either use the cursor keys or click the numbers to move them around. Pressing (S) or clicking Shuffle causes the numbers to be remixed in a random order. The object of the game is to align the numbers in order from 1 through 15.

CHAPTER

FOXPRO

2

CREATING AND DISPLAYING DATABASES

This chapter assumes that you have installed FoxPro and know how to start the program. It also assumes that you know how to make selections within dialog boxes, move and resize windows, and use the keyboard (and the mouse, if a mouse is installed). If you are unfamiliar with any of these areas, you should review the latter half of Chapter 1 before proceeding.

Creating a Database

FoxPro gives you two ways to create a database. In the Command window, you can enter **CREATE** *filename,* where *filename* is the name for the new database you wish to create. Or you can open the File menu, choose New, and then select Database from the dialog box that appears. Either method has the same result: the appearance of the Database Structure dialog box in which you define the database by entering the field names, types, and widths. For an example, you can create the sample database used throughout this chapter now by opening the File menu with Alt-F and selecting the New option. When you do this, the dialog box shown in Figure 2-1 appears.

The various options in the dialog box allow for the creation of new databases, programs, text files, index files, reports, labels, screen forms, menus, queries, or projects.

If you have already created a database, there will be additional options in the dialog box. Unless an existing database has already been opened for use, the Index option is unavailable; hence, it is dimmed.

Once you select the Database option and choose OK (or simply press Enter while the Database option is chosen), FoxPro displays a screen with highlighted blocks for the entry of field names, types of fields,

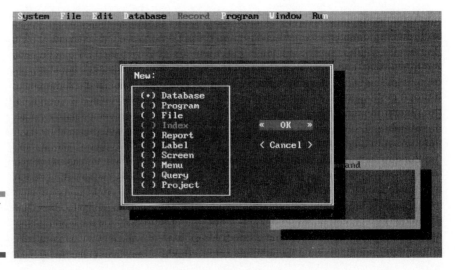

Dialog box for
a new file
Figure 2-1.

2

field widths, and the number of decimal places. This box, known as the Database Structure dialog box, is shown in Figure 2-2.

When naming a field, use a name that best describes the contents of the field. Field names can be made of letters, numbers, and underscores but must start with a letter, and spaces are not allowed. Field names can contain up to 10 characters. FoxPro does not allow the entry of field names that are too long or that contain illegal characters.

The first field on the list for the example database is the member's social security number. If you are following the example, enter **Social** for the field name. Once you press the (Enter) key, the cursor automatically moves to the field-type column. FoxPro allows for the entry of seven types of fields:

✦ *Character fields* These are used to store any characters, including letters, numbers, special symbols, and blank spaces. A character field has a maximum size of 254 characters.

✦ *Date fields* You use date fields to store dates. The default format for entering dates is *MM/DD/YY*, but this format can be changed with the SET command. FoxPro automatically inserts the slashes if you enter all six digits of a date into a date field. You must include any

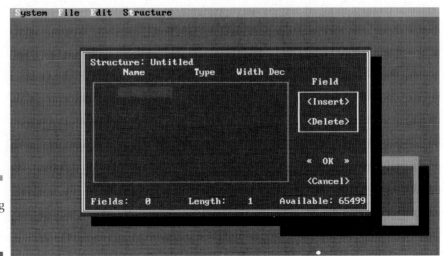

Database
Structure dialog
box
Figure 2-2.

leading zeros for the day and month; if you do not, you must type in the slashes.

✦ *Numeric fields* These use numbers, with or without decimal places. Only numbers, a decimal point, and the minus sign (the hyphen) can be entered; FoxPro does not use commas in numbers larger than 1000, although you can format reports so that the commas appear. You can enter numbers of up to 20 digits in length, and FoxPro is accurate to 15 digits, so unless you are performing scientific calculations, you shouldn't have a problem with numeric accuracy.

HINT: Use numeric fields for numbers that must be calculated. Numbers that you never need to perform calculations on (like phone numbers) should be stored in character fields.

✦ *Float fields* These are numeric fields with a floating decimal point. As with numeric fields, you can enter numbers or the minus sign, and accuracy extends to 15 digits.

✦ *Logical fields* These consist of a single letter representing a true or false value. T or Y represents true, and F or N represents false.

✦ *Memo fields* FoxPro can store large blocks of text for each record in the form of memo fields. An unlimited amount of text can be stored in a memo field (you are limited only by available hard disk space).

✦ *General fields* This type of field is provided for compatibility with FoxPro for Windows. Under the control of a FoxPro program, a general field can be used to store pictures or other binary data into a database. (For more information on FoxPro programming see Chapter 13.)

Most fields in a database are of the character or numeric type, although there may be times when you need all of the different field types that FoxPro offers.

2

When the cursor is in the Type column of the Database Structure dialog box, you can either enter the first letter of the desired field type or press (Enter) to display a pull-down menu showing the available field types. When this menu is visible, you can press the first letter of the desired field type followed by (Enter), or you can click the desired field type.

Use character fields for numbers that aren't calculated.

The social security numbers in our example database consist of numbers, so at first it might seem sensible to use a numeric field. However, this is not practical. If you include the hyphens that normally appear as part of a social security number, FoxPro ignores everything typed after the first hyphen, and the result is an incorrect entry. You will never use a social security number in a numerical calculation, so it makes sense to store entries such as social security numbers and phone numbers as character fields rather than numeric fields. A number stored in a character field cannot be used directly in a numerical calculation, although you could convert the value to a number with a FoxPro function.

Since the social security field will contain characters in the form of hyphens, the next step in the example is to choose Character. When this is done, FoxPro asks for the field width. Remember, character fields can be up to 254 characters in length, while numeric and float fields are limited to 20 digits. Logical fields are fixed at 1 character, and date fields are fixed at 8 characters. In Chapter 1, the example structure for the videos database indicated that the social security field would require 11 characters, so enter **11** as the field width and press (Enter). The cursor moves to the next field description.

For this example, enter **Lastname** for the second field name. In the field-type area, enter **Character** for the field type and **15** for the field width. The cursor moves to the third field definition. For the third item in the list of specified fields, enter **Firstname** as the field name. Again, when the cursor moves to the field-type area, enter **Character** (or press the (Enter) key to accept the existing entry), and enter **15** for the field width.

To follow the example, enter **Address** for the fourth field definition, **Character** for the field type, and **25** for the field width. For the fifth field, enter **City**, enter **Character** for the field type, and enter **15** for the width. For the next field enter **State**, enter **C** for the field type, and enter **2** for the field width.

The next field will be ZIP code. While ZIP codes contain numbers, the same reasoning used with the social security field applies, because ten-digit ZIP codes also contain hyphens. Enter **Zipcode** as the field name, **Character** as the field type, and **10** as the width.

You may recall from Chapter 1 that two of the field attributes take the form of dates: the date of birth and the date the membership expires. FoxPro lets you use date fields to enter dates. By using date fields to store dates, you can perform date arithmetic (as in subtracting one date from another to come up with the difference in days between the two). You can also arrange records chronologically based on date fields.

Enter **Birthday** for the name of the next field, and type **D** in the field-type column. Note that FoxPro automatically supplies a width of 8 for this type of field.

Enter **Expiredate** for the name of the next field, and type **D** in the field-type column to indicate a date field. For the next field name, enter **Tapelimit**. For the field type, enter **N** (for numeric). For the field width, enter **2**. This creates a numeric field with a maximum width of two digits. You will be able to store numbers from 0 to 99 in this field. (Generic Videos assumes it will never need to rent more than 99 tapes to one member.) When you specify a numeric field, the cursor moves next to the decimal heading. You could, if desired, specify a number of decimal places for the numeric field. In this example, whole numbers are used to describe the number of tapes, so you can press [Enter] to bypass the decimal entry.

Remember, numeric fields need a space for the decimal point.

Whenever you are using numeric fields to track dollar or other currency amounts (such as salaries or costs), you should include one digit in the width to contain the decimal point. For example, to track salaries of up to $999.99, you would need a numeric field with a width of 6; 3 for the dollar amount, 1 for the decimal point, and 2 for the cents values. Whenever you include decimal amounts, allow one digit for the decimal, and if you are working exclusively with decimal numbers, include one digit so the decimal point can be preceded by a zero (for example, 0.1). Thus, the minimum field width for a decimal number is 3. Note that an additional space is needed for the minus symbol if you plan to enter negative numbers in a numeric field.

If you are following the example, enter **Beta** as the next field name and choose Logical as the field type. After choosing a logical field, note that a width of 1 is assigned automatically by FoxPro.

2

Depending on the member's tastes, the Preference field may need to store a lengthy series of comments. The most economical way of storing any large group of information is to use a memo field, and Preference is designated as a memo field. Enter **Preference** as the next field name and then enter **M** (for memo) as the field type. FoxPro automatically supplies 10 as the field width.

While you are creating a database, you may notice the statistics listed at the bottom of the dialog box, as shown in Figure 2-3. In the lower-right corner of the dialog box is the number of available bytes remaining in the current record. This number is calculated by adding together the numbers in the field-width column and subtracting the total from the maximum of 65,500 bytes (characters) per record. Memo fields count as 10 spaces, but since the actual text of a memo field is stored in a different file, the limit of 65,500 characters per record will not affect the amount of text you can store in memo fields.

The number shown in the lower-left corner of the dialog box indicates the number of fields created so far. Both figures, the number of bytes remaining and the number of fields, change as you add fields to the

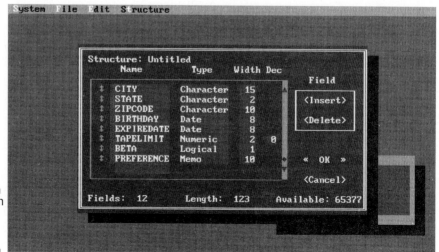

Dialog box with statistics

Figure 2-3.

database. The figure at the bottom center of the dialog box shows the combined length of all of the fields created thus far.

Correcting Mistakes

If you make any mistakes while defining the structure of the database, you can correct them before completing the database definition process. To correct mistakes, use the cursor keys to move to the field name or field type containing the offending characters, and use the Backspace key, along with the character keys, to make any desired corrections. You can use the arrow keys to move left, right, up, or down in the form. To insert new characters between existing characters, place the cursor at the desired location and then type the correction. Pressing the Ins key takes you out of insert mode. When you are not in insert mode, any characters that you type will write over existing characters. A more complete list of FoxPro editing keys is shown in Table 2-1. These editing keys also work with the Editor when you are editing memo fields.

Saving the Database

To tell FoxPro that you have finished defining the database structure, you can tab over to the OK button in the dialog box and press Enter, or

←	Cursor left one character
→	Cursor right one character
↑	Cursor up one line or one field
↓	Cursor down one line or one field
Ins	Insert mode on/off
Del	Delete character at cursor
Backspace	Delete character to left of cursor
Ctrl-T	Delete word at cursor
Ctrl-Y	Delete line at cursor
Esc	Abort operation
Tab	Move cursor right one field
Shift-Tab	Move cursor left one field

FoxPro Editing
Keys
Table 2-1.

you can click the OK button. If you just leave the field name blank and press Enter, the cursor automatically moves to the OK button and you can press Enter. (An alternative is to press Ctrl-W.) The screen displays the dialog box shown in Figure 2-4. In this box, you are prompted for a name for the file. Each database file must have a name, and the name must not contain more than eight characters. FoxPro automatically assigns an extension of .DBF to the name. Database files that include memo fields also have a corresponding file with an .FPT extension created automatically by FoxPro.

HINT: In many operations (including saving a database), Ctrl-W tells FoxPro you are ready to save.

If you have been following the example, enter **MEMBERS** as the name of the file. To save the new file structure, you must next tab over to the Save button in the dialog box and press Enter (or click the Save button). Once you have done this, you will see the following message in a new dialog box:

```
Input data records now?
< Yes >                 < No >
```

(Older versions of FoxPro may have OK and Cancel choices instead of Yes and No.) You can choose Yes (OK) or No (Cancel). Choosing No (Cancel) completes the database definition process, and choosing Yes (OK) completes the process and leaves the file open for adding new records. If you are following the example, choose Yes or OK, and FoxPro enters Append mode.

REMEMBER: Databases with memo fields are stored in two files, with .DBF and .FPT extensions. Keep this in mind if you use DOS commands to copy or erase files.

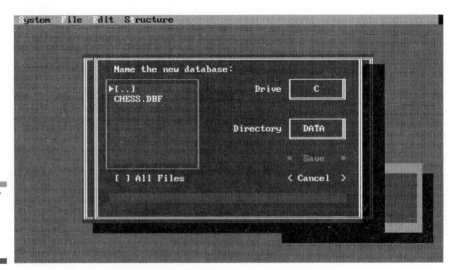

Dialog box for
naming a
database file
Figure 2-4.

Adding Information to a File

As with nearly all operations in FoxPro, you can add data by using a
menu choice or by using a command. From the Command window,
the command you use is APPEND. (Note that a database file must first
be opened with the USE command before you can use APPEND to add
data.) From the menus, you can open the File menu, select the Open
option, and then choose the file by name from the dialog box that
appears. Once the file has been opened, you open the Record menu and
choose the Append option to begin adding data.

Whether you enter **APPEND** in the Command window or choose
Append from the Record menu, the result is the same: the screen
changes to reveal a simple on-screen form (Figure 2-5), with blank
spaces beside each corresponding field name. In FoxPro, this is the
default screen used for adding and editing records. Its layout matches
the structure of the database currently in use. The default screen for
adding data may not be precisely to your liking; in Chapter 12 you
learn to create screens that differ in design from the default screens.

If you are following the example, enter the following information,
pressing Enter after each entry is completed.

2

Social: 123-44-8976
Lastname: Miller
Firstname: Karen
Address: 4260 Park Avenue
City: Chevy Chase
State: MD
Zipcode: 20815-0988
Birthday: 03/01/54
Expiredate: 07/25/94
Tapelimit: 6
Beta: F

If you make a mistake during the data entry process, you can reach the offending field with the cursor keys and use the ⌗Backspace⌗ key to correct and retype the entry. When you have entered all of the information, the cursor should be at the start of the memo field.

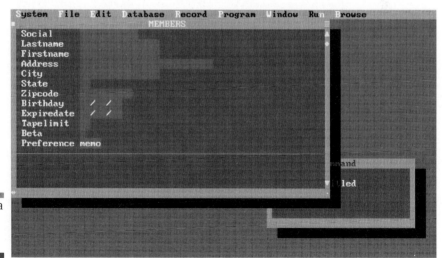

On-screen data
entry form
Figure 2-5.

Entering Data in a Memo Field

Entering data in a memo field is different from entering data in other fields. Whenever the cursor is in a memo field (as it is now), you are at the entry point for a Memo window that can hold a theoretically unlimited amount of text. (In practice, you are limited only by the available hard disk space.) You can enter the Memo window by pressing Ctrl-Pg Dn whenever the cursor is in the memo field. You can also enter a Memo window by double-clicking the field. Once you use either method, the entry form is covered by a window, and you will be editing the memo field with the FoxPro Editor.

The FoxPro Editor lets you type text as you would with any word processing software. It isn't necessary to press the Enter key at the end of every line; the Editor automatically moves the cursor to the next line. The Backspace key erases any mistakes, and you can use the arrow keys to move the cursor around the screen for editing.

The various menu options present in the Editor receive more detailed treatment in Chapter 13. For now, you'll use just the text entry capabilities and the simple editing possible with the Backspace and Del keys to add a few comments in the memo fields. As an example, type the following:

```
Prefers science fiction, horror movies. Fan of Star Trek films.
```

When you have finished typing the text, you need to get back to the data entry screen. You can do so either by choosing Close from the File menu or by clicking the close box at the upper-left corner of the window. Another, faster method is to use the Ctrl-W key combination. Use any of these methods now to get back to the data entry screen.

REMEMBER: Ctrl-Pg Dn gets you into a memo field. Ctrl-W saves the changes and gets you back out of the memo field.

You can continue adding records by using the Pg Dn key or the ↓ key to move to the next (blank) record. To follow the example, fill in the following additional records for the video members' database, using

2

Ctrl-W to complete each memo field entry and the Pg Dn or ↓ key to move to each new record as the prior one is completed.

Social: 121-33-9876
Lastname: Martin
Firstname: William
Address: 4807 East Avenue
City: Silver Spring
State: MD
Zipcode: 20910-0124
Birthday: 05/29/61
Expiredate: 07/04/94
Tapelimit: 4
Beta: F
Preference: Enjoys Clint Eastwood, John Wayne films.

Social: 232-55-1234
Lastname: Robinson
Firstname: Carol
Address: 4102 Valley Lane
City: Falls Church
State: VA
Zipcode: 22043
Birthday: 12/22/55
Expiredate: 09/05/95
Tapelimit: 6
Beta: F
Preference: Likes comedy, drama films.

Social: 901-77-3456
Lastname: Kramer

Firstname:	Harry
Address:	617 North Oakland Street
City:	Arlington
State:	VA
Zipcode:	22203
Birthday:	08/17/58
Expiredate:	12/22/94
Tapelimit:	4
Beta:	T
Preference:	Big fan of Eddie Murphy. Also enjoys westerns.

When you finish the last record, use Ctrl-W (or click the close box in the upper-left corner of the window) to close the Memo window. Then press Ctrl-W again to leave Append mode.

An Introduction to Browse

Viewing and entering records in this manner gets the job done, but as you can see, it is impossible to view more than one record on the screen at a time. FoxPro can also display information in table form, an important advantage because most users find it easier to grasp the concept of a database when it is shown in a tabular manner. It is easy to see a number of records, and the records and fields are clearly distinguished. There will be times when you prefer to see the information in the form of a table, and there will be times when you find a form like the one you have been using until now to be the best approach.

If you are following the example, open the Database menu with Alt-D and choose Browse. (You can also choose Browse from the Browse menu; however, unless you are already appending to or editing a file, the Browse menu does not appear as a menu option.) When you select the Browse option from either the Database or the Browse menu, the database in use appears in table form, as shown in Figure 2-6. (If the data does not appear as a table, open the Browse menu with Alt-B and choose Browse. Also, note that you may need to press the Pg Up key to see all of the records.) This style of display is known as Browse mode.

2

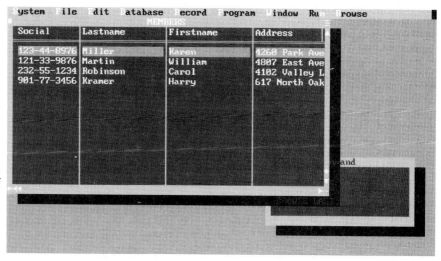

Tabular view of
record (Browse
mode)
Figure 2-6.

Another way to display data in this format is to enter the BROWSE
command in the Command window.

Moving around in the database is different when you are in Browse
mode than when you are in Append or Edit mode on the data entry
form. Try (Pg Up) and (Pg Dn), and then try using the (↑) and (↓) keys. Where
previously (in Edit mode) (Pg Up) and (Pg Dn) would move you up and
down by a record at a time, they now move you up and down by a
screenful of records. Also, the (↑) and (↓) keys now move the cursor
between records instead of between fields. You can use the (Tab) and
(Shift)-(Tab) keys to move the cursor between fields. Mouse users can click
any desired field or record to place the cursor at that location. Mouse
users can also use the scroll bars to navigate within the window; by
clicking the left, right, up, or down arrow in the window's scroll bars,
you can move in those respective directions. You can also add new
records to a database while in Browse mode with the Append Record
option of the Browse menu.

There are a number of options for using Browse mode, and these are
covered in detail in the next chapter. Remember, you can press (Alt)-(R) at
any time for the Records menu and then choose Append from the
menu to continue adding records to the database. If you are following
along with the example, use the Append Record option of the Browse
menu to add the remaining records to the table now.

Social: 121-90-5432
Lastname: Moore
Firstname: Ellen
Address: 270 Browning Ave #3C
City: Takoma Park
State: MD
Zipcode: 20912
Birthday: 11/02/64
Expiredate: 11/17/96
Tapelimit: 6
Beta: F
Preference: Drama, comedy.

Social: 495-00-3456
Lastname: Zachman
Firstname: David
Address: 1617 Arlington Blvd
City: Falls Church
State: VA
Zipcode: 22043
Birthday: 09/17/51
Expiredate: 09/19/94
Tapelimit: 4
Beta: T
Preference: Science fiction, drama.

Social: 343-55-9821
Lastname: Robinson
Firstname: Benjamin
Address: 1607 21st Street, NW
City: Washington

State:	DC
Zipcode:	20009
Birthday:	06/22/66
Expiredate:	09/17/95
Tapelimit:	2
Beta:	T
Preference:	Westerns, comedy. Clint Eastwood fan.
Social:	876-54-3210
Lastname:	Hart
Firstname:	Wendy
Address:	6200 Germantown Road
City:	Fairfax
State:	VA
Zipcode:	22025
Birthday:	12/20/55
Expiredate:	10/19/94
Tapelimit:	2
Beta:	T
Preference:	Drama, adventure. Likes spy movies, including all James Bond series.

After the last memo field entry has been made, you can use Ctrl-W or click the close box to close the window.

Getting a Quick Report

You can create *quick reports* by selecting a few menu options. The options you use are part of the report creation process that is described in detail in Chapter 7. However, the example in the following paragraphs demonstrates how easily this can be done.

To create a quick report, you open the File menu with Alt-F and choose New. The New File dialog box that appears (Figure 2-7) offers a

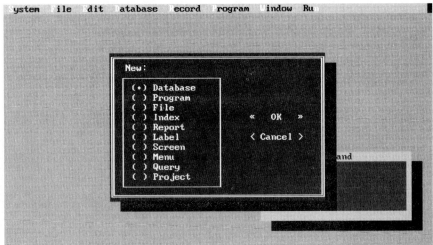

New File dialog
box
Figure 2-7.

the R key. Then, tab over to the OK box and press Enter.

Once you have selected the OK button, the report design screen
appears. This screen can be used to create custom reports, a process
detailed in Chapter 7. For a quick report, you simply choose Quick
Report from the Report menu, and the report is designed automatically
for you. Open the Report menu (note that the hot key here is Alt-O,
not Alt-R), and choose Quick Report from the menu. The Quick Report
dialog box appears, as shown in Figure 2-8.

The Column Layout and Form Layout options allow you to select either
a columnar layout, with data appearing in columns, or a form layout,
where each record appears with one field under another. For the
purposes of this example, choose Form by pressing F. (The Title option
can be used to turn on or off the appearance of field names as titles,
and the Field option is used to select specific fields for inclusion in the
report. You can ignore these options if all fields are desired in the
report, as is the case here. The Add Alias option is used with reports of a
relational nature. Such reports are covered in detail in Chapter 11.)

2

Tab over to OK and press Enter. You will see a report design appear, with field names laid out in a form fashion. Open the File menu with Alt-F and choose Save.

You must now enter a name for the report file. Enter **RSAMPLE** and then tab over to the Save button and press Enter. You will be asked whether you want to save the environment information; if so, answer Yes. Finally, choose Close from the File menu to exit the report design process.

To run the report, you use the Report option of the Database menu. Open the Database menu with Alt-D and choose Report. When the Report dialog box appears, tab to (or click) the form entry, and enter **RSAMPLE**. If you would like the report printed as well as displayed on your screen, tab down to the To Print check box, and press the Spacebar to check the box. (The remaining options in this dialog box are explained in Chapter 7.) Don't forget to turn on your printer if you choose the To Print option. The report will appear on the screen, and if you checked the To Print box, the report will be printed. Finally, tab over to OK and press Enter.

You can produce far more detailed reports in FoxPro. Such reports can include customized headers and footers, customized placement of fields, word-wrapping large amounts of text, and numeric results based on calculations of fields. These report features are covered in Chapters 7 and 10.

Command-Level Options for Displaying a Database

A few shortcuts for displaying your data with commands may prove useful. While using the commands from the Command window requires a precise recall of how the commands should be entered, many users find commands to be faster than menu options.

When you first start FoxPro, you must choose a database file for use. This action can be performed with the USE command. The syntax for this command is

USE *filename*

If you now enter

```
USE MEMBERS
```

FoxPro opens the MEMBERS database file. (Since the file was previously open, this step was unnecessary; however, if you were just starting FoxPro, you would need the USE command or its menu to open a file before working with that file.)

Viewing a Database

You can use the LIST or DISPLAY command to examine the contents of a database. Typing **LIST** by itself shows the entire contents of a database unless you specify otherwise, but you can limit the display to certain fields by including the field name after the word LIST. If you specify more than one field, separate them by commas. For example, if you are using the example database and you enter

```
LIST LASTNAME, EXPIREDATE
```

FoxPro shows only the last names and expiration dates contained in the database, as shown here. If you had entered **LIST** without any field names, you would have seen a list of all the fields.

```
Record#    LASTNAME     EXPIREDATE
      1    Miller       07/25/94
      2    Martin       07/04/94
      3    Robinson     09/05/95
      4    Kramer       12/22/94
      5    Moore        11/17/96
      6    Zachman      09/19/94
      7    Robinson     09/17/95
      8    Hart         10/19/94
```

2

The DISPLAY command lets you view selected information. By default, the LIST command shows you all records, while the DISPLAY command shows only the current record. To see more than one record with DISPLAY, you must add an optional clause, such as ALL or NEXT 5. Enter the following:

```
GO 3
DISPLAY
```

Move the Command window to see hidden records.

You will see the third record in the database. (The GO command, followed by a record number, tells FoxPro to move to that record.) Note that the record may be partially hidden by the Command window. You can move the Command window; to do so, open the Window menu with Alt-W, choose Move, and use the cursor keys to drag the window to its desired location; then press Enter to anchor the window. (Mouse users can drag the window in the usual manner, as outlined in Chapter 1.) If you try the following commands, you will see three records, beginning with record number 2:

```
GO 2
DISPLAY NEXT 3
```

You see an entire database by entering

```
DISPLAY ALL
```

There is one significant difference between DISPLAY ALL and LIST. If the database is large, the LIST command causes the contents to scroll up the screen without stopping. If you use the DISPLAY ALL command, the screen pauses after every 20 lines, and you can press any key to resume the scrolling.

The DISPLAY command can also be used to search for specific information, if it is followed by a specific condition. For example, you could display only the name, city, state, and tape-limit fields for all members with a tape limit of four or more by entering

```
DISPLAY FIELDS LASTNAME, FIRSTNAME, CITY, STATE,
TAPELIMIT FOR TAPELIMIT > 3
```

(This command appears on two lines here, but you must enter it all on one line in the Command window.)

You can find more detailed coverage on performing selective queries in Chapter 5, "Performing Queries."

Searching Within a Field

There may be occasions when you want to search for information that is contained within a field, but you know only a portion of that information. This can cause problems, because FoxPro does not search "full text," or within a field, unless you give it specific instructions to do so. To demonstrate the problem, if one of the Generic Videos managers calls and asks for the name of "that member who lives on North Oakland Street," how do you find "that" record? The manager can't recall the member's name.

Try searching for a member who lives on North Oakland Street by entering the following:

```
DISPLAY FOR ADDRESS = "North Oakland"
```

Don't feel that you've done something wrong when the record does not appear. FoxPro normally begins a search by attempting to match your characters with the first characters of the chosen field. In our database, there is no record that begins with the characters "North Oakland" in the Address field. As a result, FoxPro failed to find the data.

To get around this problem, you can search within a field. The normal layout, or syntax, for the necessary command is

DISPLAY FOR "*search text*" $ *fieldname*

2

where *search text* is the actual characters that you want to look for and *fieldname* is the name of the specific field that you wish to search. To try an example, enter the following command:

```
DISPLAY FOR "North Oakland" $ ADDRESS
```

This time, FoxPro will find the desired information.

You can use this technique to search for data within the text of a memo field. For example, the command

```
DISPLAY LASTNAME, PREFERENCE FOR "comedy" $
PREFERENCE
```

displays all records containing the word "comedy" anywhere in the Preference field.

Keeping Track of Records

Whenever FoxPro looks at a database, it examines one record at a time. Even when you list all of the records in the database, FoxPro starts with the first record in the file and then examines each additional record, one by one. The program keeps track of where it is by means of a pointer. The FoxPro pointer is always pointing to a particular record whenever you are using a database. You can move the pointer to a specific record with the GO command.

Enter **GO TOP**, and then enter **DISPLAY**. The pointer will be at the first record in the file:

```
1   123-44-8976 Miller      Karen       4260 Park Avenue...
```

To move the pointer to the fourth record, enter **GO 4**. Enter **DISPLAY**, and you will see the fourth record:

```
4   901-77-3456 Kramer      Harry       617 North Oakland Street...
```

You can go to the first record by entering **GO TOP**, or you can go to the end of a database by entering **GO BOTTOM**. If you don't know the record number but need to find a particular record, you can use the LOCATE command to find it. The use of the LOCATE command is detailed in the following chapter.

If this is a good time for a break, enter **QUIT**. The QUIT command saves any work in progress and exits the program. For your reference, the menu alternative to leave FoxPro is to open the File menu and choose Quit.

Now that you have a file containing data, you'll want to know how you can manipulate that data to better obtain the results you want. The next chapter covers this area in more detail.

CHAPTER

FOXPRO

3

CHANGING YOUR DATABASE

FoxPro has a number of menu options and commands that you can use to change records and fields. You can edit information in a record, such as a person's name or phone number on a mailing list, and you can change the structure of a database, adding fields for items that you did not plan for or deleting fields that you no longer use. You can also shorten or expand the width of a field. Let's begin by editing records in the Generic Videos database.

Editing a Database

From the menus, you can use the Change option of the Record menu to make changes to records. (This assumes that you are already at the desired record, but there are many ways to find a record you wish to change; you will learn more about that later.) After opening a database for use, you open the Record menu and select Change. This menu option is equivalent to entering **CHANGE** at the command level. With either method, a record in the database appears within the default form, as shown in Figure 3-1.

At this point you are in Change mode, and you can make changes to the data within the chosen record. If you repeatedly press the arrow keys, you will note that each keypress moves the cursor either one character or one row at a time. If you keep pressing the ⬇ key, FoxPro takes you to the next record in the file. Pressing the ⬆ key repeatedly eventually takes you to the prior record in the file, unless you are already at the first record. You can use the arrow keys to move the cursor to any location in the record.

While you are in Change mode, you can also use the (Pg Up) and (Pg Dn) keys to move around in the database. The (Pg Dn) key takes you one record forward, and the (Pg Up) key takes you one record back. At the first

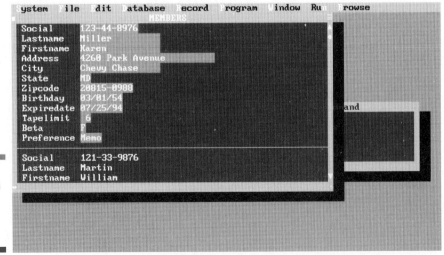

Result of
Change option
or CHANGE
command
Figure 3-1.

record in the file, (Pg Up) has no effect, and at the last record in the file, (Pg Dn) has no effect.

As an example of changing a file, an address change might be needed for Ms. Ellen Moore, a member of the video club. You could open the MEMBERS file with the Open option of the File menu or by entering **USE MEMBERS** in the Command window. You could then enter **CHANGE** or choose the Change option from the Record menu. You would next use the (Pg Dn) key to find the record for Ms. Ellen Moore. The final step in the correction would be to place the cursor in the Address field, use the ⊡ key to move to the apartment number, and use the (Backspace) key to delete the old apartment number. You would then enter **#2A** as the new apartment number.

Once you make changes you can save them either by pressing (Ctrl)-(W) or by moving to another record (with the mouse, the arrow keys, or the (Pg Up) and (Pg Dn) keys). For now, consider the menu options available for changing records.

If you press (Alt)-(R), the Record menu opens (Figure 3-2). This menu contains options that are useful when you are changing a database. The Append option puts you in the Append mode, allowing the addition of new records as detailed in the previous chapter. The Change option

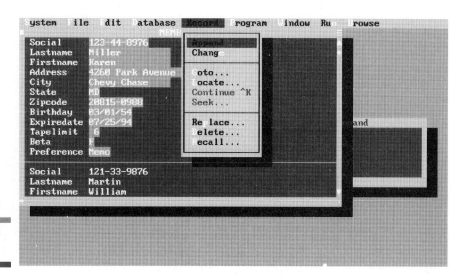

Record menu
Figure 3-2.

puts you in Change (or Edit) mode, allowing records to be edited. The Goto and Locate options can be used to quickly find a record for editing. Goto can take you to a specific record by record number, and Locate can perform a search based on the contents of a particular field. The Goto and Locate options are covered in more detail in Chapter 5; however, a brief introduction to the Locate option is useful for the task of finding records to edit.

When you select Locate from the Record menu, another dialog box appears. It contains three options: Scope, For, and While. For your basic search, all you need is the For option (Scope and While are covered in Chapter 5). When you select For, another dialog box appears (Figure 3-3). The use of all the options in this dialog box are covered in detail in Chapter 5. For the purposes of a simple search, you should know that you can enter a search expression in the For Clause window and then tab to or click the OK button. A *search expression* is simply a combination of field name, operator (usually an equal sign), and search term you are looking for. For example, say you are seeking the record for Ms. Robinson. Enter the expression

```
LASTNAME = "Robinson"
```

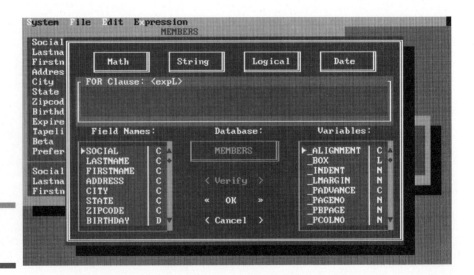

For Clause
dialog box
Figure 3-3.

in the For Clause window, and then tab to the OK button and press
[Enter]. The For Clause dialog box disappears, and the previous dialog box
(with the Scope, For, and While choices) is again visible. You next tab
over to the Locate button in this dialog box and press [Enter] to begin the
Locate operation. Assuming you are still in Change mode, the desired
record appears, as shown in Figure 3-4.

Note that the cursor stays in the field it was in when you initiated the
search. If the cursor was in the Address field, for example, after you
edited Ellen Moore's address, it would move to the Address field of
Robinson's record, and you would need to press the [↑] key twice to see
the name.

You can use similar search expressions to find any desired record. For
example, within the For Clause window you could enter

```
TAPELIMIT = 4
```

to find the first record in the database with a value of 4 in the Tapelimit
field. And you could use an expression like

```
LASTNAME = "Smith" .AND. FIRSTNAME = "Susan" .AND. CITY =
"Raleigh"
```

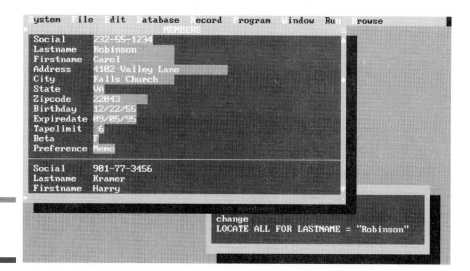

Results of
search
Figure 3-4.

to find a person with that name living in that specific city. (Chapter 5 offers more details on the use of the .AND. clause in expressions.)

The Locate option finds the first occurrence of the search term; if you wish to look for additional records meeting your search criteria, choose Continue from the Record menu. For example, after the earlier Locate operation, you could use the Continue option from the Record menu to find each successive record in which the value of Tapelimit was 4. If FoxPro could not find any records meeting the search criteria, you would see the message "End of Locate scope" on the screen (it may be hidden by the window).

Locate finds the first matching item.

If you know the record number of the desired record, you can use the Goto option of the Record menu to find the desired record. For example, if you want to edit record number 6, press (Alt)-(R) to open the Record menu. Select the Goto option, and from the dialog box that next appears, choose Record and enter **6** in response to the prompt. Tab to the Goto button in the dialog box and press (Enter). You will see that FoxPro jumps to record 6, which happens to be the record for Mr. David Zachman.

As with all menu operations, you can also perform these tasks with commands. From the Command window, once you have opened a file for use with the USE command, you can edit records by using the command CHANGE *n*, where *n* is the record number of the record you want to edit. Users who are familiar with the dBASE language may know that EDIT is an equivalent command. Entering **EDIT 5** accomplishes the same result as entering **CHANGE 5**: record number 5 appears, ready for editing.

You can also use the command GO *n*, where *n* is the record number of the record you wish to edit, and then enter the CHANGE or EDIT command without any record number after the command. For example, you could enter

```
GO 3
CHANGE
```

to edit the contents of record number 3. Once in Change mode, you can save your changes by using (Ctrl)-(W) or by clicking the close box.

From the Command window, you can also use the LOCATE command to perform a search in a manner similar to the search options of the

3

menus. By default, LOCATE starts its search from the top of the file rather than from the current record. However, you can conduct a forward search by using the CONTINUE command after the LOCATE command. For example, if you use the command

```
LOCATE FOR LASTNAME = "Robinson"
```

and the name you find is not the Robinson you want, you can then enter

```
CONTINUE
```

to find additional occurrences of the same last name.

Editing in Browse Mode

Another useful way of editing data is from Browse mode, which was introduced in the previous chapter. Browse mode displays more than one record at a time on the screen, so you can conveniently access a number of records for editing. To use Browse mode, enter **BROWSE** at the command level or choose the Browse option of the Database menu. You'll see a screenful of records, as shown in Figure 3-5 (you may need to press (Pg Up) to see all of the records).

Browse mode displays as many fields as will fit on the screen and can display up to 20 records (more if you are using special display drivers and hardware) in a horizontal format. If there are more fields in a record than will fit on a screen, only the first fields appear, as is the case with the Generic Videos database. With the default Browse window size, fields after the Address field are hidden from view. Even if you resize the window to the full width of the screen, you won't see past the City field. All that the Browse mode can show you in this case is the Social, Lastname, Firstname, and Address fields, and part of the City field. The other fields are to the right of the display. When in Browse mode, you can scan across the database to bring the other fields into view by using the (Tab) and (Shift)-(Tab) key combinations.

Mouse users have quite a bit of flexibility, thanks to the scroll bars at the right and bottom edges of the window. Using the scroll bar at the right edge, you can click the up and down arrows (they are triangular in shape) to scroll the database vertically. You can also drag the diamond-shaped indicator anywhere in the scroll box; this provides a vertical movement

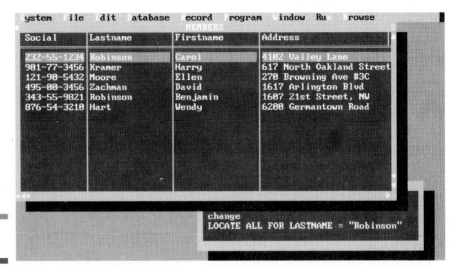

Browse mode
Figure 3-5.

relative to the location of the indicator. For example, if you drag the indicator three-fourths of the way down the scroll bar and release it, you will be positioned about three-fourths of the way down the database.

The scroll bar at the bottom edge works in a similar manner for horizontal movement. Clicking on the triangular-shaped left and right arrows moves the database columns horizontally, and dragging the diamond-shaped indicator within the scroll box provides a horizontal movement relative to the location of the indicator. Other mouse features work the same with Browse as they do with other windows; you can resize the window by dragging on the size indicator (lower-right corner), and you can zoom the window to full screen and back by repeatedly clicking the zoom indicator (upper-right corner).

Press the Tab key four times. The fields shift from right to left, with the Social field disappearing off the left side of the screen and the State field coming into view on the right side of the screen. If you continue to press the Tab key, fields on the screen disappear as remaining fields come into view.

Press Shift-Tab repeatedly, and you'll notice the opposite effect. The fields that disappeared at the left of the screen reappear, the fields on the right side disappear. Continue pressing [Shift]-[Tab] until the Social field returns to the screen.

Try using the [Pg Up] and [Pg Dn] keys. These two keys move the cursor through the database one screenful at a time. Since Generic Videos' list of members is rather short, pressing [Pg Dn] moves the cursor to the end of the database. To move the cursor up or down by one record, use the [↑] and [↓] keys.

You can also edit the records while in Browse mode. You can type changes in a field, and they will take effect just as they did when you were using Edit mode. However, since Browse mode displays a screenful of records and not just one record at a time, it is easier to access a particular field when in Browse mode.

From the Browse menu, use Append Record to add records.

In Browse mode records can be added to a database in one of two ways. You can add records to the end of the file by opening the Browse menu with [Alt]-[B] and choosing Append Record. When you choose this option, a new, blank record appears at the end of the file, and the cursor appears in the first field of that record. You can enter the desired information and exit Browse mode when you are done by choosing Close from the File menu, by pressing [Ctrl]-[W], or by clicking the close box.

The other way to add a record in Browse mode is with the INSERT command, which lets you place a new record anywhere in the database. There is no equivalent menu option; you simply enter **INSERT** as a command (you have to switch to the Command window with [Ctrl]-[F1] to enter it). This causes a new record to be inserted into the database at the present cursor location, and all existing records are pushed down by one record.

Browse Menu Options

While in Browse mode, note that a new option, Browse, has been added to the menu bar at the top of the screen. Press [Alt]-[B] to open the Browse menu (Figure 3-6).

Its options are covered in detail in the following pages, and here is a brief overview of them.

♦ *Change* This option shows the database in the Browse window but in full-screen (edit) format, similar to the display that appears with the CHANGE or EDIT command.

♦ *Grid Off* This option hides the vertical lines that normally appear between columns. Once selected, the name of this option changes to Grid On, and it can be reselected to restore the lines.

♦ *Unlink Partitions* When a window is split into two parts or partitions, this option "unlinks" the two portions of the window, allowing independent movement in each.

♦ *Change Partition* When a window is split into two partitions, this makes the active partition of the window inactive and the inactive partition active.

♦ *Size Field* This resizes the field containing the cursor. Tab to the desired field, select the option, and use the arrow keys to change the size; then press any key (except the arrow keys) to complete the resizing.

♦ *Move Field* This moves a field to a new location. Tab to the desired field, select the option, and use the ⊟ or ⊞ key to relocate the field. When done, press any key except the ⊟ or ⊞ key.

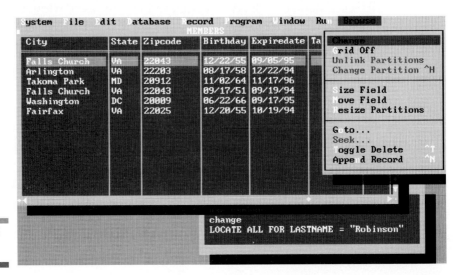

Browse menu

Figure 3-6.

◆ *Resize Partitions* This lets you split a window into two parts, or if it is already split, lets you change the size of the partitions. You also use this option to restore a split window back to a single window. Choose the option, and then use the ← and → keys to open, close, or change the size of the partitions. When done, press any key except the ← or → key.

◆ *Goto* This option is the equivalent of the Goto option of the Change menu; you can use it to go to a specific record.

◆ *Seek* This option is used with indexed files to quickly find a record. The subject of indexed files is covered in the next chapter.

◆ *Toggle Delete* This lets you mark a record for deletion while in Browse mode. Place the cursor at the desired record, and then choose Toggle Delete to mark the record for deletion.

◆ *Append Record* This adds a blank record to the end of the database.

Before proceeding, you will find it helpful to have a database to work with that contains more records than the sample one you created earlier. There is a simple way to create such a database: you can create a new file based on the existing one and copy records from the existing Videos file into the new file a number of times. Press Esc to exit the Browse window, and use the following commands now to create a larger database for use with Browse:

```
COPY STRUCTURE TO BIGFILE
USE BIGFILE
APPEND FROM MEMBERS
APPEND FROM MEMBERS
APPEND FROM MEMBERS
```

This creates a file with 24 records, enough to fill a screen while in Browse mode. Enter **BROWSE** to get back into Browse mode now.

Manipulating the Window

Ctrl-F10 also zooms a window.

A significant plus of FoxPro's implementation of Browse is the ability to manipulate the size and contents of the Browse window. Open the Window menu and choose Zoom (↑) (or click the zoom indicator) now to open the window to full-screen size (Figure 3-7), which allows the

System	File	Edit	Database	Record	Program	Window	Run	Browse

BIGFILE

Social	Lastname	Firstname	Address	City
123-44-8976	Miller	Karen	4260 Park Avenue	Chevy C
121-33-9876	Martin	William	4807 East Avenue	Silver
232-55-1234	Robinson	Carol	4102 Valley Lane	Falls C
901-77-3456	Kramer	Harry	617 North Oakland Street	Arlingt
121-90-5432	Moore	Ellen	270 Browning Ave #3C	Takoma
495-00-3456	Zachman	David	1617 Arlington Blvd	Falls C
343-55-9821	Robinson	Benjamin	1607 21st Street, NW	Washing
876-54-3210	Hart	Wendy	6200 Germantown Road	Fairfax
123-44-8976	Miller	Karen	4260 Park Avenue	Chevy C
121-33-9876	Martin	William	4807 East Avenue	Silver
232-55-1234	Robinson	Carol	4102 Valley Lane	Falls C
901-77-3456	Kramer	Harry	617 North Oakland Street	Arlingt
121-90-5432	Moore	Ellen	270 Browning Ave #3C	Takoma
495-00-3456	Zachman	David	1617 Arlington Blvd	Falls C
343-55-9821	Robinson	Benjamin	1607 21st Street, NW	Washing
876-54-3210	Hart	Wendy	6200 Germantown Road	Fairfax
123-44-8976	Miller	Karen	4260 Park Avenue	Chevy C
121-33-9876	Martin	William	4807 East Avenue	Silver
232-55-1234	Robinson	Carol	4102 Valley Lane	Falls C
901-77-3456	Kramer	Harry	617 North Oakland Street	Arlingt

Browse window
after Zoom
Figure 3-7.

display of a maximum of 20 records at a time. You can now try the
Pg Up and Pg Dn keys to move throughout the database.

You can split the window into two portions with the Resize Partitions
option. If you open the Browse menu and choose Resize Partitions, the
small rectangle at the lower-left corner of the window begins flashing.
Begin pressing the → key repeatedly, and the window splits in two.
Continue pressing the right arrow key until the Social, Lastname, and
Firstname fields are visible. Then press any key (other than the arrow
keys) to complete the operation.

HINT: You can also use function key shortcuts for manipulating
windows: Ctrl-F7 to move, Ctrl-F8 to resize, and Ctrl-F10 to
zoom.

Mouse users can split a window by dragging the *split indicator* in the
bottom scroll bar to the desired location. The split indicator is normally
shaped like an arrow with two heads; when you choose the Resize

Partitions option from the menu, it temporarily changes to a flashing rectangle.

Use Ctrl-H
*to change
partitions.*

With the window split, the portion of the window containing the cursor is the active portion. You can change partitions by choosing Change Partition from the Browse menu. Note that there is a shortcut key (Ctrl-H) for this menu option. Try repeatedly pressing Ctrl-H now to see how you can change partitions. Mouse users can change partitions simply by clicking anywhere in the desired partition.

3

Using Edit in Browse

The Change option of the Browse menu can be used to display a record in Edit mode while you are still in a Browse window. This is particularly useful for seeing records in both a tabular form and a full-record form at the same time (which you can do once you split a window). Make the right partition active now by clicking anywhere in the right partition or by pressing Ctrl-H. Next, choose Change from the Browse menu. Note that the screen display in the right partition changes to Edit mode, as shown in Figure 3-8.

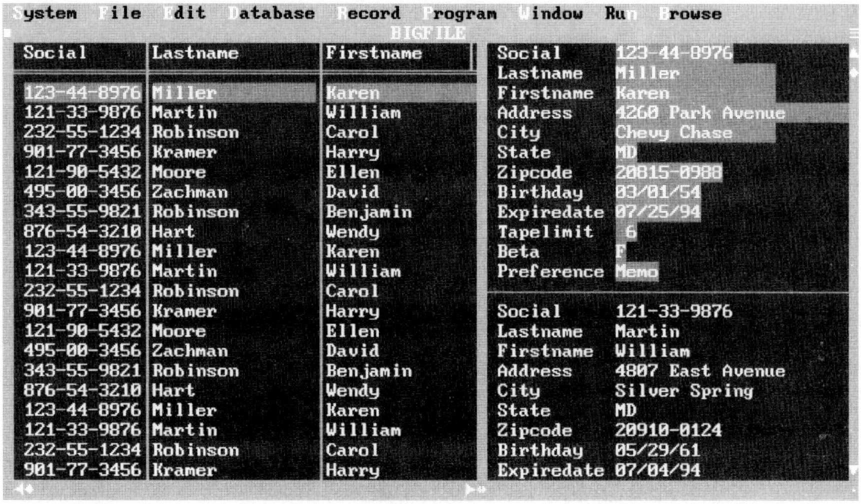

Edit mode in
Browse window
Figure 3-8.

A major advantage of this type of display is that you can easily find records in the left partition and see all of the fields for that corresponding record in the right partition. Press Ctrl-H to make the left partition the active one, and try using the ↑ and ↓ keys to view different records. As you do this, you will see the same record appear in the right partition. Note that once you are using the Edit style of display in Browse, the first option on the Browse menu changes to Browse. (This is only the case if the Change partition is the active partition.) You can then use the menu option to change the display back to a browse-style display.

The Grid Off option of the Browse menu can be used to remove the vertical lines that normally appear between fields when you use the browse style of display. Once the lines have been removed, you can restore them at any time by choosing Grid On from the Browse menu.

Unlinked Partitions

As you move the cursor between records, both partitions display a corresponding movement. This happens because partitions are normally *linked,* or tied together with respective records. There may be times when you prefer to maintain independent control over the partitions. You can do so by choosing Unlink Partitions from the Browse menu. Once you do so, you can switch between partitions with Ctrl-H or the mouse and move around in each partition independently. Mouse users will note that when partitions are unlinked, a second vertical scroll bar appears. The center scroll bar now controls movement in the left partition, and the right scroll bar controls movement in the right partition.

Open the Browse menu again, and you will note that the Unlink Partitions option has changed to Link Partitions. Choose it now to restore the link before proceeding. Then use Ctrl-H or the mouse to make the left partition the active one.

Changing Field Sizes and Positions

You can change field widths and rearrange the position of the fields while you are in Browse mode. (Changing the position of the field does not affect the field's position in the database; only the screen display is affected.) You change field widths with the Size Field option of the Browse menu, and you change field locations with the Move Field option. Place the cursor in the Firstname field now, and choose Size Field from the Browse menu. Use the ◄ key to narrow the field size to roughly ten characters, and then press Enter to complete the resizing. The results will resemble those shown in Figure 3-9.

The normal procedure for moving a field is to tab over to the desired field, choose Move Field from the Browse menu, and relocate the field with the ◄ or ► key. You can try this by placing the cursor in the Address field, choosing Move Field from the Browse menu, and pressing the ► key three times. This places Address between Zipcode and Birthday. Finally, press Enter to end the process. If your window is still split between a browse-style display and an edit-style display, note that the field position has changed in both, as shown in Figure 3-10.

Before proceeding, press Esc to exit Browse mode.

Using Browse with Commands

You can enter the BROWSE command at the command level to get into Browse mode, and the same Browse menu options and key combinations described earlier can then be used to update records.

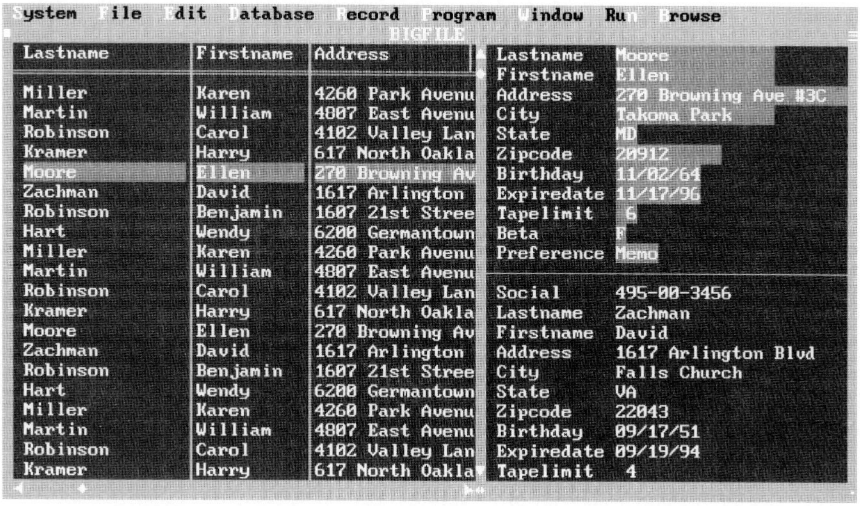

Fields after
resizing
Figure 3-9.

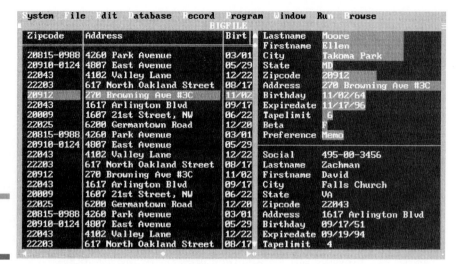

Fields after
movement
Figure 3-10.

There are also options that can be specified along with the BROWSE command when entered at the command level. These options provide ways to lock certain fields in place so that they are not lost from view when you pan with the [Ctrl] and cursor keys. Other command-level options let you show or edit selected fields when using BROWSE.

HINT: The BROWSE options available at the command level give you more flexibility than Browse from the menus.

Using the FIELDS option of the BROWSE command, you can name the fields that you want to display with BROWSE. This option is particularly helpful when you want to edit specific information while using BROWSE. The syntax for this form of the command is

BROWSE FIELDS *field1, field2,...field3*

As an example, you might wish to change the tape-limit amounts to reflect new tape limits among some video club members. You want to see only the names and tape-limit amounts. Use Esc to get to the command level, and then try this command:

```
BROWSE FIELDS LASTNAME, FIRSTNAME, TAPELIMIT
```

The resulting display (Figure 3-11) shows only those fields that you named within the command. Since these are the only fields that are displayed, they are the only fields that can be edited at the present time.

The FREEZE option of the BROWSE command lets you limit any editing to a specific field. This is a useful command to know, because there is no equivalent from the Browse menu. The FREEZE option comes in particularly handy when you must change one field in a number of records; when you do not use the option, Enter moves you to the next column rather than the next field. When you use FREEZE, other fields are displayed, but only the specified field can be changed. The syntax for the command is

BROWSE FREEZE *fieldname*

To try the effect of this option, press Esc to exit the current Browse window, and then enter

```
BROWSE FREEZE EXPIREDATE
```

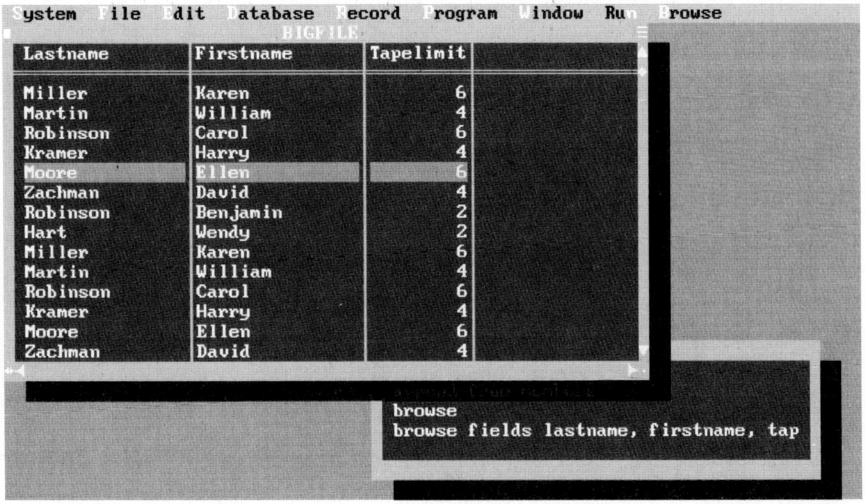

Selected fields within BROWSE
Figure 3-11.

You will see that only the Expiredate field can be edited.

You can use the command-level options of the BROWSE command in combination with each other. For example, the command

```
BROWSE FIELDS LASTNAME, CITY, STATE, EXPIREDATE
FREEZE EXPIREDATE
```

results in a display with the Lastname, City, State, and Expiredate fields visible, and just the Expiredate field available for editing.

Before proceeding, press (Esc) to close the Browse window. Then enter **USE MEMBERS** as a command to close the larger file you created earlier and get back into the video database.

Deleting Records

FoxPro uses a combination of two menu options, or equivalent commands, to delete records. From the menus, these are the Delete option of the Record menu and the Pack option of the Database menu. From the command level, the two commands are DELETE and PACK.

REMEMBER: Records you mark for deletion are still visible (unless you use SET DELETED ON). You must perform a PACK to permanently remove the records.

The Delete option of the Record menu (or its command-level equivalent, the DELETE command) prepares a record for deletion but does not actually delete the record. This method allows you to mark as many records as you wish at one time for later deletion. By letting you identify records in this manner, FoxPro provides a built-in safeguard: you have the opportunity to change your mind and recall the record.

To mark a single record for deletion, first find the desired record with any of the search techniques discussed previously. Then open the Record menu with (Alt)-(R) and choose the Delete option. A dialog box appears, as shown in Figure 3-12. If you just want to mark the current record for deletion, you can ignore all of the options, tab over to the

```
System  File  Edit  Database  Record  Program  Window  Run
Record = 3
            8 records added
            8 records added
            8 records added




            [ ] Scope...
                                    « Delete »
            [ ] For...
                                    < Cancel >
            [ ] While...




                              browse
                              browse fields lastname, firstname, tap
                              use members
                              go 5
```

Delete dialog
box
Figure 3-12.

Delete button, and then press Enter to delete the record. For your
information, the Scope option lets you choose a larger group of records
for deletion; you can choose All records, Next n, where *n* is a number
(such as the next five records), Record n where *n* is the record number
of the record to be deleted, or Rest, which deletes all records from the
current record to the end of the file. The While option of the dialog box
is used with indexed files; it is discussed in Chapter 5, but it is actually
not appropriate for use with simple deletions.

You can repeat the technique just described as often as necessary,
deleting unwanted records. The records remain in the database until
you use the Pack option of the Database menu to make the deletions
permanent. (If you are using the example database, do *not* permanently
remove any records with Pack—they are used in additional examples
later in the text.) Because the Pack option involves copying all records
not marked for deletion to a temporary file, it can be quite time
consuming with large databases.

Command users can use the LOCATE command to find desired records,
followed by the DELETE command to mark the records for deletion. To
see how this works, press Ctrl-W to exit Change mode. You may recall

Include quotes when using LOCATE with character fields.

from earlier in the chapter that the format of the LOCATE command, when used with a simple search, is

LOCATE FOR *fieldname* = "*search-term*"

If you are searching a character field, you must surround the search term with quotes. Capitalization must also match inside the quotes; you will not find the desired record if you enter **Jackson** when what's really stored within the field is "jackson". If you are searching a numeric field, enter the number alone without any quotes. (The syntax for searching dates and memo fields is discussed in Chapter 5.) As an example, if you are working with the video database, try the following:

```
LOCATE FOR LASTNAME = "Hart"
```

FoxPro should respond with the message "Record = 8." If you instead see an error message or the message "End of Locate scope," recheck your spelling of the command or the last name, and try the command again. Then, since record 8 is the one you want to mark for deletion, enter

```
DELETE
```

You will see the confirmation "1 record(s) deleted."

If you know the record number, you can specify the command DELETE RECORD *n*, where *n* is the number of the record to be deleted. Suppose that Mr. Kramer, listed in record 4, also needs to be removed from the list. Enter the command

```
DELETE RECORD 4
```

Again, the "1 record(s) deleted" message appears. Now enter the command

```
LIST LASTNAME, FIRSTNAME
```

and you will see that the marked records have not been removed from the database. When the LIST command is used, an asterisk appears beside the marked records, indicating that the records are marked for deletion.

If you decide that deleting a record is not the thing to do, you can use the RECALL command to undo the damage. For example, enter the following command to recall the fourth record:

```
RECALL RECORD 4
```

The confirmation "1 record recalled" appears. Now reenter the LIST LASTNAME, FIRSTNAME command. A shortcut is available here: by pressing the ⬆ key, you can move the cursor within the Command window to the commands you entered earlier. When you see the desired command (in this case, LIST LASTNAME, FIRSTNAME), just press (Enter) to repeat the command. Once you do so, the database shows that only record 8 is still marked for deletion. Note that the RECALL ALL command can be used to recall all records marked for deletion. (For now, leave record 8 marked for deletion.)

Use SET DELETED to hide deleted records.

When a record has been marked for deletion, it remains in the database, and operations like SUM and COUNT (which are covered later) can still use the record in calculations as if it had never been deleted. Also, the deleted record will still appear in your reports, which may not be what you had in mind. To avoid displaying and using records that have been marked for deletion, you can use the SET DELETED command. Enter

```
SET DELETED ON
```

Now repeat the LIST LASTNAME, FIRSTNAME command by pressing the ⬆ key until you are at the command and then pressing (Enter). You will see that record 8, which is still marked for deletion, does not appear. To make the record visible again, enter

```
SET DELETED OFF
```

When you try the LIST command again, the record marked for deletion will be visible in the database.

There is no need to delete records one by one with the DELETE command. You can mark more than one record for deletion by specifying the number of records to be deleted. For example, enter the commands

```
GO 5
DELETE NEXT 2
LIST LASTNAME, FIRSTNAME
```

GO 5 moves the pointer to record 5; then DELETE NEXT 2 marks records 5 and 6 for deletion.

The RECALL command can be used in the same manner. Enter

```
GO 5
RECALL NEXT 2
LIST LASTNAME, FIRSTNAME
```

and records 5 and 6 will be unmarked. Before proceeding, enter the command

```
RECALL ALL
```

to recall any records that are still marked for deletion. Remember that after deleting records in your files, you must enter **PACK** (or choose the Pack option of the Database menu) to make your deletions permanent.

NOTE: A pack operation can be time consuming with large databases.

Deleting Files

You can also delete files from within FoxPro. From the command level, you can use the DELETE FILE command. For example, the command

```
DELETE FILE NAMES2.DBF
```

would erase a file called NAMES2.DBF from the disk. Use such options for deleting files with care, because once a file has been deleted, you cannot recall it without special programs or techniques that are beyond the scope of this book.

Global Replacements with Commands

Suppose that you wanted to replace the five-digit ZIP codes with the new nine-digit ZIP codes for both members named Robinson. You can change the ZIP code for every Washington, D.C., entry by adding options to the CHANGE command. With these options, you need to use CHANGE only once because it becomes a global command. A *global command* performs the operation of the command on the entire database, not just on a single record.

When used with the global options, the CHANGE command consists of a two-step process: first, CHANGE finds the proper field, and then it asks you to enter the correction. The format of the command is

CHANGE FIELDS *fieldname* FOR *keyfield* = "*keyname*"

where *fieldname* is the field where you want the changes to occur, and *keyfield* is the field where CHANGE searches for the occurrence of *keyname*. You must surround *keyname* with quotes.

In the following example you use the CHANGE command to change the Zipcode field for each occurrence in the database that has the word "Robinson" within the Lastname field. Enter the following:

```
CHANGE FIELDS LASTNAME, ZIPCODE FOR LASTNAME =
"Robinson"
```

The first record containing Robinson in the Lastname field appears. Notice that FoxPro displays only the fields that you named as part of the CHANGE command.

The cursor is flashing in the Lastname field, so you can move down to the Zipcode field and enter **22043-1234** as the new ZIP code for this record. After you fill the field, you see the next record with Robinson in the Lastname field. Enter **20009-1010**, press Ctrl-W, and the screen form vanishes. To see the results, enter

```
LIST LASTNAME, CITY, ZIPCODE
```

The new ZIP codes you entered are displayed, as shown here:

```
Record#    LASTNAME    CITY            ZIPCODE
      1    Miller      Chevy Chase     20815-0988
      2    Martin      Silver Spring   20910-0124
```

3	Robinson	Falls Church	22043-1234
4	Kramer	Arlington	22203
5	Moore	Takoma Park	20912
6	Zachman	Falls Church	22043
7	Robinson	Washington	20009-1010
8	Hart	Fairfax	22025

Use REPLACE to quickly change a group of records.

REPLACE operates very much like CHANGE, except that REPLACE doesn't ask you to type in the change after it finds the field. Instead, you specify the change within the command, and it is made automatically. The format of the command is

REPLACE [*scope*] *fieldname* WITH *field-replacement* FOR *condition*

The *scope* parameter is optional and is used to determine how many records REPLACE will look at. If ALL is used as the scope, REPLACE looks at all records; but if NEXT 5 is used as the scope, REPLACE looks only at the next five records from the pointer's current position. NEXT is always followed by the number of records REPLACE will look at. The *fieldname* parameter is the field where the change will occur, and *field-replacement* is what will be inserted if *keyfield*, which is the field REPLACE is searching for, matches *keyword*.

There is plenty going on with REPLACE, so it might be best described by an example. Enter the following:

```
REPLACE ALL CITY WITH "Miami" FOR CITY = "Falls Church"
```

This means "Search for all City fields containing the words 'Falls Church' and then replace those fields with the word 'Miami'." Next, enter

```
LIST LASTNAME, CITY
```

You'll see that the Falls Church members have been relocated to Miami. They probably would not enjoy the commute to work, so let's move them back. Enter the command

```
REPLACE ALL CITY WITH "Falls Church" FOR CITY = "Miami"
```

Again, enter

```
LIST LASTNAME, CITY
```

Now the City field is correct. The REPLACE command is very handy for updating salaries or prices on a global basis. If every employee in a personnel file is to receive a 50-cent per hour increase, do you really want to manually update each record? It is much faster to use the REPLACE command to perform the task. Assuming a field named Salary in a personnel file, you could use a command like

```
REPLACE ALL SALARY WITH SALARY + .50
```

to quickly increase all salary amounts by 50 cents.

HINT: The REPLACE command can be used much like a word processor's search-and-replace feature. You can change values in a group of records, or in all records, depending on the structure of the REPLACE command.

As you work with FoxPro, you'll find that REPLACE is a handy command for changing area codes, dollar amounts, and for other similar applications. But you should be careful: REPLACE can wreak havoc on a database if used improperly. If you doubt whether REPLACE will have the desired effect, make a copy of the database file under a different name and experiment on the copy instead of the original. Or you can use the CHANGE command as described earlier. CHANGE is a better command to use when you want to see the data and exercise some discretion regarding the changes.

Modifying the Structure of a Database

You'll often use a database for a while and then decide to enlarge a field, delete a field, or add a field for another category. You can make these changes in the structure of a database. From the command level, this is done with the MODIFY STRUCTURE command. From the menus, you choose the Setup option of the Database menu; when the dialog box appears, you select Structure—Modify. When you change the structure of a database, FoxPro creates a new, empty database according to your instructions and then copies the old database into the new database.

If the manager at Generic Videos suddenly decides that the database should include all of the members' phone numbers, you can add a field for them. To make this change, from the command level enter

MODIFY STRUCTURE

or open the Database menu with [Alt]-[D] and choose the Setup option. When the dialog box appears, select Structure—Modify. With either approach, you will see the structure of the Generic Videos database (Figure 3-13).

Since you want to add a field, move the cursor to the Birthday field with [Tab] and the [↓] key. You will enter the field name, type, and width exactly as you did when you created the database in Chapter 2, but before you do, you need room to add a new field. While it is easiest to add new fields at the end of the existing list of fields, you can add them anywhere you desire by using the Insert and Delete buttons at the right side of the dialog box or with the [Ins] and [Del] keys.

Use the [↓] key to go to the Birthday field and press the [Ins] key, and a new field appears above the Birthday field. Since you want to enter phone numbers, the word "phone" would be a good title for the field. Enter **Phone**. Once you press [Enter], the cursor moves to the field type

The Generic Videos database structure **Figure 3-13.**

category. You want to use C for the character types (since phone numbers are never used in calculations, they need not be numeric), so press Tab to move on to the next category.

At the Width category, enter **12**. This leaves room for a ten-digit phone number and two hyphens. You could, if needed, change any of the field widths for the existing fields by moving to the desired field and entering a new value in the Width column.

3

Moving Fields

While it is not necessary in this example to move a field to a different location in the structure, you can easily do so if you desire. To move an existing field, delete the field at its old location, and then insert the same field name and specifications at the new location.

Saving the Changes

Remember, saved changes to a database are permanent.

When you modify a database, data is returned from the fields of the temporary file to the fields in the modified database automatically only if the field names and field types match. If you change the type of a field, FoxPro may not restore the data in that particular field, since it doesn't always know how to convert the data type. FoxPro makes the conversion when it can. For example, if you change a character field into a numeric field, all valid numeric entries are converted. However, if you were to change a numeric field into a logical field, the data in the numeric field would be lost because the two field types have nothing in common.

Once you have completed your desired changes to the database structure, tab to or click the OK button in the dialog box. You will see the following confirmation prompt:

```
Make structure changes permanent?
<< Yes >>                    << No >>
```

This indicates that FoxPro is ready to copy the data from the old file into the modified database. Select Yes or OK from the prompt, and after a short delay (during which FoxPro automatically rebuilds the database), the Structure dialog box disappears. You can tab to the OK button in the remaining dialog box to exit the operation. Now enter the command

```
BROWSE FIELDS LASTNAME, FIRSTNAME, PHONE FREEZE PHONE
```

Press (Pg Up), and you'll see that all of the Phone fields are present but empty. To complete the database, type in the phone numbers for the members as shown here:

Lastname	Firstname	Phone
Miller	Karen	301-555-6678
Martin	William	301-555-2912
Robinson	Carol	703-555-8778
Kramer	Harry	703-555-6874
Moore	Ellen	301-555-0201
Zachman	David	703-555-5432
Robinson	Benjamin	202-555-4545
Hart	Wendy	703-555-1201

Had this field been planned in advance during the database design stage outlined in Chapter 1, you wouldn't have the inconvenience of returning to each record to type in a phone number.

NOTE: If you rename a field and change its location in the database structure at the same time by inserting or deleting fields, FoxPro doesn't restore the data in that particular field because it doesn't know where to find the data. FoxPro uses either the field name or the position of the field in the database structure to transfer existing data. If both are changed, the existing data is discarded. If you need to change both the name of a field and its location in a database structure, perform the task in two steps. Change the field name and exit the Modify Structure process; then repeat the MODIFY STRUCTURE command and make any other changes to the file structure.

Creating the Rentals File

Before proceeding to the next chapter, you should create an additional database. This database, called RENTALS, will contain a listing of videotapes rented by the members of Generic Videos. Later chapters make use of this file along with various examples for working with more than one database file.

To create the file, enter the command

```
CREATE RENTALS
```

When the Database Structure window appears, enter the following field information.

Field	Field Name	Type	Width
1	Social	Character	11
2	Title	Character	30
3	Dayrented	Date	8
4	Returned	Date	8

Once the fields have been entered in the structure, save the new database structure by pressing Ctrl-W. When the "Add new records now?" message appears, choose OK to begin adding new records to the file. Add the following records, and then press Ctrl-W to exit Append mode when you are done.

SOCIAL	TITLE	DAYRENTED	RETURNED
123-44-8976	Star Trek VI	03/05/93	03/06/93
121-33-9876	Lethal Weapon III	03/02/93	03/06/93
232-55-1234	Who Framed Roger Rabbit	03/06/93	03/09/93
901-77-3456	Doc Hollywood	03/04/93	03/05/93
121-90-5432	Fried Green Tomatoes	03/01/93	03/06/93
495-00-3456	Wayne's World	03/04/93	03/09/93
343-55-9821	Prince of Tides	03/06/93	03/12/93
876-54-3210	Lethal Weapon III	03/07/93	03/08/93

3

SOCIAL	TITLE	DAYRENTED	RETURNED
123-44-8976	Friday 13th Part XXVII	03/14/93	03/16/93
121-33-9876	Mambo Kings	03/15/93	03/17/93
232-55-1234	Prince of Tides	03/17/93	03/19/93
901-77-3456	Coming to America	03/14/93	03/18/93
121-90-5432	Prince of Tides	03/16/93	03/17/93
495-00-3456	Star Trek VI	03/18/93	03/19/93
343-55-9821	Wayne's World	03/19/93	03/20/93
876-54-3210	Mambo Kings	03/16/93	03/18/93

CHAPTER

FOXPRO

4

SORTING AND INDEXING A DATABASE

When you want to produce reports from your data, you seldom want the data coming out to be in the same order as the data going in. Most databases contain records entered in a random manner; as different customers sign up or as different employees are hired, new records are added to the database. When you want a report, on the other hand, you usually want it in a specific order—perhaps alphabetically by name or by expiration date. With an inventory database, you may want to see the records arranged by part number. For a mailing list, a database might need to generate labels by order of ZIP code.

Databases can be arranged in a number of ways, with the SORT and INDEX commands. The first portion of this chapter teaches you how to sort and discusses some disadvantages that accompany the sorting process. The second portion of the chapter covers indexing, which offers some advantages over sorting while accomplishing the same overall result.

Most of the commands in this chapter are executed at the command level, rather than through the menus. You can perform sorting and indexing tasks with either method, but many of the more complex sorting and indexing operations can be performed more quickly with commands. Once you are familiar with the syntax of the commands, you can use them within your own FoxPro programs. Because it is good to have an idea of both methods, the chapter includes both methods; use whichever method you are comfortable with for your own use.

Sorting

When FoxPro sorts a database, it creates a new file with a different file name. If you were to sort a database of names in alphabetical order, the new file would contain all the records that were in the old file, but they would be arranged in alphabetical order, as shown in Figure 4-1.

The format for the SORT command is

SORT ON *fieldname [/A/C/D] TO new-filename*

From the menus, you open the Database menu, choose the Sort option, and then fill in the desired fields for the sort order. A new file by the name of *new-filename* is created, sorted by the field that you specify. If you specify the /A option, the file will be sorted in *ascending order.* This order places character fields in alphabetical order, numeric fields in numerical order, and date fields in chronological order (earliest to latest). If you use the /D option, character fields are sorted in *descending order* (Z to A), numeric fields from highest to lowest, and date fields in reverse chronological order (from latest to earliest). You cannot sort on memo fields. If you do not use either /A or /D, FoxPro assumes that ascending order is your preference. Sorts are also normally in ASCII order, with uppercase letters treated differently than lowercase letters.

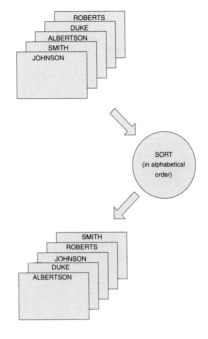

Sorting records
in a database
Figure 4-1.

ASCII order ascending specifies A through Z, then a through z. ASCII order descending specifies Z through A, then z through a. If you want uppercase and lowercase letters to be treated equally in the sorting order, include the /C option for character/dictionary.

Use the SORT command to alphabetize the Generic Videos database by members' last names. Enter the following:

```
USE MEMBERS
SORT ON LASTNAME TO MEMBERS2
```

The file has been sorted, but you are still using the original MEMBERS file at this point. To see the results, you must open the new file. Try the following commands:

```
USE MEMBERS2
LIST LASTNAME
```

The results are shown here:

```
Record#    LASTNAME
       1   Hart
       2   Kramer
       3   Martin
       4   Miller
       5   Moore
       6   Robinson
       7   Robinson
       8   Zachman
```

The old file, MEMBERS, still exists in its unchanged form. The sorting operation has created a new file (called MEMBERS2) that is in alphabetical order. Remember, a file cannot be sorted into itself in FoxPro; each time a sort is performed, a new file must be created. Enter **USE MEMBERS** to switch back to the original file.

Now try a sort option from the menus. Open the Database menu with Alt-D and choose Sort. The Sort dialog box is displayed (Figure 4-2). In the upper-left part of the dialog box is the Database Fields list box, which lets you choose desired fields on which the sort will be based. The center portion of the dialog box contains a Field Options box; this

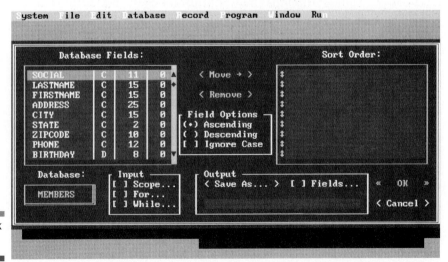

Sort dialog box
Figure 4-2.

Rememeber, FoxPro sorts in ascending order unless told otherwise.

lets you select ascending or descending order and whether FoxPro should ignore case (sorting upper- and lowercase letters together) or sort uppercase before lowercase. As you select fields from the Database Fields list box, they are added to the Sort Order box on the right side of the dialog box.

The Input box at the bottom center of the dialog box lets you add a Scope, For, or While clause to limit records included in the sorted file. The Output box at the lower-right corner of the dialog box contains a Save As entry for the file name to be assigned to the sorted file, along with a Fields option. When chosen, the Fields option lets you specify a list of fields that will be included in the sorted file. When this option is chosen, all fields are included in the sorted file (the default).

For this example, a sort is needed on the expiration-date field. Tab to the Database Fields list box and select Expiredate with the cursor and (Enter) keys. (Mouse users can click on the Expiredate field, then click the Move button.) Once selected, the field name, preceded by the database name (MEMBERS), appears in the Sort Order list box. Ascending order, which is the default shown in the Field Options box, is fine for this example. No Scope or For clauses are needed, since all records are desired. Tab to the entry space after the Fields button, and enter **MEMBERS3** as the file name. Then select OK from the dialog box.

In a few moments, you'll see a message indicating the completion of the sorting process. Enter

```
USE MEMBERS3
LIST LASTNAME, EXPIREDATE
```

You will then see the following:

```
Record#      LASTNAME     EXPIREDATE
      1      Martin       07/04/94
      2      Miller       07/25/94
      3      Zachman      09/19/94
      4      Hart         10/19/94
      5      Kramer       12/22/94
      6      Robinson     09/05/95
      7      Robinson     09/17/95
      8      Moore        11/17/96
```

4

It shows that the records in this new file are arranged in the order of expiration date, with the earliest dates first.

Enter **USE MEMBERS** and try the SORT command with the /D option (for descending order) on the Lastname field by entering

The /D option sorts a file in descending order.

```
SORT ON LASTNAME /D TO MEMBERS4
```

To see the results, you need to list the new file you created. Enter this:

```
USE MEMBERS4
LIST LASTNAME
```

The results should be as follows:

```
Record#       LASTNAME
      1       Zachman
      2       Robinson
      3       Robinson
      4       Moore
      5       Miller
      6       Martin
      7       Kramer
      8       Hart
```

Return to MEMBERS by entering **USE MEMBERS**. For an example of numerical sorting, enter

```
SORT ON TAPELIMIT TO MEMBERS5
```

When the sorting process is complete, enter

```
USE MEMBERS5
LIST LASTNAME, TAPELIMIT
```

You should then see the following:

```
Record#       LASTNAME    TAPELIMIT
      1       Robinson    2
      2       Hart        2
      3       Martin      4
      4       Kramer      4
      5       Zachman     4
      6       Miller      6
```

```
7       Robinson    6
8       Moore       6
```

This shows the records arranged by the contents of the Tapelimit field, in ascending order.

REMEMBER: Sorting always creates a duplicate of the original file. You must put the new file in use to view or print the sorted records.

4

Before going on to consider the topic of sorting on multiple fields, you may want to perform some housekeeping by deleting the example files you just created. This can easily be done from the command level. First, enter

```
USE MEMBERS
```

to close the file you are currently working with and open the original MEMBERS database. (Database files must be closed before you can erase them.) Then enter these commands to erase the database and accompanying memo field files:

```
DELETE FILE MEMBERS2.DBF
DELETE FILE MEMBERS3.DBF
DELETE FILE MEMBERS4.DBF
DELETE FILE MEMBERS5.DBF


DELETE FILE MEMBERS2.FPT
DELETE FILE MEMBERS3.FPT
DELETE FILE MEMBERS4.FPT
DELETE FILE MEMBERS5.FPT
```

NOTE: You can also erase files with the Filer. The use of the Filer is covered in Chapter 8.

Sorting on Multiple Fields

FoxPro lets you sort on any combination of field types (except memo).

Sometimes you may need to sort on more than one field. For example, if you alphabetize a list of names that is divided into Firstname and Lastname fields, you would not want to sort only on the Lastname field if there were three people with the last name of Williams. You would also have to sort on the Firstname field to find the correct ordering of the three Williamses. Fortunately, FoxPro can sort on more than one field. From the command level, this can be done by listing the fields as part of the SORT command, separating them with commas. The field that is sorted first would be listed first. From the menus, you can sort on multiple fields by choosing more than one field name from the dialog box for the database fields. You can also sort on a combination of different types of fields, such as a numeric field and a character field, at the same time.

As an example, consider the recent sort shown by tape limit. While the tape limits were in order, there were a large number of members with the same tape limit, and the members within the tape-limit group fall in random order. Sorting the file in order of tape limit, and within equal tape-limit groups by order of their last names, would provide a more logical listing.

First try it from the menus. Open the Database menu and choose Sort. When the dialog box appears, tab to the Database Fields list box, highlight Tapelimit, and press (Enter). Then highlight Lastname and press (Enter). The Tapelimit and Lastname fields will appear in the Sort Order list box at the right side of the dialog box. This indicates that the sort will take place by tape limit, and where the tape limits are the same, by last name.

Tab to the output portion of the dialog box, and enter **MEMBERS2** as the file name. Then select OK. When the sorting process is complete, choose Open from the File menu, and choose MEMBERS2 as the name of the new file to open. Next, open the Database menu and choose Browse. You will see the data sorted in order of tape limit and last name, as shown in Figure 4-3. (In the figure, the Browse window has been split to allow the Lastname and Tapelimit fields to be viewed at the same time.) When you're done viewing the data, press (Esc) to get out of Browse mode.

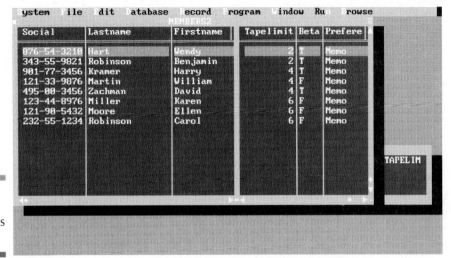

4

File sorted by
Tapelimit and
Lastname fields
Figure 4-3.

To do this type of sort from the command level, the format for the
command is

SORT ON *1st-field* [/A/C/D],*2nd-field* [/A/C/D]...\line *last-field*
[/A/C/D] TO *new-filename*

so you could perform the same sort by getting to the command level
and entering commands like this:

```
USE MEMBERS
SORT ON TAPELIMIT, LASTNAME /C TO MEMBERS2
```

The database would be sorted on both fields, in ascending order
because the /D option has not been specified. The /C option was
included, so the sort would be in character/dictionary rather than ASCII
order.

To see the results of a descending-order sort on multiple fields, enter
the following commands:

```
USE MEMBERS
SORT ON TAPELIMIT /D, LASTNAME /D TO MEMBERS2
```

Because you are now trying to overwrite a file you've already created (MEMBERS2.DBF), you will see a dialog box warning you that the file exists. Select Yes from the dialog box to tell FoxPro that you want to overwrite the previous file, and the sort will occur. To see the results, enter

```
USE MEMBERS2
LIST LASTNAME, TAPELIMIT
```

The results this time resemble the following:

```
Record#      LASTNAME      TAPELIMIT
      1      Robinson      6
      2      Moore         6
      3      Miller        6
      4      Zachman       4
      5      Martin        4
      6      Kramer        4
      7      Robinson      2
      8      Hart          2
```

The file is sorted in descending order by tape limit and, where the entries in the Tapelimit field are equal, in descending order by last names. In this sort, the Tapelimit field is the primary field. A *primary field* is the field that will be sorted first by the SORT command. After the database has been sorted by the primary field, if there is any duplicate information in the first field, SORT will sort the duplicate information by the second field listed in the command, known as the *secondary field*. It is possible to sort further with additional secondary fields; you can, in fact, sort with all fields in the database. For example, the commands

```
USE MEMBERS
SORT ON STATE, CITY, TAPELIMIT, LASTNAME TO MASTER
```

would create a database called MASTER that alphabetizes records by states, sorts each state by city, and sorts each city by tape-limit amounts. If there were any duplicate entries at this point, the last names would be sorted in ascending order. In this example, State is the primary sort field, while City, Tapelimit, and Lastname are secondary sort fields.

Sorting a Subset of a Database

Adding a qualifying FOR statement to a SORT command lets you produce a sorted file that contains only a specific subset of the records in the database. The format for the SORT command when used in this manner is

SORT ON *fieldname* [A/C/D] TO *new-filename* FOR *condition*

For an example, let's produce a new database sorted by last names and containing only those records with Virginia addresses. Enter the following commands:

```
SORT TO VAPERSON ON LASTNAME FOR STATE = "VA"
USE VAPERSON
LIST LASTNAME, STATE
```

The results are shown here:

```
Record#      LASTNAME      STATE
      1      Hart          VA
      2      Kramer        VA
      3      Robinson      VA
      4      Zachman       VA
```

This display shows the result of the qualifying FOR condition. The new database contains only the records of members located in Virginia.

More examples of conditional use of the SORT command include the following:

```
SORT TO MYDATA ON LASTNAME, TAPELIMIT FOR TAPELIMIT < = 4
SORT TO PACIFIC ON ZIP FOR ZIP >="90000"
```

Once you know the syntax of these commands, using them can be much faster than using the menus. To do this type of selective sort from the menus, you would have to select various field names and For clauses from the pick lists within the dialog box. In the time it takes to get through half the options, you could have entered the entire command from the command level to do the job.

Sorting Selected Fields to a File

Sort selected fields to create files for use with other software.

You can create a sorted file that includes selected fields from a database by including a list of fields with the SORT command. This can be quite useful for creating files that will be used by other software, such as a word processor for creating form letters. You might want to create a file in alphabetical order, containing only names and addresses and excluding all other fields. The syntax of the SORT command, when used in this manner, is

SORT TO *filename* ON *expression* FIELDS *list-of-fields*

As an example, you could create a file with only the names and addresses from the MEMBERS database with a command like the following:

```
SORT TO MYFILE ON LASTNAME, FIRSTNAME FIELDS LASTNAME,
FIRSTNAME, ADDRESS, CITY, STATE, ZIPCODE
```

The resultant sorted file, called MYFILE, would contain only the Lastname, Firstname, Address, City, State, and Zipcode fields.

Why Sort?

Remember, sorting files doubles the disk space used.

Once you've learned all about sorting with FoxPro, you should know why you should *not* sort a database—at least not very often. Sorting can be very time consuming, particularly when you are sorting large files. Sorting also uses a lot of disk space. Each time a sort occurs, FoxPro creates a new file that will be as large as the original unless you limit the fields included or the records processed with a For clause. For this reason, you must limit the database to no more than half the free space on the disk if you are going to sort it.

Adding records to a database merely complicates matters. After you add records, chances are that the database must be sorted to maintain the desired order. If you are sorting multiple fields, the sorting time can become noticeable. However, there is a more efficient way of arranging a database alphabetically, numerically, or chronologically: by using index files.

Indexing

An *index file* consists of at least one field from a database. The field is sorted alphabetically, numerically, or chronologically, and with each entry in the field is the corresponding record number used to reference the record in the *parent database* (Figure 4-4). In effect, an index file is a virtual sort of the parent database, since none of the records in the parent database are sorted.

Just as a book index is a separate section that indicates where information is located, a FoxPro index file is a separate file that contains information regarding the location of individual records in the parent database. When the database file is opened along with the index file, the first record to be retrieved is not the first record in the parent database; instead, it is the first record listed in the index. The next record retrieved is the second record listed in the index, and so on. Remember, indexing does not affect the order of the parent database.

4

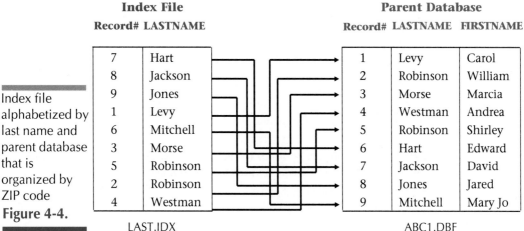

Index file alphabetized by last name and parent database that is organized by ZIP code

Figure 4-4.

Types of Indexes

Compound index files are compatible with newer versions of FoxPro.

All versions of FoxPro from version 2 on can maintain index information in one of two ways; either method accomplishes the same result of keeping things in order. The first method uses a *compound index file* with an extension of .CDX. This file maintains information on the different indexes that you create within a single file. FoxPro can have more than one compound index file open at a time, and each compound index (.CDX) file can contain data about more than one index. However, only one index file—the active index file—controls the order of the records you see. (You will learn more about this later in the chapter.)

By default, the TAG option of the INDEX command (which is discussed shortly) stores the index information in a compound index file that is automatically given the same name as the database. This .CDX file, known as the *structural .CDX file,* is opened and updated automatically whenever the database is opened.

Individual index files are compatible with earlier FoxPro products.

The second method of indexing your files is to create individual .IDX index files for each index desired. With this approach, the information for each index is stored in a separate file. If you wanted to index a file on last names and also on ZIP codes, you would need two separate .IDX files to do this. The individual .IDX files can be one of two types: compact .IDX files and noncompact .IDX files. The compact .IDX files take up less disk space than the noncompact types, but the noncompact .IDX files are compatible with other Fox Software products.

The two methods of indexing exist for an important reason: compatibility with earlier versions of FoxPro. The first method of indexing, using the compound index file to hold all the index information, is more efficient. However, FoxPro version 1.*x* cannot use the compound index files. Therefore, versions of FoxPro from version 2 on provide menu options and commands that let you work with .IDX index files, which are the style of index files used with all versions of FoxPro below version 2. If you must share data with other users of FoxPro, you may want to create and use the .IDX-style index files to maintain compatibility. Keep in mind that you must use noncompact .IDX index files if you want to use the index files with FoxBase+, FoxBase Mac, or FoxPro version 1.*x*.

From the command level, the general format of the INDEX command is similar to the format of the SORT command:

INDEX ON *expression* TO *index-filename*
[FOR *condition*][UNIQUE][COMPACT]

This variation of the index command produces a single .IDX index file containing the index information. FoxPro appends the extension .IDX to all index files. Note that Borland International's dBASE III and III PLUS products use an .NDX extension for index files. dBASE IV can use index files with either an .NDX extension or an .MDX extension. If you attempt to open a dBASE database and accompanying .NDX index file under FoxPro, FoxPro immediately rebuilds the index, using its own .IDX extension.

4

A simple use of the syntax

INDEX ON *fieldname* TO *index-filename*

creates an index file based on the named field, with all records included in the index. The UNIQUE clause, if added, causes a *unique index* to be constructed. Such an index will not contain any duplicates of the index expression. You would use this type of index to intentionally hide any accidental duplicate records. For example, if a social security field were used to build the index and two records contained the same social security number, the second occurrence would be omitted from the index. The FOR expression lets you build a selective index, which contains only those records that meet a specified condition. The COMPACT clause, if added, causes the index file to be stored as a compact-type .IDX file. If omitted, a noncompact .IDX file is created. Users of FoxPro versions 2 and above can use the TAG statement with the INDEX command, to add index tags to a compound index file. The general format of the INDEX command then becomes

INDEX ON *expression* TAG *index-tag name* [FOR *condition*]
[UNIQUE] [COMPACT]

This version of the INDEX command adds an index tag to the structural compound (.CDX) index file. If the file does not exist, it will be created; if it exists, the new index tag will be added to the file.

Creating an Index

Suppose you need to arrange the membership list in order by city for Generic Videos. You can create an index file by entering the following commands:

```
USE MEMBERS
INDEX ON CITY TO TOWNS
```

Enter **LIST LASTNAME, CITY** and you will see the result of the new index file:

```
Record#      LASTNAME      CITY
      4      Kramer        Arlington
      1      Miller        Chevy Chase
      8      Hart          Fairfax
      3      Robinson      Falls Church
      6      Zachman       Falls Church
      2      Martin        Silver Spring
      5      Moore         Takoma Park
      7      Robinson      Washington
```

With version 2, you can accomplish the same results by using the command

```
INDEX ON CITY TAG TOWNS
```

The only difference is that the index data is stored in a compound index file.

Notice that the record numbers that indicate the order of the records in the database itself are not in order. The command you entered creates an index containing the index information. Any index you create is automatically made active immediately after its creation; so the order of the records displayed with the LIST command is now controlled by the new index.

It's good practice to give index files or index tags a name related in some manner to the field that has been indexed. This helps you and others keep track of how the file was indexed and what field was used.

From the menus, you can index a file by choosing the New option of the File menu. When the dialog box appears, choose Index, and then choose OK. This causes the Index On dialog box to appear, as shown in Figure 4-5. The dialog box contains a field list from which you can select a field to base the index on. If you need to base the index on an expression (such as a combination of fields), you can manually enter the expression in the Expr window. Or you can tab over to Expr and press (Enter) to bring up the Expression Builder to create the index expression. Expressions can be complex and can include field names, functions, and operators. (Examples of indexing with complex expressions are provided later in this chapter.) After you enter the expression used to build the index, you choose OK from the dialog box to exit the Expression Builder and return to the Index On dialog box.

The Unique check box lets you select a unique index, in which duplicate entries of the indexed field or expression are ignored. (This is equivalent to the UNIQUE clause used with the INDEX ON command.) The For entry lets you specify an expression to limit records that are stored in the index; this is the equivalent of adding a FOR clause to the INDEX ON command. For example, entering an expression like

```
STATE = "MD"
```

in the For window would limit the resultant index to those records with MD in the State field.

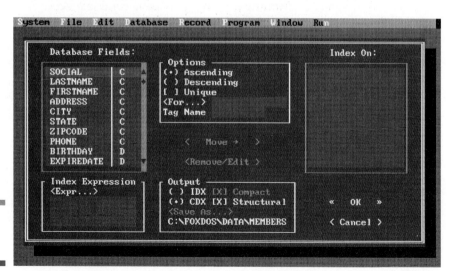

Index On
dialog box
Figure 4-5.

At the lower center of the dialog box is an area with Output options; this controls what type of index is created. You can select .IDX (normal) or .CDX (compound) index files, and you can choose compact-type index files by checking the Compact check box. (Remember, compact indexes take up less space but are not compatible with earlier versions of FoxPro.) If you choose compound (.CDX) type files, you can also choose whether the tag will be added to the structural compound index (the .CDX file having the same name as the database).

To try indexing from the menus, select New from the File menu. When the dialog box appears, choose Index, and then choose OK. In a moment, the Index Dialog Box will appear. Tab to or click Lastname in the Database Fields list box at the left side of the dialog box. When you highlight the name and press Enter, you see the field name appear in the list box at the right side of the screen. You may also notice that Lastname appears by default as a tag within the Options area of the dialog box. While you can change this to any tag that you desire, for this example you can leave the tag name as is.

At the lower center area of the screen, you may notice that a compact structural compound (.CDX) index file is chosen as the default. You can leave the options in this area as is for now. Select OK to create the index. When the indexing is completed, choose Browse from the Database menu to view the file. It will appear in order by last name. Before continuing, press Esc to leave Browse mode.

Selective Indexing

You can use the FOR clause with the INDEX ON command (or the For Expression window of the Index On dialog box) to add a clause that limits the records stored in the index. When used from the command level, the syntax for this INDEX command is

INDEX ON *expression* TO *filename* FOR *condition*

where the condition used with FOR is any expression that evaluates to a logical true or false. You can also use the FOR clause with compound index files, by using a similar syntax.

INDEX ON *expression* TAG *tagname* FOR *condition*

This is a powerful FoxPro option that can, in effect, filter unwanted records from the database and place records in order at the same time. The SET FILTER command along with a simple use of the INDEX command would accomplish the same result, but assuming an updated index already exists, using FOR with INDEX ON is faster than using SET FILTER. As an example, if you wanted to produce a report of members in the videos database who lived in Maryland or Virginia, indexed in ZIP code order, you could use a command like this to accomplish such a task:

4

```
INDEX ON ZIPCODE TO ZIPS FOR STATE = "MD" .OR. STATE = "VA"
```

Indexing on Multiple Fields

Remember, you cannot directly index on multiple fields of different types.

You can index files based on several fields. The process is similar to sorting on multiple fields. There is a limitation, however; you cannot directly index on multiple fields that are not of the same field type. For example, you could not index by Lastname and Tapelimit, because Tapelimit is a numeric field and Lastname is a character field. However, there is a way to do this; you use special operators known as functions. (This technique is discussed shortly.)

To see how indexing on multiple fields works and to be sure the index file or tag that you created earlier is still active, take a look at the Lastname and Firstname fields by entering **LIST LASTNAME, FIRSTNAME**. Now notice that Carol Robinson is listed before Benjamin Robinson, which is not correct. Because you indexed the file on last names only, the order of the first names was ignored. To correct the situation, enter

```
INDEX ON LASTNAME + FIRSTNAME TAG ALLNAMES
```

Records having the same last name are now indexed by last names and then by first names. To see the results, enter

```
LIST LASTNAME, FIRSTNAME
```

HINT: Press the ⬆ key to repeat the LIST command you used earlier.

The listing should be as follows:

```
Record#      LASTNAME      FIRSTNAME
       8     Hart          Wendy
       4     Kramer        Harry
       2     Martin        William
       1     Miller        Karen
       5     Moore         Ellen
       7     Robinson      Benjamin
       3     Robinson      Carol
       6     Zachman       David
```

You can use this technique to create an index file on any number of fields within a record. The plus symbol (+) is always used with the INDEX command to tie the fields together. For example, the command

```
INDEX ON ZIPCODE + LASTNAME + FIRSTNAME TO ZIPNAMES
```

would result in a database that is indexed three ways: by ZIP codes, by last names for records having the same ZIP code, and by first names for records having the same last name. As you might expect, multiple indexes are valuable aids when you are dealing with a large database and must organize it into comprehensible subgroups.

Indexing on Multiple Fields from Menus

When you want to index on multiple fields by using the menu options, you can manually enter the expression in the Expr portion of the dialog box, or you can click on <Expr...> in the dialog box to bring up the Expression Builder, and use the Expression Builder to enter the expression.

To try this, select New from the File menu. When the dialog box appears, choose Index, then choose OK. In a moment, the Index On dialog box will appear. Tab to or click in the Tag Name text box, and enter **NEWNAMES** as a name for the tag. Then, tab to <Expr...> and press ⌜Enter⌝, or click on <Expr...>, to bring up the Expression Builder. In the INDEX ON window of the Expression Builder, enter the following

```
LASTNAME + FIRSTNAME
```

then select OK to close the Expression Builder, and again select OK to close the Index On dialog box and build the new index.

The new index file, arranged in order of the fields that you specified, will be created. When the indexing is complete, you can examine the results by entering **BROWSE** to view the file. When you are done, press ⌜Esc⌝ to exit Browse mode.

REMEMBER: As with sorting, when you index on multiple fields, the first field named takes priority.

Indexing on Fields of Different Types

One limitation of the basic use of the INDEX command, as noted earlier, is the inability to directly index on combinations of fields that are of different types. For example, you cannot index on a combination of the Lastname and Tapelimit fields in the Generic Videos database. To see the problem, at the command level, try either of the following commands:

```
INDEX ON LASTNAME + TAPELIMIT TO TEST
INDEX ON LASTNAME + BIRTHDAY TO TEST
```

The resulting error message, "Operator/operand type mismatch," tells you that FoxPro cannot index on a combination of fields that are of differing data types (such as date and character fields). The secret to indexing on fields that are not of the same type is to use functions to convert fields that are not character fields into character fields. Functions perform special operations that supplement the normal FoxPro commands. They are explained in greater detail in the programming portion of this text. For now, it is sufficient to know about two functions; the DTOS (Date-To-String) function and the STR (String) function.

The DTOS function converts the contents of a date field into a string of characters that follow a year-month-day format. The STR function converts the contents of a numeric field into a string of characters. You can use the DTOS and STR functions in combination with your INDEX commands to accomplish the same results as indexing on combinations of different types of fields.

The normal format for an index command, when combined with these functions, is

INDEX ON *character-field* + STR(*numeric-field*) + DTOS(*date field*) TO *index-filename*

As with all indexing commands, you can use a combination of additional fields, in whatever order you prefer, to build the index. For an example of using these functions to build an index file that is indexed in alphabetical order by state and in numeric order by tape limit within each group of states, enter this command:

```
INDEX ON STATE + STR(TAPELIMIT) TO TEST
```

Enter **LIST LASTNAME, STATE, TAPELIMIT** to see the results of the index file; they should resemble the following.

Record#	LASTNAME	STATE	TAPELIMIT
7	Robinson	DC	2
2	Martin	MD	4
1	Miller	MD	6
5	Moore	MD	6
8	Hart	VA	2
4	Kramer	VA	4
6	Zachman	VA	4
3	Robinson	VA	6

In any version of FoxPro, you can also use these functions within the menus by manually entering the functions along with the field names in the index Expr window.

NOTE: For more details on functions, see the programming portion of this text. For a complete list of functions, see Appendix B.

Opening Databases and Index Files

When opening databases with the USE command, you can simultaneously open one or more index files by adding the word INDEX and the index file names after the USE *filename* portion of the command. The syntax for the USE command, when used with the INDEX option, becomes

> USE *filename* INDEX *index-name1* [,index-name2]

and users of versions 2 and above can optionally use the command

> USE *filename* TAG *tagname*

You could simultaneously open the MEMBERS database along with the TOWNS and ALLNAMES index files with a command like

```
USE MEMBERS INDEX TOWNS, ALLNAMES
```

If you are working with a compound index file with the same name as the database (or the structural compound index file), you need not specify the index file name along with the USE command. The structural compound index file, if it exists, is automatically opened by FoxPro whenever you open a database. If you choose to add index tags to compound index files that have other names, you can activate such an index file at the same time that you open the database with this variation of the USE command:

> USE *filename* INDEX .cdx *filename*

The compound index file named as part of the command will be opened along with the database.

4

Note that the first index file you list (when working with separate index files) is the controlling index, so in this example the TOWNS index file would control how the records were displayed or printed in a report.

Using SET INDEX

Use SET INDEX to make an index active.

In many cases you'll create and work with more than one index for a database, but the order in which the records appear or are printed is controlled by only one index. For an index to control the order of the records, it must be active. An index that has just been created is active, and the SET INDEX command makes a dormant index active. The SET INDEX command is the command-level equivalent of choosing Open from the File menu and then selecting Index from the Type button in the dialog box that appears.

Suppose that you need three lists from the MEMBERS database. The first list must be in order by tape limit, another list by last name, and a third list by ZIP codes. Create the indexes from these three fields now with the following commands:

```
INDEX ON LASTNAME TO NAME
INDEX ON TAPELIMIT TO TAPES
INDEX ON ZIPCODE TO ZIP
```

These commands create three indexes on your hard disk: NAME, TAPES, and ZIP. Each index file contains the appropriate field from each record and the corresponding record numbers. NAME, for example, contains last names in alphabetical order and the matching record numbers for each last name.

Since ZIP was the last index created, it is the active index. By using the SET INDEX command, you can activate any index. For example, to activate and display the database organized by tape limit instead of by ZIP code, enter

```
SET INDEX TO TAPES
LIST LASTNAME, TAPELIMIT
```

The display should appear as follows:

```
Record#      LASTNAME      TAPELIMIT
      7      Robinson      2
```

```
8       Hart         2
2       Martin       4
4       Kramer       4
6       Zachman      4
1       Miller       6
3       Robinson     6
5       Moore        6
```

Now try the same method to activate and display the ZIP file:

```
SET INDEX TO ZIP
LIST LASTNAME, ZIPCODE
```

4

The display should appear as follows:

```
Record#     LASTNAME     ZIPCODE
      7     Robinson     20009-1010
      1     Miller       20815-0988
      2     Martin       20910-0124
      5     Moore        20912
      8     Hart         22025
      6     Zachman      22043
      3     Robinson     22043-1234
      4     Kramer       22203
```

Remember, ZIP codes are stored as characters, so they are indexed "alphabetically," which explains why the nine-digit ZIP codes are not at the bottom of the list.

Using SET ORDER

When you are working with multiple tags in a compound index file, you can make any index tag the active index with the SET ORDER command. For an index tag to control the order of the records, it must be active; the SET ORDER command makes a dormant index tag active.

As an example, consider the MEMBERS database. If you have followed the example, there is already an index tag called ALLNAMES in your structural compound index file; it is organized on a combination of last and first names. Suppose that you need another list from the Generic Videos database, and it must be in order of expiration date. Create the needed index now by entering the following command:

```
INDEX ON EXPIREDATE TAG DAYS
```

Use SET ORDER to make an index tag active.

By using the SET ORDER command, you can activate any tag in the index file. For example, the index tag based on expiration dates is currently active because you created it last. To activate and display the database organized by names instead of by expiration dates, enter

```
SET ORDER TO TAG ALLNAMES
LIST LASTNAME, FIRSTNAME, EXPIREDATE
```

The display should appear as follows:

```
Record#        LASTNAME     FIRSTNAME      EXPIREDATE
      8        Hart         Wendy          10/19/94
      4        Kramer       Harry          12/22/94
      2        Martin       William        07/04/94
      1        Miller       Karen          07/25/94
      5        Moore        Ellen          11/17/96
      7        Robinson     Benjamin       09/17/95
      3        Robinson     Carol          09/05/95
      6        Zachman      David          09/19/94
```

Since the ALLNAMES index tag is active, the members are arranged in order of names. Now try the same method to activate the index tag based on expiration dates, and display the data in that order:

```
SET ORDER TO TAG DAYS
LIST LASTNAME, FIRSTNAME, EXPIREDATE
```

The display should appear as follows:

```
Record#        LASTNAME     FIRSTNAME      EXPIREDATE
      2        Martin       William        07/04/94
      1        Miller       Karen          07/25/94
      6        Zachman      David          09/19/94
      8        Hart         Wendy          10/19/94
      4        Kramer       Harry          12/22/94
      3        Robinson     Carol          09/05/95
      7        Robinson     Benjamin       09/17/95
      5        Moore        Ellen          11/17/96
```

Open Index Files

Use DISPLAY STATUS to see which index is active.

Although only one index can be active at a time, you can have up to seven open *files*. You can easily tell which indexes are in use at any time by using the LIST STATUS or DISPLAY STATUS command. If an index file is open, any changes you make to the parent database are updated automatically in that index file. For example, adding a record to MEMBERS places the Lastname field of the new record and the record number in the NAMES index and then realphabetizes the index file, provided that the NAME.IDX index file is open.

You can also open an index file with either the USE *filename* INDEX *index-names* command, or the SET INDEX command. You can open a database and index files at the same time with USE *filename* INDEX *index-names*. For example, the command

```
USE MEMBERS INDEX NAME, ZIP
```

opens the MEMBERS database, along with the NAME.IDX and ZIP.IDX index files. SET INDEX TO NAME, ZIP also opens the NAME.IDX and ZIP.IDX files if they are not already open. (You do not have to supply the .IDX extension to the command.) An active index file is also an open index file, so using SET INDEX opens a file that is closed. If you list more than one file with SET INDEX, all files are opened, but only the first is active.

Once you have opened index files, an alternative method of making any particular index active is the SET ORDER command. When using SET ORDER with any version of FoxPro prior to version 2, you must use numbers, as in SET ORDER TO 3. The number indicates the order in which the index file was originally opened. If, for example, you entered **USE MEMBERS INDEX NAME, ZIP** to open the files, the ZIP index would be the second index opened; therefore, entering **SET ORDER TO 2** would make ZIP the active index file. As discussed earlier, users of version 2 and above can also use the TAG clause along with the SET ORDER command to make any index tag of a compound index active.

In general, use the USE *filename* INDEX *index-names* command to open your databases along with as many index files as needed; once they are

4

open, use the SET INDEX command to make different index files active. For example, if you need three lists, one in order of name, one in order of ZIP code, and one in order of tape limit, you could use commands like these:

```
USE MEMBERS INDEX NAME, ZIP, TAPES
SET INDEX TO NAME
LIST LASTNAME, FIRSTNAME, CITY, ZIP, TAPELIMIT
SET INDEX TO ZIP
LIST LASTNAME, FIRSTNAME, CITY, ZIP, TAPELIMIT
SET INDEX TO TAPES
LIST LASTNAME, FIRSTNAME, CITY, ZIP, TAPELIMIT
```

To get an idea of why it is important to keep needed index files open, you can use the index files you created earlier, NAMES and TAPES. Use the SET INDEX command to open these files by entering this command:

```
SET INDEX TO TAPES, NAME
```

The two index files (TAPES.IDX, containing Tapelimit, and NAME.IDX, containing Lastname) are now open. Now enter **LIST LASTNAME, TAPELIMIT**. The display shows that the index you specified by naming the TAPES file first is the active index, but NAMES.IDX is also open. This is important if you add or edit records in the database because as long as the index files are open, they are updated automatically. See how this works by entering

```
APPEND
```

When the new blank record appears, enter this data:

Social:	111-22-3333
Lastname:	Roberts
Firstname:	Charles
Address:	247 Ocean Blvd
City:	Vienna
State:	VA
Zipcode:	22085
Tapelimit:	3

The remaining fields in the record may be left blank for now. Press
Ctrl-W to store the new record and get back to the command level. Now
enter this command again:

```
LIST LASTNAME, TAPELIMIT
```

The index file now includes the new entry, in the proper order of tape
limits, as shown here:

```
Record#      LASTNAME      TAPELIMIT
      7      Robinson      2
      8      Hart          2
      9      Roberts       3
      2      Martin        4
      4      Kramer        4
      6      Zachman       4
      1      Miller        6
      3      Robinson      6
      5      Moore         6
```

This brings up an important point: speed. Whenever you make changes
or add records to a database, FoxPro automatically updates all open
index files. This may slow down the entire operation, particularly if
more than one index file is open at once. If you wish, you can close all
open index files without closing the database with the CLOSE INDEX
command.

Using REINDEX

If you changed a database and didn't remember to open an index file,
you can update the index with the REINDEX command. You will want
to do this with the ZIP index file, for example; because you did not
open the ZIP index file, it does not include the newly added record. You
can verify this by using the ZIP index and looking at names in the
database. Enter the following:

```
SET INDEX TO ZIP, NAME, TAPES
LIST LASTNAME
```

The name Roberts does not appear in the following database because
the ZIP index was not open when you added the record:

4

```
Record#     LASTNAME
      7     Robinson
      1     Miller
      2     Martin
      5     Moore
      8     Hart
      6     Zachman
      3     Robinson
      4     Kramer
```

Try the REINDEX command now by entering

```
REINDEX
```

To display the updated result, enter **LIST LASTNAME.** The results are shown here:

```
Record#     LASTNAME
      7     Robinson
      1     Miller
      2     Martin
      5     Moore
      8     Hart
      6     Zachman
      3     Robinson
      9     Roberts
      4     Kramer
```

The Roberts entry is now in the indexed ZIP file. Mr. Roberts is no longer needed in the database. Enter **DELETE RECORD 9** and then enter **PACK** to remove him from the list. Since the ZIP, NAME, and TAPELIMIT index files are open, the entry for Roberts will be removed from each of the index files. If you are using version 2 or above, you will notice that the tags in the structural compound index file are also updated.

REMEMBER: The PACK command automatically reindexes all open index files.

NOTE: A power failure or hardware malfunction can damage an index file. If this happens, REINDEX may not work properly. Use the INDEX command instead to rebuild the index from scratch.

Using CLOSE INDEX

If you decide that you do not want to use any index file (other than the structural compound index under version 2), use the CLOSE INDEX command to close the index file and leave the associated database open. To execute the command from the command level, you enter

```
CLOSE INDEX
```

Note that the REINDEX command is available from the menus, while the CLOSE INDEX command is not. To rebuild an index file while at the menus, open the Database menu and choose the Reindex option. To close an index file through the menus, you could choose the Open option of the File menu and open the same database a second time, without opening the corresponding index file.

Searching for Specifics

You can use two additional FoxPro commands with indexed files: FIND and SEEK. These commands quickly find information in an indexed file. The commands are discussed briefly here, since they do pertain to indexed files. Chapter 5, which deals with querying your database, covers these commands in additional detail.

Both commands operate only on the active index. The format for the FIND command is FIND *character-string,* where *character-string* is a group of characters that do not have to be surrounded by quote marks. The format for SEEK is SEEK *expression.* Here, *expression* can be a number, a character string (which must be surrounded by single or double quotes), or a variable (variables are discussed in the programming portion of this text).

FIND and SEEK search the active index file and find the first record that matches your specifications. The record itself is not displayed; the FIND and SEEK commands simply locate the record pointer at the desired record. If no match is found, FoxPro responds with a "Find not successful" error message. To try the FIND command, enter

```
SET INDEX TO NAME
FIND Moore
DISPLAY
```

The result is as follows:

```
Record #     SOCIAL         LASTNAME  FIRSTNAME  ADDRESS...
        5    121-90-5432    Moore     Ellen      270 Browning Ave...
```

To try the SEEK command, enter

```
SET INDEX TO TAPES
SEEK 4
DISPLAY
```

The result is as follows:

```
Record#      SOCIAL         LASTNAME  FIRSTNAME  ADDRESS...
        2    121-33-9876    Martin    William    4807 East Avenue...
```

REMEMBER: The menu equivalent of the SEEK command is available by choosing SEEK from the RECORD menu.

The FIND and SEEK commands offer the advantage of speed over the LOCATE command (introduced in Chapter 3). LOCATE is simple to use but slow. In a database containing thousands of records, a LOCATE command can take several minutes. A FIND or SEEK command can accomplish the same task in a matter of seconds.

When you are searching for a character string, both FIND and SEEK allow you to search on only the beginning of the string. However, you should keep in mind that both the FIND and SEEK commands search for an exact match, in terms of capitalization. For example, if the Generic Videos database index is set to NAME, the two commands

```
FIND Mo
FIND Moore
```

would both find the record for Moore. However, the command

```
FIND mo
```

would not find the record, because FoxPro considers uppercase and lowercase letters to be different characters. As far as FoxPro is concerned, "Moore" and "moore" are different names. One way of preventing problems with the case-significance of FoxPro is to design entry forms that store your character data as all uppercase letters. Another method is to use a FoxPro function called the UPPER function. The use of this function is discussed later in this chapter.

Index Tips and Unusual Cases

With all the different ways to arrange a file, you may occasionally run into some unusual requests relating to indexing. The following sections cover some of the more unusual areas of indexing, along with hints for making your indexing as efficient as possible.

The Multiple Numeric Field Trap

With multiple numeric fields, things may not always turn out as you expect because of the way FoxPro builds an index expression. Consider a database of department store sales, with fields for customer name, high credit amounts, and balance amounts. You are preparing a mailing, and you want to target customers who have high credit lines and low account balances; they are likely prospects for heavy spending. You'd like to get an idea of who these customers are, so you prepare a report showing records sorted by high credit amounts. Where the high credit amounts are the same, you'd like to order the records by outstanding balance. If you use the INDEX command to do something like

```
USE SALES
INDEX ON HIGHCREDIT + BALANCE TO MAILER
LIST STORE, CUSTNAME, CUSTNUMB, HIGHCREDIT, BALANCE
```

The results will look like this:

```
STORE           CUSTNAME      CUSTNUMB   HIGHCREDIT    BALANCE
Collin Creek    Artis, K.     1008        1200.00        0.00
Oak Lawn        Jones, C.     1003         900.00      350.00
Galleria        Johnson, L.   1002        1200.00      675.00
Six Flags       Keemis, M.    1007        2000.00        0.00
Collin Creek    Williams, E.  1010        2000.00        0.00
Prestonwood     Smith, A.M.   1009        2000.00      220.00
Prestonwood     Allen, L.     1005        2000.00      312.00
Downtown        Walker, B.    1006        1300.00     1167.00
Prestonwood     Smith, A.     1001        2000.00      788.50
Downtown        Jones, J.     1011        2000.00      875.00
Collin Creek    Jones, J.L.   1004        2000.00     1850.00
```

Rather than concatenating the two numbers, FoxPro has added them
and indexed in the order of the sum, which may not be what you had
in mind. To FoxPro, the plus symbol means something different for
numeric expressions than for string (character-based) expressions. The
plus symbol adds numbers, but it combines character expressions. If
you instead use the SORT command, with commands like

```
USE SALES
SORT ON HIGHCREDIT,BALANCE TO SALES1
USE SALES1
LIST STORE, CUSTNAME, CUSTNUMB, HIGHCREDIT, BALANCE
```

You will get these results

```
STORE           CUSTNAME      CUSTNUMB   HIGHCREDIT    BALANCE
Oak Lawn        Jones, C.     1003         900.00      350.00
Collin Creek    Artis, K.     1008        1200.00        0.00
Galleria        Johnson, L.   1002        1200.00      675.00
Downtown        Walker, B.    1006        1300.00     1167.00
Six Flags       Keemis, M.    1007        2000.00        0.00
Collin Creek    Williams, E.  1010        2000.00        0.00
Prestonwood     Smith, A.M.   1009        2000.00      220.00
Prestonwood     Allen, L.     1005        2000.00      312.00
Prestonwood     Smith, A.     1001        2000.00      788.50
Downtown        Jones, J.     1011        2000.00      875.00
Collin Creek    Jones, J.L.   1004        2000.00     1850.00
```

What you get is what was expected: a file in numeric order by high
credit, and where high credit is the same, in order of the outstanding
balance. The unexpected results when using INDEX occur because the

INDEX command, when used with multiple fields, depends on a math expression. In this case, FoxPro is adding the amounts, building the index on a value that is the sum of the amounts. To index on the combined numeric fields and get the desired results, you would have to first convert the numeric expressions into string values and then use the plus symbol to combine the string values. In the previous example, you could issue a command like

```
INDEX ON STR(HIGHCREDIT) + STR(BALANCE) TO CSALES
```

to accomplish the same result as the SORT command.

4

Using Functions to Standardize Case

Use the UPPER and LOWER functions to avoid problems with case.

The UPPER function and, less commonly, the LOWER function are often used to avoid problems arising from the case-sensitive nature of FoxPro. These functions can also be used as part of an index expression, resulting in an index containing characters that are all uppercase or all lowercase. The potential problem that can arise when the data entry people are not consistent with methods of data entry is shown in the following example. In this database of names, some of the names start with initial capital letters, some are entered as all caps, and some are all lowercase:

```
USE SAMPLE
INDEX ON NAME TO NAMES
LIST
```

Record#	NAME	AGE
1	ADDISON, E.	32
2	Addison, a.	28
3	Carlson, F.	45
4	McLean,R.	28
5	Mcdonald, s.	47
7	Smith, S.	55
8	Smith, b.	37
10	adams, j.q.	76
6	de laurentis, m.	25
9	edelstein, m.	22

Unless told otherwise, FoxPro puts lowercase letters after uppercase letters in the index, and the results are probably not what you had in mind. If you use the UPPER function to build the index, you get acceptable results, as shown with the following commands:

```
USE SAMPLE
INDEX ON UPPER(NAME) TO NAMES
LIST

Record#       NAME                 AGE
    10        adams, j.q.          76
     2        ADDISON, A.          28
     1        Addison, E.          32
     3        Carlson, F.          45
     6        de laurentis, m.     25
     9        edelstein, m.        22
     5        Mcdonald, s.         47
     4        McLean,R.            28
     8        Smith, b.            37
     7        Smith, S.            55
```

To find such records in the index, simply enter all uppercase letters in the expression used along with the FIND or SEEK command. For example, the command

```
SEEK "ADDISON"
```

would find the records in this database, regardless of the case of the letters in each actual record.

Indexing on a Date Field

When you need an index based partially on a date field, FoxPro can present a bit of a challenge. It's no problem when you want to see the database in order by just one date field. Consider the example of a small medical database, containing patient names and a field with the date of admission to a hospital. You can use commands like these, with the results shown:

```
USE PATIENT
INDEX ON ADMITTED TO DATESIN
LIST PATIENT, ADMITTED

Record#       PATIENT      ADMITTED
     1        Smith, A.    04/05/85
     2        Johnson, L.  04/15/85
     3        Jones, C.    04/15/85
```

```
 4       Jones, J.L.   04/15/85
 5       Allen, L.     05/20/86
 6       Walker, B.    05/20/86
 7       Keemis, M.    05/20/86
 8       Artis, K.     05/20/86
 9       Smith, A.M.   05/20/86
10       Williams, E.  06/14/86
11       Jones, J.     06/22/86
```

You get a database indexed in the order of the entries in the date field. Things get more complex, however, when you want a database indexed on a combination of fields, and one of the fields is a date field.

4

Since FoxPro doesn't let you index directly on multiple fields of different types, you must use functions to convert the date into a character string. Assuming the database contains a date field named Diagnosed and a character field named Patient, and you want it indexed by date and then by the name of the patient, you would use the DTOS function. This function is specifically designed to store date values in true chronological order. It converts a date value to a character value of *YYYYMMDD*, where *YYYY* is the year, *MM* the month, and *DD* the day. When an index is built with the DTOS function, the result comes out in true chronological order. Using the sample database just described, the commands:

```
USE PATIENT
INDEX ON DTOS(DIAGNOSED) + PATIENT TO COMBO
LIST PATIENT, DIAGNOSED
```

provide an index based on date and patient name, in the correct chronological order:

```
Record#    PATIENT        DIAGNOSED
      3    Jones, C.      02/08/85
      4    Jones, J.L.    03/02/85
      2    Johnson, L.    03/06/85
      1    Smith, A.      03/17/85
      9    Smith, A.M.    02/03/86
      7    Keemis, M.     02/23/86
      8    Artis, K.      04/19/86
      5    Allen, L.      05/12/86
      6    Walker, B.     05/16/86
```

```
10    Williams, E. 06/01/86
11    Jones, J.    06/13/86
```

Tips for Indexing

A few tips when you are using index files will help speed things along in FoxPro.

Performance improves with short index keys.

✦ *Use short keys when you don't need long ones* Most indexes are directly based on a series of character fields, and in real life, most character fields get unique around the tenth character, if not sooner. If you can get by with indexing on fewer characters, do so. FoxPro will manage the index in less time. Let's look at a real-world example. You are building a customer file for a store in a medium-sized city of about 100,000 people, so you do not need to deal with the duplication of names that you get in New York or Los Angeles. The customer base is manageable: you might see a maximum of 5000 to 10,000 records in the file over the next ten years. The store manager despises labels with names cut off for lack of field width, so you've specified a width of 30 characters each for the Lastname and Firstname fields. You are going to index on a key field of customer number as the primary index, but you also want an index based on a combination of last and first names so you can quickly find a record when a customer is on the phone and does not have his or her customer number handy.

In this situation, do you really need an index based on the Lastname and Firstname fields? Quite likely not, but this is often done out of force of habit, and FoxPro must work harder for it. If you instead do something like

```
INDEX ON LEFT(LASTNAME,10) + LEFT(FIRSTNAME,10)
```

the use of the LEFT function results in an index that contains 20 characters per entry, as opposed to an index that contains 60 characters per entry. Given the customer base, having the first ten characters of the last and first names should be more than enough to keep the records in order and find a given record. Also, the index file uses considerably less disk space.

Store identification numbers in character fields.

✦ *Store numbers in character fields if you are never going to perform calculations on those numbers*   If you use numbers as unique identifiers (as in part numbers, employee numbers, invoice numbers, and so on) and you plan to use this data as a part of the index, don't store it in a numeric field. Use a character field instead. It makes a difference to FoxPro, because FoxPro does a better job of indexing on character fields than on numeric fields. When you try indexing with very large files, it becomes apparent that FoxPro takes longer to index a numeric field than a character field of equivalent size. Assuming you are not going to calculate such fields, they don't need to be numeric fields.

✦ *Perform routine maintenance often*   When FoxPro must perform sequential operations while your index files are open, it has to work harder. You can cut down processing times by regularly putting your database files back in their natural order. To do this, open the file along with the index you most often use for sequential reporting or processing, and use the COPY TO *filename* command to copy the contents of the file to another file. Then delete the original database, give the new database the same name as the original database, and rebuild the necessary indexes. In applications using large files that are regularly updated, this simple step can make a dramatic difference to users in terms of response time when they are performing any reporting or processing based on sequential operations in FoxPro. Part of the speedup may also be due to the fact that the creation of a new database with the COPY command results in a new file under DOS, which may have its data arranged in sectors located side by side on the hard disk. Often, when a file has been updated over months of time, it is arranged in sectors that are scattered all over the hard disk. You can use the technique just described to reduce such fragmentation of files over a hard disk, or you can use one of the many "disk optimizer" software packages available to clean up your hard disk and make all of your files more accessible to your software.

CHAPTER

FOXPRO

5

PERFORMING QUERIES

This chapter covers an important subject: getting the desired data out of your database. Performing queries, or the fine art of asking questions, is the most common task done with computer databases. With so much time spent in this area, it pays to know the best ways to query a database in FoxPro. There are many ways to get desired data out of a database in FoxPro. Some are faster than others, and different ways are often best suited to different tasks.

As with most activities in FoxPro, data can be retrieved with the menus and with commands. When it comes to queries, you're likely to see a distinct advantage in the use of commands over menus. The commands, once learned, tend to be faster to implement; querying a database through the menus often involves a large number of menu selections. Also, the command structure can be used as an integral part of programs written in FoxPro, and the programming language (which you will begin to learn about in Chapter 12) is a major resource of FoxPro. The first portion of this chapter highlights queries performed through menu selections, and the second half covers queries performed with commands.

Performing Queries with the Menus

All of your data retrieval tasks will involve one of two scenarios: either you will need to select a single record or you will need to isolate a subgroup of records (a process often followed by the printing of a report). If a single record is all you need, the Goto, Locate, and Seek options, found on the Record menu, are what you are after.

Using Goto

The Goto option lets you move to the top or bottom of the file, move by a set number of records, or move to a specific record (by record number). For example, if you know that record 7 needs to be edited, you can (after opening the database with a USE command or with the Open option of the File menu) open the Record menu and choose Goto. When you do this, the dialog box shown in Figure 5-1 appears. Four options are provided: Top, Bottom, Record, and Skip. You must choose an option, then tab over to the Goto button in the dialog box, and press [Enter] (or click the button) to implement your choice.

Choosing Top moves the record pointer to the top of the database, while the Bottom option moves the record pointer to the last record in the database. The Skip option lets you move the record pointer by a certain number of records. If you choose Skip, the number 1 appears in an entry field, because the Skip option assumes you want to skip forward by one record. You can enter any other number you want, including negative numbers; for example, entering **−5** would move you back five records in the database, and entering **42** would move you forward 42 records. If you choose the Record option, the number 1

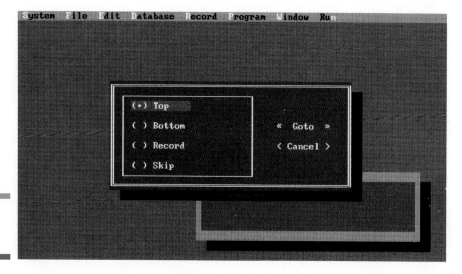

System File Edit Database Record Program Window Run

(•) Top

( ) Bottom   « Goto »

( ) Record   < Cancel >

( ) Skip

Goto dialog
box
Figure 5-1.

appears in an entry field, and you can enter the record number of the
desired record. Once you make your choice of ways to move the record
pointer, you can tab over to the Goto button and press (Enter), and the
pointer will move to the desired record.

These methods are fine when you know by its record number where a
record is located. Unfortunately, this is usually not the case; most users
performing queries have no idea where a desired record may be. Thus,
you need some sort of search operation. Searches can be performed
with the Locate, Continue, and Seek options, also found on the Record
menu. The Seek option assumes the use of an index, and the resulting
search must be performed based on the field or fields used to build the
index. Therefore, if you wanted to perform a seek based on the last
name, the database would need to be indexed on the Lastname field (or
on a combination of fields that begins with the Lastname field). Locate
and Continue do not need an index, but with large databases, they are
considerably slower than Seek.

Using Locate

To find a record without an index in use, open the Record menu and
choose Locate. The dialog box shown in Figure 5-2 appears. This dialog
box provides you with three options: Scope, For, and While.

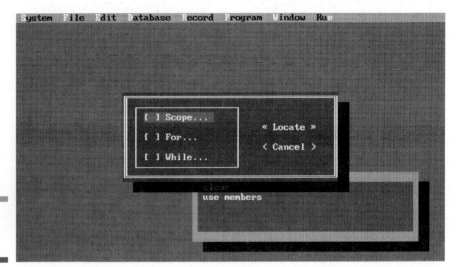

Locate dialog
box
Figure 5-2.

The Scope option reveals yet another dialog box with four options: All,
Next, Record, and Rest. The optional use of a scope lets you define a
further limit to the operation of the Locate option. You can choose All
to specify that the use of Locate should span all records; this is the
default. You can choose Next and then enter a number that specifies a
group of records starting with wherever the pointer is now located; for
example, entering **10** tells FoxPro to limit its use of Locate to the next
ten records. You can choose Record and enter a number, which again
selects a specific record by its record number. (In the case of Locate, this
is a useless option, since if you knew the record number, you wouldn't
need a search.) Or you can choose Rest, which limits the use of Locate
to all records located between the pointer and the end of the file.
Again, none of these options are much help unless you know
something about where the desired record is located.

The For and While options that appear after you choose Locate are the
options likely to prove most useful. The While option works best with
an index, but the For option can easily be used on any field, whether an
index exists or not. Choose For from the dialog box, and the Expression
Builder containing a For Clause window next appears (Figure 5-3). In
this window, you enter the expression that will locate the record you
want. An *expression* is a combination of field names, operators, and
constants that evaluate to a certain value. The term

```
LASTNAME = "Morris"
```

is an expression, as is

```
TAPELIMIT > 3
```

which evaluates to a tape limit of more than 3. If the parts of the expression do not make sense at this point, don't be too concerned; they are explained in more detail later in this chapter.

Field names, which are normally used to build search expressions, can be selected from the Field Names box in the lower-left corner of the dialog box. Once a name is selected, it appears in the For Clause window. (As an alternative, you may choose to enter the field name in the For Clause window by typing it.) The next step is usually to enter an operator, such as an equal sign. You can choose most of the commonly used operators by clicking the Logical box and selecting the operator from a pull-down menu; however, it is usually faster just to type the symbol into the For Clause box. Finally, enter the desired search value. Text expressions are always entered with quotes surrounding them; numbers are entered exactly as they are stored in the numeric field; and dates may be entered with the CTOD function. For example, CTOD("12/20/93") would be evaluated as a date value of

5

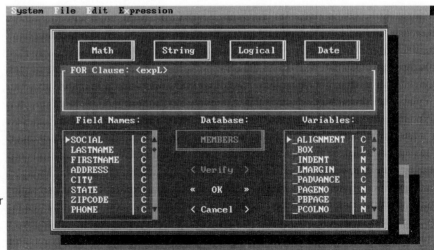

Expression
Builder with For
Clause window
Figure 5-3.

12/20/93. You can also use memo fields within your conditions when searching for a value.

You will make use of logical operators (covered in more detail in later chapters) to apply multiple conditions to a search. Two common logical operators are .AND. and .OR., which specify whether all conditions must be met (.AND.) or whether either condition can be met (.OR.). For example, the condition

```
LASTNAME = "Robinson" .AND. TAPELIMIT = 2
```

specifies that the last name must be Robinson, and the tape limit must contain a value of 2. The condition

```
CITY = "Falls Church" .OR. CITY = "Arlington"
```

specifies that the City field must contain either Arlington or Falls Church. Note that the logical operators are always surrounded by periods.

You can check your expression for correct syntax, if desired, by tabbing to or clicking the Verify button. If the expression is a valid one, FoxPro displays an "Expression is valid" message. Finally, tab to or click the OK button to finish your entry. The Locate dialog box will reappear, with the For option selected. You can now tab to or click the Locate button to implement the search. Remember, the process only locates the record—it does not display it. You can now choose the Change option of the Record menu to view the record.

REMEMBER: With large databases, LOCATE can be slow. If the field you are searching is indexed, use FIND or SEEK instead.

Consider a simple example, which you can duplicate if you've created the MEMBERS database outlined in Chapter 2. Perhaps you need to locate Mr. Kramer, a member of the video club. Assuming the MEMBERS file is open, you can open the Record menu with Alt - R, choose Locate, and select the For option when the Locate dialog box (shown in Figure 5-2) appears. The For Clause dialog box next appears

(Figure 5-3); your desired expression will be LASTNAME = "Kramer".
You can simply type this into the For Clause window, or you can select
Lastname from the list of fields, type an equal sign or choose one from
the pull-down menu that appears when you tab to the Logical menu
and press the (Spacebar) (or click the Logical menu), and then type
"Kramer" (you must include the quotation marks). For mouse users,
an alternative to typing the quotation marks is to click the String box
and select Text from the pull-down menu that appears, and then type
the name; but again, it is usually faster to just type in the quotation
marks manually.

Once all this is done, the For Clause dialog box resembles the example
shown in Figure 5-4. (If you entered the field name manually, you
probably won't have the filename prefix (MEMBERS.) in your example;
it is added if you select the field name from the list box. Such prefixes
are needed for working with multiple files, as covered in Chapter 10;
when you are working with just one file, it does not matter whether
they are included or not.

You next select the OK button, and the Locate dialog box reappears.
Finally, click the Locate button in the Locate dialog box to implement
the search. If you then choose Change from the Record menu, the
desired record appears.

5

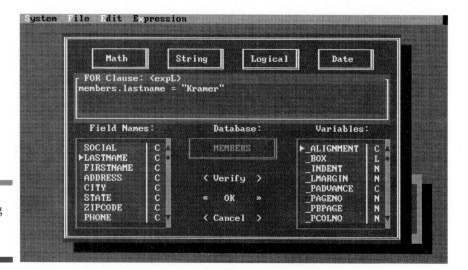

Filled-in For
Clause dialog
box
Figure 5-4.

Probably the strongest argument for using commands in place of the menu options appears in the Command window after you've completed the operation just described. These two commands are shown in the window:

```
LOCATE ALL FOR members.lastname = "Kramer"
CHANGE
```

They could have been entered from Command mode to perform the same task. Even the "members." could have been omitted, as this combination of the database name, and period identifies the file, and such identifiers are optional when you have only one file open. Hence, the command

```
LOCATE ALL FOR LASTNAME = "Kramer"
```

would have worked just as well as the menu options.

When you use Locate, FoxPro searches by examining the characters in your search term from left to right, so you need enter only as much of the term as necessary to find the record. For example, the command

```
LOCATE FOR LASTNAME = "Jo"
```

would be enough to find a person named Jones if there were no other names with "Jo" as the first two letters of the name.

When selected, the While option in the Locate dialog box (see Figure 5-2) causes the same Expression Builder to appear; the only difference is the window that will contain the expression is labeled "While Clause." Figure 5-5 shows an example of the Expression Builder containing the While Clause window. Using the While option takes a little more planning than using the For option, because the While clause is effective only "while" a condition exists. For example, if you were to enter **LASTNAME = "Kramer"** as an expression in the While Clause dialog box, FoxPro would locate the record only while the condition was true; in other words, the database pointer would need to already be at a record with Kramer in the Lastname field.

While clauses are normally used with indexed files, where you want to locate all records while a certain condition is true. For example, with a database indexed by tape limit, you could find the first record with a tape limit of 6 and then perform a Locate operation while the tape limit was 6.

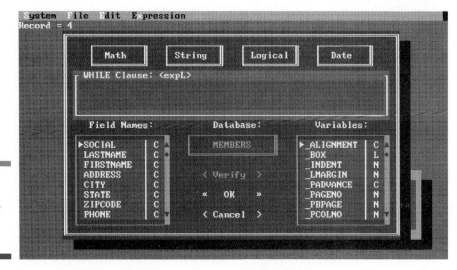

Expression
Builder with
While Clause
window
Figure 5-5.

5

Using Continue

The Locate option finds the first occurrence of what you are looking
for. If there is more than one occurrence, you can use the Continue
option to find successive records with the same search term. For
example, your database might contain two persons with a last name of
Robinson, and the use of Locate might turn up the wrong one. You can
again open the Record menu with [Alt]-[R] and choose Continue. The
Continue option is available from the menu only after you have used
the Locate option. It continues the search, seeking the next record that
meets the condition you specified when using Locate. If no further
records meet the specified condition, you will see an "End of Locate
scope" message on the screen. (You will see the same error message if an
initial use of Locate fails to find a record.)

REMEMBER: You can use the CONTINUE command only after using
a LOCATE command.

Using Seek

If a file has been indexed, you can search the index with the Seek option. When you open the Record menu and choose Seek, the Expression Builder appears, containing a Value to Seek window (Figure 5-6). Again, the operation of the Seek option's Expression Builder is like that used with the For and While options of Locate. Seek simply works much faster with large files, because it takes less time to search an indexed file.

You enter the desired expression into the Value to Seek window. However, you need enter only the expression itself, since FoxPro knows which field (or fields) the index is based on. For example, instead of entering LASTNAME = "Kramer" as was done with Locate, you would only enter "**Kramer**" in the Value to Seek window, assuming the active index is based on Lastname. Remember that since Seek is designed to work with an index, you must search for data based on the index. (You could not, for example, use Seek to search for a last name if the database were indexed only by social security number.)

Text expressions are always entered surrounded by quotes; numbers are entered exactly as they are stored in the numeric field; and dates may be entered with the CTOD function. As an example of Seek, if the video database were indexed on the Tapelimit field, you could enter **4** in the

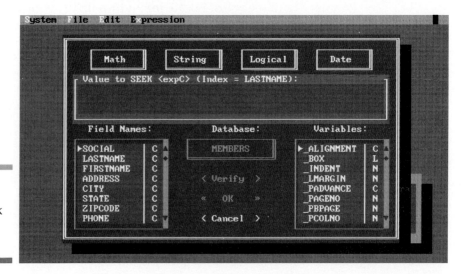

Expression
Builder with
Value to Seek
window
Figure 5-6.

Value to Seek window, and the Seek option would find the first record with a value of 4 in the Tapelimit field. If the database were indexed on the Expiredate field, you could enter **CTOD("12/20/93")** in the Value to Seek window to find the first record with the expiration date of 12/20/93.

After entering the search value, tab to or click the OK button, and the seek will take place. You can then use the Change option of the Record menu to view the desired record. Keep in mind that the Seek option finds the first occurrence in the index. If there are duplicate occurrences of that index expression (such as more than one last name of Robinson in a file indexed on Lastname only), you may want to use Browse to aid you in finding the desired record.

Selecting Subsets of Data

You can also select subsets of data with FoxPro's RQBE window. (See chapter 6 for details.)

Often, a query involves selecting a group of records. (You should note that such queries can be done by using the techniques that follow or by using FoxPro's RQBE (Relational Query By Example) window. The use of RQBE to create queires is covered in the following chapter.) For example, you may want to see all members who live in Maryland or Virginia. From the menus, this can be done with the Setup option of the Database menu. This option, among other things, lets you set a filter that restricts the available records; in effect, the records shown must meet the conditions of the filter that you specify.

When you open the Database menu and choose Setup, the Setup dialog box appears (Figure 5-7). This dialog box is used for many tasks; the one this chapter is concerned with is the Filter option, shown in the lower-left corner of the dialog box. If you choose Filter (by pressing the highlighted letter L or by tabbing to it or clicking the option), the Expression Builder containing a Set Filter Expression window appears (Figure 5-8). By now, the design of the Expression Builder should be quite familiar; you enter an expression in the same manner as with the For option of the Locate command. Field names can be selected from the Field Names box in the lower-left corner of the dialog box. Once a name is selected, it appears in the Set Filter Expression window. (As an alternative, you can enter the name in the Set Filter Expression window by typing it.) Next, you enter the desired operator, such as the equal sign. Finally, enter the desired search value. Remember to surround text

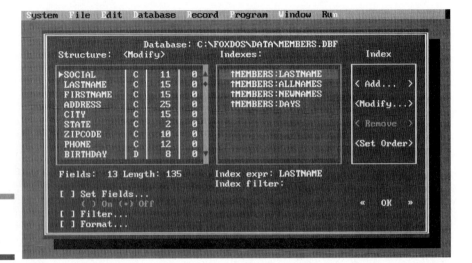

Setup dialog
box
Figure 5-7.

expressions with quotes and enter any dates with the CTOD function.
As an example, the expression

```
TAPELIMIT = 6
```

would select a group of records with a value of 6 in the Tapelimit field.
The expression

```
STATE = "MD" .OR. STATE = "VA"
```

would select records with either Maryland or Virginia in the State field.

Once you enter the expression and choose the OK button, the Database
Structure dialog box reappears. Choose the OK button in this dialog
box, and the needed SET FILTER command appears in the Command
window. You must press (Enter) to execute the command. You can then
proceed to perform a browse to see your records meeting the condition,
or you can use the LIST command to produce a simple on-screen report.

Again, consider a simple example. Perhaps you need a list of all
customers in the video database who live in Maryland or Virginia. You
would open the Database menu with (Alt)-(D), choose Setup, and select
Filter from the dialog box that appears. The Expression Builder would
next appear, as shown in Figure 5-8. You would next enter the
following expression in the Set Filter Expression window:

```
STATE = "MD" .OR. STATE = "VA"
```

Then you would select the OK button and again select the OK button in the next dialog box that appears. The resultant command, which is

```
SET FILTER TO STATE = "MD" .OR. STATE = "VA"
```

now appears in the Command window. Note that if you are using any version of FoxPro prior to version 2, you must press Enter to implement the command, and the filter is set. At this point, you could choose Browse from the Database menu to see the records meeting your filter condition.

Reporting Needs

5

If you need a report based on a select group of data, one method is to use the menu options just described for setting a filter as a part of a three-step process. First, design and save a report, as detailed in Chapters 7 and 10 (this needs to be done only once). Then use the menu options just described to set the desired filter conditions. Finally, select the Report option from the Database menu to print the report.

Another method works well if a simple columnar report with no fancy headings will suffice. Set the filter as described earlier, then use the LIST

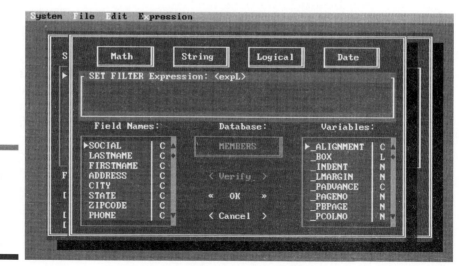

Expression
Builder with
Set Filter
Expression
window
Figure 5-8.

command with the desired fields, and add the TO PRINT option to route the output to the printer. For example, after setting the filter condition described in the prior example, you could enter the command

```
LIST LASTNAME, FIRSTNAME, STATE, EXPIREDATE TO PRINT
```

to produce a columnar listing of the above named fields at the printer. Such a list would resemble the example shown here:

```
Record#     LASTNAME    FIRSTNAME    STATE    EXPIREDATE
      1     Miller      Karen        MD       07/25/94
      2     Martin      William      MD       07/04/94
      3     Robinson    Carol        VA       09/05/95
      4     Kramer      Harry        VA       12/22/94
      5     Moore       Ellen        MD       11/17/96
      6     Zachman     David        VA       09/19/94
      8     Hart        Wendy        VA       10/19/94
```

You will find additional details on the use of the LIST command with the TO PRINT option in Chapter 7.

Before proceeding, enter the command

```
SET FILTER TO
```

with no expression following the command, and press Enter. This clears the effects of the previous filter.

Performing Queries with Commands

There are four commands you can use to search for items in FoxPro: LOCATE, CONTINUE, FIND, and SEEK. The LOCATE and CONTINUE commands perform a sequential search (checking one record at a time) and work with any database. The FIND and SEEK commands perform a much faster search than LOCATE but work with indexed files only.

Using LOCATE

The LOCATE command can be used to find the first occurrence of a record. The syntax for the command is

LOCATE [*scope*] FOR *condition*

where *condition* is a logical expression (such as LASTNAME = "Morris") that defines your search. The scope, which is optional, can be used to limit the number of records searched. If the scope is omitted, FoxPro assumes that you want to search all of the records in the file. You can enter **ALL** to specify that the use of LOCATE should span all records; this is the default. You can enter **NEXT** and then enter a number that specifies a group of records starting with wherever the pointer is now located; for example, entering **NEXT 10** as the scope would tell FoxPro to limit its use of LOCATE to the next ten records, starting with the current record. Or you can enter **REST**, which limits the use of LOCATE to all records from wherever the pointer is located to the end of the file.

Note that LOCATE does not find all matches, or even the second match—only the first match. Its companion command, CONTINUE, is used to continue the search as many times as desired, assuming the first record found was not the one you really wanted. LOCATE and CONTINUE carry on a sequential search until either a record is found or you reach the end of the database. If a LOCATE or CONTINUE command is unsuccessful, you get the message, "End of LOCATE scope."

For an example, a simple search can be entered in the Command window to search the Tapelimit field of the video database:

```
LOCATE FOR TAPELIMIT = 4
DISPLAY
```

The result, shown partially here, shows that the record found indeed contains a value of 4 in the Tapelimit field:

```
121-33-9876   Martin    William    4807 East Avenue...
```

If this is not the desired record, the search can be continued with the CONTINUE command. As an example, if you enter the commands

```
CONTINUE
DISPLAY
```

the result shows that the CONTINUE command found the next occurrence of the desired record:

```
901-77-3456   Kramer    Harry    617 North Oakland Street...
```

5

You can add the logical conditions .AND. and .OR. to get closer to the precise data you want. (The periods must be included around the words AND and OR when used as part of an expression.) The .AND. condition specifies that both conditions on each side of the word AND must be true, while .OR. specifies that either one or the other condition must be true. As an example, if you needed to find a record where the last name was Miller and the tape limit was 6, you could try the command

```
LOCATE FOR LASTNAME = "Miller" .AND. TAPELIMIT = 6
```

If you were seeking a record with an expiration date of 12/31/92 or 1/1/93, you could try the following command:

```
LOCATE FOR EXPIREDATE = CTOD("12/31/92") .OR.
EXPIREDATE = CTOD("01/01/93")
```

When using LOCATE, keep in mind that FoxPro searches by examining the characters in your search term from left to right. Therefore, you need to enter only as much of the term as necessary to find the proper record. For example, the command

```
LOCATE FOR LASTNAME = "Jon"
```

would be enough to find a person named Jones if there were no other names with "Jon" as the first three letters of the name. Sometimes, this left-to-right tendency of a search may be troublesome; for example, the command

```
LOCATE FOR LASTNAME = "Mills"
```

would locate names like Millson or Millsap, which might not be what you had in mind. If you want FoxPro to look for your precise search term, you can first enter the command

```
SET EXACT ON
```

and then enter the desired LOCATE command. The SET EXACT command tells FoxPro to execute any LOCATE, FIND, or SEEK operation using the same length for the search term and the actual data. You can later enter **SET EXACT OFF** to disable this effect.

Using FIND and SEEK

Rememeber
that FJND
and SEEK
require that
an index is
active.

FIND and SEEK work very differently than LOCATE and CONTINUE. Both FIND and SEEK make use of index files to perform a very fast search. (FoxPro may not find anything, but you will know about it very quickly!) Either a record matching the condition supplied is found or the end of the database is reached. This type of search is common with database management software; it is popular because it is extremely fast. Even with a very large database, FoxPro can usually find a record in this manner in well under two seconds. The time that a LOCATE command takes, by comparison, grows progressively worse as the database grows in size.

The syntax for both commands is similar:

> FIND *character-string*
> SEEK *expression*

where *character-string* is a group of characters that do *not* need to be surrounded by quotation marks.

The expression can be a number, a character string (which *must* be surrounded by quotation marks), or a variable. The expression can also be a combination of constants, variables, and operators (including functions).

The FIND and SEEK commands search the active index file and find the first record matching your specifications. The record itself will not be displayed; the FIND and SEEK commands simply move the record pointer to the desired record. Try the commands with the sample video database, entering the following:

```
USE MEMBERS
INDEX ON LASTNAME TO NAMES
FIND Moore
DISPLAY
```

The result is as follows:

```
#5    121-90-5432 Moore     Ellen    270 Browning Ave #2A...
```

To try the SEEK command, enter

```
USE MEMBERS
INDEX ON TAPELIMIT TO TAPES
SEEK 4
DISPLAY
```

The result is shown here:

```
#2      121-33-9876 Martin      William      4807 East Avenue...
```

Note that the index need not be created in every case; if an index already exists, you need only ensure that it is opened before you attempt to use FIND or SEEK.

Comparisons, Comparisons: FIND and SEEK Versus LOCATE and CONTINUE

LOCATE is slower than FIND and SEEK but does not require an index.

Since FIND and SEEK are usually so much faster than LOCATE, why not use FIND or SEEK in every case? Simplicity sometimes plays a part. First, remember that none of these commands is guaranteed to find what you really want. In many cases, it is easier for novice users to get close with LOCATE and CONTINUE than with FIND or SEEK, because FIND and SEEK find only the first matching record. If you're searching for Jim Smith in a 12,000-name mailing list with 75 Jim Smiths, a FIND command will find the first one. It's then up to you to figure out how to find the one you want. This can be done by using a WHILE qualifier along with the LOCATE command, which will then tell FoxPro to start its search at the current position in the database. As an example, you could use commands like these, assuming that the database is indexed by last names:

```
FIND "Smith"
LOCATE WHILE LASTNAME = "Smith" FOR FIRSTNAME = "Jim"
.AND. CITY = "New York"
```

This helps you narrow the search down to the desired record without wasting a great deal of time. An inherent advantage to LOCATE and CONTINUE is that these commands find every matching record (and, sooner or later, the desired one).

Another advantage of LOCATE is its ability to search within a field, using the $ operator. For example, the statement

```
LOCATE FOR "East Avenue" $ ADDRESS
```

would search for the words "East Avenue" inside the Address field. If you are using FIND or SEEK, you must know the starting characters or values in the index key; you cannot search for something in the middle of a field with FIND or SEEK.

HINT: You can use LOCATE to search the contents of memo fields.

5

One more problem with FIND and SEEK is the index file requirement. Logically, for reasons of efficiency, you want to index your files on something. The problem arises when you need to make a search based on something different. Suppose you index by social security number as well as by a combination of last and first name, and you pride yourself for being efficient. Then a coworker comes along and wants to find "this customer I spoke with last week, and I can't remember her name, and I don't know her social security number, but she lives somewhere on Myterra Avenue." Armed with this knowledge, your index files are fairly worthless. And FoxPro spends ten minutes on a command like

```
LOCATE ALL FOR "Myterra Ave" $ ADDRESS
```

while you mutter under your breath, thinking there must be a better way. This is brought out to emphasize one point: the LOCATE and CONTINUE commands are in the language because there may be times you would need them. There are times you will need FIND and SEEK, and there are times you may need LOCATE and CONTINUE (although with good planning, you can minimize those times). Knowing how to effectively use all of the available commands reduces the amount of time FoxPro must spend searching for your data.

The secret to a quick find, if one can be said to exist, is to use an index file and a FIND or SEEK rather than a LOCATE. This may seem like elementary knowledge to some, but it is surprising how many users of the dBASE language are still using LOCATE when it isn't necessary. When indexing on one field, using FIND or SEEK is rarely a problem. If, for example, a personnel list is indexed by last names and you are looking for Ms. Samuels, you simply use

```
FIND Samuels
CHANGE
```

and unless the database is a sizeable one, you're probably at the record or close enough to use (Pg Dn) to get to it. The problem arises when you have large databases and you index on multiple fields to get a more precise match.

Let's say you're working with a large mailing list, and you index on a combination of Lastname + Firstname + City. The Lastname and Firstname fields are each 15 characters long. This means that the records in the index get stored like this:

Smith	Art	Raleigh
Smith	Louise	Tampa
Smith	Louise	Washington
Sodelski	Thomas	St. Louis

The contents of the index precisely match the structure of the field, spaces and all. To use FIND or SEEK from the Command window with such an index and be assured of finding the correct record, you would have to enter something like

```
FIND Smith        Louise        Washington
```

including the exact number of spaces to match the index; otherwise, you get a "no find." There are ways to get around this when writing programs that find records. However, if you do much of your work from the command level, you should be aware of this potential problem. One simple way around it is to search the first field in the index (in this case, Lastname) with a FIND command; when the first matching record is found, use BROWSE to visually scan for the exact record desired.

Using SET FILTER with Commands

The SET FILTER command is a popular one in the dBASE language, and it is one that has its advantages and disadvantages. SET FILTER hides

5

records that do not meet the condition described. The syntax for the command is

> SET FILTER TO *condition*

where *condition* is a logical expression (such as LASTNAME = "Morris") that defines your search. Once the command is entered, other database commands that would normally use records from the entire database will instead use only records that meet the condition specified by the filter. In effect, this lets you work with a subset of a database as though it were the entire database. A command like

```
SET FILTER TO CITY = "Washington" .AND. STATE = "DC"
```

limits a database to those records located in Washington, D.C. In effect, this is the equivalent of the Filter option available from the Database/Setup menu choices. You can isolate a group of records by issuing a SET FILTER command; then you can use the LIST or BROWSE command to view the data, or the REPORT FORM command (covered in the next chapter) to produce a printed report.

As an example, consider the following commands, used with the video database:

```
USE MEMBERS

SET FILTER TO EXPIREDATE >= CTOD("01/01/93") .AND.
EXPIREDATE <= CTOD("12/31/93")

LIST LASTNAME, FIRSTNAME, SOCIAL, EXPIREDATE
```

(The second command appears on two lines here due to printing limitations, but you enter the entire command on a single line.) The SET FILTER command in this example restricts the listed records to only those with expiration dates that fall in the year 1992. You can enclose parts of the expression in parentheses to build very complex expressions. For example, the command

```
SET FILTER TO ( EXPIREDATE >= CTOD("01/01/93") .AND.
EXPIREDATE <= CTOD("12/31/93") ) .OR. STATE = "MD"
```

would limit the records available to those with an expiration date sometime in 1993 or those with the letters MD in the state field.

Rememeber to turn off the filter when done with SET FILTER TO.

You can see whether a filter is in effect at any time by using the LIST STATUS or DISPLAY STATUS command. The listing that results from either of these commands will include the filter condition for any filter that is in effect. And you can cancel the effects of an existing filter by entering

```
SET FILTER TO
```

without including a condition in the command, as shown here.

One point sometimes overlooked, until you get used to this abnormality, is that when you set a filter, the current record is not immediately affected by the filter. The filter does not take effect until you move the record pointer. If the next command causes the record pointer to move before data is displayed or printed, fine. If not, you may wind up with a record you don't really want. This problem can be illustrated by the use of a large personnel database containing a Lastname field. When the following commands are entered, note the result:

```
SET FILTER TO LASTNAME = "Robinson"
LIST LASTNAME NEXT 10

Record#   LASTNAME
      1   Miller
      3   Robinson
      7   Robinson
     11   Robinson
     15   Robinson
     19   Robinson
     23   Robinson
     27   Robinson
     31   Robinson
     52   Robinson
```

The first name in the display obviously isn't Robinson—it is the name in the record that was current when the LIST command was entered. Once any action that causes movement of the record pointer is taken, the invalid record disappears.

You'll have to think about whether the commands you use immediately after the SET FILTER command will move the record pointer before displaying any data. The REPORT FORM and LABEL FORM commands move the pointer to the top of the database before printing any reports or labels, so you will get the proper results if no NEXT or WHILE clauses are included in the REPORT FORM or LABEL FORM command. Similarly, a LIST command normally moves the pointer before a display of data, but it won't if you include a NEXT or WHILE scope along with the command. If you try a command like LIST NEXT 20 immediately after a SET FILTER command, you will get 19 records that meet the condition, and one that may not. The solution, simple enough, is to move the record pointer with a GO TOP command immediately after the SET FILTER command. This moves the record pointer to the first record meeting the filter condition, and you can then use the desired commands.

SET FILTER can be slow with large, indexed files.

Before you become too fond of the SET FILTER command, you should be aware of its disadvantages. The SET FILTER command appears to perform a rapid sequential qualification of every record in the database, starting from record 1 and moving to the highest record number. Because FoxPro performs a rapid internal search during this process, it is not a problem if the record numbers happen to be in sequential order (which means that no index files are open). If an index file is open, and one usually is, FoxPro examines each record sequentially in index order. Since this involves checking both the index and the database for each record, any operation that uses SET FILTER will be terribly slow for a large, indexed database. Understandably, the larger the database, the more interminable the delays with an indexed file.

You can avoid opening the index files while using SET FILTER, which is fine if you don't mind the problems of trying to keep the indexes updated after changes have been made. Then, too, what happens when you want a report with an odd selection of certain records? You probably want it in some kind of sorted order, and the alternative of sorting the database and then setting a filter is about as appealing as the slow index.

The answer, like so many things in life, is a compromise. When using indexes, stay away from filters wherever possible; when using filters, stay away from indexes wherever possible. If you want to find records for editing and updating, don't use filters. Open indexes and use FIND

5

or SEEK instead. Save the SET FILTER command for showing lists of data and for serving your reporting needs. It is less annoying to see a delay during reporting; most users turn on the printer, choose the report, and go off to do something else while FoxPro does all the work. Also, in reporting needs, often a large percentage of your records may meet the filter criteria, and performance improves as more records match the criteria outlined with the SET FILTER command. An alternative to the use of SET FILTER is to use the FOR clause with the INDEX command to build a selective index file. This topic was covered in detail in Chapter 4.

Using View Files

The conditions placed in effect with a SET FILTER command can be stored in the form of a *view file* for additional use at a later time. A view file will also contain a record of any open database and index files, as well as any screen format file in use at the time the view file was created. You can think of a view file as a "snapshot" of your open database files, index files, a filter condition, and any screen format file in use. The view file can be created with the command CREATE VIEW *filename* FROM ENVIRONMENT. Once you have opened your database and index files, placed any desired format file into use, and set a filter condition with a SET FILTER command, you enter

    CREATE VIEW *filename* FROM ENVIRONMENT

where *filename* is the name for the view file. Once you have done this, you no longer need to repeat the same set of commands for the opening of files and the setting of the filter during a later session with FoxPro. Instead, you can simply use the SET VIEW command, using the following syntax:

    SET VIEW TO *filename*

Filename is the name of the view file saved earlier, and FoxPro will open the same database, index files, and screen format file (if any). Any filter condition that was in effect when the view file was created will be placed back into effect.

Not only is this useful for saving yourself the tedious entry of a number of commands, but it can also be used with reports. As Chapter 7 shows, an ENVIRONMENT option of the REPORT FORM command automatically opens and places into effect the settings in a view file before a report is produced. And a view file will also contain any relations that have been established between multiple files. (Relations between multiple files are covered in Chapter 11.)

5

CHAPTER

FOXPRO

6

CREATING QUERIES WITH RQBE

As mentioned in the last chapter, a significant part of managing your data consists of finding specific groups of information, or making queries. The commands and menu options detailed in the last chapter can be used to find records and to isolate groups of records. However, users of FoxPro version 2 and above can also make use of FoxPro's RQBE feature to quickly isolate groups of records for browsing or reporting needs.

An important advantage of RQBE over the methods described in the prior chapter is speed. When you use RQBE to implement a query, FoxPro interprets your selections within the RQBE window as SELECT commands. (The SELECT command is a command in a computer language called SQL, originally implemented by IBM on mainframe computers in the 1970s.) FoxPro uses advanced technology to optimize the query, creating the most efficient type of SELECT command for your particular query. Hence, queries performed by using selections from the RQBE window (or the equivalent SELECT commands) are likely to execute much faster than any commands you enter by using the LOCATE and SET FILTER commands described in the previous chapter.

HINT: Queries designed by using the RQBE window operate much faster than selections implemented with SET FILTER commands or FOR clauses.

Creating a Query with RQBE

Creating a query is a simple matter with RQBE. The basic steps involved in this process are as follows:

1. Choose New Query from the Run menu, or enter the CREATE QUERY command.
2. Choose the database for use in the query (if you already have a database open, it is chosen by default).
3. Choose the fields that you want to see in the results of the query.
4. If desired, change the order of the fields for the results.
5. Choose the desired destination for the results (by default, the output is to a Browse window).
6. Specify any selection criteria for the records.
7. Perform the query.
8. Save the query (if desired) for reuse later.

As mentioned, queries are designed by using the RQBE window (Figure 6-1). You can get to this window in one of three ways. You can choose the New Query option from the Run menu. Or, you can choose New from the File menu. When the dialog box appears, you can select Query and then choose OK. Or from the command level, you can enter the command CREATE QUERY. Either method results in the display of the RQBE window.

The upper-left portion of the RQBE Window contains a list box for databases that are to be used by the query. (Chapter 11 shows how you can perform a query using more than one database file; for now, only the MEMBERS database is used.) The upper-center portion of the window displays a list box called Output Fields. This list box is used to determine which fields should be included in the results of the query. At the upper-right side of the window, the Output To pull-down menu is used to control where the results of the query are sent. By default, the results appear in a Browse window; however, you can have them appear in the form of a printed report or as a new database file.

The lower portion of the window is the Select Criteria area. In this area, you choose the conditions that will limit the records provided by the query, such as "all members living in Maryland" or "all employees earning more than $9.00 per hour."

6

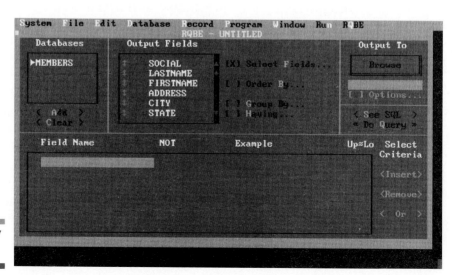

RQBE window
Figure 6-1.

Note that the RQBE window also contains a new menu among the main menu options, titled RQBE. This menu contains the same options that appear as selection buttons in the RQBE window; you can either select the desired button or choose the option from the menu. The various buttons (and their equivalent menu options) are discussed throughout this chapter.

Once you have chosen the desired options in the RQBE window, you select the Do Query button at the right side of the window, and the query is performed. Depending on your selection at the Output To menu, your results appear on screen, are printed, or are stored in a new database file.

Practice Queries

Assuming you are following along with the example of the MEMBERS database, you can perform some queries now, to see how the RQBE window is used. As an example, perhaps you need to see all members living in Virginia. Open the Run menu with Alt-N, and choose New Query. If a database is not currently open, you will see another dialog box asking you to select a database; choose MEMBERS and then choose Open if this dialog box appears.

In a moment, the RQBE window, as shown in Figure 6-1, appears. By default, the MEMBERS database appears in the Databases box. Also, notice (at the upper-center of the window) that all fields appear by default in the Output Fields box. FoxPro assumes that you want all fields available in the query; you will see how to change this assumption later.

For this simple example, all that's needed is to make the criteria selections at the bottom of the screen. Click or tab to the Field Name box and press Enter, and a menu of fields appears (Figure 6-2).

When specifying fields to control the selection criteria, you can simply pick the desired field from the menu of fields. In this case, you want all records from a particular state, so choose State from the menu. When you do so, notice that the Like clause automatically appears beside the Field Name entry.

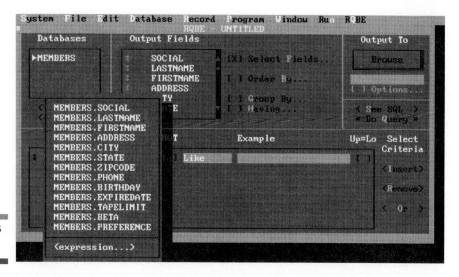

Menu of fields
Figure 6-2.

Press (Tab) twice to move into the Like entry box. For this example, this
entry is fine, but you should be aware of the possible choices here. Press
(Enter) now, and you will see a menu with choices for Like, Exactly Like,
More Than, Less Than, Between, and In. You can use this menu to
further refine the conditions in your queries.

Since Like is fine for this example, press (Enter). The cursor will appear in
the Example box. In this box (directly underneath the word "Example")
you enter the desired example for your query. Since you want all
records where the state is Virginia, enter **VA** in this box. At this point,
your query should resemble the example shown in Figure 6-3.

Tab to (or click) the Do Query button at the right side of the window.
In a moment, a Browse window will appear, containing the results of
the query (Figure 6-4). If you tab over to the State field within the
Browse window, you will see that only those members residing in
Virginia have been included in the query results.

Press (Esc) once to close the Browse window. You can remove the
existing criteria by using the Remove button at the lower-right side of
the window. Click the Remove button, or press the letter (R) if you're
not using a mouse, to remove the existing criteria. (Note that an
alternate method of clearing the criteria is to open the RQBE menu and
choose Remove.)

6

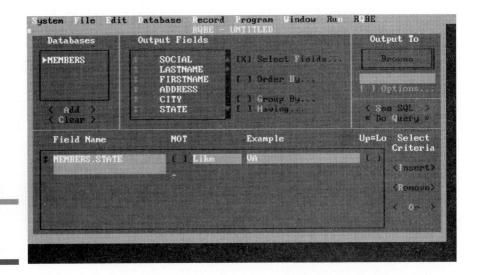

A Sample Query Using an AND Condition

By default, the RQBE window assumes that any series of conditions
should be an AND query; that is, a query where each of the named
conditions must prove true for the record to appear in the results. For
example, perhaps you need to see all members who live in Maryland

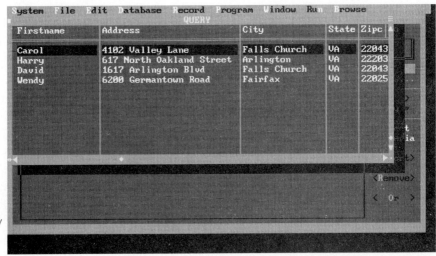

and have a value in the Tapelimit field of more than 3. This denotes an AND condition; in order for a record to qualify, the member must live in Maryland AND have a tape limit value greater than 3.

Tab to the field name box and press (Enter) (or click the Field Name box). From the menu of fields, choose State. Tab over to the Example box and enter **MD**.

You may have noticed that once an entry is made in the Field Name box, a new space appears below that entry in the same column. This space lets you enter additional conditions. Tab to the new space in the Field Name box and press (Enter) (or click the box). From the list of fields, choose Tapelimit. Tab to the next column (the one containing the Like entry), and press (Enter) to display the menu of possible choices.

Since you want all members with more than **3** in the Tapelimit field, choose More Than from the menu. When the cursor moves to the Example field, enter 3. Finally, choose Do Query to perform the query. Your results should resemble those shown in Figure 6-5.

6

A Sample Query Using an OR Condition

The other type of query you'll commonly create is an OR query; that is, a query where if any one of the named conditions proves true, the

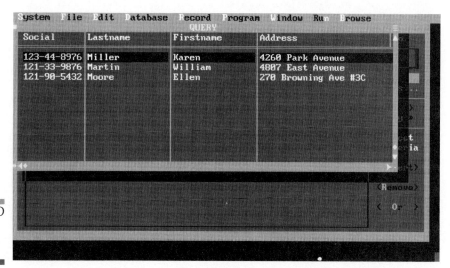

Results of AND
query
Figure 6-5.

record appears in the results. For example, perhaps you need to see all members who live in Maryland or in Washington, D.C. This denotes an OR condition; in order for a record to qualify, the member must live in Maryland OR in Washington.

Press [Esc] to clear the Browse window with the previous results, and double-click the Remove button (or press [R] twice) to clear the existing conditions.

Tab to the Field Name box and press [Enter] (or click the Field Name box). From the menu of fields, choose State. Tab over to the Example box, and enter **MD**. Then, tab to the second line of the query.

To specify an OR condition between criteria, you use the Or button at the lower-right side of the window (or the Or option of the RQBE menu). Click the Or button (or press the letter [O]). You should see a line with the designation "or" appear under your existing criteria.

Tab to the space in the Field Name box underneath the line that just appeared, and press [Enter] (or click the box). From the list of fields, again choose State. Tab over to the Example box, and enter **DC**. Finally, choose Do Query to perform the query. Your results should resemble those shown in Figure 6-6.

A Sample Query Using a Date Range

You've seen sample queries using both text (the names of states) and numbers (the contents of the Tapelimit field); you should be aware that you can also build queries that use dates as conditions. For example, you might want to see all members whose video memberships expire in 1994; this would help you to prepare a letter encouraging renewal of memberships. Press [Esc] to clear the Browse window of the prior results, and press [R] repeatedly until the conditions have been cleared from the criteria area. Tab to the Field Name area and press [Enter], or click the Field Name area, and choose Expiredate from the fields list. Tab to or click the column containing the Like entry, and choose More Than from the menu. In the Example column, enter **12/31/93**.

Tab to or click the second Field Name area, and again choose Expiredate from the fields list. Tab to or click the column containing the Like entry, and choose Less Than from the menu. In the Example column, enter **1/1/95**. Finally, choose Do Query. The results should resemble

Results of OR
query
Figure 6-6.

those shown in Figure 6-7; note that the contents of the Expiredate
fields for these records are all from 1994. Before continuing, press [Esc]
to clear the Browse window.

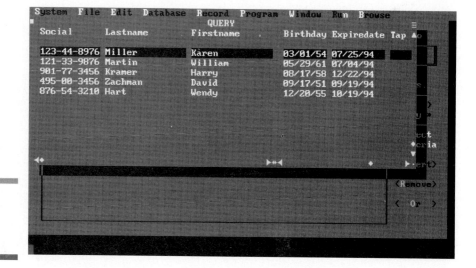

Results of
date-based
query
Figure 6-7.

Adding a Sort Order to Query Results

You can easily specify that the results of a particular query appear in a certain order. To do this, use the Order By button (or the Order By choice of the RQBE menu). When you do this, a dialog box appears, and you can select the field or fields that will control the order of the results. For example, if you wanted the records in a query to appear in order of last name, you could choose the Lastname field from the dialog box.

To see how this works, you can reuse the example that was last entered. With the criteria still entered in the lower half of the screen, open the RQBE menu with Alt-Q, and choose Order By. You will see the Order By dialog box, shown in Figure 6-8.

To define the order in which the records should appear, you simply select the desired field or fields and use the Move button to move the field name into the Ordering Criteria box at the right side of the screen. In this example, select Lastname (you can highlight it with the Tab and cursor keys and press Enter, or you can click the field name and then click the Move button). The field (Members.Lastname) will appear in the Ordering Criteria box on the right side of the screen.

For this example, ordering on the basis of last names only suffices. However, note that you could add additional field names if desired; for

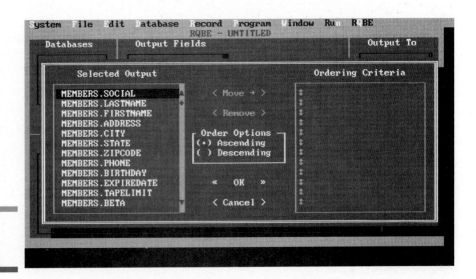

Order By
dialog box
Figure 6-8.

example, choosing Lastname followed by Firstname would result in an order based on last names, and where last names were the same, on first names.

Tab to or click the OK button. When the Order By dialog box disappears, choose Do Query from the RQBE window. The same records (with an expiration date of 1994) will appear. But this time, they will appear in alphabetical order, by last names. Before continuing, press Esc to clear the Browse window.

Selecting Fields for Query Results

You can choose to select certain fields for the results of a query, omitting all fields that you did not select. To do this, click the Select Fields button (or choose the Fields option of the RQBE menu). When you do this, a dialog box appears, and you can add or remove fields that will then appear in the results.

As an example, perhaps you are only interested in the member's name, city, and expiration date. For this example, you can again use the criteria that were previously entered. Open the RQBE menu with Alt-Q, and choose Fields from the menu. In a moment, the dialog box that appears shows that all fields have been selected for output (Figure 6-9).

First, click the Remove All button in the dialog box (or press the letter L) to remove the selected fields from the right side of the dialog box.

6

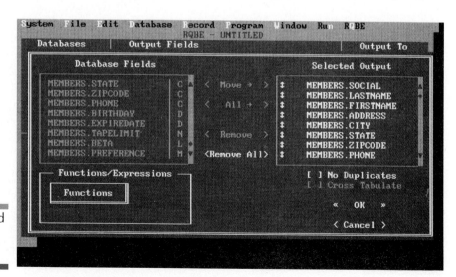

Fields selected
for output
Figure 6-9.

With no fields selected, you can now proceed to highlight the desired fields at the left side of the dialog box and use the Move button (or just press (Enter) while the desired field is highlighted) to move the field to the right side of the dialog box. Using the combination of the (Tab) and cursor keys followed by (Enter), or the mouse, choose the Lastname, Firstname, City, and Expiredate fields. When you are done, the four named fields should be the only fields visible in the Selected Output box at the right side of the screen.

Tab to or click OK, and then choose Do Query. The results, shown in Figure 6-10, contain only those fields you selected. Before continuing, press (Esc) to clear the Browse window of the results.

Changing the Output of a Query

Until now, all of your queries have appeared in the form of a Browse display. But you are likely to need to see the results of many queries in printed form. To do this, you can use the available options in the Output To area of the RQBE window.

As an example, with the criteria for the last sample query still present in the window, tab over to the Browse pop-up under the Output To area (the upper-right corner of the window). Press (Enter), and a menu appears with five choices: Browse, Report/Label, Table/DBF, Cursor, and Graph.

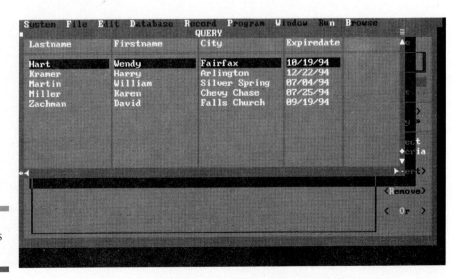

Query with
selected fields
Figure 6-10.

The first choice is the one that you have been using; this causes the output of the query to appear in a Browse window. The Cursor choice is for advanced programming use and is not discussed here. The last choice, Graph, requires the use of FoxGraph, which is optional; see your FoxGraph documentation for details. The second choice Report/Label, can be used to direct the output in the form of a report or as mailing labels. The third choice, Table/DBF, is used if you want the results of the query to be stored as a new database file.

You'll learn more about designing reports and labels in later chapters, and these options provide more flexibility once you know how to design reports or labels. For now, note that you can generate a printed copy of the results of a query by using the Reports/Labels option of this menu and then choosing Options from the dialog box. To see how this works, select Report/Label now, and then click the Options button (or press the letter Ⓞ). In a moment, the RQBE Display Options dialog box appears, as shown in Figure 6-11.

Most of the options in this dialog box will make more sense after you have considered the material in Chapters 7 and 10. For now, all you need to keep in mind is that the Output Destinations area at the right side of the dialog box can be used to get a printed copy of the results of your query.

Tab to or click the To Printer option under Output Destinations, and then click OK. Make sure your printer is ready, and choose Do Query.

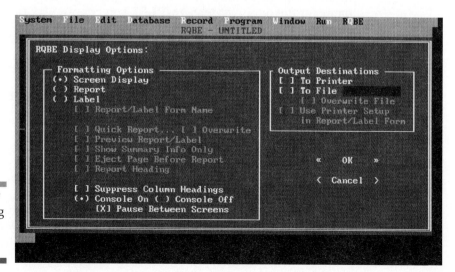

RQBE Display Options dialog box
Figure 6-11.

This time, the results are printed instead of appearing in a Browse Window. (Note that if you are using a laser printer, you may have to press your printer's On Line button, followed by the Form Feed button, to get the page to eject from the printer.)

Saving Queries for Reuse

FoxPro lets you save queries for repeated use. This feature proves useful if you perform the same queries often, such as when printing the same type of report on a daily or weekly basis. You can choose Save As from the File menu, and FoxPro will prompt you for a name for the query. Or you can simply press (Esc) or click the close box; before exiting, FoxPro always asks if you want to save a query that has not been saved. As an example, with the RQBE window still visible, press (Esc) now. You will see the following prompt:

```
Save changes to
C:\FOXPRO\DATA\UNTITLED.QPR?

<Yes>          <No>          <Cancel>
```

Choosing Yes causes another dialog box to appear, prompting you for a name for the query. Choosing No discards the current query without saving it. And choosing Cancel returns you to the RQBE window.

In this case, choose Yes. The next dialog box that appears will ask for a name for the query. Enter **SAMPLE1** and choose Save from the dialog box; the query will be saved under the name SAMPLE1. (All queries are saved with an extension of .QPR.)

REMEMBER: You must save your queries if you want to reuse them later without reentering all of the information.

Performing Saved Queries

You can run a query either by choosing Query from the Run menu, or by using the DO command level. To run an existing query from the menus, open the Run menu, and choose Query. A dialog box appears, displaying the names of all saved queries in the current directory. Select the desired query by name, then select the Run button within the dialog box to run the query.

To repeat the results of a query you have saved from the command level, use the command

>   DO *query-name*.QPR

where *query-name* is the name of the stored query. Hence, if you wanted to repeat the results of the stored query SAMPLE1, you could enter the command

```
DO SAMPLE1.QPR
```

in the Command window.

6

Modifying Existing Queries

If you want to modify an existing query, use the MODIFY QUERY command. At the command window, enter the command

>   MODIFY QUERY *query-name*

where *query-name* is the name of the stored query. The RQBE window appears, and you can make whatever changes are desired to the query. Remember that you must save the query again if you want to keep a permanent copy of the modifications.

A Note About RQBE and the SELECT Command

As noted earlier, the RQBE feature of FoxPro translates your selections into equivalent SELECT commands. If you are familiar with the use of the SELECT command and the SQL language that the command is derived from, you may prefer to enter your own SELECT commands at the command level. You can enter a SELECT command by typing it directly into the Command window, just as you enter any other command in FoxPro.

If you are not familiar with the SQL language, you can still get an idea of what FoxPro is doing behind the scenes by choosing the See SQL option of the RQBE menu after you have designed a query. When you design a query and then choose See SQL from the RQBE menu, a window containing the equivalent SQL command appears. If you want to see how this works, bring the query you just saved back into the RQBE window now by entering the command

```
MODIFY QUERY SAMPLE1
```

Queries can be entered by typing SELECT commands into the Command window.

When the RQBE window appears, open the RQBE menu with Alt-Q, and then choose See SQL. The window that appears contains the SELECT command that is equivalent to the stored query. If you followed the example, it should read something like this:

```
SELECT MEMBERS.LASTNAME, MEMBERS.FIRSTNAME, MEMBERS.CITY,;
MEMBERS.EXPIREDATE;
FROM MEMBERS;
WHERE MEMBERS.EXPIREDATE > 12/31/93;
AND MEMBERS.EXPIREDATE < 01/01/95;
ORDER BY MEMBERS.LASTNAME;
TO PRINTER NOCONSOLE
```

If you were to type this SELECT command into the Command window, the query would be performed. And as you will learn in later chapters, the contents of one FoxPro window can be copied into another; hence, the command that you see in the window now could be copied into another window where a program was being designed. (You can get rid of the window and the query now by pressing the Esc key twice.)

Most users of FoxPro will probably find it easier to compose queries using the RQBE window. But keep in mind that FoxPro offers you the option of direct entry of SELECT commands. If you are not familiar with the SQL language, you can learn much about how SELECT commands should be structured by designing queries in the RQBE window and using the See SQL option of the RQBE menu to view the equivalent SELECT command.

CHAPTER

FOXPRO

7 INTRODUCING REPORTS

Creating reports is, for many users, what database management is all about. You can readily perform queries to gain immediate answers to specific questions, but much of your work with FoxPro will probably involve generating reports. Detailed reports are easy to produce with FoxPro, thanks in part to the program's Quick Report option, which can be combined with selective commands such as SET FILTER and SET FIELDS to obtain reports of selective data.

FoxPro also provides several ways to print reports. You can design and print quick reports with a few steps. From the command level, you can also use a combination of the LIST and DISPLAY commands to print information. You can use FoxPro's sophisticated Report Generator to create customized reports. And you can print form letters or mailing labels.

This chapter provides an introduction to the many ways you can produce reports. More advanced reporting topics, including mailing labels and form letters, are covered in Chapter 10. Before going any further, be sure that your printer is turned on and ready; otherwise, you may lock up your system when you try to print.

Reports available using the Report Generator in FoxPro can be divided into two overall groups: quick reports and customized reports. FoxPro creates *quick reports* immediately, when you start the Report Generator and choose the Quick Report option from the Report menu. Quick reports normally contain all of the fields in the file. (You can limit the fields available in the report with the SET FIELDS command, covered later in this chapter.) The field names supplied during the database design phase are used as headings for the fields.

Custom reports, by comparison, are reports that you create or modify to better fit your specific needs. A significant plus of the Report Generator is that it doesn't force you to design custom reports from scratch, starting with a blank screen. You can use the Quick Report option to create a report layout containing all fields and then proceed to modify that layout as you wish, deleting fields, moving the location of fields, changing headings, or adding other text. Custom reports that you design with the Report Generator can contain any data you desire from the fields of the database. They can include numeric information, such as totals or other calculations based on numeric fields. Reports can also include headings that contain the specified title of the report, the date (as determined by the PC's clock), and the page number for each page. Such headings are commonly used with columnar reports. The following shows an example of a report in a columnar layout. *Columnar layouts* contain the data arranged in columns.

```
SOCIAL          TITLE                          DAYRENTED  RETURNED
123-44-8976     Star Trek VI                   03/05/93   03/06/93
121-33-9876     Lethal Weapon III              03/02/93   03/06/93
232-55-1234     Who Framed Roger Rabbit        03/06/93   03/09/93
```

```
901-77-3456   Doc Hollywood              03/04/93   03/05/93
121-90-5432   Fried Green Tomatoes       03/01/93   03/06/93
495-00-3456   Wayne's World              03/04/93   03/09/93
343-55-9821   Prince of Tides            03/06/93   03/12/93
876-54-3210   Lethal Weapon III          03/07/93   03/08/93
123-44-8976   Friday 13th Part XXVII     03/14/93   03/16/93
121-33-9876   Mambo Kings                03/15/93   03/17/93
232-55-1234   Prince of Tides            03/17/93   03/19/93
901-77-3456   Coming to America          03/14/93   03/18/93
121-90-5432   Prince of Tides            03/16/93   03/17/93
495-00-3456   Star Trek VI               03/18/93   03/19/93
343-55-9821   Wayne's World              03/19/93   03/20/93
876-54-3210   Mambo Kings                03/16/93   03/18/93
```

Here is an example of a report in a form layout. *Form layouts* often resemble paper-based forms.

```
SOCIAL        123-44-8976
TITLE         Star Trek VI
DAYRENTED     03/05/93
RETURNED      03/06/93

SOCIAL        121-33-9876
TITLE         Lethal Weapon III
DAYRENTED     03/02/93
RETURNED      03/06/93

SOCIAL        232-55-1234
TITLE         Who Framed Roger Rabbit
DAYRENTED     03/06/93
RETURNED      03/09/93

SOCIAL        901-77-3456
TITLE         Doc Hollywood
DAYRENTED     03/04/93
RETURNED      03/05/93

SOCIAL        121-90-5432
TITLE         Fried Green Tomatoes
DAYRENTED     03/01/93
RETURNED      03/06/93
```

7

*Use the
Quick
Report
option for
fast reports.*

One of the fastest ways to produce printed reports in FoxPro is to enter the Report Generator and use the Quick Report option, since this report needs no designing in advance. To produce a quick report, simply open the desired database and enter **CREATE REPORT** *filename* as a command. (This command starts the Report Generator and is equivalent to choosing New from the File menu and then selecting Report.) When the Report Generator design screen appears, open the Report menu with [Alt]-[O] and choose Quick Report. From the dialog box that next appears, select Column Layout (if a columnar-style report is desired) or Form Layout (if a form-style report is desired). Select the OK button, and then choose Save from the File menu (or press [Ctrl]-[W]). Exit the Report Generator by choosing Close from the File menu, and the stored report is ready for use. You can display the report on the screen or print it at any time with the REPORT FORM command. Entering **REPORT FORM** *filename* as a command displays the report on the screen, while entering **REPORT FORM** *filename* **TO PRINT** sends the report to the screen and printer at the same time. The menu equivalent for generating the report is to open the Database menu and choose Report; then enter the name of the stored report in the dialog box, check any desired options in the dialog box that appears (see the next section), and select the OK button to produce the report.

The first report shown was produced from the RENTALS database created in Chapter 2 by means of the Quick Report option. It illustrates the design of a columnar-style quick report. Field names appear as column headings, and the data appears in single-spaced rows beneath the headings.

If you generate your own quick report by opening the MEMBERS file (not the RENTALS file) and following the procedure described in the preceding paragraphs, you may notice one trait of a quick report that may not be very appealing to you. Depending on the number of fields in the file, one or more columns of data may be cut off at the right margin. You could solve this problem by changing the widths or moving the locations of columns in a customized report. The right margin is set at 80, so you can't fit more data in the report by printing in compressed mode or using wide paper. You can, however, change the right margin as described later in this chapter.

If you don't want all the fields in the report, you can obtain a quick report with the selected fields you desire by using the SET FIELDS command. Briefly, the syntax of this command is

SET FIELDS TO *field1, field2, field3,...fieldx*

This command makes the database appear to contain only the fields you specify in the list of fields. Therefore, if you wanted a quick report of the MEMBERS database with only the name, city, state, and expiration date fields in the report, you could first open the database and use the command

```
SET FIELDS TO LASTNAME, FIRSTNAME, CITY, STATE,
EXPIREDATE
```

and then proceed to create and save the report; the report would contain only the fields named in the command. After you have created the report, you can make the rest of the fields available for use again by closing and reopening the database or by entering **SET FIELDS TO ALL** without any list of fields after the command.

The Report Dialog Box

When you choose the Report option of the Database menu to print a report, the default selections that appear in the Report dialog box (Figure 7-1) cause the data to be displayed on the screen only. You can choose instead to direct the output of a report to the printer or to a disk file as *ASCII* (American Standard Code for Information Interchange) text.

In the Form window you enter the name of the report, which was created and saved earlier with the Report Generator. The Environment check box tells FoxPro to use any environmental settings that were in effect while the report was being designed. When you create and save a report, FoxPro automatically saves the environment settings to a view file with the same name as the report (see Chapter 5 for more on view files).

The Scope, For, and While options let you limit the records that appear in the report. Scope can be used to limit the number of records that qualify for the operation. If the scope is omitted, FoxPro assumes that you want to use all records in the file. You can enter **ALL** (to specify

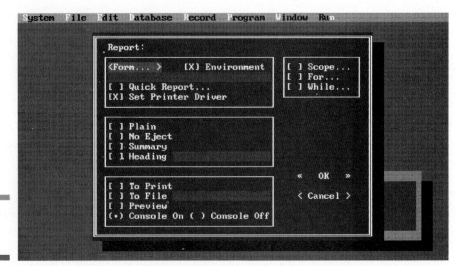

Report dialog
box
Figure 7-1.

the use of all records; this is the default scope). You can enter **NEXT**
and then enter a number, which specifies a group of records starting
with the current pointer position; for example, entering **NEXT 10** as
the scope tells FoxPro to limit its selections to the next ten records. Or
you can enter **REST**, which limits the operation to all records from the
current pointer position to the end of the file.

The For and While options are used to further limit your records, as
described in Chapter 5. The While option works best with an index, but
the For option can easily be used on any field, whether an index exists
or not. When you choose For from the dialog box, the Expression
Builder (discussed in Chapter 5) appears. Using the Expression Builder,
you can enter an expression that limits the records available to the
report. The use of the While option also results in the display of the
Expression Builder, which can be used in the same manner.

Checking the Plain box produces a plain report with no headings. The
No Eject option tells FoxPro not to send a page-eject code before
printing the report. The Summary option tells FoxPro to produce a
summary report only. In this case, individual records do not appear in
the report; only summary totals appear. (This option makes sense when
you have included summary fields in your report; a subject covered
later in the chapter.) Checking the To Print option routes the report to
the printer, while checking the To File option and entering a file name

in the corresponding text box stores the report output in the form of an ASCII text file. Such files can be read by most word processors and all popular desktop publishing packages.

The Preview option causes an on-screen representation of the report to appear. This is useful for checking the visual appearance of a report before you begin printing. The Set Printer Driver option determines whether the default printer driver should be in effect. (You can specify printer drivers by choosing File/Printer Setup, and clicking the Printer Driver Setup check box.)

The Heading option, when chosen, causes the Expression Builder to appear, this time containing a window for a heading, as shown in Figure 7-2. You can use this window to enter a custom heading of your choice, or you can build an expression that results in a desired heading. If you want to enter text in your heading, surround the text in quotes. Fields are normally used as headings with multiple groupings in reports, a topic covered later in the chapter.

Once you enter the name of the report form, check the desired options and select the OK button. The report will be produced in accordance with your chosen options.

7

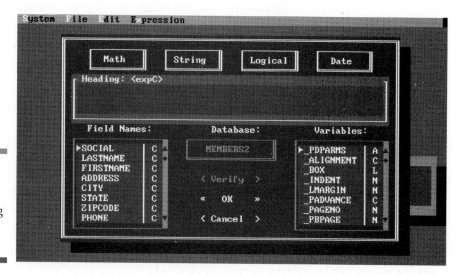

Expression
Builder
containing
report heading
window
Figure 7-2.

Producing Selective Reports with Ease

If you want maximum results in a minimum amount of time, keep in mind the flexibility that FoxPro provides with the SET FIELDS, INDEX ON...FOR, and SET FILTER commands; these can be used to provide selective views of data. Assuming you are using version 2 or above, you can also use the Report/Labels menu option in the RQBE window to produce reports based on a selected query, as described in Chapter 6. You can use the SET FILTER command, described in Chapter 5, or you can add a FOR clause to the REPORT FORM command, to limit the records included in your reports. (An alternative way to do this is to produce the report using the menu options rather than commands; when you use the menu option, the dialog box appears, and you can use the For clause to specify which records will appear in the report.) With large databases, you may find it less time consuming to build a query as described in Chapter 6 or to limit available records by building a selective index with the INDEX ON...FOR command. Details of this technique are found in Chapter 4.

In many cases, you can solve formatting problems by including selected fields and omitting unwanted fields with the SET FIELDS command. Take the quick report produced if you use the MEMBERS file, create a report, and choose the Quick Report option from the Report menu. Obviously, there are far too many fields to fit on a standard sheet of paper. Perhaps all you are really interested in are the Lastname, Firstname, City, and Tapelimit fields, and you know that these will comfortably fit on a standard sheet of paper. To create a Quick Report with only these fields, enter **USE MEMBERS** if the file is not already open, and enter the following SET FIELDS command:

```
SET FIELDS TO LASTNAME, FIRSTNAME, CITY, TAPELIMIT
```

Next, create a new report by entering the command

```
CREATE REPORT SAMPLE
```

to get into the Report Generator. Open the Report menu with Alt-O, and choose Quick Report. Select OK, and notice that the report that is produced contains only those fields listed with the SET FIELDS command, as shown in Figure 7-3.

Save the report with Ctrl-W (answer Yes to the prompt to save the environment information when you are asked), and enter the command

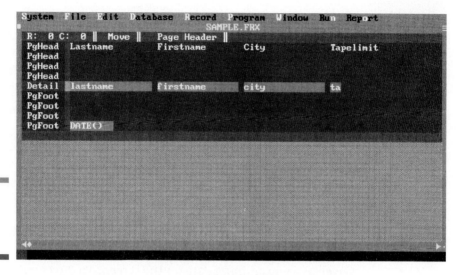

Report design
resulting from
SET FIELDS
Figure 7-3.

REPORT FORM SAMPLE

7

to display the report on the screen. The resulting report should contain all of the records from the MEMBERS database, but only the desired fields, as shown here:

LASTNAME	FIRSTNAME	CITY	TAPELIMIT
Miller	Karen	Chevy Chase	6
Martin	William	Silver Spring	4
Robinson	Carol	Falls Church	6
Kramer	Harry	Arlington	4
Moore	Ellen	Takoma Park	6
Zachman	David	Falls Church	4
Robinson	Benjamin	Washington	2
Hart	Wendy	Fairfax	2

Before proceeding, be sure to enter

SET FIELDS TO ALL

to restore the use of all fields in the database for subsequent operations.

If you wanted specific records in the report, you could use the methods described in Chapters 5 and 6 to produce a subset of records available to the report. Also, if you wanted to see the records within the Quick

Report in some specific order, you could use the indexing or sorting techniques covered in Chapter 4, apply any desired filter conditions, and print the report. Using these techniques, you can generate detailed reports based on complex conditions with little or no custom report designing.

HINT: If you are using the RQBE window to design a query that will produce a report, be sure to design and save the report first, before designing or implementing the query.

Generating Reports with Commands

From the command level, the LIST command is useful for printing data as well as for examining data on the screen. To direct output to the printer, use the TO PRINT option with the LIST command. This avoids having all your command words print on the page along with the desired data. The normal format of the command with this option is

LIST [*field1, field2...fieldx*] TO PRINT

To try this command, enter

```
LIST LASTNAME, CITY, STATE TO PRINT
```

to print all the Name, City, and State fields for each record in the database. If you are using a laser printer, you may also need to enter an EJECT command to cause the printed sheet to feed out of the printer.

You can be selective by specifying a FOR condition with the LIST command and still send output to the printer with TO PRINT. For example,

```
LIST LASTNAME, FIRSTNAME, CITY FOR LASTNAME =
"Robinson" TO PRINT
```

prints the last names, first names, and cities of both members named Robinson. The command

```
LIST LASTNAME, CITY, STATE, TAPELIMIT FOR TAPELIMIT < 6
```

provides a printed listing like the one shown here, with the last names, cities, states, and tape limits for all members with a tape limit of less than 6.

```
Record#      LASTNAME    CITY             STATE      TAPELIMIT
      2      Martin      Silver Spring    MD         4
      4      Kramer      Arlington        VA         4
      6      Zachman     Falls Church     VA         4
      7      Robinson    Washington       DC         2
      8      Hart        Fairfax          VA         2
```

You can use curly braces surrounding a date to tell FoxPro that the enclosed set of characters should be read as a date value. The date value can then be used to form a conditional command for printing a report. This is a very handy tool for printing reports that indicate activity within a certain time period. For example, the command

```
REPORT FORM SAMPLE FOR EXPIREDATE <= {10/01/93} TO PRINT
```

produces a report of all records with expiration dates earlier than October 2 of 1993. A report of all members with expiration dates within a particular month could be produced with a command like this one:

```
REPORT FORM SAMPLE FOR EXPIREDATE > {09/30/93} .AND.
EXPIREDATE < {11/01/93} TO PRINT
```

You can also generate stored reports with commands. The REPORT FORM command uses the following syntax:

> REPORT FORM *filename* [*scope*]
> [FOR *expression*]
> [WHILE *expression*]
> [TO PRINT / TO FILE *filename*]
> [PLAIN] [SUMMARY] [NOEJECT]
> [HEADING *character-expression*]
> [ENVIRONMENT]

The SCOPE, FOR, and WHILE options work as discussed earlier in this text; see Chapter 5 for a full discussion on these options. If the TO PRINT clause is added to the command, the report is routed to the printer and to the screen. If TO PRINT is omitted, the report is displayed only on the screen.

If the TO FILE option is included, the report is sent to a file in the form of ASCII text. You can use either TO PRINT or TO FILE, but you cannot use both options in the same REPORT FORM command.

The PLAIN option prints a plain report without the standard headings. The SUMMARY option prints a report with summary fields only. The NOEJECT option suppresses the normal page ejects (form-feed codes) that are sent to the printer. The HEADING option lets you add a custom heading; character expressions must be enclosed in quotes.

The ENVIRONMENT option can be used to specify a view file that will control the records available for processing, which fields appear, and any relationships between other files. When you save a report, FoxPro automatically saves the current environment to a view file with the same name as the report. Adding this clause to the REPORT FORM command therefore saves you the trouble of opening a database and index file if they are not already open. For example, you could load FoxPro from DOS or OS/2 and enter one command such as

```
REPORT FORM MYFILE ENVIRONMENT
```

to open the database and any index files, and to produce the report.

Manual Margin Settings and Page Ejects

You can change your printer's left margin with the SET MARGIN command. FoxPro normally defaults to a printer margin value of 0. Entering **SET MARGIN TO 12**, for example, causes the printer to indent 12 spaces at the beginning of each line. (This command affects only the left margin. The right margin cannot be set with a command in FoxPro.) The EJECT command, as mentioned earlier, causes the printer to perform a form feed, which advances you to the top of the next sheet. The EJECT command is not available from the menus; it must be entered as a command. An alternative is to use the Form Feed button on your printer to accomplish the same task.

Designing Customized Columnar Reports

When you prefer to place fields in various locations, add custom headers and footers, and change formatting attributes, you can design customized reports. Depending on how complex your needs are, the precise steps involved in the report's design will vary in complexity.

The description that follows illustrates the basic process in creating a customized report with a columnar format.

To start the process, open the database in question, and then enter **CREATE REPORT** *filename* (or choose New from the File menu and select Report). In a moment, the design screen of the Report Generator will appear (Figure 7-4). The screen contains the menu bar, which includes one new option, titled Report, and the *report specification,* or layout of the report.

The Report Specification

The report specification is made up of several parts, as illustrated in Figure 7-5. FoxPro views each portion of the report as a horizontal area known as a *report band.* Every report contains a Page Header band, a Page Footer band, and a Detail band. There can also be an optional Title band or Summary band, and there can be optional Group bands; in the figure, the band containing the name of a field, State, is a Group band.

The Page Header band appears once for each page of the report. In many cases, you'll place such information as the date or time of the report and a report title in this area. The Page Footer band at the bottom of the report specification has the same purpose as the header

7

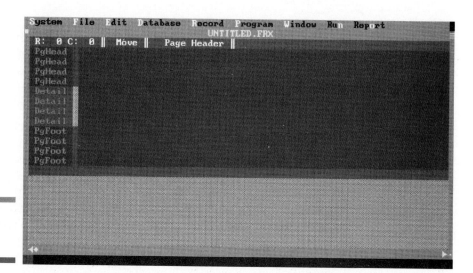

Report specification
Figure 7-4.

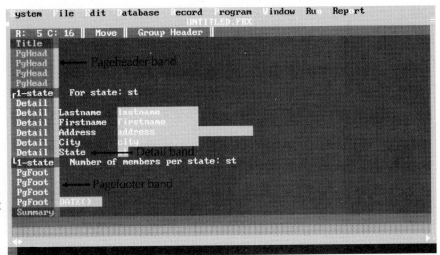

Parts of a report
specification
Figure 7-5.

but is for footers, the information that typically appears at the bottom
of each page.

Title bands, when used, contain any information that should appear
only at the start of the report (as opposed to at the start of each page).
Summary bands, when used, contain information that should appear at
the end of the report. You'll usually use Summary bands for totals of
numeric fields.

The Detail band is used to define the actual information (usually fields)
that will appear in the body of the report. The values in the Detail band
are represented by highlighted blocks containing the name of the field
or expression. While fields are most common, expressions can also be
used; such expressions might contain a function representing the
current date, or a calculated value based on a numeric field.

Group bands, which are optional, are printed once for each group of
records in a report. Group bands provide a means of grouping records
in a report. Such grouping often includes some type of header
identifying the group, along with subtotals of numeric data. You may
or may not want to group records in a report; as an example of
grouping, you might decide to print a list of members of the video
database by state. If you decide to include groups, FoxPro lets you add
an unlimited number of groups to a single report.

Making Changes to the Report's Design

Once the report specification appears on the screen, you can use various options of the Report menu to add, rearrange, or remove fields; to add new lines, boxes, or text; and to change the layout or format of the report in general. If you press Alt-O while the report specification is visible, the Report menu opens (Figure 7-6).

The Page Layout option of this menu lets you change specifications that affect the layout of the printed page. When you choose this option, the Page Layout dialog box appears (Figure 7-7). Use the Page Length option to change the length of the printed page. The default value of 60 allows 6 blank lines at the end of a normal 8 1/2-by-11-inch sheet of paper. Legal-size (14-inch-long) paper works well with a setting of 82. For the various European paper sizes, you may need to experiment to obtain the best results.

The Top Margin option lets you specify a top margin, or the number of lines down from the top edge where printing will begin. Laser-printer users should note that this is in addition to the default top margin set internally by your printer; see your printer manual for details on the printer's default top margin. In a similar fashion, the Bottom Margin option provides a setting for the bottom margin, or the number of lines up from the bottom edge. Data does not appear beyond this setting.

7

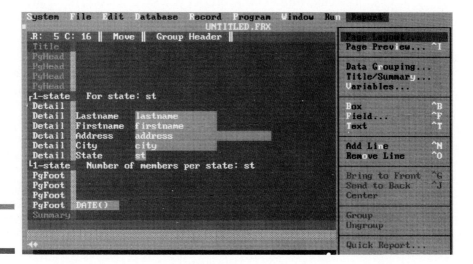

Report menu
Figure 7-6.

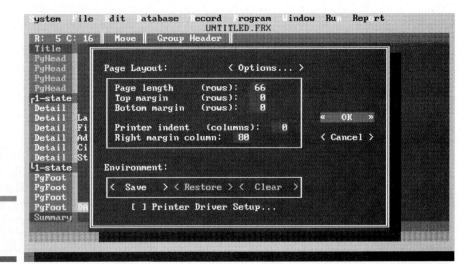

Page Layout
dialog box
Figure 7-7.

The Printer Indent option lets you enter the number of spaces by which all data in the report should be indented. The Right Margin Column option lets you specify a number for the right margin. This is particularly useful with printers that allow compressed print. When using the compressed-print mode of most dot-matrix printers, you can enter 132 as a margin when using 8 1/2-inch-wide paper, and you can enter 240 as a margin when using the larger computer-fanfold paper. The environment buttons let you save, restore, or clear the *environment* (the databases, indexes, and filters that are currently in effect). Once all your desired options have been entered, select the OK button to exit the dialog box.

The Page Preview option of the Report menu lets you see what a report will look like before you save the report and exit the Report Generator. After laying out the desired fields and other data, choose Page Preview from the Report menu, and a visual representation of the printed report appears on the screen (Figure 7-8). Two options, Done and More, appear at the bottom of the screen. Choose More to view successive pages of the report (if there are any); choose Done to exit back to the report specification. This option is quite useful for checking your design; you can go back into the report specification, make changes to the report, and try Page Preview again until you are satisfied with the design of the report.

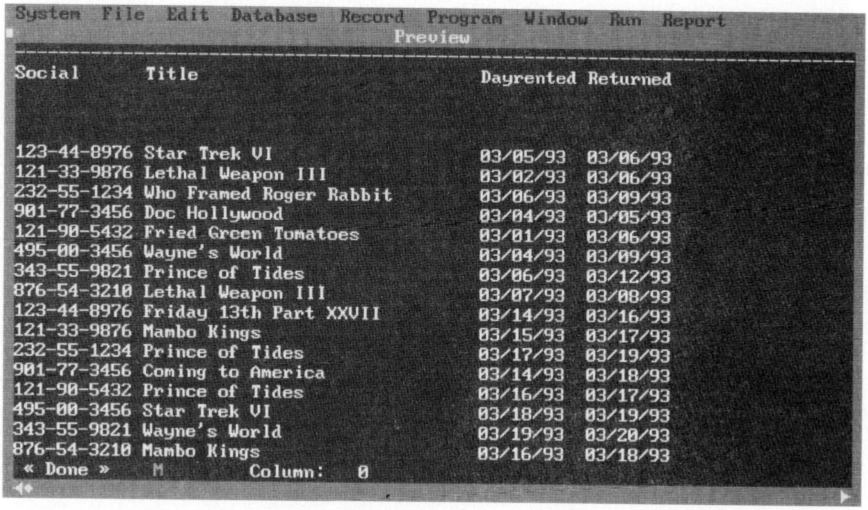

Screen preview
of report
Figure 7-8.

The Data Grouping option of the Report menu lets you add groups to a report. This topic is covered later in this chapter. The Title/Summary option lets you add Title bands or Summary bands to a report. When you choose this option, the Title/Summary dialog box appears (Figure 7-9). You can check the boxes that affect both the Title band and the Summary band. Selecting Title Band adds the Title band, while selecting Summary Band adds the Summary band. The bands, once added, are empty; you must then add any desired text or fields to the bands. The New Page option tells FoxPro to start the band on a new page. Once you check the desired boxes and choose OK, you are returned to the report specification.

The Variables option lets you add memory variables to a report. This is an advanced programming technique that is not covered in this chapter.

The Box, Field, and Text options are used to add boxes, fields, and text to the report. The added items will then appear in the report, in accordance with the band where you add them. For example, adding an item in the Detail band will cause it to appear once for each record of the report; adding an item in the Page Head band will cause it to appear once each time the Page Head prints, and so on.

Selecting Box from the Report menu causes a box to appear. You can then move and size the box as desired. Keyboard users can move the cursor to the upper-left corner for the box, choose Box from the Report

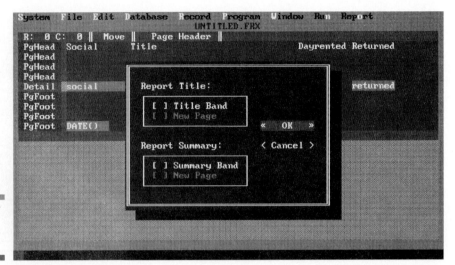

Title/Summary
dialog box
Figure 7-9.

menu, stretch the box with the cursor keys, and press ⌨Enter to complete the box. Mouse users can click the upper-left corner of the box, and drag to the desired lower-right corner.

Use the Field option of the Report menu (or its shortcut key, ⌨Ctrl-F) to place fields or expressions (such as combinations of fields or calculations based on fields) at the cursor location. Choosing Field from the menu causes the dialog box shown in Figure 7-10 to be displayed. In the Expression box, you enter the name of the field or expression that you want to place at the cursor location. If you need help in building the expression, tab to Expr and press ⌨Enter to bring up the Expression Builder. As an expression, you can enter a calculation based on a field; an example, in the case of a numeric field named Cost, might be

```
COST * .06
```

which would result in a sales tax figure that is 6% of the value contained in the Cost field.

Applying Formats and Style Options to a Field

At Format you can press ⌨Enter to display the Format dialog box (Figure 7-11). This provides various formatting options that you can select by checking the boxes. One of the Character, Numeric, Date, and Logical

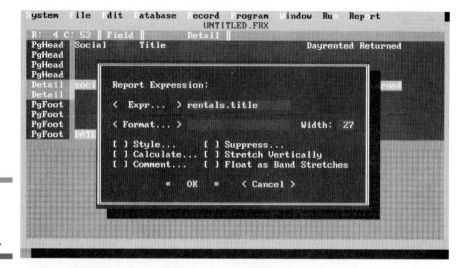

Report
Expression
dialog box
Figure 7-10.

options will be chosen based on the field type; however, if your field is based on an expression, you may want to change this option according to your preference. The list of available formatting options that you see will vary, depending on the data type. The editing options may be checked according to your wishes for that field. Table 7-1 shows the results of the various formatting options. Once you choose the desired options and select the OK button, the Report Expression dialog box reappears.

7

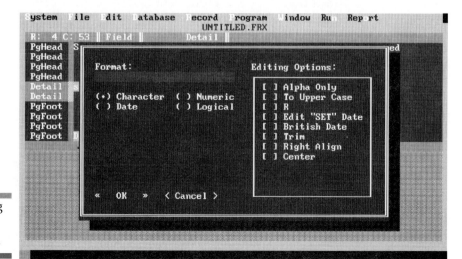

Format dialog
box
Figure 7-11.

Option **For Character Data**	**Results**
Alpha Only	Only alphabetic characters permitted
To Upper Case	All characters converted to uppercase
R	Characters are displayed but not stored
Edit SET date	Prints data as date that follows the current SET DATE format
British Date	Prints data following the British (European) date format
Trim	Removes leading and trailing blanks
Right Align	Prints data flush right in field
Center	Prints data centered in field
For Numeric Data	**Results**
Left justify	Aligns numeric data flush left in field
Blank if zero	Does not print output if field contents contains zero
(Negative)	Negative numbers are enclosed in parentheses
Edit SET date	Prints data as date that follows the current SET DATE format
British Date	Prints data following the British (European) date format
CR if positive	CR (for Credit) appears after a number if the number is positive
DB if negative	DB (for Debit) appears after a number if the number is negative
Leading zero	Leading zeros are printed
Currency	Values are printed in Currency format
Scientific	Values are printed using scientific notation
For Date Data	**Results**
Edit SET date	Prints data as date that follows the current SET DATE format
British Date	Prints data following the British (European) date format

Formatting
Options
Table 7-1.

In the Width box of the Report Expression dialog box (see Figure 7-10), you can enter a maximum width for the field. This is useful if you have a long field and you want to restrict its length in a particular report.

The Style option, when chosen, displays another dialog box with choices for various printing styles: Normal, Bold, Italic, Underline, Superscript, and Subscript. You will also see options for Condensed and Double, and a Code entry box, where escape codes for condensed or other special effects can be entered. Choose any of these by checking the desired box and then selecting OK; you can choose more than one option at a time. (Your printer must support the chosen options.)

The Stretch Vertically option of the Report Expression dialog box lets you stretch the contents of a long character field or a memo field vertically. This permits the wrapping of text past more than one line in the report, making the option quite useful with memo fields. If you do not select this option, a memo field placed in a report will not take more than one line per record printed; any excess text gets cut off when the field ends at the width you specified. If you select the Stretch Vertically option, FoxPro uses as many lines as necessary to print the complete contents of the memo or character field.

The Float as Band Stretches option is used along with the previous option. When you choose this option, the field will be printed on the line that follows the last line of data in the Vertically Stretched field. You can use this option to prevent a field from overwriting a prior field that has been stretched vertically.

Users of very early versions of FoxPro may see a Totaling option. The Totaling option, when chosen, reveals a choice of totals. This option allows you to define a numeric summary field. Once you check the Totaling box, FoxPro allows you to select whether the total will be a count of the number of records, the sum of the numeric data, an average, the lowest value in any of the records, or the highest value in any of the records.

Also shown when you select the Totaling option is a Reset option, which determines when the totaling field will be reset. Tab to this menu and press (Enter), and you are provided with reset choices of End of Report, End of Page, and the name of the field or expression you are using (in other words, each time the value of that field or expression changes, the total is printed).

7

Users of version 2 and above will see a Calculate option and a Comment option. When the Calculate option is chosen, another dialog box appears, and you can choose whether the calculation based on the field will be a total (sum), a count of records, an average value, a maximum or minimum value, a standard deviation, or a variance. Also shown when you select the Calculate option is a Reset option, which determines when the calculating field will be reset. Tab to this menu and press Enter, and you are provided with reset choices of End of Report and End of Page.

The Comment option, when chosen, displays a comment box. You can enter any desired comments that help you identify the report's purpose in this box.

The Suppress option (in version 1.*x*, called the Suppress Repeated Values option) of the Report Expression dialog box tells FoxPro not to print repeated values within the report. If this option is selected and the field value is the same for more than one consecutive record, the value is printed for the first record but not for successive records. Note that the Suppress option also has a reset feature for End of Page or End of Report. The End of Report option is the default.

Once you have chosen the desired options within the Report Expression dialog box, select OK. The dialog box closes, revealing the report specification underneath. You can modify the formatting and style settings for an existing field at any time: just place the cursor anywhere in the field and press Enter. Doing so redisplays the Report Expression dialog box. You can make the desired modifications to the formatting and style options and then choose OK to implement the changes.

HINT: Use the Style option in the Report Expression dialog box to apply bold or italic styles to a field or other selected object of a report. Remember that your printer must support these options to get the proper results.

Adding Text or Lines and Overlaying Object

The Text option of the Report menu can be used to add text at the cursor location. Choose the Text option, and then begin typing your desired text. Complete the entry by pressing (Enter). Note that you do not need this menu option to enter text; if you move to any blank area in the report specification and begin typing, FoxPro assumes that you want to enter text.

The Add Line After and Remove Line options of the Report menu are used to add or delete lines (rows) from the report specification. To add a line, place the cursor anywhere in the desired row location and choose Add Line from the menu; the new line is inserted at the cursor location. To remove a line, place the cursor anywhere in the unwanted line and choose Remove Line from the Report menu. Note that there are shortcut keys for these options; you can use (Ctrl)-(N) for Add Line After and (Ctrl)-(M) for Remove Line.

The Bring to Front, Send to Back, and Center options of the Report menu are used when, for one reason or another, you choose to overlay one object (such as a box) with another object (such as a field). For example, it is possible to drag a field so it partially covers a box or a title you have entered as text. If you then select one of the objects (such as the text) with the (Tab) key or the mouse and choose Bring to Front from the Report menu, the selected object appears over the object it partially covers. If you select Send to Back, the selected object is placed under the other object. You may find these options useful when you are combining text labels and boxes; you might, for example, type a few words as a descriptive label and later add a box whose position covers the label. If you select the box and choose Send to Back from the Report menu, the text overlays the box. The Center option of the Report menu centers the selected object within the left and right edges of the report.

The Group and Ungroup options can be used to group together selected objects for further operations (such as moving a group of fields at once).

The Quick Report option provides an immediate report based on either a columnar or a form layout, as detailed earlier in this chapter.

Moving and Deleting Objects

You can move or delete existing objects (fields, boxes, or text) within a report. This can be particularly useful in modifying a quick report to serve as a customized report. To move an object to another location, place the cursor anywhere within the desired object, and press the (Spacebar) to select the object. Once selected, the object is highlighted.

7

Use the cursor keys to move the object to its new location, and press (Enter) to complete the movement. Mouse users can simply click and drag the desired object to its new location. To delete an object, first select the object as just described. Then open the Edit menu with (Alt)-(E) and choose Cut from the menu to delete the object.

Note that the Edit menu's Cut, Copy, and Paste options provide an alternative method for moving objects, as well as a method for duplicating objects in the report. You can select an object with the techniques just described and choose Cut from the Edit menu to remove the object from its existing location. Then place the cursor at the new location and choose Paste from the Edit menu to insert that same object at the new location. (The Paste option always inserts whatever was deleted last with the Cut option.)

You can make duplicates of objects with the Copy option of the Edit menu. Just select the object using the methods described, and choose Copy from the Edit menu. Place the cursor where the duplicate of the object is to appear, and choose Paste from the Edit menu.

Saving and Running the Report

Once you have made your desired changes to the report design, press (Ctrl)-(W) or choose Save from the File menu (and enter a name, if prompted for one, in the dialog box that appears). To run a report from the menus you can open the Run menu and choose Report, or you can choose Report from the Database menu and enter the report's name in the dialog box that appears. You can also run a report from the command level by entering the command

    REPORT FORM *filename* TO PRINT

where *filename* is the name with which you saved the report. Omit the TO PRINT designation if you simply wish to view the report on the screen.

Practice Designing a Customized Report

As an example of the steps involved in creating a customized report, consider the case of the Generic Videos membership file. The company needs a report with the name, city, and state of each member, along with the phone number, expiration date, tape limit, and beta information. Below all of this data, a listing of the comments in the Preferences field should appear. They also want a title and the current date and time on the report. For now, the report will contain a single group of data; later, the report will be broken into separate groupings of members by state.

To begin designing the report, enter

```
USE MEMBERS
CREATE REPORT MEMBERS
```

The report specification will appear. Let's begin with the headings. The date and time need to appear in the upper-right corner of the first page, so these items need to be placed in the Page Header band. Move the cursor to row 1, column 50. You can tell the cursor location from the R and C designations shown in the upper-left corner of the report specification; mouse users can quickly move the cursor by clicking the desired area of the screen.

Open the Report menu and choose Field. The Report Expression dialog box now appears (Figure 7-12). You could enter a field name here, but in this case a field isn't desired; the date is what's wanted. If you knew

7

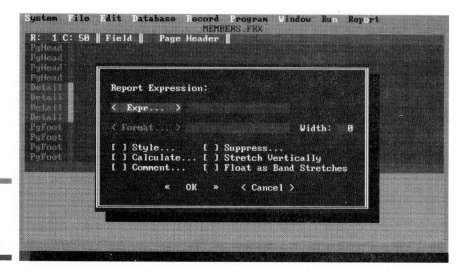

Report Expression dialog box
Figure 7-12.

the syntax for the date function, you could type it in here; however, if you cannot recall the syntax, the Expression Builder can be used as an aid. If you tab to the Expr heading in the dialog box and press (Enter) or click the Expr heading, you see the Expression Builder, as shown in Figure 7-13. Here you can select field names, functions, and math, string, or logical symbols to build a desired expression.

In this case, all that's needed is the appropriate function for the current date. Tab over to the Date menu box, press the (Spacebar) to open the menu (or click the Date box and drag down the menu of choices), and select DATE as the desired function. The DATE function, when used, provides the current date as read from the system clock.

Press (Ctrl)-(W) (or choose OK from the dialog box), and then choose OK when the Report Expression dialog box reappears. You should see the DATE function, now located at row 1, column 50.

Move the cursor down to row 2, column 50; the TIME function will be inserted here, to provide the time when the report is run. Open the Report menu and choose Field. This time when the Report Expression dialog box appears, use the shorter method of entering the function directly. Tab to the Expr window, and enter

```
TIME()
```

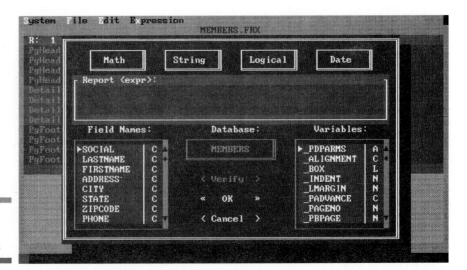

Expression Builder

Figure 7-13.

Then choose OK from the dialog box. The TIME function will appear in the report specification immediately below the DATE function.

Press `Home` to get back to the left margin, and move the cursor down to row 4, the first line in the Detail band. Type

```
Name:
```

and press `Enter` to complete the entry of text, and then move the cursor over to column 6. Open the Report menu with `Alt`-`O`, choose Field, and enter **LASTNAME** in the window as the desired field name. Select OK from the dialog box to complete the placement of the Lastname field.

Move the cursor two spaces to the right, to row 4, column 22. As a shortcut to using the Field choice of the Report menu, you might want to try the `Ctrl`-`F` key combination this time. Press `Ctrl`-`F`, and the Report Expression dialog box again appears. Tab to the window, enter **FIRSTNAME**, and then select OK from the dialog box to place the field.

Move the cursor four spaces to the right, to row 4, column 40. Enter

```
Phone:
```

7

Press `Enter` to complete the entry of text. Move the cursor one space to the right of the colon, and press `Ctrl`-`F` to open the dialog box. Tab to the window, enter **PHONE** as the field name, and select OK to place the field.

Move the cursor to the start of row 5 and enter

```
City & State:
```

as the heading. Press `Enter` to complete the entry of text. Move the cursor to row 5, column 16, open the dialog box with `Ctrl`-`F`, tab to the window, and enter **CITY**. Then select OK to place the field.

Move the cursor two spaces to the right, to row 5, column 32. Press `Ctrl`-`F`, and enter **STATE** as the field name; then select OK to place the field.

Move the cursor four spaces to the right, to row 5, column 37. Enter

```
Exp. date:
```

Then press (Enter) to complete the entry of the text. Move the cursor to row 5, column 48. Press (Ctrl)-(F), and enter **EXPIREDATE** as the field name; then select OK to place the field.

Move the cursor to the start of row 6, and enter

```
Tape limit:
```

Press (Enter) to complete the entry of the text. Move the cursor to column 12. Press (Ctrl)-(F) and enter **TAPELIMIT** as the field name; then select OK to place the field.

Move the cursor to row 6, column 20, enter

```
Uses Beta?
```

and press (Enter) to complete the entry of the text. Move the cursor to column 31. Press (Ctrl)-(F) and enter **BETA** as the field name; then select OK to place the field.

For this report, a blank line is desired between the contents of the Preference field and the next row of data. To accomplish this, you need to add another line to the Detail band. Move the cursor down to the start of row 7. Open the Report menu and choose Add Line After to add a new line. Next, enter the label

```
Preferences:
```

Then press (Enter) to complete the entry of the text. Move the cursor to column 13. Press (Ctrl)-(F) and enter **PREFERENCE** as the field name. Since this is a memo field, you can use the Stretch Vertically option, which allows long text entries to use up as much vertical space as is needed. Tab over to the Stretch Vertically option and press the (Spacebar) to select it. Then select OK to place the field. At this point, your screen should resemble the one shown in Figure 7-14.

To enable more data to fit on each page, the staff has decided that the default of four lines for a Page Footer band isn't really necessary. Move the cursor to row 9 (the first line in the Page Footer band) and choose Remove Line from the Report menu. Choose the same option two more times, which leaves one line remaining in the Page Footer band.

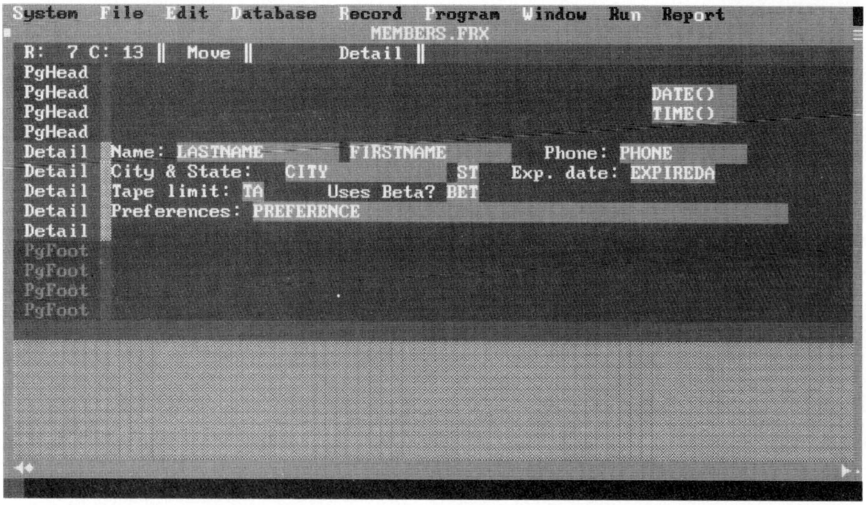
System File Edit Database Record Program Window Run Report
MEMBERS.FRX
R: 7 C: 13 ‖ Move ‖ Detail ‖
PgHead
PgHead DATE()
PgHead TIME()
PgHead
Detail Name: LASTNAME FIRSTNAME Phone: PHONE
Detail City & State: CITY ST Exp. date: EXPIREDA
Detail Tape limit: TA Uses Beta? BET
Detail Preferences: PREFERENCE
Detail
PgFoot
PgFoot
PgFoot
PgFoot

Report specification with fields added
Figure 7-14.

The staff has decided that a summary field showing the number of members in the video club would be a nice addition; for this, you need a summary field based on a count of records (members) in the database. Open the Report menu and choose Title/Summary. From the dialog box that appears, choose Summary Band by highlighting the option and pressing the Spacebar. Then choose OK from the dialog box.

This step adds the Summary band at the bottom of the report specification; you must still add any desired text or fields in the Summary band. At the start of the Summary band, type the heading

```
Number of Members:
```

and press Enter to complete the text entry. Move the cursor over to column 19, and press Ctrl-F to open the Report Expression dialog box. Because you will request a total count of the number of entries, you could use any field that would always have an entry. Since the Social field will always contain an entry for each record, enter **SOCIAL** as the field name. Then Tab to the Calculate option (or, under version 1.x, the Totaling option) and press the Spacebar to select it (or click the entry).

You will see a dialog box similar to the one shown in Figure 7-15. This dialog box lets you base the contents of a summary field on a count of records, a numeric sum, an average, or a lowest or highest value. (The appearance of the dialog box will differ slightly from the illustration if you are using version 1.*x*, but the options discussed are the same.) The Sum, Average, Lowest, and Highest options apply only to numeric fields, while the Count option can count the occurrences in any type of field. Select Count by tabbing to it and pressing the (Spacebar) or by using the mouse. Then select OK within the dialog box. When the Report Expression dialog box reappears, change the Width entry to 3. (This prevents a count of 8 members appearing as 8.000000000 in the Summary band.) Finally, select OK from the dialog box to complete the placement of the field.

Save the report by pressing (Ctrl)-(W). When asked, answer Yes to the environment prompt. When you are back at the command level, enter

```
REPORT FORM MEMBERS
```

or, if your printer is connected and turned on, you might want to instead try

```
REPORT FORM MEMBERS TO PRINT
```

You should see (or print) a report similar to the following example:

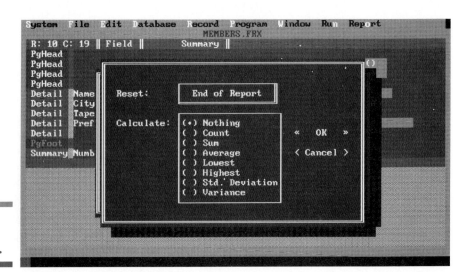

Calculate
dialog box
Figure 7-15.

```
                                         12/06/93
                                         16:35:37

Name: Miller          Karen            Phone: 301-555-6678
City & State:   Chevy Chase     MD    Exp. date: 07/25/94
Tape limit:  6        Uses Beta? .F.
Preferences: Prefers science fiction, horror movies. Fan of
             Star Trek films.

Name: Martin          William          Phone: 301-555-2912
City & State:   Silver Spring   MD    Exp. date: 07/04/94
Tape limit:  4        Uses Beta? .F.
Preferences: Enjoys Clint Eastwood, John Wayne films.

Name: Robinson        Carol            Phone: 703-555-8778
City & State:   Falls Church    VA    Exp. date: 09/05/95
Tape limit:  6        Uses Beta? .F.
Preferences: Likes comedy, drama films.

Name: Kramer          Harry            Phone: 703-555-6874
City & State:   Arlington       VA    Exp. date: 12/22/94
Tape limit:  4        Uses Beta? .T.
Preferences: Big fan of Eddie Murphy. Also enjoys westerns.

Name: Moore           Ellen            Phone: 301-555-0201
City & State:   Takoma Park     MD    Exp. date: 11/17/96
Tape limit:  6        Uses Beta? .F.
Preferences: Drama, comedy.

Name: Zachman         David            Phone: 703-555-5432
City & State:   Falls Church    VA    Exp. date: 09/19/94
Tape limit:  4        Uses Beta? .T.
Preferences: Science fiction, drama.

Name: Robinson        Benjamin         Phone: 202-555-4545
City & State:   Washington      DC    Exp. date: 09/17/95
Tape limit:  2        Uses Beta? .T.
Preferences: Westerns, comedy. Clint Eastwood fan.

Name: Hart            Wendy            Phone: 703-555-1201
City & State:   Fairfax         VA    Exp. date: 10/19/94
Tape limit:  2        Uses Beta? .T.
```

7

```
Preferences: Drama, adventure. Likes spy movies, including all
             James Bond series.

Number of Members:   8
```

Using the Group Menu Options

You can use the various group options of the Report menu to work with groupings of records within a report. You will probably need to arrange reports broken down by groups. For example, you might need to see all members divided into groups by state of residence. Using the Data Grouping option of the Report menu, you can define multiple levels of grouping.

While many more than three levels of groups may seem like overkill to some, it is nice to know that FoxPro is accommodating when you must base a complex report on a large number of subgroups. Multiple groupings can be quite common in business applications. In something as simple as a national mailing list, for example, you might need to see records by groups of states, and within each state group by city, and within each city group by ZIP code. That represents three levels of grouping alone. Cut the data in the table more specifically—by other categories like income levels, for example—and you can quickly come to appreciate FoxPro's ability to perform effective grouping.

When you choose the Data Grouping option from the Report menu while designing a report, the Group dialog box shown in Figure 7-16 is displayed. You use the Add, Change, or Delete button to add, change, or delete Group bands from a report. When you choose Add, you see the Group Info dialog box (Figure 7-17). You can use this dialog box to enter a field name (or other expression) to base your group on.

If you want to establish the group by field (as in groups of records from the same state or with the same assignment), you enter the name of that field. You can also group records based upon a valid FoxPro expression. For example, if you were using an index based on a combination of Lastname + Firstname to control the order of the records, you could enter the expression **LASTNAME + FIRSTNAME** to define the grouping. Once you add a Group band, you can then enter text or fields into that band within the report specification. After selecting the desired type of grouping, FoxPro inserts a new starting Group band and a new ending Group band for the group. Group bands must fall outside of the Detail bands.

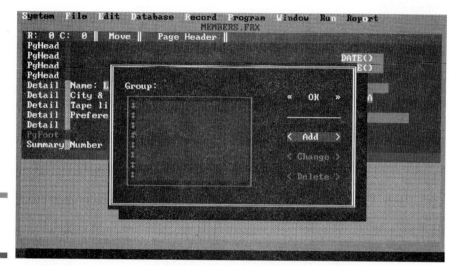

Group dialog
box
Figure 7-16.

The Swap Page Header option tells FoxPro to place group headers
instead of page headers on all pages where the group header appears.
The Swap Page Footer option does the same for footers; when chosen,
each page containing a group footer prints the group footer at the
bottom of the page in place of the page footer. You can use the Reprint

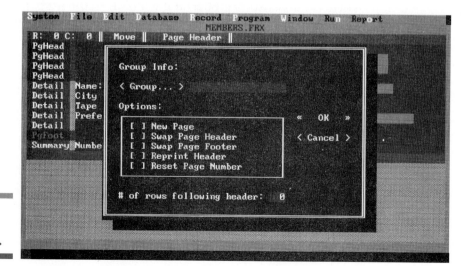

Group Info
dialog box
Figure 7-17.

Header and Reset Page Number options to reprint a header or to start new page numbering whenever a group changes.

Once you've placed the desired group, you can check to see if the results are what you desire by pressing (Alt)-(O) for the Report menu and choosing Page Preview. The resulting report will be divided by group. Note that the file must be sorted or indexed on the field you are grouping by to get the records in the proper group order; you may need to save the report, index or sort the file from the menus or command level, and then run the report. Or you can create a query, set an order for that query, and generate the report from the RQBE window. When you are satisfied with the results, save the report specification by pressing (Ctrl)-(W).

Adding Grouping by State to the Membership Report

Try adding a group by state to the existing membership report you created earlier in the chapter. From the command level, you can enter **MODIFY REPORT MEMBERS**. The report specification for the report you designed earlier will appear.

To add the group to the report, first place the cursor on the line above the Detail band. Next, open the Report menu with (Alt)-(O), and choose Data Grouping to insert a new group. The Group dialog box appears. There are no existing groups in the report, so the list box is empty. Select Add from the dialog box to add a group. Doing so reveals the Group Info dialog box (Figure 7-17).

In the Group box, you enter the field name or expression that will control the grouping. (When you can't remember the name of a field, you can tab to or click the Group heading and use the Expression Builder to select field names or parts of expressions.) In this case, enter

STATE

in the text box, and then select OK. When you choose OK, you see the Group dialog box uncovered; note that it now contains the designation

STATE

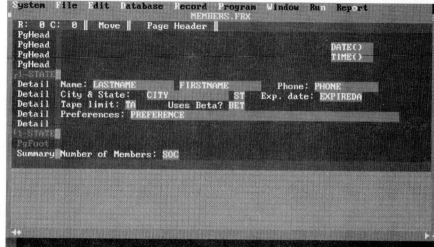

Report
specification
with single
level of
grouping added
Figure 7-18.

in the list box, showing that there is one level of grouping based on the State field. Again, select OK from the dialog box. The new Group bands will appear in the report specification, as shown in Figure 7-18.

Save the report by pressing Ctrl-W. Then create an index file that will control the order of the grouping by entering the following command:

```
INDEX ON STATE TO STATES
```

The file will be indexed in the order needed to provide the groups within the report. Next, turn on your printer and enter the command

```
REPORT FORM MEMBERS TO PRINT
```

The report will be printed and should resemble the following listing:

```
                                          12/06/93
                                          16:42:59


Name: Robinson        Benjamin          Phone: 202-555-4545
City & State:    Washington      DC   Exp. date: 09/17/95
Tape limit:   2       Uses Beta?  .T.
Preferences: Westerns, comedy. Clint Eastwood fan.
```

7

```
Name: Miller          Karen              Phone: 301-555-6678
City & State:   Chevy Chase     MD    Exp. date: 07/25/94
Tape limit:  6        Uses Beta? .F.
Preferences: Prefers science fiction, horror movies. Fan of
             Star Trek films.


Name: Martin          William            Phone: 301-555-2912
City & State:   Silver Spring   MD    Exp. date: 07/04/94
Tape limit:  4        Uses Beta? .F.
Preferences: Enjoys Clint Eastwood, John Wayne films.


Name: Moore           Ellen              Phone: 301-555-0201
City & State:   Takoma Park     MD    Exp. date: 11/17/96
Tape limit:  6        Uses Beta? .F.
Preferences: Drama, comedy.


Name: Robinson        Carol              Phone: 703-555-8778
City & State:   Falls Church    VA    Exp. date: 09/05/95
Tape limit:  6        Uses Beta? .F.
Preferences: Likes comedy, drama films.


Name: Kramer          Harry              Phone: 703-555-6874
City & State:   Arlington       VA    Exp. date: 12/22/94
Tape limit:  4        Uses Beta? .T.
Preferences: Big fan of Eddie Murphy. Also enjoys westerns.


Name: Zachman         David              Phone: 703-555-5432
City & State:   Falls Church    VA    Exp. date: 09/19/94
Tape limit:  4        Uses Beta? .T.
Preferences: Science fiction, drama.


Name: Hart            Wendy              Phone: 703-555-1201
City & State:   Fairfax         VA    Exp. date: 10/19/94
Tape limit:  2        Uses Beta? .T.
Preferences: Drama, adventure. Likes spy movies, including all
             James Bond series.

Number of Members:    8
```

If you are observant, you will immediately notice a problem here. The
actual contents of the State field do not appear with each group, so the
meaning of the grouping is not obvious. To add a heading indicating

the grouping, you need to place the field where you want it to appear. You can place the field used to control the group within the Group band, and it will then print once for each occurrence of that group. To see how this works, enter

```
MODIFY REPORT MEMBERS
```

to get back into the report specification. Place the cursor inside the starting Group band for the State field. At the far left margin, type the heading

```
For State:
```

and press Enter to complete the entry of the text. Then move the cursor to the right two spaces (to column 11). Press Ctrl-F to get to the Report Expression dialog box, enter

```
STATE
```

as the expression, and select OK from the dialog box. A field template representing the State field will appear in the Group band.

Place the cursor at the start of the ending Group band (row 10). A count of members per group would be desirable here, so enter the text

```
Members per State:
```

and press Enter. Move the cursor over to column 19 and press Ctrl-F. Tab to the Expr window, and enter **SOCIAL** as the field to base the count upon. Tab down to the Calculate option (or under version 1.*x*, the Totaling option), and press the Spacebar to select the option.

At the next dialog box that appears, tab over to the Count option and press the Spacebar to select it. If you're using version 1.*x*, tab back up to the Reset menu, and press Enter to open the menu. Select State from the menu. This tells FoxPro to reset the member count for each state group. (Users of versions 2 and above will see that State is selected by default.)

Choose OK in the dialog box. In the Report Expression dialog box that reappears, tab over to the Width box and enter **3**. Finally, choose OK from the Report Expression dialog box.

7

Save the report by pressing Ctrl-W. To see the results, enter

```
SET INDEX TO STATES
REPORT FORM MEMBERS TO PRINT
```

The report will appear or be printed, and this time the contents for the State field will appear along with each group:

```
                                              12/06/93
                                              16:47:18


For State: DC
Name: Robinson        Benjamin           Phone: 202-555-4545
City & State:   Washington      DC   Exp. date: 09/17/95
Tape limit:  2        Uses Beta? .T.
Preferences: Westerns, comedy. Clint Eastwood fan.


Members per State:    1
For State: MD
Name: Miller          Karen              Phone: 301-555-6678
City & State:   Chevy Chase     MD   Exp. date: 07/25/94
Tape limit:  6        Uses Beta? .F.
Preferences: Prefers science fiction, horror movies. Fan of
             Star Trek films.


Name: Martin          William            Phone: 301-555-2912
City & State:   Silver Spring   MD   Exp. date: 07/04/94
Tape limit:  4        Uses Beta? .F.
Preferences: Enjoys Clint Eastwood, John Wayne films.


Name: Moore           Ellen              Phone: 301-555-0201
City & State:   Takoma Park     MD   Exp. date: 11/17/96
Tape limit:  6        Uses Beta? .F.
Preferences: Drama, comedy.


Members per State:    3
For State: VA
Name: Robinson        Carol              Phone: 703-555-8778
City & State:   Falls Church    VA   Exp. date: 09/05/95
Tape limit:  6        Uses Beta? .F.
Preferences: Likes comedy, drama films.
```

```
Name: Kramer         Harry              Phone: 703-555-6874
City & State:   Arlington      VA    Exp. date: 12/22/94
Tape limit:   4        Uses Beta? .T.
Preferences: Big fan of Eddie Murphy. Also enjoys westerns.

Name: Zachman        David              Phone: 703-555-5432
City & State:   Falls Church   VA    Exp. date: 09/19/94
Tape limit:   4        Uses Beta? .T.
Preferences: Science fiction, drama.

Name: Hart           Wendy              Phone: 703-555-1201
City & State:   Fairfax        VA    Exp. date: 10/19/94
Tape limit:   2        Uses Beta? .T.
Preferences: Drama, adventure. Likes spy movies, including all
             James Bond series.

Members per State:   4
Number of Members:   8
```

REMEMBER: You must create or activate an index, or sort the file, before a report containing groups will print properly.

7

Creating a Report with Multiple Groups

You can insert additional groups to further refine your reports. As an example, consider the RENTALS database, which contains records of the tapes rented by the members. If what is needed is a report grouped by the name of the movie and by the rental date within each group of movie names, you must create a report containing more than one group.

Enter **USE RENTALS** to open the RENTALS database. Next, enter **CREATE REPORT RENTS** to begin a new report. Open the Report menu, choose Quick Report, and leave the Column Layout option selected as the desired layout. Select OK from the dialog box to create a standard columnar report. The standard report format will do for this example.

In this case, what is wanted is a report grouped by movie name and, within each movie name, by groups of rental dates. Place the cursor at the start of the last Page Header band, just above the Detail band. Press [Alt]-[O] to get to the Report menu, and choose Data Grouping to insert a new group; from the dialog box that appears, choose Add. In the next dialog box, enter **TITLE** as the field name, and then select OK.

To add a second level of grouping, you simply select Add from the Group dialog box again. Choose Add now, and the Group Info dialog box again appears. The field controlling the second level of grouping is the Dayrented field, so enter **DAYRENTED** as the field name and select OK. Once you select OK, the DayRented field name appears under Title in the list box. Choose OK in the Group dialog box to get back to the report specification.

Press [Home] to move the cursor to the left margin, and move down into the first Group band (labeled "1-Title"). Choose Add Line from the Report menu to add another line; this provides blank space when the report is produced. Move the cursor down one line and type the heading

```
Movie name:
```

[Ctrl]-[F] can be used to place fields anywhere in a report.

Press [Enter] to complete the text entry, and then press the [→] key twice. Press [Ctrl]-[F] to open the Report Expression dialog box, and enter **TITLE** as the field name. Then choose OK.

Move the cursor down one line and press [Home] to get back to the left margin of the second Group band (labeled "2-dayre," short for "day rented"). Again, choose Add Line from the Report menu, and then move the cursor down one line. Type the heading

```
Rental date:
```

and press [Enter] to complete the text entry, and press the [→] key twice. Press [Ctrl]-[F] to open the Report Expression dialog box, and enter **DAYRENTED** as the field name. Then choose OK.

Since the movie title will appear as a group heading in the first Group band, it is not needed in the Detail band. Place the cursor anywhere in the Title field that is inside the Detail band (*not* the one in the 1st Group band), and press the [Del] key.

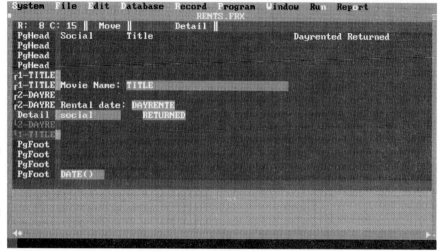

Report
specification
containing
multiple groups
Figure 7-19.

The Dayrented field is also in a Group band, so it is not needed in the Detail band. Place the cursor anywhere in the Dayrented field that is inside the Detail band (*not* the one in the 2nd Group band), and press the ⌦ key. Then move over to the Returned field and press ⌦ again. Move the cursor back to column 15 (just to the right of the Social field), press Ctrl-F, tab to the window, and enter **RETURNED** as the field name; then choose OK from the dialog box. Your screen should resemble the one shown in Figure 7-19.

Because the report will be grouped by movie title and then by rental date, the database must be sorted or indexed on a combination of the Title and Dayrented fields for the groupings to appear in the correct order. Save the report by choosing Save As from the File menu; use RENTS2 as a report name. Choose Close from the File menu to exit the Report Generator. Then enter the following command:

```
INDEX ON TITLE + DTOS(DAYRENTED) TO DAYFILE
```

The file will be indexed in the order needed to provide the groups within the report. As you may recall from Chapter 4, the DTOS function allows indexing on two fields of different types when one of the fields is a date field.

To see the results, enter the following command:

```
REPORT FORM RENTS2 TO PRINT
```

The report will be printed and should resemble the following:

```
Movie Name: Coming to America

Rental date: 03/14/93
901-77-3456    03/18/93


Movie Name: Doc Hollywood

Rental date: 03/04/93
901-77-3456    03/05/93


Movie Name: Friday 13th Part XXVII

Rental date: 03/14/93
123-44-8976    03/16/93


Movie Name: Fried Green Tomatoes

Rental date: 03/01/93
121-90-5432    03/06/93


Movie Name: Lethal Weapon III

Rental date: 03/02/93
121-33-9876    03/06/93

Rental date: 03/07/93
876-54-3210    03/08/93


Movie Name: Mambo Kings

Rental date: 03/15/93
121-33-9876    03/17/93

Rental date: 03/16/93
876-54-3210    03/18/93


Movie Name: Prince of Tides

Rental date: 03/06/93
343-55-9821    03/12/93
```

```
Rental date: 03/16/93
121-90-5432     03/17/93

Rental date: 03/17/93
232-55-1234     03/19/93

Movie Name:  Star Trek VI

Rental date: 03/05/93
123-44-8976     03/06/93

Rental date: 03/18/93
495-00-3456     03/19/93

Movie Name:  Wayne's World

Rental date: 03/04/93
495-00-3456     03/09/93

Rental date: 03/19/93
343-55-9821     03/20/93

Movie Name:  Who Framed Roger Rabbit

Rental date: 03/06/93
232-55-1234     03/09/93
```

7

Generating Reports from the RQBE Window

Assuming you are using version 2 or above, you can generate your reports from within the RQBE window, detailed in Chapter 6. This is generally the most efficient way to obtain selective groups of data in the form of a report. Simply design your desired report, using the techniques covered in this chapter, and save the report. Then, design your selective query, using the techniques covered in Chapter 6. Then, open the query (if it is not already open) with the MODIFY QUERY command or with the Open option of the File menu. Once you are in the RQBE window, use the menu in the Output To area to select Report/Labels, and then choose the Options button. When the next dialog box appears, select Report in the Formatting Options area, enter the name of your stored report, and choose your output options (usually to the printer).

To see how this works, you can combine a query from the RQBE window with the membership report you designed earlier in this chapter, called MEMBERS.

First, enter **USE MEMBERS**, then enter **CREATE QUERY** in the Command window. The RQBE window will appear. In the Output To area at the upper-right corner of the screen, choose Report/Label from the menu if it is not already chosen. Then, select the Options button by clicking it or pressing the letter Ⓟ. In a moment, the RQBE Display Options dialog box will appear.

Under Formatting Options, choose Report (by clicking the button or pressing Ⓡ). Tab to or click the Report/Label Form Name box, and enter **MEMBERS**. Tab down to the Preview Report/Label option, and turn this option off by pressing the [Spacebar]. Then, tab over to the Output Destinations area, and turn on the To Printer option. Finally, choose OK from the dialog box.

When the RQBE window reappears, tab to or click the Field Name box, and choose State as the field. In the example box, enter **VA**. Finally, make sure your printer is ready, then choose Do Query from the RQBE window. The results will be printed; in this case, you get a selective query (only those members living in Virginia) printed, using the custom report you designed. For this example, you can exit the query without saving, by pressing [Esc] and answering No to the Save prompt. Remember, any time you want to save a query for repeated use with reports, you can do so by choosing Save As from the File Menu.

Report Design

Before you start to design your custom reports, you should plan the design of the report. This may mean asking the other users of the database what information will actually be needed from the report. In the case of Generic Videos, you would consider what information the managers need from the report and how the report should look.

In many cases, you'll find it advantageous to outline the report contents and format on paper. Once the report has been designed on paper, your outline should resemble the actual report that is produced by FoxPro. You may also find it helpful to print a list of fields from the database structure, particularly if you are designing a report that contains a large number of fields. This can be done with the LIST STRUCTURE TO PRINT command.

CHAPTER

FOXPRO

8

MANAGING YOUR FILES

This chapter's topic is file operations—copying, renaming, and erasing files, and using more than one database file at a time. Although some file operations usually are performed from your operating system (DOS or OS/2), these operations can also be performed without leaving FoxPro.

In addition to performing file operations without returning to the operating system, you can also transfer information between database files. You can transfer all the data in a file, or selected data. You can also open and work with more than one file at once. The use of multiple files is common in a relational database manager like FoxPro, and you will find it a virtual necessity for performing some types of tasks, such as inventory and complex accounting functions.

Using the Filer

Various options for managing files are available through the Filer option of the System menu. If you open the System menu and choose Filer, the Filer appears, as shown in Figure 8-1. Its list box shows all files in the current directory. Also shown at the bottom of the Filer are options such as Find, Copy, Move, and so forth. These options can be selected (by typing the highlighted letter within the option or by clicking the option) to perform various file operations. At the upper-right side of the Filer are two menus for your disk drives and directories. You can tab to either menu and press Enter to display an additional menu that lists available disk drives or directories. Using these menus, you can navigate within other drives and directories.

Underneath the menus is the Files Like entry box. You can enter filenames or DOS wildcards here to restrict the types of files displayed in the list box. For example, entering ***.DBF** in the Files Like box would restrict the files shown to database files only.

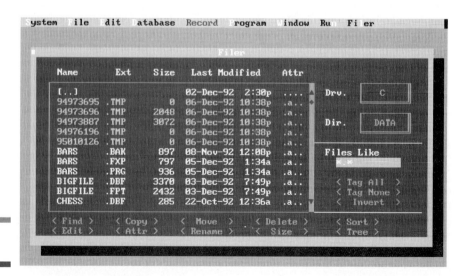

The Filer

Figure 8-1.

The list box is divided into five columns: Name, Ext, Size, Last Modified, and Attr (for Attribute). The Name and Ext columns show the file name and extension (if any) of the file. Directories and subdirectories are displayed within brackets; In a directory, the file name [..] at the top of the list denotes the parent directory.

The Size column shows the size of each file in bytes, and the Last Modified column shows the DOS date and time stamp on the file. The Attr column shows the attributes of the file, as determined by your operating system. Up to four letters can appear in this column: A, for archive; H, for hidden; R, for read-only; and S, for system. More information about file attributes can be found in your DOS manual.

Moving Around the Files List

You can use the ⬆ and ⬇ keys and the Pg Up and Pg Dn keys to move the cursor within the files list. Try Pg Dn and your ⬇ key now to see the effect. As you highlight a particular file, you can press Enter to *tag* (place a marker) beside the file. Once a file has been tagged, you can use the options at the bottom of the Filer to perform a desired operation (such as copying or erasing) on the tagged file.

Use Shift + Spacebar to tag multiple files.

You can tag multiple files by keeping the Shift key depressed while moving to different files and pressing the Spacebar. Mouse users can tag individual files by clicking the desired file in the List box. To tag multiple files with a mouse, hold down the Shift key while dragging the mouse.

Files that are currently open, such as database files, appear dimmed. You cannot select open files for other operations (such as copying or erasing).

Note the Tag All, Tag None, and Invert options at the right side of the Filer. You can select Tag All to tag all files, and you can select Tag None to remove all tags from files. Selecting Invert reverses the order of existing tags; all tagged files are untagged, and all untagged files are tagged. You may find that using the Tag All option along with the Files Like entry box is useful for selecting groups of files of the same type. For example, you could delete all backup (.BAK) files by entering ***.BAK** in the Files Like box, selecting Tag All, and then selecting Delete.

8

You are not limited to working within the current directory. By tabbing to the Dir menu at the right side of the Filer and pressing (Enter), you can display directories above the current one. Highlight the desired directory and press (Enter) to switch to that directory, or highlight the drive letter to switch to the root directory. When you do this, the Files list box shows the directory you have switched to. You can highlight any directory in the Files Box and press (Enter) to switch to that directory.

After experimenting with moving around, be sure to get back to the subdirectory that contains your working files (it is probably FOXPRO\DATA, unless you set up your hard disk differently at the start of this book). If you somehow get lost and can't find your way back, just exit the Filer by pressing (Esc) and restart the Filer by choosing Filer from the System menu. FoxPro automatically puts you back in the working directory. You can exit the Filer at any time by pressing the (Esc) key or by clicking on the close box in the upper-left corner of the window.

Deleting Files

You can delete files by tagging the files (highlighting the file and pressing (Enter) to tag it) and then choosing the Delete option. When you do this, a dialog box warns you that the file will be deleted. You must then choose Delete from the dialog box to delete the file. If multiple files have been tagged, the dialog box contains two additional options: Skip and Delete All. You can confirm the deletion, or you can choose Skip to skip to the next tagged file. If you choose Delete All, all tagged files are deleted without any further confirmation.

NOTE: Exercise care when deleting files. FoxPro does not prevent you from deleting its own program files or other program files.

Renaming Files

You can rename a file by tagging the file and choosing the Rename option. When you do this, a dialog box displays the old name and asks you for the new name. Enter the new name and choose Rename from the dialog box to rename the file.

Finding Files

The Find option lets you find files based on a name or extension and tag those files. When you choose Find, the Find Files Like dialog box appears (Figure 8-2).

In the text box, you can enter the name and/or extension for the type of file that you want to find and tag. For example, entering ***.TXT** would cause the Filer to find and tag all files with a .TXT extension. Note that you can enter more than one file extension at a time by separating the extensions with semicolons. As an example, you could enter ***.TXT; *.COM; *.EXE** in the text box.

Note that the Find Files Like dialog box also contains two options that add to its power; they are the check boxes labeled Specify text to search for and Search subdirectories. If you select Specify text to search for, another dialog box appears, and you can enter up to three text strings (of a maximum of 256 characters). If you use this option, the Filer tags only those files found containing the text strings. The Search

Find Files
Like dialog box
Figure 8-2.

subdirectories option tells Filer to search all subdirectories in the current directory. Hence, if you start at the root directory, the Find option searches the entire drive. (This may take some time if you have a lot of files on your hard disk.)

When the Filer completes its search, you are placed back in the Files list, and all files matching your file name or extension are tagged. If you chose the Search subdirectory option, any directories that contain a file that matched the specification are also tagged. You can proceed to use the other Filer buttons to choose an option for the tagged files. If you are performing a destructive operation such as a Delete, it may be a wise idea to check the names of the tagged files before performing the operation.

Editing Files

Do not try to edit database or program files.

You can edit a file with the Edit option. (This should only be attempted with text files, such as programs you write in FoxPro; you should not attempt to load nontext files, such as databases or indexes, into the Editor.) To edit a file, highlight the desired file in the list box and choose Edit. The uses of the Editor are covered in more detail in Chapter 13.

Copying and Moving Files

You can copy files with the Copy option. To copy a file, tag the desired file or files and choose Copy. A dialog box appears, asking for a name for the new file. Enter the file name, choose Copy from the dialog box, and the file or files are copied to the new file name or file names. (Note that you can tab to or click the Target Directory button to pick a different directory from a list box as the destination for the copied file.) You can copy multiple files by using wildcards in the file specification; for example, if you tagged all files with a .DBF extension, you could enter a file specification of *.DBK, and all tagged files would be copied to new files having the same name and a .DBK extension. Two options in the dialog box, Replace Existing Files and Preserve Directories, let you specify whether any existing files at the destination having the same name should be overwritten, and whether the directory structure should be copied as well as the files.

The Move option lets you move a file or files from one location to another. It operates just like the Copy option, with one difference: when the tagged file or files have been copied to the new location, they are removed from the old location. FoxPro does this quickly, because it does not actually copy and delete the files from the hard disk; it instead performs a sophisticated renaming operation that appears to "move" the files between directories.

Changing File Attributes

You can change the DOS attributes of a file with the Attr option. When you tag a file and then select Attr, a dialog box appears with the four attribute choices: Archived, Hidden File, Read-Only, and System. The check boxes for the choices will already be selected or unselected, depending on the file's current status; for example, if you have tagged a read-only file, the Read-Only check box will be filled in with an X. You can press the highlighted letters of your choice or click the check boxes with the mouse to change any file attributes as desired. The Change All button at the bottom of the dialog box can be used to tell FoxPro to change the attributes for all tagged files, without stopping to display the dialog box for each file you have tagged.

NOTE: You should not change file attributes without being aware of possible consequences, particularly with files that are part of the program or the operating system. If you were to change the attributes of files that make up the actual FoxPro program or of your system (DOS) files, the results could be disastrous. Your computer could fail to operate normally.

Using Size and Tree

Use the Size option to display statistics on the size of a file. To use the option, select the desired file in the list box and choose Size. A dialog box containing information on the size of the file will appear.

The Tree option can be used to display a Tree Panel (a visual representation of the layout of files within your directories). You can perform operations on entire directory structures from the Tree Panel. Choose Tree, and FoxPro takes a few moments to scan your entire hard disk. When this is done, a Tree Panel appears displaying the files and directories on your hard disk.

To navigate within the Tree Panel, use the scroll bars and the mouse, the ⬆ and ⬇ keys, or the [Pg Up] and [Pg Dn] keys. You can tab over to or click the Drv. (Drive) pop-up menu to display and select from all available disk drives. For your information, the lower-right portion of the Tree Panel shows the number of files on the drive, the disk space used, and the remaining free space on the drive.

You can create and rename directories from the Tree Panel.

You can use the buttons shown at the bottom of the Tree Panel to rename directories, make directories, and change directories. You can also copy or move directories, delete directories, and determine the size (disk space used) for a particular directory.

Keep in mind that when you are working in the Tree Panel, you are working with entire directories, so the potential for accidental damage is great. It is a wise idea to back up files before performing any deletions of entire directories. You also should not casually rename directories without considering what effect this could have on other programs on your system; if, for example, you are using Microsoft Windows and you casually rename certain directories using FoxPro's Filer, you could wreak havoc when Windows later looks for directories that no longer exist.

Using Sort

Use the Sort option to sort the files in the files list. When you choose the Sort option, a dialog box lets you select the sort criteria. You can choose to sort by name, extension, size, date, or file attributes. You can also choose whether the list will be sorted in ascending or descending order. After choosing the desired options from the dialog box, choose OK, and the files in the list box will be sorted. This in no way affects the order of the files on the disk; only the appearance of the files in the list box is affected.

Commands for Managing Files

If you prefer to stick with commands, you can use a number of different commands for file management. You can even run a DOS command from the command level within FoxPro. You can also perform selective copying of records within a database file to another file.

The RUN Command

To exit FoxPro temporarily and run a DOS command, use the RUN command. The syntax for this command is

> RUN *DOS command or program name*

It causes FoxPro to suspend itself temporarily in memory and exit to DOS. Note that a substantial portion of FoxPro remains in memory when you do this. On a 640K machine, between 128K and 256K of memory will be available (the exact amount varies with your version of DOS and hardware configuration). So while you can technically run other programs, you will probably find few programs that fit in the available memory.

The RUN command is primarily useful for executing DOS commands you may be familiar with, such as COPY, DIR, and RENAME. To see how this works, enter the following command:

```
RUN DIR/P
```

8

You see the current directory displayed just as if you had entered **DIR/P** at the DOS prompt. When the command completes, you are returned to the Command window within FoxPro.

Note that you should never attempt to run a program that will modify your PC's memory with the RUN command. All memory-resident programs fall into this category, as does the PRINT command in DOS.

The COPY FILE Command

You can use the COPY FILE command as an equivalent to the COPY command in DOS to make copies of entire files. The format for this command is

> COPY FILE *source-filename* TO *destination-filename*

You must include any extensions when using this command. As an example, if you wanted to make a copy of a file named LETTER1.TXT and the copy was to be named MYFILE.TXT, you could use the following command:

```
COPY FILE LETTER1.TXT TO MYFILE.TXT
```

Drive identifiers and path names are optional and can be included before the file names.

Note that if you use this method to copy a database file, be sure to also copy any .FPT (memo field) file that may accompany the database. Remember, whenever a database contains memo fields, it is made up of two files, one with a .DBF extension and another with a .FPT extension.

NOTE: With very large fields, using COPY at the DOS level is much faster than using COPY FILE within FoxPro.

The COPY Command

The COPY command copies all or parts of a database file. Its format is

COPY TO *filename*

where *filename* is the name of the new file that you want the records copied to. You must first use the USE command to open the file that you want to copy from. For example, try the following commands now:

```
USE MEMBERS
COPY TO FILE1
USE FILE1
LIST
```

All of the records in the MEMBERS database will be copied to the new file, FILE1.

One advantage of the COPY command is that you need not worry about copying the memo field (.FPT) file; it is copied automatically. A disadvantage of COPY is that with large databases, it is much slower than the COPY FILE command.

The COPY command offers significant flexibility when you choose to copy specific fields. To select the fields to be copied, use the format

COPY TO *filename* FIELDS *fieldlist*

By adding the word FIELDS after the file name and then adding a list of fields, you tell FoxPro to copy only the fields that you place in the list to the new database. As an example, you can copy just the Lastname, Firstname, City, and State fields in FILE1 by entering

```
COPY TO FILE2 FIELDS LASTNAME, FIRSTNAME, CITY, STATE
USE FILE2
LIST
```

The listing shows that only the fields you specified by name in FILE1 are copied to FILE2.

You can also use a FOR clause to copy specific data from a database. When used with the COPY command, the optional FOR clause limits the records that are copied to the new file; only the records meeting the condition specified by the FOR clause are copied. The format for the COPY command when used with the FOR clause is

COPY TO *filename* FIELDS *fieldlist* FOR *condition*

Using the FOR clause as part of the COPY command, you can copy the Lastname and Tapelimit fields from FILE1 for all records in which the Tapelimit field contains a value greater than 3. To do this, enter

```
USE FILE1
COPY TO FILE3 FIELDS LASTNAME, TAPELIMIT FOR TAPELIMIT
> 3
```

The FOR condition specified before the Tapelimit field results in the new file, FILE3, containing only those members with a tape limit of more than 3. To see the results, enter

```
USE FILE3
LIST
```

You can perform this type of copying from the menus, if desired, by choosing the Copy To option of the Database menu. The dialog box that appears when you choose this option lets you specify a For or While condition to limit the records copied, as well as a scope or a list of fields to be copied to the new database.

Work Areas and Active Files

When you work with multiple files, each file is open in a different work area.

FoxPro can access any database file that is open, up to a limit of 255 database files at the same time. Opening a database file is equivalent to telling FoxPro, "I am ready to work with a database file that is stored on disk; now go get it." FoxPro can read any information in the database from an open database file. However, if you want to change, add, or delete any information in a database, the database file must not only be open; it must be active as well. Commands like CHANGE or EDIT, APPEND, and DELETE normally operate on active database files. FoxPro allows only one active database at a time, so out of a possible ten open files, only one can be active.

Opening a database file from disk requires that it be assigned to a *work area*. No database file can be open unless it resides in a work area. As you might have guessed, there are ten work areas in FoxPro, numbered from 1 to 255. Assigning a database file to a work area, or opening a database file, is a two-step process. You tell FoxPro what work area you want the file opened in, and you open the file in that work area. The SELECT command enables you to choose the work area, and the USE command opens the file. For example, if you wanted to open the MEMBERS file in work area 2, you could first select the work area by entering

```
SELECT 2
```

To load the MEMBERS file into the current work area, you would enter

```
USE MEMBERS
```

As an alternative, you could perform both steps—specifying the work area and opening the file—on a single command line by using the IN clause along with the USE command. For example, the following command tells FoxPro to open MEMBERS in work area 2:

```
USE MEMBERS IN 2
```

If you had specified a different file name—for example, RENTALS instead of MEMBERS—that file (RENTALS) would have been loaded into work area 2. In fact, any database file that you now load with the USE command will be loaded in work area 2 until you use the SELECT command to choose a different work area. Note that the USE *filename* IN *work-area* syntax of the USE command does *not* select a work area; it only loads the file in the named work area. If the current work area happened to be work area 1 and you entered **USE MEMBERS IN 2**, the MEMBERS file would be loaded in work area 2, but you would still be using work area 1.

The current work area is always the last area you chose with the SELECT command. The active database file is the last database file you loaded into the current work area. For an example, open the RENTALS file in work area 1 and the MEMBERS file in work area 2 by entering the following commands:

```
SELECT 1
USE RENTALS
SELECT 2
USE MEMBERS
```

8

MEMBERS is now the active database, because work area 2 was the last work area selected; thus, FoxPro is pointed to MEMBERS. FoxPro can now change or access any information in the MEMBERS file but can only access information from the RENTALS file. If you wanted RENTALS to be the active file, you would enter **SELECT 1** after opening both databases. The active database would switch from MEMBERS to RENTALS, although MEMBERS would remain open.

You can see the effects of having multiple work areas open if you now enter the following commands:

```
SELECT 1
LIST TITLE, DAYRENTED
```

```
Record#  TITLE                       DAYRENTED
      1  Star Trek VI                03/05/93
      2  Lethal Weapon III           03/02/93
      3  Who Framed Roger Rabbit     03/06/93
```

```
 4   Doc Hollywood                03/04/93
 5   Fried Green Tomatoes         03/01/93
 6   Wayne's World                03/04/93
 7   Prince of Tides              03/06/93
 8   Lethal Weapon III            03/07/93
 9   Friday 13th Part XXVII       03/14/93
10   Mambo Kings                  03/15/93
11   Prince of Tides              03/17/93
12   Coming to America            03/14/93
13   Prince of Tides              03/16/93
14   Star Trek VI                 03/18/93
15   Wayne's World                03/19/93
16   Mambo Kings                  03/16/93
```

See Chapter 12 for more on working with multiple databases.

```
SELECT 2
LIST LASTNAME, FIRSTNAME


Record#   LASTNAME      FIRSTNAME
      1   Miller        Karen
      2   Martin        William
      3   Robinson      Carol
      4   Kramer        Harry
      5   Moore         Ellen
      6   Zachman       David
      7   Robinson      Benjamin
      8   Hart          Wendy
```

You can see, from this example, that with two database files open simultaneously in different work areas, you can use commands to obtain information from both of the databases. This technique for working with multiple databases will prove useful in Chapter 12.

The CLOSE DATABASES Command

Another command that you will use often is the CLOSE DATABASES command. It closes all database and index files and returns FoxPro to work area 1. Enter

```
CLOSE DATABASES
```

to close all of the database files that you opened earlier.

Combining Files

FoxPro lets you transfer records from one database file to another by using a variation of the APPEND command that you have used to add records to a database. However, the format of the command is somewhat different when it is used for transferring records from another database. Instead of simply entering APPEND, you must enter the command in the format

APPEND FROM *filename*

where *filename* is the name of the file from which you wish to transfer records. The file to which you are adding the records must be the active database file.

As an example, to transfer records from the newly created FILE3 database to the FILE2 database, you should first activate FILE2. Enter

```
USE FILE2
```

You can append the records to FILE2 with

```
APPEND FROM FILE3
```

8

When you list the database to see the appended records, your display should resemble this:

Record#	LASTNAME	FIRSTNAME	CITY	STATE
1	Miller	Karen	Chevy Chase	MD
2	Martin	William	Silver Spring	MD
3	Robinson	Carol	Falls Church	VA
4	Kramer	Harry	Arlington	VA
5	Moore	Ellen	Takoma Park	MD
6	Zachman	David	Falls Church	VA
7	Robinson	Benjamin	Washington	DC
8	Hart	Wendy	Fairfax	VA
9	Miller			
10	Martin			
11	Robinson			
12	Kramer			
13	Moore			
14	Zachman			

One characteristic of the APPEND FROM command becomes apparent when you examine the list: only fields having the same names in both databases are appended. Remember, you gave different structures to these files as a result of the selective use of the COPY command. FILE2 contains the Lastname, Firstname, City, and State fields, while FILE3 contains the Lastname and Tapelimit fields. When you appended from FILE3 to FILE2, FoxPro found just one field in common between the two files: Lastname.

Even if the field name is the same, FoxPro may or may not append the field if the data type is different. If FoxPro can make sense of the transfer, it appends the data. For example, a numeric field will transfer to a character field of another database, with data appearing in the character field as numbers. A character field, if it contains only numbers, will transfer to a numeric field. A memo field will not transfer to any other type of field. In addition, if the field being copied has a field size larger than the field receiving the record, character data is truncated and asterisks are entered for numeric data that does not fit within the new field size.

The file that you appended from does not have to be a FoxPro database file. The APPEND FROM command is also commonly used to transfer data from other programs like spreadsheets or word processors. This aspect of using FoxPro is discussed in more detail in Chapter 18.

Copying a Database Structure

Another helpful FoxPro command, COPY STRUCTURE, lets you make an identical copy of the database structure (in effect, an empty database). You can use COPY STRUCTURE to create empty copies of a database on multiple floppy disks that others can use at their machines (provided they have FoxPro) to add records. Later, the records can be combined at a single site with the APPEND FROM command.

Use COPY STRUCTURE to copy files for use on other PCs.

To use this command, first open the database you want to copy the structure from with the USE command. Then use the command

COPY STRUCTURE TO *filename*

where *filename* is the desired name of the file. You can precede the file name with a path or a drive identifier if desired. As an example, the command

```
USE MEMBERS
COPY STRUCTURE TO A:REMOTE
```

copies an empty database containing the structure of MEMBERS to a file called REMOTE.DBF on the disk in drive A. If the file contains memo fields, both a .DBF and an .FPT file are copied under the new name.

8

CHAPTER

FOXPRO

AUTOMATING YOUR WORK WITH MACROS

FoxPro provides macros, which are combinations of keystrokes that can automate many of the tasks you normally perform while within FoxPro. Macros let you record a sequence of characters in a single key combination. You can save the macro and later use it to play back those key sequences by pressing the same single key combination. When the macro is played back, FoxPro performs as if you had just manually performed the actions that are contained within the macro.

Save time by saving repetive actions to macros.

When you use macros, a single key combination can hold a complex series of menu choices or commands. You can store frequently used phrases, names, or complete paragraphs of text in a macro. And you are not limited to one key combination; you can use various combinations of letter and function keys for macros. If you must print daily reports or perform similar repetitive tasks, you can save many keystrokes by using macros.

If you use commercially available keyboard enhancers like SuperKey and ProKey, you are familiar with the advantages of automating your work with macros. Users of other keyboard enhancers may wonder whether they should simply continue to use such products instead of using FoxPro's macro capability. The advantage of using the macro capability within FoxPro is twofold. First, you will not consume additional memory that could be used by the program because you have loaded a memory-resident keyboard enhancer. FoxPro requires a minimum of 512K of RAM. Unless your memory-resident keyboard enhancer can use extended or expanded memory, you may run into "insufficient memory" messages when trying to use it with FoxPro. Second, you will avoid any possible conflicts between the operation of FoxPro and the memory-resident keyboard enhancer. Memory-resident programs have, in the past, been known to conflict with other software such as FoxPro. During the writing of this book, Borland's SideKick did at times conflict with FoxPro, depending on the number of SideKick features loaded simultaneously with FoxPro.

Creating Macros

To create a macro, follow these four steps:

1. Press Shift-F10 to display the Macro Key Definition dialog box. (An alternate method for this step is to choose the Macros option of the System menu and then choose New from the dialog box that appears.)

2. Press the Ctrl or Alt key with the letter key or function key that is to be assigned to the macro. You can use Ctrl or Alt plus any of the 26 letters or 10 function keys. (Note that if you use Alt with a letter key that normally opens a menu, the key combination overrides the menu choice. For example, if you assign Alt-F to a macro, you

will not be able to use Alt-F to open the File menu while that macro is loaded.)

3. Enter the keystrokes that will make up the macro. If you make an error, press Shift-F10, choose Discard from the dialog box to end the recording, and start again.

4. Once all the keystrokes have been entered, press Shift-F10, and then select OK to stop the macro recording.

Once the macro has been recorded, you can press the Ctrl- or Alt- key combination to play back the macro at any time.

For a quick example of what macros can do for you, consider editing within the MEMBERS database. Perhaps you regularly update records by splitting a Browse window just past the three leftmost fields and performing a forward search in the Lastname field for a desired last name. A macro would automate much of this process.

Press Shift-F10 and then press Ctrl-A to designate that key combination for the macro. Select OK. In the message that appears you will see

```
Recording Ctrl A. Shift-F10 stops.
```

indicating that FoxPro is now recording each of your keystrokes in the form of a macro. Enter **USE MEMBERS** to open the file, and enter **BROWSE** to enter Browse mode. Press Alt-B to open the Browse menu, and press R to choose the Resize Partitions option. Press the → key repeatedly until the window is split just past the Firstname field. Then press Enter to complete the resizing. Press Ctrl-H to move the cursor to the left partition of the Browse window. Press Ctrl-F10 to zoom the Browse window to full size.

Open the Record menu with Alt-R and choose Locate. From the dialog box that appears, choose For. In the Expression window, enter the following (note the pair of quotes):

```
LASTNAME = " "
```

Then press the ← key once so the cursor is between the quotes. Press Shift-F10, and choose OK from the dialog box to stop the recording of the macro.

9

To try the macro, first press (Esc) and choose Yes from the dialog box. Then press (Esc) twice to exit the menus and exit Browse mode. Assuming that you now want to open the file, enter Browse mode, split the window past the first three fields, and search for a particular name. You could use the macro to carry out all steps except the final ones of entering the name to search for, choosing OK from the dialog box, and then choosing Locate. Press (Ctrl)-(A) now to play back the macro. All the keystrokes are entered from the macro, and you are presented with the prompt for a last name to search for.

Go ahead and enter any last name in the database. Then choose OK and choose Locate from the next dialog box to appear. When the search is complete, press (Esc) to exit Browse mode.

Saving Macros

Macros that you create are saved in temporary memory, not permanently on the disk. If you want to keep a permanent record of your macros, you must use the Save option, which appears in the Keyboard Macros dialog box when you choose Macros from the System menu. Open the System menu now with (Alt)-(S) and choose Macros. From the dialog box that appears, choose Save. FoxPro asks you to name the macro file; enter **MYMACROS** as the file name. Then choose Save from the dialog box.

Once the file has been saved, you can exit FoxPro. When you return to the program, you can reload the macros you saved by choosing Macros from the System menu and then selecting Restore from the Keyboard Macros dialog box.

NOTE: While recording this macro, the (Alt)-key shortcuts to menu choices were used on purpose. You could have used the cursor keys and the (Enter) key to choose menu options, but when you are building macros it is a good idea to get into the habit of avoiding the cursor keys whenever possible. Not only does this use fewer overall keystrokes in the macro, but there is also less chance of an error during playback due to a list of available options being different than it was during recording. This can be a particular problem when choosing file names from a pick list, because the list changes as files are added to or deleted from your directory.

Command-level Use and Macros

Macros can also be used to repeat a series of commands, but this is not the speediest way to carry out a series of commands. You could start a macro with [Shift]-[F10], assign a key to the macro, enter a series of commands at the command level, and then stop the recording and save the macro. When you played back the macro, all of those commands would be repeated just as if you had typed them. However, FoxPro executes a series of commands much faster if they are stored in a command file or program. Details on creating programs begin with Chapter 13.

Macro Menu Options

When you choose the Macros option of the System menu, a dialog box called Keyboard Macros appears (Figure 9-1). In the center of this box is a list containing all macros currently in memory and the keys assigned to those macros. The upper portion of the list displays the macros that are assigned to the letter keys, and the lower portion shows the macros that are assigned to the function keys.

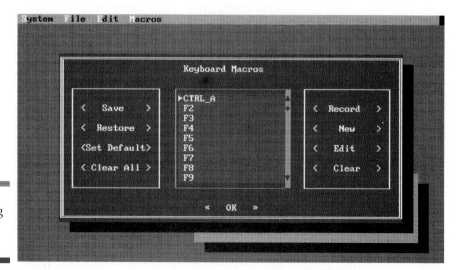

Keyboard
Macros dialog
box
Figure 9-1.

The Save and Restore options let you load a set of macros into memory or save the current macros in memory to a macro file. The command-level equivalents for these options are RESTORE MACROS FROM *macro-filename,* which loads the macro file, and SAVE MACROS TO *macro-filename,* which saves the current macros to the named file. The Set Default option stores the macros currently in memory to a startup macro file. The macros stored in this manner are loaded automatically into memory whenever FoxPro is started.

The New option begins the creation of a new macro; selecting this option is equivalent to pressing `Shift`-`F10` and causes the dialog box requesting the key combination for the new macro to appear. To record a macro, press the combination of `Alt` or `Ctrl` and the function or letter key you want to assign to the macro. If that key was used earlier, FoxPro asks for confirmation before overwriting the old macro in memory. After pressing the desired key, you can proceed to perform the actions desired in the macro. When you are done, press `Shift`-`F10`, and then choose OK to stop the recording.

The Clear option clears the highlighted macro from memory. To use this option, first highlight the unwanted macro in the list box. Then choose Clear to clear the macro. The Clear All option clears all existing macros from memory.

The Record and Edit options (versions 2 and above only) let you begin recording a macro (the equivalent of `Shift`-`F10`) or edit an existing macro.

Since you can save different sets of macros under different file names, you can have an unlimited number of macros. One helpful hint in keeping track of your macro files is to give them the same name as the associated database file. Macros are saved to a file with an extension of .FKY.

Adding to Existing Macros

You can add to the end of an existing macro by pressing `Shift`-`F10` to start a macro and then pressing the same key combination as the existing macro. For example, if you have already defined `Ctrl`-`A` as a macro and want to add more keystrokes to the end of it, you can press `Shift`-`F10`, which reveals the Macro Key Definition box. Press `Ctrl`-`A` as the key to define, and choose OK. The dialog box shown in Figure 9-2 appears.

The dialog box presents you with three options: Overwrite, Append keystrokes, and Cancel. You can now choose Append keystrokes to add your keystrokes to the end of the existing macro. Selecting Overwrite clears the old macro and assigns the key combination you picked to a new macro; Cancel exits the macro definition without adding any changes.

Adding Pauses to Macros

FoxPro lets you add pauses to a macro. This is useful for allowing a user to enter an item that changes from day to day. A good example is the macro you created earlier, which searches for a record based on a last name. A pause could be added to let the user enter a last name in the dialog box; then the macro could perform the final steps of selecting OK from the dialog box and selecting Locate from the next dialog box to appear. To try this now, you need to be at the spot where the search

9

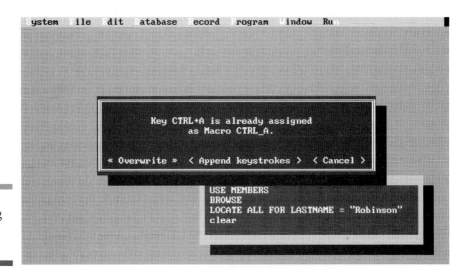

Overwrite
Macro dialog
box
Figure 9-2.

process ends; you can easily get there by replaying the macro. Press Ctrl-A to replay the macro. When the macro ends, you should be in the dialog box for the search expression, with the cursor flashing between the double quotes.

Press Shift-F10. When the Macro Key Definition box appears, press Ctrl-A to add to the existing macro. Next, choose OK from the dialog box. From the next dialog box to appear, choose Append keystrokes. You will see the message "Recording CTRL_A" in the upper-right corner of the screen.

Press Shift-F10 again to display the Stop Recording dialog box. Choose Insert Pause from the dialog box. It will vanish, leaving the Expression Builder still visible underneath. Choose OK from the Expression Builder dialog box. From the next visible dialog box choose Locate. Then press Shift-F10 and choose OK from the next dialog box to stop recording the macro. Press Esc to exit Browse mode.

Try playing the macro by pressing Ctrl-A. When the macro pauses, enter any last name in the database, and then press Shift-F10 to continue the macro. This time the macro will complete the search process by locating the record.

Rules and Limitations of Macros

A macro should never be made a part of itself. (For example, if a macro can be called with the Macro menu's Play option followed by the letter J, you cannot call up the Macro's menu, choose Play, and enter the letter J within the macro.) Such a technique would set up an anomaly known in programming as a *recursive loop,* where the program chases its own tail. FoxPro lets you get away with this, but only to a point. The macro repeats itself until an internal limit is reached, and an error message then results.

Allowable key combinations for assigning macros are Alt or Ctrl plus the function keys F1 through F9, or the alphabetic keys. Any attempt to assign a macro to other keys is ignored.

CHAPTER

FOXPRO

10

ADVANCED REPORT TOPICS

Chapter 7 began the process of covering how FoxPro can meet your reporting needs by allowing you to create quick reports and customized reports. This chapter continues with that topic, describing the use of form letters, labels, and other report topics in detail.

Using Expressions and Functions

You can coax much flexibility out of your reports and labels by using various expressions within the entry window of the Expression Builder. You usually enter a field in this window, but you can use any valid expression, including memory variables, field names, fields with alias names for related database files (see Chapter 11), and combinations of fields with or without spaces added.

Combinations of character fields are routinely used. As an example, consider a database with fields called Lastname, Firstname, and Midname (it contains the middle initial of a person). With such a database, the expression

```
TRIM(FIRSTNAME)+" "+LEFT(MIDNAME,1)+". "+TRIM(LASTNAME)
```

STR and DTOC functions convert numbers and dates to character strings.

would yield a name like Thomas A. Harris. This expression uses the LEFT function to get the leftmost character of a field and the TRIM function to trim excess spaces from the Firstname and Lastname fields. In this example, if there were no entry in the middle initial field, you would get an unwanted space and a period. However, this can be cured by including the IIF function in the Expr window, a topic that is covered later in this chapter. Combine names like this to save space in the report; if you can safely assume that 25 characters is enough for any reasonable combination, you can set the Width entry within the Report Expression dialog box to 25, regardless of the actual field widths. If 25 characters turns out to be too small for a given name, the Report Generator drops the excess characters.

You can also combine various expressions of different types by converting the noncharacter portions of the expressions to characters with string functions (discussed in detail in Chapter 13). For example, you could enter an expression like

```
STR(AMOUNT) + " " + DTOC(DATESOLD)
```

to combine a numeric amount and a date field into the contents of a single column. This example uses the STR function, which converts a numeric value into a string of characters, along with the DTOC function, which converts a valid date into a string of characters.

Using the IIF Function in Expressions

The Immediate IF function, IIF, is also quite useful as a part of an expression within reports or labels when you want to display one set of data if a condition is true and another set if a condition is false. In a personnel report, you may want to indicate the number of weeks of vacation that an employee gets; the company gives two weeks for employees with fewer than five years employment, and three weeks for all others. Assuming five years is equivalent to 365 days multiplied by 5 plus 1 day for at least one leap year, this means that any employee who has over 1826 days with the firm from the hire date to the date on the computer's clock gets three weeks' vacation. This is simple enough to calculate; for a given record in the personnel database with a date field called Hire_Date, the expression

```
IIF((DATE()SY-HIRE_DATE) < 1826, "two weeks", "three weeks")
```

would return the character string "two weeks" if less than 1826 days have passed since the date of hire, and "three weeks" if 1826 or more days have passed since the date of hire. You could place the entire expression into the Expression Builder window for a field within the report, and the report would display the appropriate number of weeks of vacation for that employee.

As an example of another use of the IIF function, recall that an earlier example of the combination of fields in a report expression had the problem of an unwanted period if no initial was entered into the middle-initial field. To cure such a deficiency, you could use an expression like the following:

```
TRIM(FIRSTNAME) +" " + IIF(LEFT(MIDNAME) <> " ",
LEFT(MIDNAME,1))+". ","") + TRIM(LASTNAME)
```

If the leftmost character of the Midname field is a space (indicating no middle initial), a space appears instead of the middle initial and a period.

Yet another common use for the IIF function within a report is to blank out numeric amounts that are equivalent to zero. For example, to

10

display hyphens in place of zero if a numeric field called Balance in a sales database contains a zero, you could use the following expression:

```
IIF(BALANCE=0,"   ---",STR(BALANCE,7,2))
```

The results are shown in this sample report:

```
                     Credit Sales
                     Account Report
Customer Name Cust.        High          Account
              Number       Credit        Balance
Smith, A.     1001         2000.00         788.50
Johnson, L.   1002         1200.00         675.00
Jones, C.     1003          900.00         350.00
Jones, J.L.   1004         2000.00        1850.00
Allen, L.     1005         2000.00         312.00
Walker, B.    1006         1300.00        1167.00
Keemis, M.    1007         2000.00         ---
Artis, K.     1008         1200.00         ---
Smith, A.M.   1009         2000.00         220.00
Williams, E.  1010         2000.00         ---
Jones, J.     1011         2000.00         875.00
```

Again, if the precise syntax for these functions is unfamiliar, you can consult the material on the use of functions contained in Chapter 13.

Other Useful Functions

Always remember the availability of functions within reports and labels. A few additional functions and one system variable that may come in handy are shown here; see Chapter 13 for more details on these.

Use Ctrl-F to place functions as well as fields in a report.

*PAGENO_*   This is a special system memory variable that FoxPro interprets as the current page number. It is most useful at the top or bottom of each page of a report's design to add page numbering to the report. If you want page numbering, simply place the cursor in the Page Header band (for page numbers at the top of the page) or in the Page Footer band (for page numbers at the bottom of the page). Then press Ctrl-F to open the Expression Builder, tab to the entry window, and enter **PAGENO_** in the window. Select OK from the dialog box to place the page numbers in the report.

DATE TIME   These functions place the current date or the current time, respectively. You can place them anywhere within a report or label by placing the cursor at the desired location, pressing [Ctrl]-[F] (in reports) or [Ctrl]-[E] (in labels), and typing **DATE()** or **TIME()** as desired.

CMONTH DAY YEAR   These functions can be combined with the DATE function to produce the current month, day, or year as determined by the PC's clock. For example, the expression

```
CMONTH(DATE())
```

produces the name of the current month spelled out, while the expression

```
YEAR(DATE())
```

produces the current year. (Note that the YEAR function yields a number, so you must use it along with the STR function to combine it with character data.) You can place these functions as expressions within text in a report to produce the current date in a spelled-out fashion.

Designing Form Letters

Designing a report in the format of a form letter lets you generate form letters for names and addresses within a database. Another way to do this is to export a file for use with a word processor, but the following method has the advantage of letting you create the form letters without leaving FoxPro.

10

The basic process in designing a report to serve as a form letter is to expand the size of the Detail band and to place the text of the form letter within the expanded Detail band along with the necessary fields for the name and address. Add fields as desired at appropriate locations within the letter. Add a Summary band at the bottom of the report and turn on the New Page option for the Summary band, so that each record in the report prints on a separate page. You can see how this works by using the following steps as an example along with the MEMBERS database.

Open the database with USE MEMBERS, and create a new report by entering **CREATE REPORT LETTER**. If you examine the Report menu by pressing Alt-O, note that the Add Line option has a shortcut key, [Ctrl]-[N], and the Remove Line option also has a shortcut key, [Ctrl]-[O] (or [Ctrl]-[M] if you are using version 1.x). Move the cursor down to the first row of the Page Footer band, and press [Ctrl]-[O] (or [Ctrl]-[M] if you are using version 1.x) three times to remove three lines from the Page Footer band. (You will not be able to remove the last line; every report must have at least one line in the Page Footer band.)

Move the cursor back into the Detail band, and press [Ctrl]-[N] ten times to add ten new lines to the Detail band. The number of lines you want in your own applications will vary, depending on the amount of text that is needed in the form letter. In your applications, you may choose to type text into the Detail band and add needed new lines as you go along.

Place the cursor at row 4, column 40. (Remember, the row and column locations appear at the upper-left corner of the report specification.) Enter

```
September 1, 1993
```

and press [Enter] to complete the entry. Use [Home] to get back to the left margin, and place the cursor two lines down, at the start of row 6. Press [Ctrl]-[F] to open the Report Expression dialog box. Tab to the Expr window, and enter

```
TRIM(FIRSTNAME) + " " + LASTNAME
```

This expression causes the contents of the Firstname field (trimmed of extra blanks) to appear, followed by one space and the contents of the Lastname field. This combination of names requires sufficient room, so after you enter the expression, tab over to the Width box and enter **40** as the maximum width. Then select OK from the dialog box to place the expression in the report.

Move the cursor to the start of line 7. Press [Ctrl]-[F], tab to the Expr window, and enter **ADDRESS**. Then choose OK to place the field.

Move the cursor to the start of line 8. Press Ctrl-F, tab to the Expr window, and enter the following expression:

```
TRIM(CITY) + ", " + STATE + " " + ZIPCODE
```

Then tab over to the Width box and enter **35** as the maximum width. Select OK from the dialog box to place the expression in the report.

To fill in the rest of the Detail band, you simply type the text of the form letter. You are not using a word processor, so you must complete each line by pressing Enter, and use the Home and ↓ keys to move the cursor to the start of the next line. Use this technique to enter the following text on the lines as show:

```
Line    Text
10      Dear Member:
11        We have been pleased to have you as a member of Generic
12      Videos movie club during the past year. As a valued member,
13      we would like to extend to you the chance to renew your video
14      membership now at a special reduced rate. By returning the
15      enclosed form, you will save an additional 33% off the regular
16      membership renewal rate.
```

Note that you could intermix fields within the text of the form letter. Although it is not necessary in this case, you might find such a technique helpful in your applications. For example, if you had a database with a numeric field of a customer's past-due amounts, you could have the past-due amount appear within a sentence in the letter. To do this, you would press Ctrl-F at the point in the letter where the field is to appear, enter the field name in the Expr window, and choose OK to place the field.

10

If you are inserting numeric fields into the body of your form letters, you want to get rid of leading blanks. You can do this by converting the numeric value into a character string and using the LTRIM function to trim leading blanks. For example, if you wanted to insert the Tapelimit field into the text of the letter and trim the leading blanks, you could place the cursor at the desired location, press Ctrl-F, and enter an expression like

```
LTRIM(STR(TAPELIMIT))
```

to accomplish such a task.

One item is still needed: a Group band containing a New Page option must be added so that each record will print on a separate page. Open the Report menu with [Alt]-[O] and choose the Data Grouping option. Choose Add, tab into the Group entry box, and enter **SOCIAL**. Turn on the New Page option by tabbing to it and pressing the [Spacebar]. Finally, select OK from the dialog box to place the Group band in the report. Choose OK from the next dialog box to appear. At this point, your screen should resemble the example shown in Figure 10-1.

This completes the letter for this example, so save the report by pressing [Ctrl]-[W]. When prompted to save the environment information, answer Yes. You can use the command

```
REPORT FORM LETTER TO PRINT
```

to print a letter for every record in the database. Or in the interest of saving paper, you may want to try a more limited scope, such as

```
REPORT FORM LETTER NEXT 3 TO PRINT
```

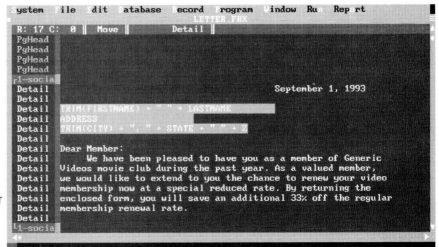

Report specification for form letters
Figure 10-1.

The results should resemble this sample:

```
                                              September 1, 1993


Carol Robinson
4102 Valley Lane
Falls Church, VA   22043-1234

Dear Member:

  We have been pleased to have you as a member of Generic
Videos movie club during the past year. As a valued member,
we would like to extend to you the chance to renew your video
membership now at a special reduced rate. By returning the
enclosed form, you will save an additional 33% off the regular
membership renewal rate.
```

You could add more text by placing as many additional Detail lines as you needed; in this example, a closing salutation could have been added in the lines following the paragraph of the form letter. You are not limited by the screen size in the number of Detail bands you place in the report; as you reach the bottom of the screen, additional lines added to the Detail band can be reached by moving the cursor down, which causes the top of the report specification to scroll off the screen as more of the bottom comes into view. In practice, a maximum of 64 lines in the Detail band, one line in the Page Header band, and one line in the Page Footer band would use up a full 11-inch sheet of paper. Fortunately, few form letters will require 64 lines of text.

Designing Invoices

10

If your printer supports the drawing of lines and boxes, you can use the capabilities of FoxPro's Report Generator to design invoices that imitate printed forms. Consider the standard invoice form, available from most office supply stores, as shown in Figure 10-2.

To follow this example, another database with a numeric field containing a billing amount would be appropriate. You can quickly create one by entering the following commands:

```
USE MEMBERS
COPY TO BILLS FIELDS LASTNAME, FIRSTNAME, ADDRESS,
CITY, STATE, ZIPCODE
```

FROM:

Date:

TO:

INVOICE No.
This bill is rendered only as
an accommodation
TERMS ARE NET CASH AND
PAYABLE ON PRESENTATION
YOUR ORDER No.

For Labor and Services Furnished on

ORIGINAL

Common invoice Figure 10-2.

```
USE BILLS
MODIFY STRUCTURE
```

When the Database Structure window appears, add a new field at the end of the database; call the field Amountdue. Make it a numeric field, with a width of 6 and 2 decimal places. Save the modified structure with Ctrl-W. Then use BROWSE to add sample amounts of your choosing to the new Amountdue fields of each record.

With the database ready for use, you can begin creating the report. Enter **CREATE REPORT BILLING** to display the report specification of a new report. With the cursor at the top of the Page Header band, press Ctrl-O (or Ctrl-M if you are using version 1.x) three times to remove three lines from the band. More lines will be needed in the Detail band to duplicate the form. Place the cursor in the first row of the Detail band, and press Ctrl-N 20 times to add 20 new lines.

You first need to place the "From" and "Date" information, as shown in Figure 10-2, so enter the following text at the positions described:

Row 1, column 2: **Generic Sales Company**
Row 2, column 2: **121 West Main Street**
Row 3, column 2: **Houston, TX 75202**

Move the cursor to row 4, column 45. Enter the text

```
Date:
```

and press [Enter]. Then move the cursor over to column 51. Press [Ctrl]-[F] to bring up the Report Expression dialog box, and tab over to the window. Enter

```
DATE()
```

Use the
DATE
function to
put the
current date
in a report.

The DATE function causes the current date, according to the PC's clock, to be displayed in this location of the report. Choose OK from the dialog box to place the expression in the report.

Place the cursor at row 6, column 1. Open the Report menu with [Alt]-[O], and choose Box. Using the arrow keys and the mouse (or, under version 1.*x*, using the [Spacebar] followed by the arrow keys or the mouse), stretch the box across and down to row 20, column 65. As you stretch downwards, you may not be able to see the end of the line beyond the bottom of the screen; however, you can use the row and column indicators in the upper-left corner of the report specification to tell the cursor location. Press [Enter] to complete placement of the box.

Place the cursor at row 10, column 2. Again, choose Box from the Report menu. Press the [↑] key once, then stretch the line directly across to row 10, column 64, and then press [Enter]. Because you stretched across and remained on the same line, a solid line is drawn instead of a box. Place the cursor at row 11, column 50. Again, choose Box from the Report menu. This time, press the [←] key once, then stretch the line directly down to row 19, column 50, and then press [Enter].

Place the cursor at row 7, column 3. Enter

```
To:
```

and complete the entry with [Enter]. Then move the cursor over to column 7 of the same line. Press [Ctrl]-[F], tab over to the Expr window of the dialog box, and enter the following expression:

```
TRIM(FIRSTNAME) + " " + LASTNAME
```

10

This causes the first and last names to appear, separated by one space. Tab over to the Width entry, and change the width to **40**, and then choose OK from the dialog box to place the expression in the report.

Move the cursor to row 8, column 7. Press Ctrl-F, tab over to the window, enter **ADDRESS**, and select OK from the dialog box to place the field.

Move the cursor to row 9, column 7. Press Ctrl-F, tab to the window, and enter the following expression:

```
TRIM(CITY) + ", " + STATE + "  " + ZIPCODE
```

Then tab over to the Width box and enter **35** as the maximum width. Select OK from the dialog box to place the expression in the report.

At row 8, column 46, enter the following text:

```
Terms are net cash
```

At row 9, column 46, enter the following text:

```
payable on receipt
```

At row 12, column 4, enter the following text:

```
Our records show the amount at the right
```

At row 13, column 4, enter the following text:

```
is PAST DUE. Please remit this amount.
```

Place the cursor at row 12, column 52. Press Ctrl-F, tab to the window, and enter **AMOUNTDUE** Select OK from the dialog box to place the Amountdue field at this location in the report.

A Group band containing a New Page option is needed so that each record will be printed as a separate invoice on its own page. Open the Report menu with Alt-O and choose the Data Grouping option. Choose Add, tab to the Group entry box, and enter **LASTNAME + FIRSTNAME** Turn on the New Page option by tabbing to it and pressing the Spacebar. Finally, select OK from the dialog box to place the Group band in the report. Choose OK from the next dialog box to appear.

At this point, your screen should resemble the example shown in Figure 10-3. In this case, the report was laid out in imitation of the form shown in Figure 10-2. In your applications, you can use the box-drawing capabilities of the Report Generator to imitate the forms commonly used in your office. Save the report with Ctrl-W, and try the report by entering

```
REPORT FORM BILLING TO PRINT
```

Note that whether the lines appear as lines depends on whether your printer has the capability to print the IBM graphic character set. Some printers will not handle graphics, and on such printers the lines may appear as symbols or letters or not appear at all.

Creating and Printing Mailing Labels

FoxPro provides a facility for designing mailing labels. You can enter various dimension parameters that allow you to use different label sizes. And you can print labels in the common three-across or four-across formats, where the labels are placed on the label sheets in rows of three or four labels each. Label designs are stored on the disk with an .LBX extension.

10

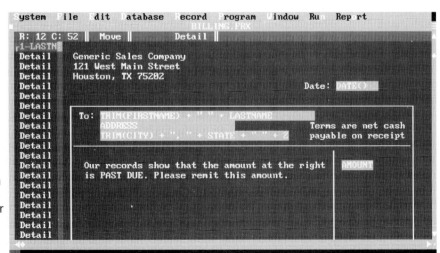

Report specification for invoices
Figure 10-3.

Creating the Label

To create a mailing label from the menus, you choose New from the File menu and select Label from the dialog box that appears. From the command level, you can enter

CREATE LABEL *filename*

where *filename* is the name assigned to the label file. When you do so, the label design screen appears, as shown in Figure 10-4.

The label design screen contains six parameters that control the overall dimensions of the labels: Margin, Width, Number Across, Height, Spaces Between, and Lines Between. In the center of the window is a label design area representing the contents of the label. In this area, you place the field names or expressions that will provide the data when the labels are printed. At the top of the screen is a Remarks window, which can contain an optional description of the label. When you create a new label, the window contains the designation shown in Figure 10-4 as a default; this is the most commonly used size and matches standard peel-and-stick labels available in office supply stores. As with other design screens in FoxPro, you can use the ⎯Tab⎯ key or the mouse to move between the various parameters and the label design area.

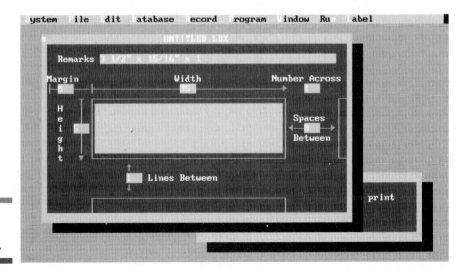

Label design
screen
Figure 10-4.

Figure 10-5 shows the relationship between the various parameters that make up the label dimensions. The Margin parameter controls the distance between the start of the leftmost label and the left edge of the sheet of labels. By default this is zero, since many labels are attached to the underlying paper at the left edge of the label sheet. Height and Width control the height and width, respectively, of the label. The default values of 35 characters for the width and 5 rows for the height match the standard 3 1/2-inch by 15/16-inch label size (assuming you are printing at the standard of 10 characters per inch and 6 lines per inch). The Number Across parameter controls the number of labels printed across a sheet of labels. With roll-fed labels, this is usually one, but with the popular sheets of three-across labels used in laser printers this value would be set to 3. The Spaces Between parameter controls the number of spaces between the labels. This value matters only when the Number Across value is set at more than 1. Finally, the Lines Between parameter controls the number of blank lines between labels. Depending on your labels, you may need to play with this option to prevent data from printing across the breaks in the labels. Table 10-1 gives some suggested settings for common label sizes.

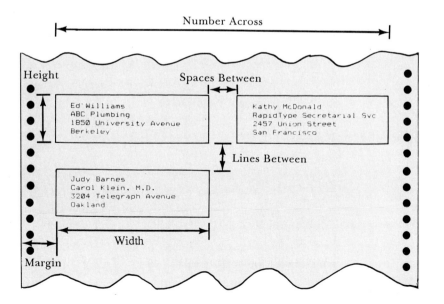

Label
dimensions
Figure 10-5.

10

Note that these sizes assume a standard printing character size of 10 characters per inch and printer line spacing of 6 lines per inch, matching that of most standard printers including Epson-compatible dot-matrix and the Courier font used with Hewlett-Packard or compatible lasers. If your printer is set to a different character size (such as compressed print) or has an unusual line spacing, you will need to experiment with different values to discover the right settings for the dimensions of your labels.

Adding Fields to the Design Area

When the dimensions of the label are set, you can add fields in the design area of the screen. To do so, place the cursor at the desired location and choose Expression from the Label menu (or press Ctrl-E). With either method, the Expression Builder appears, as shown in Figure 10-6.

Type of Label	Width	Height	Across	Margin	Line	Spaces
3 1/2 by 15/16 by 1 across	35	5	1	0	1	0
3 1/2 by 15/16 by 2 across	35	5	2	0	1	2
3 1/2 by 15/16 by 3 across	35	5	3	0	1	2
4 inch by 1-7/16 inch	40	8	1	0	1	0
1 7/16 by 5 by 1 across	50	8	1	0	1	0
Xerox Cheshire labels	32	5	3	0	1	2
Rolodex 3-inch by 5-inch	50	14	1	0	4	0
Rolodex 2-1/4 inch by 4-inch	40	10	1	0	1	0
No. 7 envelope	65	14	1	0	8	0
No. 10 envelope	78	17	1	0	8	0

Settings for Common Label Sizes

Table 10-1.

Enter the desired field name in the window, or enter an expression (such as a combination of field names). You can combine two name fields with an expression as you do with reports; for example, an expression such as

```
TRIM(FIRSTNAME) + " " + LASTNAME
```

causes the first name to be printed without any blank spaces at the end, followed by a space, followed by the last name. You can also use calculations you create based on fields. With a numeric field called Salescost, you could enter the expression

```
SALESCOST * .06
```

to calculate a charge that is 6% of the amount contained in the Salescost field. And you can use functions, such as DATE(), to produce the current date.

You can check the design of the label as you go along by opening the Label menu with Alt-L and choosing Page Preview. When you choose this option, a visual representation of the label appears, as shown in Figure 10-7.

10

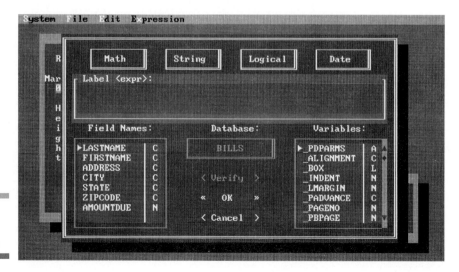

Expression
Builder
Figure 10-6.

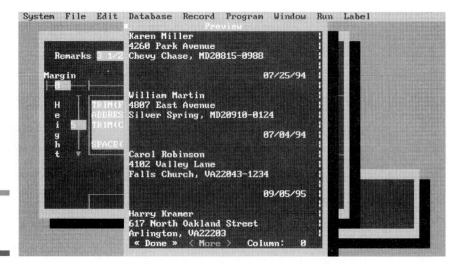

Use of Page
Preview
Figure 10-7.

Choose More to see additional labels, or choose Done when you are finished with the Page Preview option. The shortcut key Ctrl-I (or Ctrl-P with version 1.x) can be used to call up the Page Preview option.

Saving the Label Design

Once you have placed the desired fields or expressions in the label, you can save the label by choosing Save from the File menu or by pressing Ctrl-W and answering Yes to any environment prompts that appear. If you did not enter a name when you started the process, you are prompted for a file name for the label, and then you are returned to the command level.

Printing Labels

Once the label design has been saved, you can print labels by choosing Label from the Database menu or by using the LABEL FORM command. If you choose Label from the Database menu, the dialog box shown in Figure 10-8 appears.

Enter the name of the label in the Form window. You can select Scope, For, or While to limit the number of records that appear as labels; see

```
Label:

<Form....>        [X] Environment        [ ] Scope...
                                         [ ] For...
[X] Set Printer Driver                   [ ] While...

[ ] Sample                               «   OK   »
[ ] To Print
[ ] To File                              < Cancel >
(•) Console On ( ) Console Off

                 modify label members1
```

Label dialog box
Figure 10-8.

Chapter 5 for a discussion of these options. Turn on the Sample option if you want to print a sample label (containing rows of Xs) before the actual printing of data begins. This is often helpful for aligning labels in your printer before printing. Turn on the To Print option to route the labels to the printer; otherwise, they appear only on the screen. The To File option can be selected to store the output in an ASCII text file. If you choose this option, enter a name for the file in the window beside the To File option. When you are done selecting the options, choose OK to begin producing the labels. The Console On/Off determines whether you will see the labels on the screen as they are printed.

From the command level, you use the command

```
LABEL FORM filename [SCOPE] [FOR condition] [WHILE condition]
[SAMPLE] [TO PRINT] [TO FILE filename]
```

and as with other commands, all clauses within the brackets are optional. The SCOPE, FOR, and WHILE clauses are used to limit the records printed, as detailed in Chapter 5. Add the SAMPLE clause to print a sample label (composed of rows of Xs) before you print the data. Add the TO PRINT clause to route the output to the printer, and add TO FILE followed by a file name to store the output as an ASCII text file.

10

If you want the labels printed in a certain order, simply index or sort the database first and then use the LABEL FORM command (or the Label option of the Database menu). It is usually wise to print a test run of labels on plain paper first and to visually align the printout with a sheet of blank labels. After the alignment looks correct, then you can proceed to print on the labels themselves.

To print labels selectively, you can build a query (detailed in Chapter 6), you can use the SET FILTER or INDEX ON...FOR commands, or you can apply view files (as detailed in Chapter 5) that will specify a group of records for which you want to print labels. From the command level, you can combine conditional FOR clauses to print labels for specific records, just as you did with reports. For example, assuming the use of a label file based on the MEMBERS database, the command

```
LABEL FORM MEMBER1 FOR STATE = "VA" TO PRINT
```

prints mailing labels for members in Virginia. The command

```
LABEL FORM MEMBER1 FOR YEAR{EXPIREDATE} = 1993 TO
PRINT
```

prints mailing labels only for those members whose memberships expire in 1993.

An Example Label

To try creating a label for use with the MEMBERS database, enter the commands

```
USE MEMBERS
CREATE LABEL MEMBERS1
```

The label design screen shown earlier in Figure 10-4 appears. For this example, the default parameters will suffice. With the cursor on the first line of the design area, press Ctrl-E to open the Expression Builder. The first line should contain a combination of first and last names, separated by a space. Enter the following expression in the window to accomplish this:

```
TRIM(FIRSTNAME) + " " + LASTNAME
```

Then choose OK from the dialog box to place the expression. The expression will appear on the first line. Move the cursor down to the second line of the design area.

Press `Ctrl`-`E` again, and enter **ADDRESS** in the window of the Expression Builder. Select OK from the dialog box to place the expression, and move the cursor down to the third line. Open the Expression Builder with `Ctrl`-`E`, and enter the following expression:

```
TRIM(CITY) + ", " + STATE + " " + ZIPCODE
```

Then select OK from the dialog box, and move the cursor down to the last line of the label.

Press `Ctrl`-`E` again, and this time enter the following expression:

```
SPACE(25) + DTOC(EXPIREDATE)
```

Use TO PRINT along with the LABEL FORM command to print the labels.

This particular expression uses the SPACE function to insert 25 blank spaces, followed by the DTOC function to convert the contents of the Expiredate field to a character expression. The end result will be 25 blank spaces, followed by the member's expiration date, appearing at the bottom of the label. Choose OK from the dialog box when you are done to place the expression.

Save the label with `Ctrl`-`W`. (Answer Yes to any save prompts that appear.) Try the labels by entering the command

```
LABEL FORM MEMBERS1
```

and add the TO PRINT option at the end of the command if you want to see a printed version. Your results should resemble those shown here:

10

```
Karen Miller
4260 Park Avenue
Chevy Chase, MD 20815-0988


                            07/25/94


William Martin
4807 East Avenue
Silver Spring, MD 20910-0124


                            07/04/94
```

```
Carol Robinson
4102 Valley Lane
Falls Church, VA 22043-1234

                09/05/95

Harry Kramer
617 North Oakland Street
Arlington, VA 22203

                12/22/94
```

Modifying Existing Labels

To change an existing label, use

MODIFY LABEL *filename*

at the command level, where *filename* is the name of the label you wish to change. Or you can choose Open from the File menu, and from the Type menu in the dialog box that appears choose Label. Then select the desired label by name from the list box. With either method, the label design screen appears, as shown earlier in Figure 10-4.

Keep in mind that you can make changes to existing fields by placing the cursor in the field and pressing `Enter` to display the Expression Builder. When the changes are completed, press `Ctrl`-`W` or choose Save from the File menu to save the changes.

CHAPTER

FOXPRO

11

USING FOXPRO'S RELATIONAL POWERS

FoxPro is a relational database manager, which means that it offers you the ability to use more than one database file at a time and to define relationships between two or more database files. This chapter describes a number of ways you can take advantage of the relational capabilities of FoxPro. By using the SET RELATION command, you can link multiple database files by means of a common field that exists in each database file. The examples in this chapter make extensive use of the MEMBERS and RENTALS databases created in Chapters 2 and 3. If you did not create those database files as outlined earlier, do so now before proceeding.

Consider the MEMBERS and RENTALS files. The RENTALS file contains records of the videotapes rented by each member. However, it does not contain the names of the members. The MEMBERS file, on the other hand, contains the full name of each member but no record of the tapes that were rented.

The purchasing manager at Generic Videos needs a report in a format illustrated by Figure 11-1. A report with this kind of information is a *relational report* because it draws its information from more than one file. The MEMBERS file contains the Lastname and Firstname fields. The RENTALS file contains the Title, Dayrented, and Returned fields. In order to produce a report based on these fields, you can establish a relationship that permits the retrieval of data from both files. The data provided through the link can then be used to produce the desired report.

Relational reports require data from multiple files.

The key to retrieving data from a relational database is to link the desired records on some sort of matching, or common, field. In this context, the term *common field* is used to indicate a field that is common to both database files. Consider an example of two files; one contains records of computer parts, and the other contains purchasers who have ordered certain parts. These files (in this example, called PARTS and ORDERS) are typical examples of database files that benefit from the use of relational commands.

Last Name	First Name	Title	Day Rented	Day Returned
Miller	Karen	Star Trek VI	3/5/93	3/6/93
Martin	William	Lethal Weapon III	3/2/93	3/6/93
Robinson	Carol	Who Framed Roger Rabbit	3/6/93	3/9/93

Desired relational report
Figure 11-1.

The PARTS file contains part numbers, descriptions, and the costs of each part:

Field Name	Type
Partno	Numeric
Descript	Character
Cost	Numeric

The ORDERS file, on the other hand,, contains the names and customer numbers of the customers who order computer parts, as well as the part numbers and quantities of the parts that have been ordered:

Field Name	Type
Custno	Numeric
Custname	Character
Partno	Numeric
Quantity	Numeric

Avoid unneeded duplication of data by using relational databases.

If you had a single database file with all of the fields present in these two files, each time one customer ordered a part number that had been previously ordered by another customer, you would have to duplicate the part description and part cost. To avoid such duplication, you can use two files and link the files together based upon the contents of the common Partno field, as illustrated in Figure 11-2.

With all relational databases, establishing a link between common fields allows you to match a particular record in one file with a corresponding record in another file. Take Generic Videos' problem of the rental tapes again. If you needed to know which tapes Carol Robinson rented, you could do this visually by looking at the data from the two files, shown in Figure 11-3. To find the answer manually, you would first look at the listing from the MEMBERS file and find the social security number for Ms. Robinson, which is 232-55-1234. You would then refer to the listing of the RENTALS file and look for all the records with the matching social security number. The process of matching social security numbers between the files could be repeated for every member in the database.

11

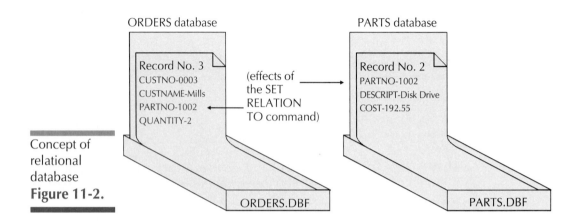

ORDERS database   PARTS database

Record No. 3
CUSTNO-0003
CUSTNAME-Mills   (effects of
PARTNO-1002   the SET
QUANTITY-2   RELATION
                        TO command)

Record No. 2
PARTNO-1002
DESCRIPT-Disk Drive
COST-192.55

ORDERS.DBF   PARTS.DBF

Concept of
relational
database
Figure 11-2.

The important point to realize is that without a field that contains matching data in each of the database files, such a relational link is not possible. This is one reason that designing complex, relational databases is not a process to be taken lightly. Unless you include matching fields in the files you want to link, you will find it impossible to access multiple files in the desired manner. As Figure 11-3 illustrates, the Social field makes it possible to access data simultaneously from both files. While relational links are usually established by using a single field, it is possible to establish such links based on a combination of fields.

How to Relate Files

The relational powers provided by FoxPro are easily implemented from the command level. You can link databases together with the SET RELATION command. It links the files together by means of a common field. In our example, you will draw a relation between the RENTALS database and the MEMBERS database by linking the common Social field. Then, whenever you move to a record in the RENTALS database, the record pointer in the MEMBERS database will move to the record that contains the same social security number as is contained in the record in the RENTALS database. As you will see shortly, this link allows you to display matching data from two files with a LIST command. You can also take advantage of a relational link within the reports or labels you create.

Record#	SOCIAL	LASTNAME	FIRSTNAME	CITY	STATE
1	123-44-8976	Miller	Karen	Chevy Chase	MD
2	121-33-9876	Martin	William	Silver Spring	MD
3	232-55-1234	Robinson	Carol	Falls Church	VA
4	901-77-3456	Kramer	Harry	Arlington	VA
5	121-90-5432	Moore	Ellen	Takoma Park	MD
6	495-00-3456	Zachman	David	Falls Church	VA
7	343-55-9821	Robinson	Benjamin	Washington	DC
8	876-54-3210	Hart	Wendy	Fairfax	VA

Record#	SOCIAL	TITLE	DAYRENTED	RETURNED
1	123-44-8976	Star Trek VI	03/05/93	03/06/93·
2	121-33-9876	Lethal Weapon III	03/02/93	03/06/93
3	232-55-1234	Who Framed Roger Rabbit	03/06/93	03/09/93
4	901-77-3456	Doc Hollywood	03/04/93	03/05/93
5	121-90-5432	Fried Green Tomatoes	03/01/93	03/06/93
6	495-00-3456	Wayne's World	03/04/93	03/09/93
7	343-55-9821	Prince of Tides	03/06/93	03/12/93
8	876-54-3210	Lethal Weapon III	03/07/93	03/08/93
9	123-44-8976	Friday 13th Part XXVII	03/14/93	03/16/93
10	121-33-9876	Mambo Kings	03/15/93	03/17/93
11	232-55-1234	Prince of Tides	03/17/93	03/19/93
12	901-77-3456	Coming to America	03/14/93	03/18/93
13	121-90-5432	Prince of Tides	03/16/93	03/17/93
14	495-00-3456	Star Trek VI	03/18/93	03/19/93
15	343-55-9821	Wayne's World	03/19/93	03/20/93
16	876-54-3210	Mambo Kings	03/16/93	03/18/93

RENTALS, MEMBERS database files **Figure 11-3.**

11

The format of the SET RELATION command is

SET RELATION TO *(key-expression)* INTO *(alias)*
[ADDITIVE]

The *key-expression* is the common field present in both databases. The *alias* is usually the name of the other database that the active database is to be linked to. Note that ADDITIVE is an optional clause, needed only when you are setting a relation in more than one file at a time.

The overall process of linking two databases using a common field involves the following steps:

1. Open the file from which you want to establish the relation in one work area.
2. In another work area, open the file you wish to link to the first file.
3. Activate an index file based on the field (or expression) that is the basis of the relationship.
4. Use the SET RELATION command to establish the link.

Once the link has been established, any movement of the record pointer in the active file results in a corresponding movement of the pointer in the related file. The nature of such a relationship can be seen in the example shown in the following paragraphs.

One important requirement of the SET RELATION command is that you must index the related file on the common field. In our case, the MEMBERS database must be indexed on the Social field. Enter the following commands now to create an index file for the MEMBERS database, based on the social security field:

```
USE MEMBERS
INDEX ON SOCIAL TO SOCIALS
```

To work with multiple database files, you need to open more than one database file at a time. As mentioned in Chapter 8, you do this by using different work areas, which contain the database files. You choose the work area with the SELECT command; for example, entering **SELECT 2** at the command level chooses work area 2. (If no SELECT command is used, work area 1 is chosen by default.)

Open the RENTALS and MEMBERS database files by using the following commands:

```
CLOSE DATABASES
SELECT 1
```

```
USE RENTALS
USE MEMBERS IN 2 INDEX SOCIALS
```

An explanation of the last command is in order. The USE MEMBERS IN 2 portion of the command line tells FoxPro to open the database file MEMBERS, but to open it in work area 2 without actually switching work areas (hence the "in 2" designation). The INDEX SOCIALS option tells FoxPro to open the SOCIALS index file you just created.

It is now possible to link the files, by the Social field, with the SET RELATION TO command. The RENTALS database is the active database, so you will link the MEMBERS database to the RENTALS database. Enter

```
SET RELATION TO SOCIAL INTO MEMBERS
```

No changes are immediately visible, but FoxPro has linked the files. To see the effects, enter the commands

```
GO 3
DISPLAY
```

and you see the third record in the RENTALS database. The record indicates that a member having the social security number of 232-55-1234 rented *Who Framed Roger Rabbit.* To see just who this member is, enter these commands:

```
SELECT 2
DISPLAY
```

The MEMBERS database (open in work area 2) becomes the active database. The record pointer will be at record 3 (the record containing the social security number 232-55-1234), showing that the member in question is Carol Robinson.

Get back to the RENTALS database with these commands:

```
SELECT 1
GO 2
DISPLAY
```

Again, you can see that because of the relation, FoxPro has automatically found a matching social security number in the MEMBERS database by entering the following commands:

11

```
SELECT 2
DISPLAY
```

Use the alias name and pointer to retrieve related data

Wherever you move in the RENTALS database, FoxPro will try to move the record pointer to a matching social security number in the MEMBERS database. If FoxPro cannot find a match according to the relation that you have specified, the record pointer will be positioned at the end of the database. (At the end of a file, all fields are blank. You can use this fact to test for failures to find a match by listing key fields from both databases.)

You can retrieve data in the related file by including the alias name and pointer (*filename.*) along with the field name. In the expression

```
MEMBERS.FIRSTNAME
```

the file name MEMBERS is the alias, while FIRSTNAME is the field name. The period is used as the pointer. To see how this works, try the following commands:

```
SELECT 1
LIST MEMBERS.LASTNAME, TITLE, DAYRENTED, RETURNED
```

the results are shown here:

Record#	MEMBERS.LASTNAME	TITLE	DAYRENTED	RETURNED
1	Miller	Star Trek VI	03/05/93	03/06/93
2	Martin	Lethal Weapon III	03/02/93	03/06/93
3	Robinson	Who Framed Roger Rabbit	03/06/93	03/09/93
4	Kramer	Doc Hollywood	03/04/93	03/05/93
5	Moore	Fried Green Tomatoes	03/01/93	03/06/93
6	Zachman	Wayne's World	03/04/93	03/09/93
7	Robinson	Prince of Tides	03/06/93	03/12/93
8	Hart	Lethal Weapon III	03/07/93	03/08/93
9	Miller	Friday 13th Part XXVII	03/14/93	03/16/93
10	Martin	Mambo Kings	03/15/93	03/17/93
11	Robinson	Prince of Tides	03/17/93	03/19/93
12	Kramer	Coming to America	03/14/93	03/18/93
13	Moore	Prince of Tides	03/16/93	03/17/93
14	Zachman	Star Trek VI	03/18/93	03/19/93
15	Robinson	Wayne's World	03/19/93	03/20/93
16	Hart	Mambo Kings	03/16/93	03/18/93

This shows that such use of the SET RELATION command to establish the relational link, combined with the use of the alias and pointer, can be a powerful tool for obtaining data of a relational nature. You could add the TO PRINT option at the end of the LIST command to generate a printed list like this one.

When working with related files in this manner, keep in mind that you can test for mismatched records (such as an entry in the RENTALS file with no matching social security number) by listing the common field from each of the related files. For example, the command

```
LIST RENTALS.SOCIAL, MEMBERS.SOCIAL, MEMBERS.LASTNAME
```

should produce a listing with a matching member for each entry in the RENTALS file. If a member name and social security number turn up blank next to an entry in the RENTALS listing, it is clear that a mismatch exists. Such a mismatch could be caused by a social security number entered incorrectly in the RENTALS file.

A Warning About Index Files

When you are working with related files, it is completely up to you to make sure your indexes that allow the use of the SET RELATION command are kept updated. If you or another user open a database without using an accompanying index file and add or edit records, the resulting incomplete index files can cause incorrect results when you are trying to establish relationships or generate relational reports. If in doubt, use REINDEX to rebuild any indexes you are using.

Using View Files to Store Relations

Save relationships with the CREATE VIEW FROM ENVIRON-MENT command.

If you are going to establish relationships from the command level (as opposed to creating them by running a program), keep in mind the use of the CREATE VIEW FROM ENVIRONMENT command. This command, introduced in Chapter 5, stores a record of all open databases, index files, and any existing relationships. You can save much repetitive typing by saving the relationship as part of a view file, and then using the SET VIEW command to open the database files and

11

index files and establish the relationship at the same time. You save the environment, including the relational link, by entering the command

CREATE VIEW *filename* FROM ENVIRONMENT

where *filename* is the name you assign to the view file. Later, you open the databases, index files, and the relational link by entering the command

SET VIEW TO *filename*

where *filename* is the name that you gave to the view file earlier. If you followed the prior example in establishing a relational link between MEMBERS and RENTALS, you can save that information in a view file now. Enter the following command:

```
CREATE VIEW RELATE1 FROM ENVIRONMENT
```

Then enter **CLOSE DATABASES** to close all the open files. If you now enter the commands

```
USE RENTALS
LIST MEMBERS.LASTNAME, TITLE, DAYRENTED
```

you get an "Alias not found" error message, because the RENTALS file is not open and no relationship exists. Enter **CLOSE DATABASES** again to close the open file and start from scratch. (This is not a requirement, but doing so makes it clear that the SET VIEW command will be all you need to open all files and reestablish the link.) Enter the command

```
SET VIEW TO RELATE1
```

Then retry the earlier command:

Use the SET VIEW TO command to restore previously saved relationships.

```
LIST MEMBERS.LASTNAME, TITLE, DAYRENTED, RETURNED
```

The results show that the files are open and the relationship has been reestablished. You can verify this in another way with the DISPLAY STATUS command. Enter **DISPLAY STATUS** now. The display you see should resemble the following:

```
Processor is INTEL 80386
Currently Selected Database:
Select area:  1, Database in Use: C:\FOXDOS\DATA\RENTALS.DBF  Alias: RENTALS
Structural CDX file:    C:\FOXDOS\DATA\RENTALS.CDX
        Index tag:    SOCIAL    Key:  SOCIAL
        Index tag:    TITLE    Key:  TITLE
        Index tag:    DAYRETURNED    Key:  DAYRETURNED
        Index tag:    RETURNED    Key:  RETURNED
    Lock(s):  Exclusive USE
    Related into:    MEMBERS
        Relation:    SOCIAL
```

The first lines of the listing show the names of the open databases, the index files and/or tags in use, and the relationship between the files.

Creating Relational Reports

As shown earlier, you can use the LIST...TO PRINT command to generate simple listings of relational data; you must include the file name and pointer when you are retrieving data that is in the related file. The same technique can be used for designing relational reports. When you enter a field name or an expression into the Expr window during the creation of the report, you must again include the file name and pointer symbols to indicate a field that is in a related database.

As an example, consider a report similar to the one shown in Figure 11-1, but using a form-oriented format. You could quickly construct such a report by opening the files, establishing the relationship, creating a new report, and adding the Lastname and Firstname fields to the report design along with the file name and pointer.

To try this, the relationship described in the prior example should still be in effect (if not, use the SET VIEW TO RELATE1 command). Enter

```
CREATE REPORT RELATE1
```

to start a new report. Open the Report menu with Alt-O, and choose Quick Report. Select the Form Layout option, and then choose OK from the dialog box. The report appearing on the screen resembles the one shown in Figure 11-4.

Because the RENTALS file is the active database, the quick report placed all fields from that database into the report specification. Using the file

11

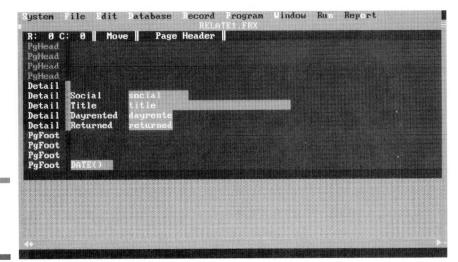

Quick report
based on
RENTALS file
Figure 11-4.

name and pointer combination, you can replace the rather ambiguous social security field with the actual name of the member from the related MEMBERS file. Move the cursor to the word SOCIAL and press the (Del) key to delete it; then move the cursor into the Social field and press (Del) to remove the field.

Press (Home) to get back to the left margin, and enter this text:

```
Member
```

Then press (Enter) to complete the text entry. Move the cursor over to column 11 and press (Ctrl)-(F) to add an expression. Press (Enter) to bring up the Expression Builder. (This provides room to enter and view a long expression.) In the window, enter the following:

```
TRIM(MEMBERS.FIRSTNAME) + " " + MEMBERS.LASTNAME
```

Choose OK from the dialog box to close the Expression Builder. Tab over to the Width box and change the width to **25** (this should provide ample width for a combination of last and first names). Choose OK from the dialog box to complete the entry.

For aesthetics' sake, you may want to change the field heading "Dayrented" to two words, "Day rented." Move the cursor to the Dayrented label and press the Del key. Then type in the text

```
Day rented
```

Press Enter to complete the entry. Next, save the report with Ctrl-W, and enter

```
REPORT FORM RELATE1
```

to see the results. They should resemble those shown here:

```
Member      Karen Miller
Title       Star Trek VI
Day rented  03/05/93
Returned    03/06/93


Member      William Martin
Title       Lethal Weapon III
Day rented  03/02/93
Returned    03/06/93


Member      Carol Robinson
Title       Who Framed Roger Rabbit
Day rented  03/06/93
Returned    03/09/93


Member      Harry Kramer
Title       Doc Hollywood
Day rented  03/04/93
Returned    03/05/93


Member      Ellen Moore
Title       Fried Green Tomatoes
Day rented  03/01/93
Returned    03/06/93


Member      David Zachman
Title       Wayne's World
Day rented  03/04/93
Returned    03/09/93
```

11

```
Member     Benjamin Robinson
Title      Prince of Tides
Day rented 03/06/93
Returned   03/12/93

Member     Wendy Hart
Title      Lethal Weapon III
Day rented 03/07/93
Returned   03/08/93

Member     Karen Miller
Title      Friday 13th Part XXVII
Day rented 03/14/93
Returned   03/16/93

Member     William Martin
Title      Mambo Kings
Day rented 03/15/93
Returned   03/17/93

Member     Carol Robinson
Title      Prince of Tides
Day rented 03/17/93
Returned   03/19/93

Member     Harry Kramer
Title      Coming to America
Day rented 03/14/93
Returned   03/18/93

Member     Ellen Moore
Title      Prince of Tides
Day rented 03/16/93
Returned   03/17/93

Member     David Zachman
Title      Star Trek VI
Day rented 03/18/93
Returned   03/19/93

Member     Benjamin Robinson
Title      Wayne's World
Day rented 03/19/93
Returned   03/20/93
```

```
Member     Wendy Hart
Title      Mambo Kings
Day rented 03/16/93
Returned   03/18/93
```

If desired, you could improve a report like this one by adding grouping to the report, as described in Chapter 7. You could index the RENTALS file on the Social field and then group the report on the Social field, using the member name in the group heading. You can use this same technique with labels, if desired. Just include the file name and pointer whenever you are referencing a field that is not in the active database.

Re-establish relationships before generating reports.

Remember that all needed files must be open and the relationship established before you can generate a relational report or label. If, for example, you now enter **CLOSE DATABASES** and then open just one database, such as MEMBERS, and try to print this same report, you will get an "Alias not found" error message. This indicates that because the related file has not been opened and the relationship established, the report cannot locate the data it needs.

The use of SET VIEW combined with stored reports provides you with a powerful capability for generating relational reports when needed. You can continue to add and edit data within the databases; and whenever a relational report is needed, you could use commands like

```
SET VIEW TO RELATE1
REPORT FORM RELATE1 TO PRINT
```

to generate the needed data. Note that there is no need to name your view files and your reports with the same name, but it often is helpful in keeping track of which files are used with which reports. Also, when you save your report, a view file with the same name as the report is automatically created. This lets you use the ENVIRONMENT clause along with the REPORT FORM command. If you enter

```
REPORT FORM RELATE1 TO PRINT ENVIRONMENT
```

the ENVIRONMENT clause at the end of the command tells FoxPro to look for the view file with the same name as the report. That view file is put into effect automatically before the report is generated.

11

Because a view file is automatically created when you save the report, you should make sure any desired relationships exist *before* you create a relational report. It is possible to create and save a relational report without having established the relationships by manually entering the file names and pointers in your expressions. But if you do this, the saved view file won't contain the relationships, and the REPORT FORM...ENVIRONMENT command will result in an error message.

A Warning About SET FIELDS and dBASE

Those who are familiar with various versions of dBASE may be aware of the use of the SET FIELDS command to eliminate the need for file names and pointers. In dBASE III PLUS or dBASE IV, you can use SET FIELDS to establish fields from related files once; from then on, you can drop the file name and pointer prefix, and dBASE will still find the data. As a brief example, using the same databases that have been used throughout this text, you could enter the following commands in dBASE IV:

```
SELECT 1
USE RENTALS
USE MEMBERS IN 2 INDEX SOCIAL
SET RELATION TO SOCIAL INTO MEMBERS
SET FIELDS TO MEMBERS.LASTNAME,
MEMBERS.FIRSTNAME, TITLE, DAYRENTED
```

You could then access the Lastname, Firstname, Title, or Dayrented field without using any file names or pointers in the case of the Lastname and Firstname fields. You could also create reports without using the file name and pointer in the report expressions.

What's important to note is that FoxPro and its predecessor, FoxBase Plus, do *not* support this relational use of the SET FIELDS command. You can enter the SET FIELDS command as just shown in FoxPro, and you will not get an error message. However, if you try to access the fields without the prefix of file name and pointer, you will not be able to do so. If you plan to use dBASE programs that contain such use of the SET FIELDS command, you need to make changes to those programs so that they use the file name and pointer method instead.

Getting Selective Data from Related Files

You can use the same techniques covered in Chapters 5 and 6—the SET FILTER, FOR, and WHILE clauses, the use of queries, and the INDEX ON...FOR command—to retrieve selective data from multiple files. One of the biggest challenges in working with multiple files at the same time is in keeping track of where you are. This is particularly true when you want to retrieve specific data, because the commands you use will apply to the active file unless you include file names and pointers as a prefix. If, for example, you use the commands

```
SELECT 1
USE RENTALS
USE MEMBERS IN 2 INDEX SOCIALS
SET RELATION TO SOCIAL INTO MEMBERS
```

SET FILTER can be used with related files.

to establish a relationship, and you then apply a filter with a command like

```
SET FILTER TO TITLE = "Beverly Hills Cop II"
```

you can then list or report on selective data, based on a condition you applied to the active file (RENTALS).

If you wanted to instead apply a filter to the MEMBERS file, you would need to do things a little differently. You would have to apply a filter condition within that work area. To do this, include a file name and pointer in the filter condition. For example, while the RENTALS file is active, you could enter the commands

```
SET FILTER TO MEMBERS.LASTNAME = "Kramer"
GO TOP
```

followed by a LIST command to limit rentals retrieved to only those for Mr. Kramer.

Keep in mind that a filter condition is only saved along with a view if it was established from the active work area. If you establish a filter condition with SET FILTER, switch work areas, and then save the environment to a view file, the filter condition will not be saved in the view.

11

Relating More Than Two Database Files

As many database files as you need (up to the limit of 225 possible open database files) can be linked to provide you with the results that you need in FoxPro. One common example of the type of application requiring more than two files is the tracking of customers, sales, and product inventory. A complete sales-tracking system is commonly built around at least three database files: one containing customer data such as names and addresses, one containing product data such as descriptions and prices, and a third containing a record of each item purchased by a customer. The three database structures shown here contain the fields necessary, at a minimum, to accomplish such a task:

ITEMS.DBF	ORDERS.DBF	CUSTOMER.DBF
Stockno	Custno	Custno
Descript	Stockno	Name
Cost	Quantity	Address
	Date	City
		State
		Zip

Such a database system, properly designed, could meet a variety of needs. Inventory could be tracked by using the ITEMS file; reports summarizing total sales could be generated by using the ITEMS and ORDERS files; mass mailings to customers could be handled with the CUSTOMER file. The task of generating customer invoices is a prime example of a relational application demanding the use of three files; the data listed in an invoice would need to come from three different databases, as illustrated in Figure 11-5.

An example of the needed relationships can be demonstrated if you duplicate the following database structures and the sample data contained in the files. (If you decide to duplicate this example, enter a CLEAR ALL command first, to clear the previous view.) The structure of ITEMS.DBF is as follows:

Field Name	Type	Width	Decimals
Stockno	character	4	
Descript	character	25	
Cost	numeric	7	2

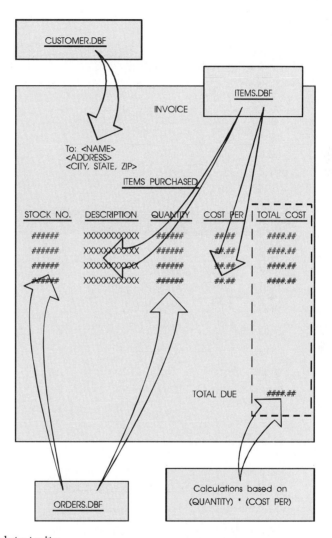

Invoice and
supporting
databases
Figure 11-5.

11

Add this data to it:

Stockno	Descript	Cost
2001	leather handbag, black	89.95
2002	attache case	139.95
2003	suitcase, overnighter	159.95
2004	carry-on bag, leather	69.95

The structure of ORDERS.DBF is shown here:

Field Name	Type	Width	Decimals
Custno	character	4	
Stockno	character	4	
Quantity	numeric	2	0
Date	date		

Add this data to it:

Custno	Stockno	Quantity	Date
9001	2001	1	03/05/93
9001	2004	1	03/05/93
9002	2002	2	03/06/93
9004	2004	1	03/04/93
9003	2001	1	03/05/93
9001	2002	1	03/05/93
9003	2003	1	03/04/93
9005	2002	1	03/06/93
9002	2004	2	03/06/93

CUSTOMER.DBF has this structure:

Field Name	Type	Width
Lastname	character	15
Firstname	character	15
Address	character	25
City	character	15
State	character	2
Zipcode	character	10
Custno	character	4

To quickly duplicate the example CUSTOMER.DBF file, you can copy existing data from the MEMBERS file with the following commands:

```
CLOSE DATABASES

USE MEMBERS

COPY TO CUSTOMER NEXT 5 FIELDS LASTNAME, FIRSTNAME,
ADDRESS, CITY, STATE, ZIPCODE

USE CUSTOMER
MODIFY STRUCTURE
```

When the Database Structure dialog box appears, add a new field:

```
CUSTNO          character      4
```

and then save the structure. Then enter

```
BROWSE FIELDS CUSTNO, LASTNAME, FIRSTNAME FREEZE
CUSTNO
```

to add customer numbers to the existing records, as shown here:

```
Custno    Name
9001      Miller, Karen
9002      Martin, William
9003      Robinson, Carol
9004      Kramer, Harry
9005      Moore, Ellen
```

Once the databases like these exist, the entry of day-to-day sales, new customers, and changes to inventory can be performed on each file individually. Screens can be created, as detailed in Chapter 12, for adding and editing data. The ability of FoxPro to display data in multiple windows can come in handy here. If, for example, you enter

11

```
SELECT 1
USE ITEMS
BROWSE
```

and then open the Window menu and choose Command (or just press Ctrl-F2) to switch back to the Command window, you can next enter

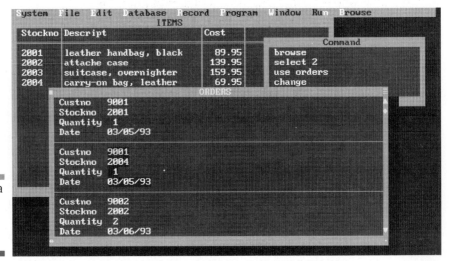

Display of data
in multiple
windows
Figure 11-6.

```
SELECT 2
USE ORDERS
CHANGE
```

You then can move the windows and add new orders while viewing the
descriptions in the inventory database, as shown in Figure 11-6. When
done, remember that you can close a window by selecting the window
by name from the Window menu and then pressing ⌈Esc⌋ once you are
in the window.

Most reports generated from this type of database will be of a relational
nature. A visual representation of the needed links appears in Figure 11-7.

Assuming you are retrieving order data for reports or invoices, you
could establish the relational links with these commands:

```
CLOSE DATABASES
SELECT 1
USE ITEMS
INDEX ON STOCKNO TO BYSTOCK
SELECT 2
USE ORDERS
INDEX ON CUSTNO TO BYCUST
SELECT 3
```

```
USE CUSTOMER
INDEX ON CUSTNO TO CUSTOM
SELECT 2
SET RELATION TO CUSTNO INTO CUSTOMER
SET RELATION TO STOCKNO INTO ITEMS ADDITIVE
```

Note the use of the ADDITIVE clause for the second SET RELATION command. Once a relation exists out of an active file, the ADDITIVE clause must be used to establish a second relation. Without the clause, the second SET RELATION command would simply override the first.

At this point, the ORDERS file is the active file. For any record located in the ORDERS file, the corresponding customer name and address can be retrieved from the CUSTOMER file, and the corresponding item cost and description can be retrieved from the ITEMS file. You can obtain a columnar listing of sales with a command like the one shown here. The OFF option turns off the record numbers, so each record will still fit on one line.

```
LIST CUSTOMER.LASTNAME, DATE, QUANTITY, ITEMS.DESCRIPT, ITEMS.COST OFF

CUSTOMER.LASTNAME  DATE       QUANTITY ITEMS.DESCRIPT        ITEMS.COST
Miller             03/05/93   1 leather handbag, black      89.95
Miller             03/05/93   1 carry-on bag, leather       69.95
Miller             03/05/93   1 attache case                139.95
Martin             03/06/93   2 attache case                139.95
Martin             03/06/93   2 carry-on bag, leather       69.95
Robinson           03/05/93   1 leather handbag, black      89.95
Robinson           03/04/93   1 suitcase, overnighter       159.95
Kramer             03/04/93   1 carry-on bag, leather       69.95
Moore              03/06/93   1 attache case                139.95
```

11

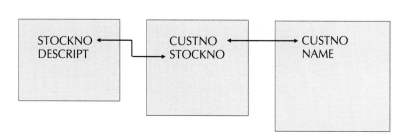

Map of
relationships
Figure 11-7.

An alternative is to lay out all desired fields in an invoice, including file names and pointers where necessary, to refer to the related files. Since the ORDERS database is the active file, any report would include one group of orders for each customer (unless you applied some type of filter first). As an example, you can create an invoice for each customer. To try this, enter **CREATE REPORT SALESINV** to start a new report. Then perform the following steps.

With the cursor in row 0, press `Ctrl`-`O` (or `Ctrl`-`M` if you are using version 1.*x*) three times to get rid of three lines in the Page Header band. Open the Report menu with `Alt`-`O`, and choose Data Grouping to add a Group band. Select Add, and then enter **CUSTNO** in the Group window as the field to group the report on. This provides a group of purchases printed for each individual customer.

Turn on the New Page option in the Group Info dialog box. Choose OK from the dialog box, and then choose OK again from the remaining dialog box.

Move the cursor into the Group band (anywhere on row 1) and press `Ctrl`-`N` four times to add four lines to the starting Group band. The customer name and address data will need to be placed here, since it should only print once for each invoice.

Move to row 1, column 1. Press `Ctrl`-`F` and `Enter` to open the Expression Builder. Enter the expression

```
TRIM(CUSTOMER.FIRSTNAME) + " " + CUSTOMER.LASTNAME
```

and choose OK from the dialog box. When the Report Expression dialog box reappears, change the width to **30**, and choose OK.

Move to row 2, column 1. Press `Ctrl`-`F` and then `Enter` to open the Expression Builder. Enter the expression

```
CUSTOMER.ADDRESS
```

and choose OK from the dialog box. When the Report Expression dialog box reappears, choose OK again to close the box.

Move to row 3, column 1. Press `Ctrl`-`F` and then `Enter` to open the Expression Builder. Enter

```
TRIM(CUSTOMER.CITY) + ", " + CUSTOMER.STATE + " " +
CUSTOMER.ZIPCODE
```

and choose OK from the dialog box. When the Report Expression dialog box reappears, change the width to **35**, and choose OK.

At row 5, column 1, enter these words:

```
Stock no    Description
```

Press (Enter) to complete the entry, and move over to column 40. Enter these words, with three spaces between them:

```
Quantity    Cost
```

Press (Enter) to complete the entry. Move over to column 60, and enter

```
Total
```

Again, press (Enter) to complete the entry.

Move to row 6, column 1, the first line in the Detail band. Add fields to the report by performing the following steps. Be sure to press (Enter) after entering each expression, and choose OK from the dialog box after each entry:

Location	Keypress	Text Entry
Row 6, column 1	(Ctrl)-(F) then (Tab)	STOCKNO
Row 6, column 10	(Ctrl)-(F) then (Tab)	ITEMS.DESCRIPT
Row 6, column 40	(Ctrl)-(F) then (Tab)	QUANTITY
Row 6, column 50	(Ctrl)-(F) then (Tab)	ITEMS.COST
Row 6, column 60	(Ctrl)-(F) then (Tab)	ITEMS.COST* QUANTITY

Move the cursor down to row 7, and press (Ctrl)-(O) twice (or (Ctrl)-(M) twice if you are using version 1.*x*) to delete two of the blank lines in the Detail band. If not removed, these would appear as blank lines in the invoice between each purchase for a customer.

11

Save the report with Ctrl-W, turn on your printer, and enter

```
REPORT FORM SALESINV TO PRINT
```

to see the results. An invoice for a single customer should be printed on each page, resembling the following:

```
Karen Miller
4260 Park Avenue
Chevy Chase, MD 20815-0988

Stock no  Description            Quantity      Cost       Total
2001      leather handbag, black 1             89.95      89.95

2004      carry-on bag, leather  1             69.95      69.95

2002      attache case           1             139.95     139.95
```

One minor point is worth noting. The commands used to establish the links also included these commands:

```
USE ORDERS
INDEX ON CUSTNO TO BYCUST
```

They constructed an index on ORDERS, the active file. This was not needed for the SET RELATION command; only the files into which the relations are set need to be indexed (in this case, CUSTOMER.DBF and ITEMS.DBF). The indexing of the ORDERS file was done only to support grouping, based on the customer number (Custno) field. Without the grouping, an invoice would be printed for each item ordered, and customers ordering more than one item would receive multiple invoices as a result.

Of more significance is the overall complexity that the day-to-day management a system of this nature involves. Adding and updating all three files as needed from the command level will require all users of such a system to be familiar with FoxPro commands. With the staff turnover typical in today's workplace, this could be a problem. Also, there is virtually no referential integrity in a relational system maintained entirely from the command level. In a nutshell, this means that there is nothing to protect users from entering corrupt data, such as an incorrect social security number, that will not support the relationship. The same problem applies to edits of existing data. For example, if a user of the system deletes a customer from the CUSTOMER file while orders still exist for that customer in the ORDERS file, later invoices will contain orders for which no matching customer name can be found.

The answer to these problems lies in programming, the subject of the chapters to follow. With programming techniques, you can build applications that guard against mistakes such as deleting customers who have existing orders. Such applications can also present menu choices to novice users, shielding them from the complexity of FoxPro commands.

Analyzing Types of Relationships

Before you delve deeply into working with relationships between multiple files, you may find it necessary to do some analysis on paper and determine the relationships that need to be drawn between the fields. The different types of possible relationships mean you may want to establish your links in different ways.

Relationships can be one-to-one, one-to-many, or many-to-many. When one field in one record of a database relates in a unique manner to a field in another record in a different database, you have a *one-to-one relationship*. An example may exist in a personnel system that contains medical and benefit information in one file and salary information in another file. Each database contains one record per employee, meaning that for every record in the medical file there is a corresponding record for the same employee in the salary file. The relationship between the files is a one-to-one relationship. Figure 11-8 shows two such databases and the relationship between them. In such a case, things are relatively simple; you use the SET RELATION command to link on the common field used between the two files (in this example, a unique employee ID number).

11

When relating files, it is often advantageous to have a field that will always contain unique data for each record such as this one; unless an incorrect entry is made, no two members ever have the same employee ID number. Customer numbers, social security numbers, and stock numbers are other types of data commonly used for the same purpose of unique identification.

EMPLOYEEID	LASTNAME	FIRSTNAME	SALARY	GRADE	HIRED
X288	Anderson	Terence	750.55	8	03/17/69
X289	Smith	Linda	890.00	10	06/25/75
G343	Robinson	James	790.40	6	08/19/86

EMPLOYEEID	LASTNAME	HEALTHCOST	DENTAL NAME	DENTAL COST
G343	Blue Cross	95.50	Prudential	33.00
X289	Kaiser	62.00	Kaiser	27.00
X288	Prudential	55.00	Kaiser	27.00

One-to-one
relationship
Figure 11-8.

In some cases, a single field with unique data may not be available; for example, you may have a list of customers, but your company may not assign customer numbers as a practice. If you can't convince management to change the way it tracks customers, you have the alternative of creating a link based on more than one field. In the case of customers, you could index on a combination of Lastname + Firstname + Address and establish the relation on the expression with a command like

```
SET RELATION TO (LASTNAME+FIRSTNAME+ADDRESS) INTO
MYFILE
```

This would work, assuming you never have two customers with the same name living at the same address.

By comparison, if one field of one record in the first file relates to a field in one or more records in the second file, you have a *one-to-many relationship.* An example is the relationship between the Generic Videos MEMBERS and RENTALS database files, as illustrated in Figure 11-9. For every member in the MEMBERS file, there are a number of records in the RENTALS file corresponding to rentals of different videotapes by that member. Again, SET RELATION is used to establish the link, as was demonstrated earlier in the chapter with the video database. However, things do get more complex with one-to-many relationships, because you must keep track of where you are when performing data retrieval operations.

SOCIAL	LASTNAME	FIRSTNAME	CITY	STATE
123-44-8976	Miller	Karen	Chevy Chase	MD
121-33-9876	Martin	William	Silver Spring	MD
232-55-1234	Robinson	Carol	Falls Church	VA
901-77-3456	Kramer	Harry	Arlington	VA
121-90-5432	Moore	Ellen	Takoma Park	MD
495-00-3456	Zachman	David	Falls Church	VA
343-55-9821	Robinson	Benjamin	Washington	DC
876-54-3210	Hart	Wendy	Fairfax	VA

Record#	SOCIAL	TITLE	DAYRENTED	RETURNED
1	123-44-8976	Star Trek VI	03/05/93	03/06/93
2	121-33-9876	Lethal Weapon III	03/02/93	03/06/93
3	232-55-1234	Who Framed Roger Rabbit	03/06/93	03/09/93
4	901-77-3456	Doc Hollywood	03/04/93	03/05/93
5	121-90-5432	Fried Green Tomatoes	03/01/93	03/06/93
6	495-00-3456	Wayne's World	03/04/93	03/09/93
7	343-55-9821	Prince of Tides	03/06/93	03/12/93
8	876-54-3210	Lethal Weapon III	03/07/93	03/08/93
9	123-44-8976	Friday 13th Part XXVII	03/14/93	03/16/93
10	121-33-9876	Mambo Kings	03/15/93	03/17/93
11	232-55-1234	Prince of Tides	03/17/93	03/19/93
12	901-77-3456	Coming to America	03/14/93	03/18/93
13	121-90-5432	Prince of Tides	03/16/93	03/17/93
14	495-00-3456	Star Trek VI	03/18/93	03/19/93
15	343-55-9821	Wayne's World	03/19/93	03/20/93
16	876-54-3210	Mambo Kings	03/16/93	03/18/93

One-to-many
relationship
Figure 11-9.

11

In this example, the MEMBERS file is the "one" file, and the RENTALS file is the "many" file. When a listing of all video rentals was needed, the RENTALS file had to be the active file, and the relation had to be set out of that file because it contained the "many" data. If the MEMBERS file had been the active file and a relation had been set out of MEMBERS into RENTALS, you could have retrieved only those rentals associated with a particular member. Depending on your needs at the time, this might be exactly what you want. The point is to keep in mind the nature of the one-to-many relationship, and plan your relationships accordingly.

Finally, a type of relationship that is not as common as the first two but occasionally arises is the *many-to-many relationship*. This relationship exists when a field in several records in one database will relate to a field in several records in another database. A classic example of a many-to-many relationship is that of student tracking at a high school or college, where many students are assigned to many different classes. To set up this or any many-to-many relationship under FoxPro, you need at least three database files. The third file serves as an intermediate or "linking" file between the other two files, which contain the "many" data.

Determine the type of relationships needed for your application.

Using the example of students and classes, a student file can be created with the name of each student, along with a unique student ID number (for simplicity's sake, social security numbers are used in this example). A database containing a unique class ID number for each class, the class name, the room number, and the teacher name is also created. Finally, a schedule file containing a record for each student's enrollment in a class is also created. Figure 11-10 shows the databases and illustrates the relationships between the files. You can duplicate the files and the data shown if you want to try the examples that follow. If you decide to duplicate the example, you can easily create the STUDENTS database by copying the first five records from the MEMBERS file and including only the Social, Lastname, and Firstname fields in the copy.

Once the databases are created, you can use the SET RELATION command to link the SCHEDULE file to both the STUDENTS file and the CLASSES file. Depending on the data you need, you could use various LIST commands or design different reports to produce the desired results. If you duplicated the preceding files, you could try these commands:

Record#	SOCIAL	LASTNAME	FIRSTNAME
1	123-44-8976	Miller	Karen
2	121-33-9876	Martin	William
3	232-55-1234	Robinson	Carol
4	901-77-3456	Kramer	Harry
5	121-90-5432	Moore	Ellen

Record#	SOCIAL	TITLE
1	123-44-8976	S100
2	123-44-8976	S102
3	123-44-8976	H101
4	123-44-8976	T101
5	121-33-9876	S102
6	121-33-9876	H100
7	121-33-9876	T100
8	232-55-1234	S101
9	232-55-1234	S102
10	232-55-1234	T100
11	232-55-1234	H100
12	901-77-3456	S100
13	901-77-3456	H100
14	901-77-3456	T101
15	121-90-5432	S102
16	121-90-5432	T101

Record#	CLASSID	TITLE	ROOM	TEACHER
1	S100	Earth Science	204	Williams, R.
2	S101	Biology	210	Sanders, B.
3	S102	Chemistry	205	Roberts, C.
4	H100	World History	114	Askew, N.
5	H101	Amer. History	121	Jones, R.
6	T100	Auto Repair	B14	Johnson, I.
7	T101	Microcomputers	B12	Jones, E.

Many-to-many
relationship
Figure 11-10.

11

```
SELECT 1
USE STUDENTS
INDEX ON SOCIAL TO STUDENTS
SELECT 2
USE SCHEDULE
SELECT 3
USE CLASSES
INDEX ON CLASSID TO CLASSES
SELECT 2
SET RELATION TO SOCIAL INTO STUDENTS
SET RELATION TO CLASSID INTO CLASSES ADDITIVE
```

If you wanted to use this relationship at a later date, it would be wise to save it with a command like

```
CREATE VIEW SCHOOL FROM ENVIRONMENT
```

You could then proceed to retrieve the needed data. As an example, a cross-list of student names and instructor names could be produced with a command like

```
LIST CLASSES.TEACHER, STUDENTS.LASTNAME,
STUDENTS.FIRSTNAME
```

The results would resemble this:

Record#	CLASSES.TEACHER	STUDENTS.LASTNAME	STUDENTS.FIRSTNAME
1	Williams, R.	Miller	Karen
2	Roberts, C.	Miller	Karen
3	Jones, R.	Miller	Karen
4	Jones, E.	Miller	Karen
5	Roberts, C.	Martin	William
6	Askew, N.	Martin	William
7	Johnson, I.	Martin	William
8	Sanders, B.	Robinson	Carol
9	Roberts, C.	Robinson	Carol
10	Johnson, I.	Robinson	Carol
11	Askew, N.	Robinson	Carol
12	Williams, R.	Kramer	Harry
13	Askew, N.	Kramer	Harry
14	Jones, E.	Kramer	Harry
15	Roberts, C.	Moore	Ellen
16	Jones, E.	Moore	Ellen

If you needed a course list for all students, you could use a command like

```
LIST STUDENTS.LASTNAME, STUDENTS.FIRSTNAME,
CLASSID, CLASSES.TITLE
```

and the results would resemble this:

```
Record#  STUDENTS.LASTNAME  STUDENTS.FIRSTNAME  CLASSID  CLASSES.TITLE
      1  Miller             Karen               S100     Earth Science
      2  Miller             Karen               S102     Chemistry
      3  Miller             Karen               H101     Amer. History
      4  Miller             Karen               S102     Chemistry
      6  Martin             William             H100     World History
      7  Martin             William             T100     Auto Repair
      8  Robinson           Carol               S101     Biology
      9  Robinson           Carol               S102     Chemistry
     10  Robinson           Carol               T100     Auto Repair
     11  Robinson           Carol               H100     World History
     12  Kramer             Harry               S100     Earth Science
     13  Kramer             Harry               H100     World History
     14  Kramer             Harry               T101     Microcomputers
     15  Moore              Ellen               S102     Chemistry
     16  Moore              Ellen               T101     Microcomputers
```

If you wanted a list of classes for a single student, you could include a FOR clause, as in the following example:

```
LIST STUDENTS.LASTNAME, STUDENTS.FIRSTNAME,
CLASSID,
CLASSES.TITLE FOR STUDENTS.LASTNAME = "Kramer"
```

The results would include only the classes for the student named:

```
Record#  STUDENTS.LASTNAME  STUDENTS.FIRSTNAME  CLASSID  CLASSES.TITLE
     12  Kramer             Harry               S100     Earth Science
     13  Kramer             Harry               H100     World History
     14  Kramer             Harry               T101     Microcomputers
```

11

You could use similar techniques to obtain listings of all students for a given teacher, as shown in the following example:

```
LIST STUDENTS.LASTNAME, STUDENTS.FIRSTNAME, CLASSID,
CLASSES.TITLE FOR CLASSES.TEACHER = "Roberts, C."
```

Record#	STUDENTS.LASTNAME	STUDENTS.FIRSTNAME	CLASSID	CLASSES.TITLE
2	Miller	Karen	S102	Chemistry
5	Martin	William	S102	Chemistry
9	Robinson	Carol	S102	Chemistry
15	Moore	Ellen	S102	Chemistry

While the management of a many-to-many application like this one gets fairly complex, it also demonstrates the power and usefulness of a well-planned relational database system. To manage this data in a single database file would call for an enormous amount of redundant data entry; student names and teacher names would be repeated needlessly dozens or hundreds of times in such a file. In spite of this, database users create single files to manage tasks like this all too often, either to avoid learning the necessary relational commands, or because the student data entry labor is cheap.

CHAPTER

FOXPRO

12

CREATING APPLICATIONS WITH FOXAPP

If you have closely followed this text, you should have a knowledge of how you can put FoxPro to work. You have created different database files, used menu options or commands for getting information from those database files, designed custom reports, and used macros to automate your work. This chapter shows how you can use an additional tool, FoxApp, to create menu-driven applications.

NOTE: This chapter assumes the use of FoxPro version 2 or above. FoxApp, the applications builder detailed in this chapter, is not available in FoxPro version 1.x. There is a combined screen design and applications design tool (called FoxView) available in versions 1.x of FoxPro; you can refer to your FoxPro documentation to learn more about the use of this tool. However, if you are interested in developing applications, you should seriously consider upgrading to the latest version of FoxPro. Versions 2 and above of FoxPro contain many useful development tools for serious developers, in addition to FoxApp. These tools include a custom menu-design system and a "build" utility that lets you create stand-alone applications that can be used without a copy of FoxPro. For the serious FoxPro developer, the tools present in the newer versions of FoxPro are a must.

Applications Defined

First, why are applications so important to database users? In a nutshell, an application makes things easier on the average user by combining a series of "building blocks," like database files, reports, and labels, into a complete system. An application is what makes an accounts receivable system different from a database containing accounts receivable information. Both deal with the same kinds of information—dollar amounts, and bills addressed to recipients that contain breakdowns of those amounts. But the accounts receivable database can only store the data, while the accounts receivable system has the database and all the other files (indexes, reports, mailing labels, and programs) needed to solve a particular business problem.

Besides helping you meet the needs of a specific task, an application binds together the building blocks of a database system. If you consider the parts of a database system—one or more database files, the indexes, the labels, and the reports—to be building blocks of a sort, the application can be thought of as a kind of glue that binds these building blocks into a complete operating unit. Applications are nothing new in the computer world, and there is a good chance that you have already used some types of specialized applications based around a database of some sort. Programs to handle mailing lists, inventory, sales tracking, and accounting are all specialized applications that make use of databases. But to use these types of applications, you had to buy a software package designed for the application (or pay a programmer to write it), and then you were often stuck with something that did most, but not all, of what you wanted. By using programming skills (which are developed in the chapters to follow) along with tools such as FoxApp, you can build custom applications designed to do precisely what you want.

To further illustrate how an application can make things easier, consider the work you've done if you have followed the examples throughout this book to create a usable system for Generic Videos. You have database files for tracking both members and rental tapes checked out by members, and you have custom reports for printing the contents of those databases. With your familiarity with FoxPro, if you want to add or edit data or generate reports, you can load FoxPro and use various menu options or commands to accomplish the desired results.

But what happens when you want to show someone else in the office how to add or edit data or how to produce reports containing certain records? That person must go through the same kind of learning curve, getting sufficiently familiar with the FoxPro menus or commands until she or he can accomplish the same kind of results that you can manage. If your office has the usual moderate to high staff turnover common in today's business world, you could be faced with having to show others how to use FoxPro for the same tasks, year in and year out. The answer to this sort of dilemma, as proven by thousands of programmers year after year, is to build custom applications with menu choices that casual users need no specialized training to understand.

Starting FoxApp

The FoxApp utility is actually a program written in the FoxPro programming language. As you will learn in the chapters to follow, you can run a program under FoxPro with the DO command or with the DO option from the Program menu. Because FoxApp is stored in the same directory as the FoxPro program files (probably C:\FOXPRO if your hard disk is drive C), it is usually easiest to start the program by selecting the proper directory from the pop-up menus after choosing the DO option of the Program menu.

12

Open the Program menu now, and choose DO. The Do Program File dialog box appears (Figure 12-1).

Do Program
File dialog box
Figure 12-1.

You may not see any programs in your list box; the contents of the list box depend on whether any programs have been stored in your current directory. If FOXAPP.APP appears in your list box, you should highlight FOXAPP.APP by name, and then choose Do from the dialog box to start FoxApp. If you do not see the program FOXAPP.APP in the list box, tab to or click the Directory pop-up and choose the same directory that contains your FoxPro program files (usually FOXPRO, unless you named it something else during the installation process).

Once you have chosen the directory that contains your FoxPro program files, you should be able to scroll down in the list box and find FOXAPP.APP. Highlight the file, and choose Do from the dialog box to start FoxApp.

When FoxApp is started, the FoxPro Application Generator screen appears (Figure 12-2).

FoxApp needs only two items to build an application: the name of the database to use and the name of a screen. (The screen controls how the data appears during the adding and editing of the database.) For this example, you can use the MEMBERS database that was created in earlier chapters. You need to design a screen that controls how the data appears; however, this can be done within FoxApp.

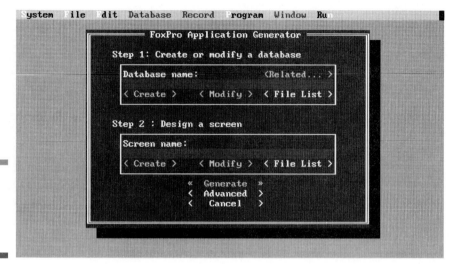

FoxPro
Application
Generator
screen
Figure 12-2.

The cursor should be flashing in the Database Name entry box; FoxApp is asking for the name of the database file that the application will use. You can either type in the file name (including the directory path name), or you can select the File List button and pick the database name from a list of files that then appears. Because you are probably running FoxApp from a different directory (the FoxPro program directory), you should use the File List button to find the proper location of the MEMBERS database.

Tab to or click the File List option under Database Name. If MEMBERS.DBF is in the list box that appears, select it by name and choose Open. If it is not visible in the list box, highlight the name of your data directory in the list box and press Enter to switch to that directory; then, highlight MEMBERS.DBF and choose Open from the dialog box.

You may notice that once a database file name has been chosen, it appears in the Database Name entry field of the FoxPro Application Generator dialog box, and a corresponding screen name appears in the Screen Name entry field (Figure 12-3). FoxApp assumes that the screen to be used by the application will be given the same name as the database. For this example, the database name will do fine, although

12

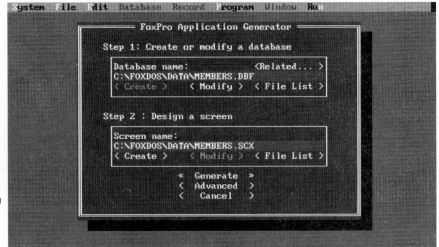

Application
Generator
dialog box with
filled-in names
Figure 12-3.

keep in mind that you can change the screen name to any name you
desire.

Relating a File

A major improvement of the FoxPro Application Generator over earlier
versions is that it allows you to create applications that make use of
relationships between two files. In the Application Generator, you click
the Related button and use the options in the dialog box that next
appears to create applications that use related files.

With relationships, one database is the *parent database,* and the other is
the *child database.* The parent database controls the child, so that
whenever you move the record pointer in the parent database, the
record pointer in the child database moves accordingly. (Refer to
Chapter 11 for further details about working with related database
files.) When you are creating a relational application with the FoxPro
Application Generator, the important point to remember is that the
parent database must be the database whose name you enter in the
Database Name entry box. When you add or edit records through the
completed application, a record in the parent database will appear
within a Change window. At the same time, all related records for the

child database will appear in a separate Browse window. (In the next step, you will see how to tell the Application Generator which file to use as the child database.)

NOTE: If you were building an application that had no relations (that is, the application used only a single database file), you could skip the following step, and continue under the heading "Creating A Screen."

Click the Related button in the dialog box now. In a moment, the Related Databases list box appears, as shown in Figure 12-4.

The parent database (in this case, MEMBERS.DBF) appears in the list box. Tab to the Add button and press (Enter) or click the Add button to add a related database. When you do so, the familiar Open File dialog box appears. RENTALS.DBF will be related as the child database, so tab to RENTALS.DBF in the file list and press (Enter), then select Open; or, click RENTALS.DBF in the file list, then click Open. This causes the Database Relations dialog box, shown in Figure 12-5, to be displayed.

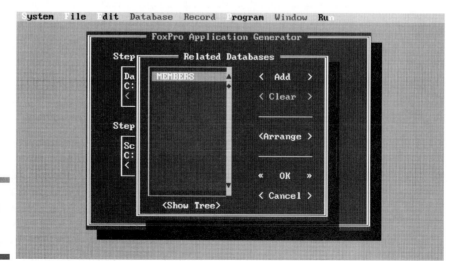

Related
Databases list
box
Figure 12-4.

12

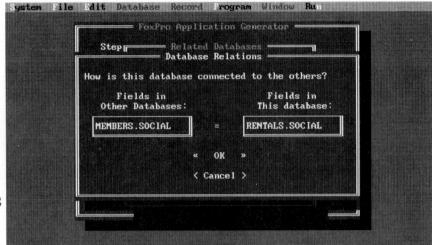

Database
Relations dialog
box
Figure 12-5.

In this dialog box, FoxPro is asking how the RENTALS file should be
related to the MEMBERS file. Note that the SOCIAL field appears in
both Fields text boxes. Because this is the only common field found in
both files, FoxPro assumes that this field should be used to establish the
relationship.

In this case, this is a correct assumption, so tab to OK and press (Enter), or
click OK. Then, again tab to OK and press (Enter) or click OK in the
Related Databases list box to close the list box. This completes the
process of establishing the relationship between the files. You are now
ready to create a data entry screen for the application.

Creating a Screen

You may notice that because a screen does not exist for this database,
the Create button is available as an option in the Screen Name area.
Before proceeding, you should have an idea of just what a *screen* is. A
screen is simply a means of controlling the appearance of database
fields during the appending and editing process. You can create a
screen during the application design process (within FoxApp) or from
elsewhere in FoxPro (by choosing File New from the menus and
selecting Screen from the dialog box that appears). Until this point in

the book, screens have not been discussed, because the use of screens under FoxPro requires either some knowledge of programming and development techniques or the use of FoxApp.

With the name MEMBERS.SCX already in the Screen Name entry field, tab to or click the Create button to begin creation of the screen. FoxApp automatically creates a screen for the editing of data, and you briefly see a confirmation message reading, "Screen has been created" in the upper-right corner.

Making Changes to the Default Screen

While FoxApp does a fine job of creating a default data entry screen, you can make changes to that screen, if desired. To see what the screen looks like (and how you can make modifications), tab to or click the Modify button under the screen name now. When you select Modify, the screen appears (Figure 12-6).

Within this design area, you can change the names used to refer to the fields; move fields to other locations in the screen; add or remove fields; and add text, lines, or boxes to the screen. Many of these topics are beyond the scope of this text, but you can find further information on

Default screen for the MEMBERS database
Figure 12-6.

12

designing screens in your FoxPro documentation, and also in more advanced texts such as *FoxPro 2.5: The Complete Reference* (Berkeley, CA: Osborne-McGraw Hill, 1993). For now, this chapter shows how you can move fields to different locations and add other text to the screen.

To move a field, you simply select the field (with the mouse or the (Spacebar)) and then move the field to the new location (with the mouse or the arrow keys). In this example, the State and Zipcode fields might look better next to the City field. Move the cursor to the State field (be sure to move to the field itself, and not to the label that says "State"), and press the (Spacebar) to select the field (or click the field with the mouse). Notice that a selected field turns a different shade from the unselected fields.

Use the cursor keys to move the State field to row 5, column 36. (You can tell the row and column locations of the field by viewing the indicators at the upper-left corner of the screen, under the System menu.) Then press (Spacebar) to deselect the field.

In a similar manner, move the cursor to the Zipcode field, and press the (Spacebar) to select it (or just click the field with the mouse). Then, use the cursor keys or the mouse to move the Zipcode field to row 5, column 48. Finally, press (Spacebar) to deselect the field.

Move the cursor to the word "State" at row 6, column 1. Press the (Spacebar) to select it, move the word to row 5, column 30 (next to the State field), and press the (Spacebar) to deselect the field.

Move the cursor to the word "Zipcode" at row 7, column 1. Press the (Spacebar) to select it, move the word to row 5, column 40 (next to the Zipcode field), and press the (Spacebar) to deselect the field.

Adding Text to a Screen

Add descriptive text to explain the use of screens to new users.

You can add descriptive text, such as headings or comments, at any location in a screen. To do this, simply place the cursor at the desired location and begin typing. When you are done entering the text, press the (Enter) key to complete the text entry. (You can later delete text that has been entered by moving the cursor to the text, pressing the (Spacebar) to select it, and then pressing the (Del) key.)

One benefit of designing a custom screen is that it allows you to add descriptive messages that may help novice users. Generic Videos employees may not instinctively understand how to enter data in a memo field. To add an explanation now, move the cursor to row 14, column 20 (underneath the Preference field). Enter the following text:

Use CTRL-PG DN to edit this memo field.

and press (Enter) when done entering the text.

Saving Changes to the Screen

As with any object in FoxPro, you want to save the changes you make to the screen. The easiest way to save the changes is with the Save ((Ctrl)-(W)) key combination, although you can also choose Save from the File menu followed by Close from the File menu. In this case, press (Ctrl)-(W) now to save the changes and return to the FoxApp dialog box.

Generating the Application

With the database name and the screen name both entered in the dialog box, you are ready to generate the application. Tab to or click the Generate button at the bottom of the dialog box. As soon as you select this button, you see another dialog box, asking for a name for your application. FoxPro assumes that you want to use the same name as the database; hence, the name MEMBERS.APP appears by default in the entry box. (All applications created by FoxApp are assigned a default extension of .APP.) Again, this name will do for this example; keep in mind that you can name your application with any file name you prefer.

With MEMBERS.APP as the application name, choose Save from the dialog box. In a moment, a message appears indicating that the application is being generated. When this process is complete, the message, "Press any key to start your application" appears in the upper-right corner of the screen. Press a key, and the application loads and displays a menu along with a data entry screen (Figure 12-7).

12

Using the Application

The completed application provides an easy way for you or others to access the data in the MEMBERS and RENTALS databases. The six options that appear at the bottom of the screen can be used to quickly

Completed
application
Figure 12-7.

move throughout the database. You can select these options by
pressing the first letter of the desired option or by clicking the option
name with the mouse. These options perform as indicated:

+ *Top* This option moves you to the first record in the database.

+ *Prior* This option moves you to the previous record. If you are
  already at the first record, a warning message appears indicating
  that fact.

+ *Next* This option moves you to the next record. If you are already
  at the last record, a warning message appears indicating that fact.

+ *Bottom* This option moves you to the last record in the database.

+ *Search* This option lets you find a record in the database, using any
  of the fields as the basis for the search. When you choose Search,
  the Search For dialog box shown in Figure 12-8 appears.

  In the entry box, enter the term you want to search for. Then, from
  the pop-up menu, choose the field that you are searching. For
  example, if you wanted to find a video club member who lived in
  Silver Spring, you would enter **SILVER SPRING** in the entry box.
  Then, you would choose City as the field to be searched from the

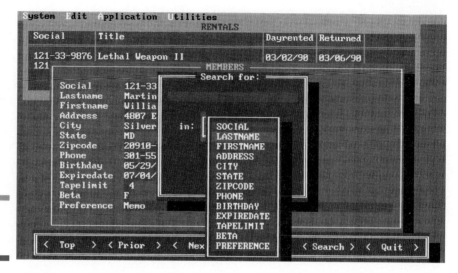

Search For
dialog box
Figure 12-8.

pop-up menu. Finally, choose OK from the dialog box, and the desired record is displayed (assuming it exists). If a record containing your search term cannot be found, the application displays a warning message to that effect.

✦ *Quit* This option exits the application, returning you to the Run Application dialog box. You can then choose Cancel to get to the FoxPro menus and command window.

Making Changes to Records

You can also add, edit, or browse among records by using the various options of the Application menu (Figure 12-9). The Application menu appears in any application created by FoxApp.

The Application menu provides various options for adding records, deleting records, and displaying a Browse window (which you can then use to quickly make edits to a record). For example, if you wanted to change a record, you could first find the desired record, using the search techniques described previously. Then, you could open the Application menu by pressing Alt-A, and choose Browse. From the Browse window that appears, you could change the record as desired.

12

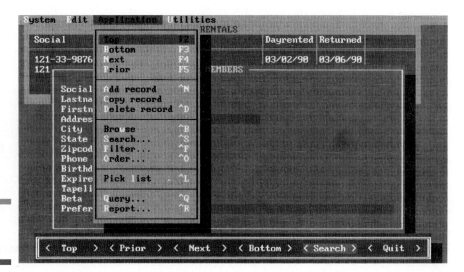

(Remember, once a Browse window is visible, you can choose Browse or Change from the Browse window to switch between a browse-style display and an edit-style display.) When you are done with your changes, press Ctrl-W to exit the Browse display and return to the application.

Generating Reports

To display or print reports from the application, open the Application menu with Alt-A and choose Report. The next menu that appears has choices labeled Print Report, Printer Setup, Create Report, and Modify Report. The Create Report and Modify Report options simply call up the report design screen, detailed in Chapters 7 and 10. The Printer Setup option, when chosen, reveals a dialog box that lets you change the print device and the margins for printing.

If you choose Print Report from the dialog box that appears, another dialog box appears, showing the names of all stored reports. Simply pick the desired report by name, and then choose the desired destination (screen, printer, or text file) from the next dialog box to appear. Choose OK, and the report is produced.

*See
Chapters 5
and 6 for
specifics on
selecting
records for
your reports.*

If you want to produce a report based on selected records (which is often the case), there are two ways you can do this from within an application. One method is to specify a filter condition, and the other is to build a query that produces a report. From the Application menu, you can choose Filter, which causes the Expression Builder to appear. As detailed in Chapter 5, you can enter an expression in the Expression Builder to limit the records available to the application. Choose OK from the Expression Builder after entering the expression. From that point on, only the records meeting the conditions specified by the expression will be available for editing or for generating reports.

If the selective reports come from large databases, you will probably get faster results with the second method, which is to build a query. Design a query, using the techniques outlined in Chapter 6, and specify Reports/Labels as the output choice during the query design. Once the query has been saved, you can use it within the application by choosing Query from the Application menu and entering the name of the query in the dialog box that appears. The conditions specified in the design of the query take effect, and the report specified during the design of the query is printed.

Other Menu Options

The remaining options on the Application menu can be used for various database management tasks. The Top, Bottom, Next, and Prior options move you around in the database; they operate in the same manner as the Top, Bottom, Prior, and Next options at the bottom of the screen. The Add Record option appends a blank record to the database, and you can then fill in the data. The Copy Record option makes a copy of the current record, and you can then make any desired changes to the new record. The Delete Record option deletes the current record.

The Search option performs in the same manner as the Search button at the bottom of the screen; use it to search for a specific record based on the contents of any field. As described earlier, the Filter option brings up the Expression Builder, and you can enter a filter expression to limit the available records. The Order option brings up an Index Order dialog box; from this box, you can choose any existing index, and it is made active. The records then appear in the order of that index.

12

The Edit and System menus are shortened versions of the Edit and System menus that normally appear in FoxPro. The available options in these menus perform the same tasks as elsewhere in FoxPro; since they have been covered earlier in this text, they are not covered here. One point worth noting is that the Quit option of this System menu does not quit FoxPro entirely; it instead quits the application and leaves you back in FoxPro.

The Utilities menu provides three options: Construct Index, Pack, and Environment. The Construct Index option rebuilds all index tags used by the application. The PACK command permanently removes all records marked for deletion. The Environment option lets you control whether the Status Bar, Clock, and extended video (on machines so equipped) are present, and whether FoxPro is in "sticky" mode (when in sticky mode, menu pop-ups remain on the screen until chosen).

Quitting the Application

To exit the application, choose the Quit button, or select Quit from the System menu. You are returned to a dialog box asking for the name of an application to run. Choose Cancel from this dialog box, and you are returned to the FoxPro menus and command window.

Just the Beginning

This chapter has given you an idea of the power and ease of use that a professional application, written with the help of the FoxPro Applications Generator, can provide. If your job can be made easier through the presence of an application, take the time to explore all the features of the applications created by FoxApp. You may want to try creating a database that matches your own needs, designing some reports and queries for that database, and then building an application. The resulting ease-of-use will be well worth the time you spend.

CHAPTER

FOXPRO

13

INTRODUCTION TO FOXPRO PROGRAMMING

Although you may not have purchased FoxPro with the intent of becoming a computer programmer, you'll find that programming with FoxPro is not as difficult as you might expect. As you will see in this chapter, you program in FoxPro through the use of command files. Using programs that automate the way FoxPro works for you is well worth the effort spent in designing and writing command files. For the most part, FoxPro is command compatible with dBASE IV and with dBASE III PLUS, so you can use programs written for them with FoxPro. And FoxPro for DOS is fully compatible with its companion product, FoxPro for Windows. dBASE IV users should note that there are a few dBASE IV commands and functions, such as SET SQL, that are not supported by FoxPro. If in doubt, compare the command listing from your dBASE IV documentation with the command listing in this book (or in your FoxPro documentation).

Any computer *program* is simply a series of instructions to a computer. These instructions are commands that cause the computer to perform specific tasks. The commands are written in a file contained on a disk, and they are performed each time the file is retrieved from the disk.

A FoxPro *command file* is made up of FoxPro commands. Each time you use a command file, FoxPro executes the list of commands in sequential order, unless you request otherwise.

HINT: If you repeat the same commands over and over in your work, command files will save you considerable effort.

Let's look at an example using the Generic Videos database. If a Generic Videos manager wanted a printed listing of members' last names, cities, states, and expiration dates, that manager could enter commands, like those you have learned to use, to produce the listing. This may not seem like a complex task; in fact, it could be done with the following two commands:

```
USE MEMBERS
LIST LASTNAME, FIRSTNAME, CITY, STATE, EXPIREDATE
```

If, however, the manager needed to reprint this list frequently, typing the same commands over and over would be a waste of time. Instead, he could place them inside a command file, and then he would type only one short command to execute all the commands in the file.

Two characteristics of command files make them a powerful feature of FoxPro:

✦ Any series of FoxPro commands entered from the command level can be stored in a command file. When the command file is run, the FoxPro commands present in the file are executed just as if they had been entered from the keyboard.

✦ One command file can call and execute another command file. Information can be transferred between command files. This means that complex systems can be designed efficiently through creating a series of smaller command files for individual tasks.

Using command files, you can create a system that provides the user with one or more menus of options. An example of a menu screen is shown in Figure 13-1. Rather than using individual commands, the user simply makes choices from the menu to retrieve and manipulate information in the database. Such a menu-driven system can easily be used by people unfamiliar with FoxPro commands.

Creating Command Files

You create command files with the MODIFY COMMAND command, using the form

MODIFY COMMAND *filename*

Generic Videos
System Menu

Add records

Edit records
Reports
Display Member Data
Quit

HIGHLIGHT OPTION, PRESS ENTER

Sample menu
for Generic
Videos
Figure 13-1.

13

MODIFY
COMMAND
adds a
default
extension of
.PRG.

Entering **MODIFY COMMAND** along with a file name brings up the FoxPro Editor. You then use the Editor to type the commands that will be stored as a command file. When you use MODIFY COMMAND, the file you create will have an extension of .PRG (for Program) unless you enter a different extension. If the file name you enter already exists on the disk, it is recalled to the screen. If the file name does not exist, a blank screen within the Editor window is displayed. You can also create command files from the menus by opening the File menu, choosing New, and then choosing Program from the dialog box that appears.

To try a simple example of a command file now, enter

```
MODIFY COMMAND TEST
```

The FoxPro Editor appears. At this point, the screen is like a blank sheet of paper. You type the commands that you wish to place in your command file, pressing (Enter) as you complete each line. If you make any mistakes, you can correct them with the arrow keys and the (Backspace) or (Del) key. The editing keys available in the Editor are listed in Table 13-1. When you use the Editor, any characters you type push any existing characters in the same position to the right unless you are in overwrite mode. You can get out of insert mode and into overwrite by pressing (Ins). When you are in insert mode, the cursor takes the shape of a thin line, and any characters to the right of the cursor are pushed to the right as you type new characters. When you are in overwrite mode, the cursor is shaped like a block, and any characters you type overwrite existing characters.

One feature of the Editor that comes in handy for programming is its ability to delete, move, and copy blocks of text. You can mark a block of text for deletion in the Editor by placing the cursor at the beginning of the text, holding down the (Shift) key, and moving the cursor to the end of the block of text while continuing to hold the (Shift) key down. The marked text appears in a different shade. You can then delete the marked text by pressing the (Del) key.

To move or copy text, you mark the block of text in the same manner, but you then use the Cut, Copy, or Paste option of the Edit menu. To copy a block of text to another location, first place the cursor at the start of the text, hold down the (Shift) key, and move the cursor to the

Key	Action
↑	Moves cursor up one line
↓	Moves cursor down one line
←	Moves cursor left one character
→	Moves cursor right one character
Enter	Inserts a new line
Ins	Turns insert mode on or off
Del	Deletes character at cursor position
Backspace	Deletes character to the left of cursor
Pg Up	Scrolls screen upwards
Pg Dn	Scrolls screen downwards
Ctrl-W	Saves file on disk
Esc	Exits Editor without saving

Editing Keys in
the FoxPro
Editor
Table 13-1.

end of the text. Open the Edit menu and choose Copy. Move the cursor to where the copied text should appear, open the Edit menu, and choose Paste. The copied text appears in the new location.

To move a block of text to another location, first place the cursor at the start of the text, hold down the Shift key, and move the cursor to the end of the text. Open the Edit menu and choose Cut. Move the cursor to where the text is to be moved, open the Edit menu, and choose Paste. The moved text appears in the new location.

Type the following series of commands now, pressing Enter after you complete each line; only one command should appear on each line. (If you don't have a printer on your system, omit the SET PRINT ON, SET PRINT OFF, and EJECT commands.)

```
USE MEMBERS
SET PRINT ON
LIST LASTNAME, FIRSTNAME, CITY, TAPELIMIT FOR STATE = "MD"
LIST LASTNAME, FIRSTNAME, CITY, TAPELIMIT FOR STATE = "VA"
LIST LASTNAME, FIRSTNAME, CITY, TAPELIMIT FOR STATE = "DC"
SET PRINT OFF
EJECT
```

13

Whenever you finish editing with the FoxPro Editor, choose Save from the File menu (or press Ctrl-W) to save the command file. (If you want to leave the Editor without saving the file, you can press Esc and then answer No in the dialog box that appears.)

HINT: You can also run programs from the menus, by choosing Do from the Program menu and entering the name of the program.

The simple command file that you have created prints a listing of each member, grouped by state, including member names, city names, and salary amounts. Make sure that your printer is turned on; then, to see the results of your work, enter

```
DO TEST
```

The commands in the file are carried out in sequential order, just as if you had entered them individually:

Record#	LASTNAME	FIRSTNAME	CITY	TAPELIMIT
1	Miller	Karen	Chevy Chase	6
2	Martin	William	Silver Spring	4
5	Moore	Ellen	Takoma Park	6
Record#	LASTNAME	FIRSTNAME	CITY	TAPELIMIT
3	Robinson	Carol	Falls Church	6
4	Kramer	Harry	Arlington	4
6	Zachman	David	Falls Church	4
8	Hart	Wendy	Fairfax	2
Record#	LASTNAME	FIRSTNAME	CITY	TAPELIMIT
7	Robinson	Benjamin	Washington	6

You can also create a command file by using other word processing programs. Although the FoxPro Editor is convenient and quite powerful, you may prefer to use your favorite word processing program. (If you do use your own editor, be sure to see "Compiling" following this paragraph.) Any word processor that can save files as ASCII text (text without any control codes) can be used to create a FoxPro command file. This includes the programs WordPerfect, MultiMate, and WordStar, as well as Microsoft Word. In WordPerfect, save the file with the [Ctrl]-[F5] then [1] key combination. In WordStar, save the file in the Nondocument mode. In Microsoft Word, save the file as Unformatted. The important points to remember are to save the file as ASCII and to use the .PRG extension when naming the file; otherwise, FoxPro won't recognize the file as a command file unless you include the extension when calling the program with the DO command.

Compiling

FoxPro uses a compiler to run programs on a compiled basis rather than an interpreted basis. (*Interpreters* convert each line of a program into machine language each time the program runs; *compilers* translate the entire program into what is known as object code once, and each time the program runs, it runs using the object code.) A compiler offers significant speed over an interpreter. Earlier versions of Ashton-Tate's dBASE, including dBASE II, dBASE III, and dBASE III PLUS, were based on interpreters. By comparison, FoxPro, FoxBase, and dBASE IV all use compilers.

When you run a FoxPro program with the DO *filename* command, FoxPro looks for a compiled object-code file with an extension of .FXP. If FoxPro finds the file, it runs the program using the already compiled object code. If FoxPro can't find the file, it looks for a "source file"—an ASCII text file of commands with a .PRG extension. FoxPro compiles this file, creating an object-code file of the same name, and then runs the program.

It is important to know this if you use your own editor to modify existing programs. When you change an existing program with the FoxPro Editor, FoxPro recompiles to a new object file when you run the program. If you use your own editor to change a program and the existing object-code file is not erased, using DO *filename* causes the old version of the program to be run.

Use SET DEVELOP-MENT ON if you use your own editor.

When making changes with your editor, you must erase the old object-code (.FXP) version of the program, or you must use the SET DEVELOPMENT ON command when you start your FoxPro session. Entering **SET DEVELOPMENT ON** tells FoxPro to compare creation

13

dates and times between source (.PRG) and object (.FXP) files; if they differ, FoxPro recompiles the program before running it.

There are various concepts associated with programming that you should know about before delving into the topic of FoxPro command files: constants, variables, expressions, operators, and functions.

Constants

A *constant* is an item of fixed data, or data that does not change. Unlike fields (whose values change, depending on the position of the record pointer), a constant's value is dependent on nothing; once established, the constant remains the same. There are numeric, character, date, and logical constants. For example, 5.05 might be a numeric constant, while the letter "a" might be a character constant. All character constants must be surrounded by quotes. Date constants must be surrounded by curly braces, and logical constants must be surrounded by periods.

Memory Variables

A *memory variable* (or simply *variable,* for short) is a memory location within the computer that is used to store data. Memory variables are referred to by their assigned names. A variable name must be ten or fewer characters. It must consist of letters, numbers, and underscores only, and it must start with a letter. You cannot use the names of commands, and it is best not to use field names. Because the contents of a memory variable are stored apart from the contents of a database, memory variables are useful for the temporary processing of values and data within a FoxPro program. Data can be stored in the form of memory variables and then be recalled for use by the program at a later time.

HINT: Think of a memory variable as a temporary place to put a piece of information that will be needed later in the program.

The STORE command is commonly used to assign data to a variable. The format is shown in the following:

STORE *expression* TO *variable-name*

An alternate way of assigning data to a variable is to use the "variable = X" format, as shown here:

variable-name = *expression*

FoxPro allows four types of variables: character, numeric, date, and logical. Character variables store strings of characters, which can be letters, numbers, or a combination of both. Numbers in a character variable are treated as characters. Numeric variables contain whole or decimal numbers. Date variables contain dates written in date format (for example, 12/16/84). Logical variables contain a logical value of T (true) or F (false), or Y (yes) or N (no).

You do not have to designate the type when creating a variable—just assign the value you will be using. Use a descriptive name to help you remember what is stored in the variable. For example, the following STORE command assigns a numeric value of 18 to the variable LEGALAGE:

```
STORE 18 TO LEGALAGE
```

If you preferred the alternate format, you could accomplish the same result with the statement

```
LEGALAGE = 18
```

You can change the value by using the STORE command again:

```
STORE 21 TO LEGALAGE
```

The contents of a field can be stored to a memory variable. As an example, the command STORE LASTNAME TO ROSTER would store the contents of the Lastname field to a memory variable named ROSTER. When a list of characters is stored in a variable, the list of characters, known as a *character string,* must be surrounded by single or double quotation marks. For example, the command

```
STORE "BILL ROBERTS" TO NAME
```

would store the character string BILL ROBERTS in the variable NAME.

13

Surround the logical variable T, F, Y, and N with periods to distinguish them from regular characters: while .T. has a logical value of true, T is simply the letter T. Logical values can also be stored in variables with the STORE command. The following command would assign a logical value of false to the variable CHOICE:

```
STORE .F. TO CHOICE
```

To initialize a date variable, surround the date with curly braces. As an example, the statement

```
STORE 11/01/91 TO MYDAY
```

would store the date 11/01/91 in a date variable named MYDAY.

Use DISPLAY MEMORY to see memory variables.

In addition to STORE, other commands assign values to variables. These commands are discussed in later chapters. To display a list of the variables you have used and their values, enter the command DISPLAY MEMORY.

You can use memory variables in direct commands and in command files. However, memory variables are only temporary: as soon as you turn off the computer, they vanish. You can make a memory variable permanent by storing the variable to a memory file on disk. As you might expect, when the values are stored on disk, they can be recalled by a FoxPro program. Each memory variable is assigned a different name.

Try entering the following:

```
STORE 25 TO QUANTITY
STORE "Jefferson" TO NAMES
STORE TIME() TO CLOCK
? QUANTITY, NAMES, CLOCK
```

The previous example displayed the values stored in memory with the STORE command. However, you can use the DISPLAY MEMORY command to take a look at all variables that have been defined in memory. Enter

```
DISPLAY MEMORY
```

to display a listing of variables, a letter designating the type of variable, and what each variable contains. The letter C indicates a character variable, N a numeric variable, D a date variable, and L a logical variable. The designation "Pub" beside each variable indicates that these are public variables, available to all parts of FoxPro. Variables can be public or private. For now, you needn't be concerned about this designation. Along with the memory variables you created, you will see information on print system memory variables that FoxPro uses; you can ignore these.

You can also use a period in place of the -> symbols.

You should keep two guidelines in mind. First, it's a good idea not to name variables after a field. If a program encounters a name that can be either a variable or a field, the field name takes precedence over the memory variable. If you must give a variable the same name as a field, use the M-> prefix ahead of the variable name so that FoxPro knows when you are referring to the variable. For example, if MEMBERS were in use, LASTNAME would refer to the Lastname field, while M->LASTNAME would refer to a variable called LASTNAME.

Second, note that you must store a value to a memory variable before you start using it in a program. This must be done because of FoxPro's firm rule that some type of value, even if it is a worthless one, must be stored to a FoxPro variable before you can begin using the variable. If you attempt to use variables in a program before defining them with the STORE command, FoxPro responds with a "Variable not found" error message.

To save variables on disk, use the SAVE TO command. The format of this command is

    SAVE TO *filename*

where *filename* is the name of the file that you want the variables saved under. The .MEM extension is automatically added to the file name.

Right now, you have at least three memory variables defined from the previous examples—QUANTITY, NAMES, and CLOCK. (You may also have other variables created from prior examples.) To save the variables currently in memory, enter the following:

```
SAVE TO FASTFILE
```

13

Once the variables have been stored, you can clear the memory of variables with the RELEASE ALL command. Enter the following:

```
RELEASE ALL
DISPLAY MEMORY
```

You'll see that the memory variables no longer exist in memory. To get the memory variables back from FASTFILE, use the RESTORE FROM *filename* command. This command restores variables from the file to memory. You do not have to include the file extension .MEM. Enter

```
RESTORE FROM FASTFILE
```

Then enter **DISPLAY MEMORY**. The variables are again in the system, ready for further use.

When you use the RESTORE FROM *filename* command, all variables currently in memory are removed to accommodate variables from the file. If you want to keep existing variables in memory while loading additional variables that were saved to a disk file, use the RESTORE FROM *filename* ADDITIVE variation of the command.

Getting back to RELEASE ALL, you can select specific variables to remove from memory by including either the EXCEPT or the LIKE option. RELEASE ALL with EXCEPT eliminates all variables except those that you list after EXCEPT. RELEASE ALL with LIKE, on the other hand, removes the variables that you list after LIKE, the opposite of EXCEPT. As an example, the command

```
RELEASE ALL LIKE N*
```

causes all memory variables starting with the letter N to be erased from memory.

You can use LIKE to erase some memory variables and leave other variables untouched. Try this:

```
RESTORE FROM FASTFILE
RELEASE ALL LIKE Q*
DISPLAY MEMORY
```

This causes all memory variables beginning with the letter Q, including the memory variable QUANTITY, to be erased from memory (the others will be untouched). Note that you can use the same LIKE and ALL options in a similar manner with the SAVE command. For example, you could enter the command

```
SAVE ALL LIKE Q* TO QFILE
```

to save all memory variables starting with the letter Q.

Expressions

An *expression* can be a combination of one or more fields, functions, operators, memory variables, or constants. Figure 13-2 shows a statement combining a field, a memory variable, and a constant to form a single expression. This statement calculates total rent over a period of months, deducting 5% for estimated utilities (water, garbage, and so on). Each part of an expression, whether that part is a constant, a field, or a memory variable, is considered an element of the expression. All elements of an expression must be of the same type. You cannot, for example, mix character and date fields within the same expression unless you use functions to convert the dates to characters. If you try to mix different types of fields within an expression, FoxPro displays an "Operator/operand type mismatch" error message.

The most common type of expression found in FoxPro programs is the math expression. Math expressions contain the elements of an expression (constants, fields, memory variables, or functions), usually linked by one or more math operators (+, −, *, /). Examples of math expressions include

```
HOURLYRATE - SALARY

COST + (COST * .05)

HOURLYRATE * 40

637.5/HOURLYRATE
```

82

13

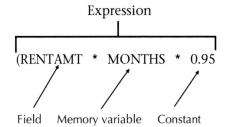

An example of
an expression
Figure 13-2.

Character expressions are also quite common in FoxPro programs.
Character expressions are used to manipulate character strings or groups
of characters. Examples of character expressions include the following:

```
"Bob Smith"

"Mr." + FIRSTNAME + " " + LASTNAME + " is behind in payments."
```

Operators

Operators, which are represented by symbols, work on related values to
produce a single value. Operators that work on two values are called
binary operators; operators that work on one value are called *unary
operators.* Most of FoxPro's operators are binary operators, but there are
a couple of unary operators. FoxPro has four kinds of operators:
mathematical, relational, logical, and string.

Mathematical Operators

Mathematical operators are used to produce numeric results. Besides
addition, subtraction, multiplication, and division, FoxPro has operators
for exponentiation and unary minus (assigning a negative value to a
number, as in –47). The symbols for math operators are as follows:

Operation	Symbol
Unary minus	–
Exponentiation	** or ^
Division	/
Multiplication	*
Subtraction	–
Addition	+

If an expression contains more than one math operator, FoxPro executes the operations in a prescribed order, known as the *order of precedence*. Unary minus is performed first, followed by exponentiation; then multiplication or division is calculated, and then addition or subtraction. In the case of operators with equal precedence—division and multiplication, subtraction and addition—calculation will be from left to right. In the case of logical operators, the order is .NOT., then .AND., and then .OR. When different types of operators are in a single expression, any math and string operators are handled first, and then any relational operators, and then any logical operators.

Use parentheses to change the order of operations.

You can alter the order of operations by grouping them with matched pairs of parentheses. For example, the parentheses in (3 + 6) * 5 force FoxPro to add 3 + 6 first and then multiply the sum by 5. You can group operations within operations with nested parentheses. FoxPro begins with the innermost group and calculates outward, as in the case of ((3 + 5) * 6) ^ 3, where 3 + 5 is added first, multiplied by 6, and then raised to the power of 3.

Relational Operators

Relational operators are used to compare character strings with character strings, date values with date values, and numbers with numbers. The values you compare can be constants or variables. The relational operators are as follows:

Operation	Symbol
Less than	<
Greater than	>
Equal to	=
Not equal to	< > or #
Less than or equal to	<=
Greater than or equal to	>=

13

Any comparison of values results in a logical value of true or false. The simple comparison 6 < 7 would result in .T. The result of 6 < NUMBER depends on the value of NUMBER.

You can also compare such character strings as "canine" < "feline", because FoxPro orders letters and words as in a dictionary. However, uppercase letters come before lowercase letters, so Z < a even though "a" comes before Z in the alphabet.

Logical Operators

Logical operators compare values of the same type to produce a logical true, false, yes, or no. The logical operators are .AND., .OR., and .NOT. Table 13-2 lists all possible values produced by the three logical operators. .AND. and .OR. are binary operators, and .NOT. is a unary operator.

String Operators

The string operator you will commonly use in FoxPro is the plus sign (+). It is used to combine two or more character strings, which is known as *concatenation*. For example, "Orange" + "Fox" would be combined as "OrangeFox" (remember, a blank is a character). Strings inside variables can also be concatenated; for example, if ANIMAL = "Fox" and COLOR = "Orange", then COLOR+ANIMAL would result in "OrangeFox".

First Value	Operator	Second Value	Result
.T.	.AND.	.T.	.T.
.T.	.AND.	.F.	.F.
.F.	.AND.	.T.	.F.
.F.	.AND.	.F.	.F.
.T.	.OR.	.T.	.T.
.T.	.OR.	.F.	.T.
.F.	.OR.	.T.	.T.
.F.	.OR.	.F.	.F.
.T.	.NOT.	N.A.	.F.
.F.	.NOT.	N.A.	.T.

Truth Table for Logical Operators .AND., .OR., and .NOT
Table 13-2.

Functions

Functions are used in FoxPro to perform special operations that supplement the normal FoxPro commands. FoxPro has a number of different functions that perform operations ranging from calculating the square root of a number to finding the time.

Every function statement contains the function name, followed by a set of parentheses. Most functions require one or more arguments inside the parentheses. A complete list of functions can be found in Appendix B. For now, it will help to know about some functions that are commonly used in command files.

EOF

The EOF function indicates when the FoxPro record pointer has reached the end of a database file. The normal format of the function is simply EOF(). To see how EOF() is set to true when the pointer is past the last record, enter

```
GO BOTTOM
```

This moves the pointer to the last record. Now enter

```
DISPLAY
```

and you will see that you are at record 8, the final record in the database. Next, enter

```
? EOF()
```

to display the value of the EOF function. FoxPro returns .F. (false), meaning that the value of the EOF function is false because you are not yet at the end of the file.

The SKIP command, discussed shortly, can be used to move the FoxPro record pointer. Enter

```
SKIP
```

to move the pointer past the last record. Next, enter

```
? EOF()
```

13

The .T. (true) value shows that the pointer is now at the end of the file.

BOF

The BOF function is the opposite of the EOF function. The value of BOF is set to true when the beginning of a database file is reached. The format is BOF(). To see how BOF operates, enter

```
GO TOP
```

The pointer moves to the first record. Now enter

```
DISPLAY
```

and the first record in the database is displayed. Next, enter

```
? BOF()
```

to display the value of the BOF function, which is .F. (false) because the pointer is at the first record and not at the beginning of the file. Enter

```
SKIP -1
```

to move the pointer above record 1. Then enter

```
? BOF()
```

The .T. (true) value shows that the pointer is at the beginning of the file.

DATE and TIME

The DATE and TIME functions are used to provide the current date and time, respectively. FoxPro provides the date and time by means of a clock built into your computer. For this reason, if the date and time set with your computer's DOS are incorrect, the date and time functions of FoxPro will also be incorrect.

The format for DATE is DATE(), and it provides the current date in the form *MM/DD/YY*. Dates follow the American date format, month followed by day followed by year, unless you use the PICTURE option (Chapter 15) or the SET DATE command to tell FoxPro otherwise. The

TIME format of the function is TIME(), and it provides the current time in HH:MM:SS format. Note that for either function you do not need to supply anything between the parentheses, since they serve only to identify TIME and DATE as functions.

From the command level, you could display the current date and time by entering

```
? DATE()
? TIME()
```

The output of the DATE and TIME functions can be stored as a variable for use within a program, as in the example shown here:

```
? "Today's date is: "
?? DATE()
STORE TIME() TO BEGIN
?
LIST LASTNAME, FIRSTNAME, TAPELIMIT, EXPIREDATE
?
? "Starting time was: "
?? BEGIN
? "Ending time is: "
?? TIME()
```

UPPER

The UPPER function converts lowercase letters to uppercase letters. This function is especially useful when you want to search for a character string and you are not sure whether it was entered in all capital letters or initial caps. UPPER can thus be used to display text and variables in a uniform format if consistency is desired. It may be used with a character field, a character string, a constant, or a memory variable that contains a character string. Here is an example:

```
? UPPER ("This is not really uppercase")
THIS IS NOT REALLY UPPERCASE

STORE "not uppercase" TO WORDS
? UPPER(WORDS)
NOT UPPERCASE
```

13

```
? WORDS
not uppercase
```

As shown from the example, the UPPER function displays characters in the uppercase/lowercase format but does not actually alter the data.

You can use the UPPER function to compare data when you are not sure whether the data was entered as all uppercase or in initial caps only. For example, a command like

```
LIST FOR UPPER(LASTNAME) = "SMITH"
```

finds a record whether the last name was entered as Smith or SMITH.

LOWER

The LOWER function is the reverse of UPPER; it converts uppercase characters to lowercase characters, as in the following example. As with the UPPER function, the LOWER function does not convert the actual data; it changes only the appearance of the data.

```
STORE "NOT CAPS" TO WORDS
? LOWER(WORDS)
not caps
```

CTOD and DTOC

CTOD and DTOC are the Character-To-Date and Date-To-Character functions, respectively. CTOD converts a string of characters to a value that is recognized as a date by FoxPro. DTOC performs the opposite function, converting a date into a string of characters.

Acceptable characters that can be converted to dates range from 1/1/100 to 12/31/9999. The full century is optional. Usually, you only specify the last two digits of the year, unless the date falls in a century other than the current one. Any character strings having values that fall outside of these values produce an empty date value if the CTOD function is used.

As an example of the CTOD function, the following command might be used within a program to convert a string of characters to a value that could be stored within a date field:

```
MYEAR = YEAR(DATE())
STORE CTOD("01/01/" + LTRIM(STR(MYEAR))) TO JAN1
```

As an example of the DTOC function, the following command combines a text string along with a date converted to a text string:

```
? "The expiration date is: " + DTOC(EXPIREDATE)
```

DTOS

Use DTOS to build indexes in correct chronological order.

The DTOS function converts a date to a character string that follows the *YYYYMMDD* format. For example, the DTOS function would convert a date of 12/03/1993 to the character string 19931203. This function is very useful when building indexes based on dates, so that any dates spanning multiple years will appear in the correct chronological order. (If you were to use the DTOC function to build the index instead, dates appear in true chronological order only if they all occurred within a single year.) As an example, the command

```
INDEX ON DTOS(EXPIREDATE) TO BYDAYS
```

creates an index in chronological order, with records arranged by order of the expiration date.

SPACE

The SPACE function creates a string of blank spaces, up to a maximum length of 254 spaces. As an example, the following commands make use of a variable called BLANKS, which contains ten spaces (the variable is created with the SPACE function):

```
STORE SPACE(10) TO BLANKS
LIST LASTNAME + BLANKS + CITY + BLANKS + STATE
```

TRIM

The TRIM function removes trailing blanks, or spaces that follow characters, from a character string. You have already used this function in expressions for reports and labels. The expression

```
TRIM(CITY) + ". " + STATE + " " + ZIPCODE
```

13

for example, was used to print the contents of the City and State fields, separated by one space.

The TRIM function also is useful as part of an expression, when displaying information with LIST or DISPLAY, to close large gaps of space that often occur between fields. For example, the commands

```
USE MEMBERS
GO 2
SET PRINT ON
? FIRSTNAME, LASTNAME, ADDRESS
```

result in an unattractive printout that looks like this:

```
William       Martin      4807 East Avenue
```

With the TRIM function, the large gaps between the fields can be eliminated, as shown here:

```
USE MEMBERS
GO 2
SET PRINT ON
? TRIM(FIRSTNAME), TRIM(LASTNAME), ADDRESS

William Martin 4807 East Avenue
```

Note that you should *not* use the TRIM function as part of an indexing expression, such as INDEX ON TRIM(LASTNAME) + FIRSTNAME TO NAMES. Such an index would result in variable-length index keys, which can cause problems in searching for data.

LTRIM

The LTRIM function performs an operation similar to that of the TRIM function, but it trims leading spaces (spaces at the start of the expression) rather than trailing spaces. The following example shows the effect of the LTRIM function:

```
STORE "          ten leading spaces here." TO TEXT
? TEXT
          ten leading spaces here.
? LTRIM(TEXT)
ten leading spaces here.
```

STR

The STR function is used to convert a numeric value into a character string. This type of conversion lets you mix numeric values with characters within displays and reports. As an example of the STR function, the command

```
? "Name is " + LASTNAME + " and limit is " + TAPELIMIT
```

produces an "Operator/operand type mismatch" error message, because Tapelimit is a numeric field and the rest of the expression contains character values. The STR function can convert the numeric value into a character value as follows:

```
? "Name is " + LASTNAME + " and limit is " + STR(TAPELIMIT)
```

Commands Used in Command Files

Some FoxPro commands are often used within command files but are rarely used elsewhere. You will be using command files with increasing regularity through the rest of this book, so these commands deserve a closer look. At the end of this chapter, you will begin using the commands to design a program.

SET TALK

SET TALK ON displays on-screen execution of the commands within a command file. When SET TALK OFF is executed within a command file, visual responses to the FoxPro commands halt until a SET TALK ON command is encountered. You can use SET TALK OFF to stop the display of messages such as the "% of file indexed" message during indexing or the record number displayed after a GO TO or LOCATE command. When you begin a session with FoxPro, SET TALK is on.

SKIP

The SKIP command moves the record pointer forward or backward. The format of the command is

SKIP [+/–*integer*]

13

The integer specified with SKIP moves the pointer forward or backward by that number of records. For example, entering **SKIP 4** moves the record pointer forward by four records. Entering **SKIP – 2** moves the record pointer backward by two records. Entering **SKIP** without an expression moves the pointer one record forward.

The values can be stored in a memory variable, which can then be used as part of SKIP. For example, entering **STORE 4 TO JUMP** assigns 4 to JUMP; then the SKIP JUMP command moves the record pointer forward by four records. If you attempt to move the record pointer beyond the end of the file or above the beginning of the file, an "End of file encountered" or a "Beginning of file encountered" error message results.

RETURN

The RETURN command halts the execution of a command file. When a RETURN command is encountered, FoxPro leaves the program and returns to the command level. If the RETURN command is encountered from within a command file that has been called by another command file, FoxPro returns to the command file that called the file containing the RETURN command.

ACCEPT and INPUT

See Chapter 15 for more ways to accept data.

Two FoxPro commands display a string of characters and wait for the user to enter a response that is then stored in a variable. These commands are ACCEPT and INPUT. The ACCEPT command stores characters; the INPUT command stores values of any data type. The format for ACCEPT is

ACCEPT "prompt" TO *variable-name*

For INPUT, the format is

INPUT "prompt" TO *variable-name*

The order of the commands is the same whether you are dealing with characters or numbers. You enter the command, followed by the question or message that is to appear on the screen (it must be enclosed in single or double quotes), followed by the word TO, followed by the memory variable you want to store the response in. For example, let's use this format with the ACCEPT statement to store a name in a memory variable. Enter the following:

```
ACCEPT "What is your last name? " TO LNAME
```

When you press (Enter), you see the message "What is your last name?" appear on the screen. FoxPro is waiting for your response, so enter your last name. When the cursor reappears in the Command window, enter the following:

```
? LNAME
```

(The ? command, as you may recall from earlier use, displays the contents of the expression following the question mark.) You'll see that FoxPro has indeed stored your last name as a character string within the memory variable LNAME.

The same operation is used for numbers, but you use the INPUT statement instead. For example, enter

```
INPUT "How old are you? " TO AGE
```

and in response to the prompt, enter your age. Next, enter

```
? AGE
```

You'll see that the memory variable AGE now contains your response.

HINT: ACCEPT works well when you want to ask for a character response, like a name. INPUT works well when you want to ask for a numeric response.

COUNT

13

The COUNT command counts the number of occurrences of a condition within a database. One condition might be to count the number of occurrences of the name Robinson in a file, another to find out how many members live in Washington. The general format is

COUNT FOR *condition* TO *variablename*

The condition often takes the form of *fieldname = value*. It can also take the form of *fieldname > value*, or *fieldname > value* .AND. *fieldname < value2*. Or, in the case of logical fields, the condition can simply take the form *fieldname*. The value to which you compare the field must be of the same data type as the field. The entire logical expression constitutes the condition. Every condition can eventually be evaluated as true or false.

The number of occurrences of the condition are stored in *variablename*. The variable can then be used in another part of the program for calculations or for printing. For example, the command

```
COUNT FOR LASTNAME = "Robinson" TO NAMECOUNT
```

counts the occurrences of the last name Robinson in the Lastname field of MEMBERS. That count is stored as a memory variable, NAMECOUNT. The FOR clause used in this example is optional. You could accomplish the same type of selective counting by setting a filter with the SET FILTER command and then simply entering the COUNT command.

SUM

The SUM command calculates the total for any numeric field. The basic format of the command is

SUM [*scope*] [*fieldlist*] [FOR *condition*] [WHILE *condition*]
TO [*variablelist*]

SUM can be used with or without conditions in a number of ways. The scope identifies the magnitude of the summation; that is, if *scope* is absent, all records are checked; if *scope* is NEXT followed by an integer, then only the specified number of records is summed, or if *scope* is ALL, all records are summed, which is the same as when no scope is

Add a condition to specify the records summed.

specified. The record pointer is considered to be at the beginning of the current record, so a command like SUM NEXT 5 sums the current record plus the next four records. If *scope* is REST, all records from the current record are summed. If the clause RECORD <*n*> is used as a scope, only the single record designated by <*n*> is summed (which is rather ridiculous, since there is nothing to add). The *fieldlist* parameter is a list of the numeric fields to be summed by the SUM command. Entering **SUM** without a field list causes FoxPro to add and display the totals of all the numeric fields within the database. Note that SUM always displays its results unless SET TALK is off. You may also want to store the results in memory variables so you can redisplay them later or use them in calculations.

The memory variable list (*variablelist*) assigns the memory variables that the values produced by SUM will be stored in. The SUM TAPELIMIT TO TOTAL command stores the total of the Tapelimit field in a memory variable called TOTAL. SUM TAPELIMIT, HOURLYRATE TO C,D stores the total of the Tapelimit field in variable C and the total of the Hourlyrate field in variable D. SUM TAPELIMIT FOR LASTNAME = "Robinson" TO E would store tape limit amounts for the name Robinson in variable E.

The WHILE clause, which is optional, is used with indexed files to sum the records while (or as long as) a particular condition is true. For example, in a file indexed by last names, you could find the first occurrence of the name Smith and then use a command like

```
SUM WHILE LASTNAME = "Smith"
```

to obtain the sum of any numeric fields for all the persons named Smith. You can use the FOR clause to accomplish the same task, but in a large database, using WHILE is considerably faster.

AVERAGE

The AVERAGE command calculates the average value of a numeric field. The basic format is

AVERAGE [FOR *fieldname*, ...] [WHILE *fieldname=condition*]
[TO *variable*, ...]

13

Here, *fieldname* must be a numeric field (there can be more than one field name). If you include a TO clause, the average of each field named is stored in *variable*.

The command AVERAGE TAPELIMIT TO F stores the average value of the Tapelimit field in variable F.

@, ?, ??, and TEXT

Four commands are commonly used to display or print text: @, ?, ??, and TEXT. The ? and ?? commands display a single line of text at a time. If ? is used, a linefeed and carriage return occur before the display. A ?? command does not include a linefeed and carriage return before the display, so the subsequent value is displayed on the current line.

If the ? or ?? command is preceded by a SET PRINT ON command, output is also routed to the printer. An example is shown in the following command file:

```
SET PRINT ON
? "The last name is: "
?? LASTNAME
?
? "The salary per 40-hour week is: "
?? SALARY * 40
SET PRINT OFF
```

You can also add the optional AT clause and a column position to the ? or ?? command to control where on the line the data appears. For example, the command

```
? "Lastname:" AT 26
```

prints "Lastname:" starting at column 26 on the current line.

See Chapter 15 for more on the @ command.

For more selective printing or display, the @ command moves the cursor to a specific location on the screen or page and, when combined with SAY, displays the information there. FoxPro divides the screen into 24 rows and 80 columns. The top left coordinate is 0,0, and the bottom right coordinate is 23,79. The general format of the @ command is

@ *row,column* [SAY *character-string*]

Omitting the SAY clause clears the designated row from the column position to column 79.

To try the use of the @ command, enter

```
CLEAR
@ 12,20 SAY "This is a display"
```

Using the @ command with the SAY option, you can generate report headings or statements at any required location. Screen formatting with the @ command will be covered in greater detail in Chapter 15.

The TEXT command is useful for displaying large amounts of text. TEXT is commonly used to display operator warnings, menu displays, and notes that appear during various operations of the program. TEXT is followed by the text to be displayed and then ended with ENDTEXT. The text does not need to be surrounded by quotes. Everything between TEXT and ENDTEXT is displayed. The following example erases the screen with CLEAR and then displays a copyright message:

```
CLEAR
TEXT
* * * * * * * * * * * * * * * * * * * * * * * * * * * * * * * * * * * * * * * * * * * * * * * * * * * * * * * * * * * * * * * * * * *

         FoxPro Copyright (C) 1989-1992 Microsoft Corporation
      Personnel Director Copyright (C) 1990 J Systems, Inc.
       For technical support, phone our offices at 555-5555
* * * * * * * * * * * * * * * * * * * * * * * * * * * * * * * * * * * * * * * * * * * * * * * * * * * * * * * * * * * * * * * * * * *

ENDTEXT
WAIT
```

In this example, the WAIT command at the end of the program causes FoxPro to display a "press any key" message and pause until the user presses a key.

The TEXT command must be used from within a command file. Any attempt to use TEXT as a direct command results in an error message.

Overview of a Program Design

13

How do you start to write a program, and after it is operational, how do you determine whether the program is efficient? Unfortunately, there is no one correct way to write a program or determine when it is efficient or good. However, most programmers have a natural tendency to follow five steps in the design of a program:

1. Defining the problem
2. Designing the program
3. Writing the program
4. Verifying the program
5. Documenting the program

As these steps imply, the process of good programming is more than just writing a series of commands to be used in a particular command file. Programming requires careful planning of the code and rigorous testing afterward.

The key to a successful application is careful planning.

If you are programming, you are probably building *applications,* which are a group of programs that perform a general task. Designing an application is somewhat similar to the process of designing a database (outlined in Chapter 1) in that careful planning is required. However, because you are designing an application and not a database, you must think about how the application will use information in the source database, how the application will produce reports, and how the application can be designed so that it is easy to use. Once these design steps have been clearly defined, you can proceed to design and create the programs that will make up the application.

Defining the Problem

The first step is to define the problem that the program is intended to solve. This step is too often skipped, even by professional programmers, in the rush to create a program. The problem may be as simple as wanting to automate a task; but in the process of defining it, you should query the people who will be using the program and find out just what they expect the program to do. Even if you will be the only user, you should stop to outline what the program must provide before you begin writing it.

Output Requirements

Output, the information the application must produce, should be considered. Output is often useful in the form of a printed report, so defining what type of output is needed is often similar to the process of defining what is needed in a report. What types of output must the application produce? What responses to queries do the users expect? What must the reports look like? Sample screen displays or reports should be presented to the users for suggestions and approval. This may sound like a time-consuming process (and it often is), but the time saved from unnecessary rewrites of an inadequate program is worth the initial effort.

In the case of Generic Videos, asking the staff to list the kinds of reports they needed revealed two specific output needs. The first is a printed summary report that shows all outstanding rented tapes by state. The second is a way to find and display all of the information about a particular member. You want to be able to display information so that it appears organized and is easy to read and visually pleasing.

Input Requirements

Ask users for suggestions when designing screens and reports.

Input, the ways in which the application will facilitate the collection of the data, also should be considered during the problem definition process. How will the information used by the application be entered and manipulated? A logical method for getting all of the information into the computer must be devised, and once the information is in the computer, you'll need efficient ways to change the data. For example, someone must key in all of the information for an inventory that is being placed on the computer system for the first time. It's easy to think, "Why not just use the APPEND command to enter a record, and let personnel type in all the data they might ever need?" Data integrity is the reason against such an approach; if the data entry screens aren't easy to understand and logically designed, and if verification of the data isn't performed, chances are you'll have a database full of errors. Good design comes from using program control to make the data entry process clear and straightforward.

13

Most database applications must encompass two specific input needs. The first is a way to add new records to the database. You will do this by using not only the APPEND command, but also other commands that make the screen display visually appealing and easy to read. The second is a way to select and edit or delete a particular record in the database. If you outline the output and input requirements of Generic Videos, the list might look like the one in Figure 13-3.

Designing the Program

Well-designed applications are a collection of smaller programs, often referred to as *modules,* each performing a specific function. For example, a payroll accounting application is thought of as one program, but most such applications consist of at least three smaller modules. One module handles accounts receivable, the process of tracking incoming funds; the second module handles accounts payable, the process of paying the bills; and the third module handles the general ledger, a financial balance sheet that shows the funds on hand (see Figure 13-4).

Small modules help you tackle large programming tasks in small steps, which is an important principle of good program design. Many tasks worth performing with a database management system are too large in scope to be done in one simple operation. An inventory system is an excellent example. At first glance, such a system may appear to be just a

Input and output operations for Generic Videos' database system
Figure 13-3.

Generic Videos
Database System

Output Operations
  1. Print summary report
  2. Display member data

Input Operations
  1. Add new records
  2. Edit existing records

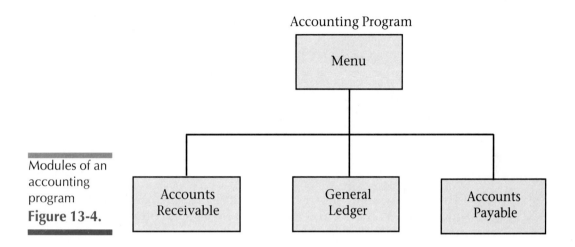

Accounting Program

Menu

Accounts
Receivable

General
Ledger

Accounts
Payable

way of keeping track of the items on hand in a warehouse. Scratch the surface, though, and you'll find that there are numerous modules in such a system. The first module in the system adds items to the inventory as they are received; a second module subtracts inventory items as they are shipped; a third module monitors inventory levels; and if the quantity of an item falls below a specific point, a fourth module alerts the user by printing a message on the screen. Modules interact and exchange information with other modules in the system, but they share one pool of information: the database itself. In addition, finding errors in the program is easier if the program is divided into modules, since the problem can be traced to the modules performing the tasks that may be in error.

It is during the design phase that the general and subsidiary functions of the program are outlined in detail. Remember: any program worth writing is worth outlining on paper. The designer should resist the urge to begin writing programs at the keyboard without first outlining the steps of the program. The outline will help ensure that the intended program design is followed and that no steps are accidentally left out. Outlines are of great help in identifying the smaller tasks to be done by your system.

You'll find that it's best to list the general steps first and then break the general steps into smaller, more precise steps. Let's use the Generic

13

Videos database system as an example. The system should perform these tasks:

✦ Allow new members and new rentals to be added

✦ Allow existing records to be changed (edited)

✦ Display data from a record

✦ Produce reports on all rentals or members

This simple outline shows what is basically required of the database management system. You then add more detail to the outline, as in Figure 13-5.

For purposes of simplicity, a specific requirement for the deleting of records has been omitted from this design. In a complete database system, you would also want to include a specific process for deleting records, as well as for performing file maintenance (such as rebuilding index files and performing a PACK from time to time).

Outline of database management system

Figure 13-5.

Outline of Program Design

1. Allow new entries to be added—APPEND

2. Change (edit) existing entries
   —Show all record numbers and names on the screen
   —Ask the user for the number of the record to edit
   —Edit the selected record

3. Display data regarding a chosen entry
   —Ask the user for the name of the member
   —Search for that name in the database
   —If name is found, print the information contained in all fields of the record

4. Produce reports of all rentals or all members
   —Use the REPORT FORM *filename* command to produce a report

Always provide a way out of your menus.

With so much to think about during the process of designing a program, you can easily overlook how the user will use it. Good program design considers users by including menus. Menus provide the user with a simple way of selecting what he or she would like to do. In a way, they are like a road map of the system; they guide the user through the steps in performing a task. For that reason, menus should be easy to follow, and there should always be a way out of a selection if the user changes his or her mind. In addition, the program should not operate abnormally or crash (stop running) in the event that the user makes an error when entering data.

Writing the Program

Now it's time to write the program. Most applications begin with a menu of choices, so the menu module should be written first. Each selection within the menu should then lead to the part of the program that performs the appropriate function. For example, a Run Report choice on a menu could result in a REPORT FORM command being issued to print a report. An Add New Entries choice could result in an APPEND command that adds data to the database. When you design your own systems, you'll find it helpful to design the menu first and then use it as a starting point for the other modules in the program. In this example, however, you will design the menu module of the program in the next chapter, because it uses various commands that are explained there.

It often helps, particularly if you are new to designing programs, to use pseudocode. Writing *pseudocode* means writing out all the steps of an operation in English. You write the program in pseudocode and then convert it into actual code. For instance, the process that would allow users to display a list of names and edit a particular name would look like this in pseudocode:

1. Open the MEMBERS database.
2. Clear screen.
3. List all names in the database.
4. Ask user for number of record to be edited, and store that number as a variable.

13

5. Edit specified record.

6. Return to main menu.

When you know what steps are needed to perform the task, you store the corresponding commands in a command file. As an example, enter

```
MODIFY COMMAND EDITMEMB
```

to create a new command file called EDITMEMB.PRG. When the Editor appears, enter the following commands and then press (Ctrl)-(W) to save the command file:

```
USE MEMBERS
CLEAR
LIST LASTNAME, FIRSTNAME
INPUT "Edit what record? " TO RECNO
CHANGE RECNO
RETURN
```

Verifying the Program

Any errors in the program are corrected during this step. You also examine the program to see if the needs of all the users have indeed been met; if not, you may need to make changes or additions to some modules. In addition, you should now make any improvements that can speed up the system or minimize user confusion.

The best way to find errors in a program is to use the program, so verify the program's operation by entering

```
DO EDITMEMB
```

The program displays a list of all member names. The corresponding record numbers are shown to the left of the names:

```
Record#    LASTNAME      FIRSTNAME
      1    Miller        Karen
      2    Martin        William
      3    Robinson      Carol
      4    Kramer        Harry
      5    Moore         Ellen
      6    Zachman       David
```

```
7   Robinson    Benjamin
8   Hart        Wendy
```

```
Edit what record?
```

The program now asks for the number of the record that you wish to edit. In response to the prompt, enter **8** (for record 8). If the program works as designed, the edit screen for record 8 should appear. Change the phone number for Wendy Hart to 555-3456, and save the change by pressing [Ctrl]-[W]. (Later, as a convenience for users unfamiliar with FoxPro, you may want to display a message explaining how to save changes.)

You should return to the command level, and for now, that is all that is expected of the program. In later chapters, you'll add commands that use more attractive designs to view and edit data.

Documenting the Program

Documentation of a program takes one of two forms: written directions (like a manual) explaining how the program operates, and comments within the program itself about how the program is designed. The use of clear and simple menus and instructions within the program can help minimize the need for written documentation. A few sentences on how to start FoxPro and run the command file that displays the menu may be sufficient. As for directions and remarks within the program, FoxPro lets you put comments, in the form of text, at any location in a command file. Comments are preceded by an asterisk (*) or by the NOTE command. You can also use the double ampersand (&&) to add comments to the right of a command. When FoxPro sees a line beginning with an asterisk or the word NOTE, no action is taken by the program. And when FoxPro sees a double ampersand at the end of a command line, FoxPro ignores everything that follows it on that line.

Comments are simply an aid to you or any other person who modifies your command files. As an example, this short command file documents the program with NOTE and the asterisk (*):

```
CLEAR
NOTE Display the employees' names
LIST LASTNAME, FIRSTNAME
NOTE Ask for a record number and store it.
```

13

```
INPUT "Edit what record?" TO RECNO
*Edit the record.
EDIT RECNO
RETURN
```

This file may seem to have an overabundance of comments because it does not need elaboration. If a command file consists of dozens of commands, however, comments become more necessary. Not only do they make the program easier to understand, but if any other person must make changes to your FoxPro program, the task will be much easier.

CHAPTER

FOXPRO

14

PROGRAM CONTROL

Using command files to automate the storing and retrieving of records provides you with even more flexibility when you use decision-making conditions to provide control of the program. A program can prompt the user for a response, and the user's response determines what the program does next. To program a condition, you need a way to evaluate user responses and, based on those responses, cause FoxPro to perform certain actions. Similarly, a program can read through a database file and perform different actions depending on the values stored in individual records. In this chapter you use the IF, ELSE, ENDIF, DO WHILE, and ENDDO commands to perform these operations within a program. A number of other commands involved in the control process, such as CANCEL, EXIT, and WAIT, are also covered in this chapter.

Going in Circles

There will be many times when your program will need to perform the same task repeatedly. FoxPro has two commands, DO WHILE and ENDDO, that are used as a matched pair to repeat a series of commands for as long as necessary. The commands that you want to repeat are enclosed between the DO WHILE and the ENDDO commands.

The DO WHILE command always begins the loop, and the ENDDO command normally ends it. The series of commands contained within the DO WHILE loop continues to execute until the condition, specified immediately next to the DO WHILE command, is no longer true. You determine when the loop should stop by specifying the condition; otherwise, the loop could go on indefinitely. The format is

DO WHILE *condition*
          [*commands...*]
ENDDO

As long as the condition within the DO WHILE command is true, the commands between the DO WHILE and the ENDDO commands are executed. Whenever ENDDO is reached, FoxPro returns to the top of the loop and reevaluates the condition. If the condition is true, FoxPro executes the commands within the loop again; if the condition is not true, FoxPro jumps to the command following the ENDDO command. If the condition is false when the DO WHILE command is first encountered, none of the commands in the loop are executed, and the program proceeds to the first command that follows the ENDDO command.

REMEMBER: ENDDO is a matching statement for DO WHILE. For every DO WHILE there must be an ENDDO, or you will encounter errors in your program.

You could use the DO WHILE and ENDDO commands in a command file that will print the names and addresses in the Generic Videos database with triple line spacing between them. Get to the command level and open a command file. Name it TRIPLE by entering

```
MODIFY COMMAND TRIPLE
```

When the FoxPro Editor comes up, you should enter the following command file:

```
SET TALK OFF
USE MEMBERS
SET PRINT ON
DO WHILE .NOT. EOF()
   ? FIRSTNAME + LASTNAME
   ? ADDRESS
   ? CITY + STATE + " " + ZIPCODE
   ?
   ?
   ?
   SKIP
ENDDO
? "Triple report completed."
SET PRINT OFF
EJECT
```

HINT: After indenting lines with [Tab] , you can get back to the left margin with the [Home] key.

Before you save this command file, take a brief look at its design. After such preliminaries as activating the MEMBERS file and routing the

14

output to the printer, the program begins the DO WHILE loop. The condition for DO WHILE is .NOT. EOF(), which simply means, "As long as the end of the file—EOF()—is not reached, continue the DO WHILE loop." The first three statements in the loop print the name and address from the current record. The next three question marks print the three blank lines between each name and address. SKIP moves the pointer down a record each time the body of the DO WHILE loop is executed. (If this command were absent, the pointer would never reach the end of the file, the condition would never be false, and the program would never leave the loop.) The ENDDO command is then reached, so FoxPro returns to the DO WHILE statement to evaluate the condition. If the pointer hasn't reached the end-of-file, the loop is repeated. Once the end-of-file has been reached, FoxPro proceeds past the ENDDO command. The final two commands in the program are executed, and you are returned to the command level.

Indenting the commands between DO WHILE and ENDDO helps you identify the body of the loop. This is especially helpful if you have *nested* DO WHILE loops—a DO WHILE loop within a DO WHILE loop.

After entering the commands in the file, press Ctrl-W to save the command file to disk; then make sure your printer is on, and enter **DO TRIPLE**. The command file will print the names and addresses, triple line spacing each, on your printer.

SCAN and ENDSCAN

Another set of commands you may encounter in working with FoxPro programs are the SCAN and ENDSCAN commands. These commands, like DO WHILE and ENDDO, are a matched pair. Also like DO WHILE and ENDDO, the SCAN and ENDSCAN commands let you create a repetitive loop in which operations are performed for a group of records in a database. The syntax for these commands is

    SCAN [scope] [FOR condition] [WHILE condition]
        [commands...]
    ENDSCAN

The SCAN and ENDSCAN commands are simpler alternatives to the DO WHILE and ENDDO commands. If you simply wish to use DO WHILE

and ENDDO to perform repetitive processing, you can often use SCAN
and ENDSCAN instead, and use slightly fewer lines of programming
code.

As an example, perhaps you want to write a program that, using a DO
WHILE loop, would print the name and tape limit for every person in
the database who has a tape limit of more than three. You could
accomplish the task with a program like this:

```
USE MEMBERS
SET PRINT ON
DO WHILE .NOT. EOF()
    IF TAPELIMIT > 3
        ? LASTNAME, FIRSTNAME
        ?? TAPELIMIT
    ENDIF
    SKIP
ENDDO
```

SCAN and ENDSCAN can save programming effort.

By comparison, you could use the SCAN and ENDSCAN commands to
accomplish the same task. An example of the program code using SCAN
and ENDSCAN is shown here:

```
USE MEMBERS
SET PRINT ON
SCAN FOR TAPELIMIT > 3
        ? LASTNAME, FIRSTNAME
        ?? TAPELIMIT
ENDSCAN
```

Because you combined FOR and WHILE clauses with the SCAN
command to specify the condition (a tape limit greater than three), the
IF and ENDIF conditions are not needed, so fewer lines of program code
accomplish the same task.

FoxPro automatically skips to the next successive record when it
encounters ENDSCAN unless you are at the end of the file. Once the
end of the file is reached, program control drops out of the loop and
moves on to the next command. Note that program control may exit
from the loop before the end of the file is reached if you include a
WHILE clause as a part of the SCAN statement.

IF, ELSE, and ENDIF

In many command files, FoxPro needs to perform different operations depending on a user's response to an option, a previous calculation or operation, or different values encountered in a database. For example, if the user has a choice of editing or printing a record in a main menu, the program must be able to perform the chosen operation. FoxPro uses the IF, ELSE, and ENDIF commands to branch to the part of the program where the chosen operation is performed. Much like the DO WHILE-ENDDO loop, the IF and ENDIF commands are used as a matched pair enclosing a number of commands. The ELSE command is optional and is used within the body of IF-ENDIF as another decision step. The IF command along with the ENDIF command can be used to decide between actions in a program.

The format of the command is

```
IF condition
      [commands...]
ELSE
      [commands...]
ENDIF
```

This decision-making command must always start with IF and end with ENDIF. The commands that you place between the IF and ENDIF commands determine exactly what will occur if the condition is true, unless an ELSE is encountered. (Again, indenting the commands within the body of IF-ENDIF makes the flow of the program easier to follow.) If an ELSE is encountered and the condition specified by ELSE is true, the commands that follow ELSE are carried out.

A good way to write IF and ELSE commands is to write them in pseudocode first and then compare them:

Pseudocode	FoxPro
If last name is Cooke, then display last name.	IF LASTNAME = "Cooke" ? LASTNAME ENDIF
If monthly rent is less than $300, then display "Reasonably priced."	IF RENTMONTH < 300 ? "Reasonably priced." ENDIF

Using IF and ENDIF alone works fine for making a single decision, but if you wish to add an alternative choice, you need the ELSE statement:

Pseudocode	FoxPro

If last name is Cooke, then print last name; or else print "There is no one by that name in this database."	IF LASTNAME = "Cooke"
	  ? LASTNAME
	ELSE
	  ? "There is no one by that name in this database."
	ENDIF

FoxPro evaluates the condition following the IF command to see if any action should be taken. If no action is necessary, FoxPro simply moves on to the next command after the ENDIF command. In this example, if SALARY is not 10, the STORE command is not executed and FoxPro proceeds to the command following ENDIF:

```
IF SALARY = 10
     STORE SALARY TO MATCH
ENDIF
```

You can also use multiple IF-ENDIF commands if you need to have the program make more than one decision. Consider this example:

```
? "Enter 1 to print mailing labels or 2 to edit."
INPUT "What is your choice?" TO CHOICE
IF CHOICE = 1
     DO TRIPLE
ENDIF
IF CHOICE = 2
     DO CHANGES
ENDIF
```

The answer that the user types is stored in a variable called CHOICE. One of three things can happen then, depending on whether the user types a 1 or a 2 in response to the question. If CHOICE equals 1, the TRIPLE program is run from disk. If CHOICE equals 2, the CHANGES program is run. If CHOICE does not equal 1 or 2, the program proceeds to the next command after the ENDIF command.

14

Nesting IF-ENDIFs

You can use the nested IF-ENDIF statements, which are the IF-ENDIF statements placed inside of the other IF-ENDIF statements. For the innermost IF-ENDIF statement to be processed, the condition tested by the outermost IF-ENDIF statement must be true. The following is an example of a nested IF-ENDIF statement:

```
INPUT "Display report on (S)creen or (P)rinter?" TO ANS
IF UPPER(ANS) = "P"
     INPUT "Ready printer, press Enter, or type C then;
     press Enter to cancel report." TO ANS2
     IF UPPER(ANS2) = "C"
          *user canceled print run.
          RETURN
     ENDIF
     REPORT FORM MEMBERS TO PRINT
     EJECT
ENDIF
```

In this example, whether the innermost IF-ENDIF is ever processed is determined by the response supplied to the outermost IF-ENDIF statement. If the user does not type P for printer, FoxPro skips ahead to the outermost ENDIF statement. If the user does respond with P for printer, FoxPro displays the "Ready printer" message, and the innermost IF-ENDIF tests for a response and takes appropriate action.

HINT: If you are going to nest IF-ENDIF statements, indenting helps you keep track of whether you have a matching statement (an ENDIF for each IF).

The Immediate IF Function

Within programs, you may want to make use of the IIF (Immediate IF) function. The syntax for the function is

IIF(*condition, expression1, expression2*)

The IIF
function can
replace many
uses of
IF-ENDIF
statements.

If the condition specified is true, FoxPro returns the first expression; if
the condition is false, FoxPro returns the second expression. As an
example, the statement

```
CREDITOK = IIF(INCOME>=15000, "yes", "no")
```

would, when processed in a program, store a character expression of
"yes" to the CREDITOK variable if the amount in INCOME was equal to
or greater than 15,000. In effect, this statement performs the same task
as the following commands:

```
IF INCOME >= 15000
    CREDITOK = "yes"
ELSE
    CREDITOK = "no"
ENDIF
```

The advantage of the Immediate IF function is that it takes fewer lines
of code to accomplish the same task, and it is executed slightly faster.

Using the IF-ENDIF Statement

You can use the IF-ENDIF statement in a command file to search for
and display the data regarding a specific entry in the database. If you
want to find a member named Zachman, you can use the ACCEPT and
IF-ENDIF commands to search for the record. (This operation can be
done faster with SEEK, but for demonstration purposes, a combination
of IF and DO WHILE is used here.)

First let's use pseudocode to outline what needs to be done:

```
USE MEMBERS database.
ACCEPT the last name.
BEGIN the DO-WHILE loop.
IF the Lastname field = the ACCEPT variable,
PRINT (on the screen) name, address, tape limit, and expiration date.
END the IF test.
SKIP forward one record.
END the DO-WHILE loop.
RETURN to the command level.
```

Now create a command file by entering

```
MODIFY COMMAND SHOWMEMB
```

When the FoxPro Editor appears, enter the following command file:

```
*This program finds and shows data in the members file.
USE MEMBERS
SET TALK OFF
CLEAR
*Begin loop that contains commands to display record.
ACCEPT "Search for what last name? " TO SNAME
DO WHILE .NOT. EOF()
     IF LASTNAME = SNAME
          ? "Last name is: "
          ?? LASTNAME
          ? "First name is: "
          ?? FIRSTNAME
          ? "Address is: "
          ?? ADDRESS
          ? CITY + STATE + " " + ZIPCODE
          ?
          ? "Tape limit is: "
          ?? TAPELIMIT
          ? "Expiration Date is: "
          ?? EXPIREDATE
          ?
     ENDIF
     SKIP
ENDDO
WAIT
RETURN
```

After saving the file with [Ctrl]-[W], try the program by entering **DO SHOWMEMB**. In response to the last-name prompt that appears on the screen, enter **Zachman**, and FoxPro searches the database for the record containing Zachman. Run the program again and enter **Robinson**. You will see the records for both Robinsons displayed.

In this search you used the ACCEPT, IF, and ENDIF commands. The ACCEPT command stored the name that you entered into the memory variable SNAME. The IF loop began a decision-making process that stated the condition, "If the memory variable SNAME contains the same name as the Lastname field, then execute the commands that follow the IF command."

There is no limit to the number of commands that you can place between IF and ENDIF in the loop. You can also link multiple IF-ENDIF and ELSE commands if multiple choices are needed within a program.

Using Case to Evaluate Multiple Choices

Your program may need to make more than two or three decisions from a single response. A series of IF-ENDIF statements could do the job, but using more than three IF-ENDIFs to test the value of one field or memory variable is unwieldy. There is an easier way: the CASE statement. With the CASE statement, the IF-ENDIF tests are made into cases, and FoxPro then chooses the first case, the second case, or another case.

The CASE statement is a matched pair of DO CASE and ENDCASE. All choices are declared between DO CASE and ENDCASE. OTHERWISE is treated exactly like the ELSE in an IF-ENDIF statement. The general format is

```
DO CASE
      CASE condition
      [commands...]
      [CASE condition...]
      [commands...]
      [OTHERWISE]
      [commands...]
ENDCASE
```

Whenever FoxPro encounters a DO CASE command, it examines each case until it finds a condition that is true; then it executes the commands below CASE until it encounters the next CASE statement or ENDCASE, whichever comes first.

If you want to create a menu that offers to display a record, print labels, edit a record, or add a record, you could create the following command file:

14

```
CLEAR
? "1. Display a membership record"
?
? "2. Print the membership database"
?
? "3. Change a membership record"
?
INPUT "Choose a selection " TO SELECT
DO CASE
     CASE SELECT = 1
          DO SHOWMEMB
     CASE SELECT = 2
          DO TRIPLE
     CASE SELECT = 3
          DO EDITMEMB
ENDCASE
```

Remember, every CASE statement requires a matching ENDCASE statement.

In this example, FoxPro queries the user for a selection with the INPUT statement (the SHOWMEMB file for the first selection was created in the last chapter). When the user enters the choice, it is stored in the SELECT variable. Then, in the DO CASE series, FoxPro examines the SELECT variable for each CASE until it finds one that matches the value of SELECT. Once a match has been found, no other CASE statement is evaluated. If no match is found, FoxPro proceeds to the next statement after the ENDCASE command. Like IF-ENDIF, the DO CASE and END-CASE commands are used in pairs. You must always end a CASE series with an ENDCASE command.

You should use DO CASE to process menu selections if you have more than three choices. For example, if you wanted to offer the same three selections from the last program using IF-ENDIF and ELSE, the command file might look like this:

```
CLEAR
? "1. Display a membership record"
?
? "2. Print the membership database"
?
? "3. Change a membership record"
?
INPUT "Choose a selection" TO SELECT
IF SELECT = 1
     DO SHOWMEMB
```

```
ENDIF
IF SELECT = 2
     DO TRIPLE
ENDIF
IF SELECT = 3
     DO EDITMEMB
ENDIF
```

Using IF-ENDIF becomes more complex than DO CASE as the number of choices increases.

Let's use a CASE statement to create a main menu for the users of the Generic Videos database. Enter **MODIFY COMMAND MENU1**, and when the FoxPro Editor appears, enter the following command file:

```
USE MEMBERS
SET TALK OFF
STORE 0 TO CHOICE
DO WHILE CHOICE < > 5
CLEAR
 * Display the menu.
? "Generic Videos Membership System Menu"
?
? " 1. Add a new entry to the database."
? " 2. Change an existing entry."
? " 3. Produce the membership report."
? " 4. Display data regarding a particular member."
? " 5. Exit this program."
INPUT "Enter selection: " TO CHOICE
DO CASE
        CASE CHOICE=1
             APPEND
        CASE CHOICE=2
             DO EDITMEMB
        CASE CHOICE=3
             REPORT FORM SAMPLE
        CASE CHOICE=4
             DO SHOWMEMB
        CASE CHOICE=5
             CLOSE DATABASES
             SET TALK ON
             RETURN
        ENDCASE
ENDDO
```

14

There are five choices, and the INPUT command stores the response in the corresponding CHOICE variable. When FoxPro finds a matching choice, it executes the command or commands that follow that choice.

Save this command file by pressing (Ctrl)-(W). When the prompt reappears, enter **DO MENU1**. Try some of the menu choices on your own to see how the system operates.

EXIT

The EXIT command is used when you are within a DO WHILE programming loop. EXIT lets FoxPro exit from a DO WHILE-ENDDO loop to the first command below ENDDO. An EXIT command arbitrarily placed within a DO WHILE loop prevents FoxPro from ever reaching the commands below EXIT to ENDDO; thus, EXIT makes sense only if it is executed conditionally. For this reason, you will frequently find EXIT commands with IF-ENDIF and CASE statements.

Consider the following example in a program that lists a name based on a desired address. The same task could be done with a LOCATE command, but to demonstrate the EXIT command, this program uses a DO WHILE loop.

```
USE MEMBERS
SET TALK OFF
GO TOP
ACCEPT "What is the address- " TO CHOICE
DO WHILE .NOT. EOF()
      IF ADDRESS = CHOICE
            ? LASTNAME, FIRSTNAME
            EXIT
      ENDIF
      SKIP
ENDDO
```

If the contents of Address, a field, match CHOICE, a variable, the EXIT command causes the DO WHILE loop to terminate. If no match is found, the commands below the IF statement are executed and finally drop from the loop when the last record is accessed.

Use EXIT commands conservatively: a program that is always jumping out of loops—and around the program, for that matter—is difficult to follow and debug and is contrary to good program design. Most DO WHILEs that have EXITs can be redesigned without them.

CANCEL

The CANCEL command exits a FoxPro command file and returns you to the command level. It can be useful when you are testing various commands and program files. However, using CANCEL in a completed FoxPro program may be unwise. CANCEL drops the user at the command level, and the inexperienced user may not know how to exit FoxPro to DOS or return to the program. QUIT is used more often to exit programs and return to the DOS prompt. You can add a selection at the main menu that allows the user to get out of FoxPro and back to the computer's operating system when the work is completed.

WAIT

The WAIT command halts execution of a FoxPro program until a key is pressed. WAIT can also display a message or prompt and store the value of the key pressed as a character variable. The normal format of the command is

```
WAIT [prompt] [TO memory-variable]
```

Both *prompt* and *memory-variable* are optional. If a prompt is not specified, FoxPro supplies the message "Press any key to continue..." as a default prompt. As an example, to display a message, halt execution of a program until a key is pressed, and store that key as a variable named ANSWER, you could use the following command:

```
WAIT "Enter Y to begin processing transactions, any other key
to continue:" TO ANSWER
```

You could then use an IF-ELSE-ENDIF structure to test the value of ANSWER and take different actions depending on the result.

ZAP

The ZAP command is a one-step command for erasing all records from a database while leaving the structure of the database intact. Using ZAP is functionally equivalent to entering **DELETE ALL** and then entering

PACK. However, ZAP operates considerably faster than a DELETE ALL command followed by a PACK command.

If you include ZAP in a program, you may want to include a SET SAFETY OFF command near the start of the program; this tells FoxPro not to ask for confirmation before erasing all records from the file.

Using Programming Macros

FoxPro has a handy macro-substitution function. It is used specifically within programs and is not to be confused with the types of macros covered in Chapter 9. Macro substitution works like this: an ampersand (&) is placed in front of a memory variable name, and the combination of ampersand and variable name becomes the FoxPro macro. Then, whenever FoxPro sees the macro, it replaces it with the contents of the memory variable.

If, for example, you had a memory variable called NAME, you could store names of people in variables at different times during a program. When you prefix NAME with an ampersand (&), it becomes a macro. Each time FoxPro encounters &NAME, it references the value of &NAME instead of the name of the variable. Try a macro operation by entering the following commands from the command level:

```
USE MEMBERS
INDEX ON LASTNAME TO NAME
STORE "Zachman" TO TEST
FIND &TEST
DISPLAY
```

Commands that use literal values require macros if they are to treat the value as a variable. One such command is FIND. With the FIND command, you are normally required to enter the literal value, or the actual name of the item to be found. With the macro function, however, you are able to substitute a variable for the actual name. In the example just shown, you could have easily specified the contents of the variable instead of creating the variable to use as a macro; using macros saves time in programming, since the variable will probably have been declared.

You can use macro substitution in response to a user's query to search a database selectively for information, and once you have found the item you can edit or delete it. An example of these techniques is used in a routine for editing records discussed in the following chapter.

CHAPTER

FOXPRO

15
PROGRAMMING FOR DATA ENTRY AND EDITING

FoxPro can help you design screen displays that won't confuse the people who use your database management system. The appearance of screen displays may at first seem like a minor point of importance, but if you were a new FoxPro system user, which screen display would be easier to use: the top screen in Figure 15-1 or the bottom screen? Obviously, the bottom screen will make more sense to the novice FoxPro user; it is clearer and less cluttered than the top screen.

Generic Video Membership System
1. Add new entries
2. Change an entry
3. Print reports
4. Display member data
5. Exit system

Generic Videos Membership Data System
Add Members
Edit Members
Print Reports
Display Member Data
Exit System

Two screen
displays
Figure 15-1.

As you will see in this chapter, you can easily create well-designed screens by storing various screen-display commands within a FoxPro command file. You'll use the @ command and the SAY and GET options to place prompts and information at selected locations on the screen, and the READ option to allow responses to the prompts displayed by the system. You can use the PROMPT and MENU TO commands to create, with relative ease, pop-up menus similar to those used by FoxPro. You'll also examine how the forms design screen can provide most of the commands needed for the formatting of screens.

Putting Information on the Screen

The @ command (commonly referred to as the "AT" command) tells FoxPro where to place the cursor on the screen. The FoxPro screen is divided into 25 lines and 80 columns, as shown in Figure 15-2. Rows are numbered from 0 to 24, and columns are numbered from 0 to 79. Row 0, column 0 is in the upper-left corner of the screen; row 24, column 79 is in the lower-right corner. The cursor can be placed in any screen position.

Columns

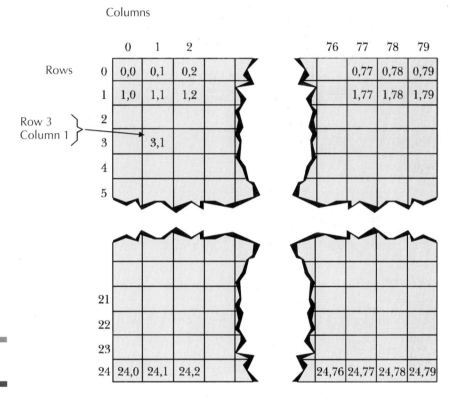

FoxPro screen
Figure 15-2.

Once the cursor has been placed in the proper position with the @ command, you can print a message with the SAY option. The SAY option causes the text or the contents of a string variable that follows the command to appear on the screen. The SAY option can be used, along with the @ command, in one of these two possible ways:

@ *row,column* SAY "*message*"
@ *row,column* SAY *varname*

In the first format, SAY is followed by one or more characters, which must be enclosed by double or single quotes. (You should use double quotes whenever there is an apostrophe in the message itself.) The characters are displayed on the screen exactly as they appear between the quotes. In the second format, *varname* is a variable name. Any value that your program stores in that variable is displayed.

To try the first format, let's display a message beginning at row 12, column 40 on the screen. Get to the command level, and then enter

```
CLEAR
@ 12,40 SAY "Enter name."
```

This displays the prompt "Enter name." beginning at row 12, column 40 on the screen.

You can try the second format by entering this:

```
STORE 1200.57 TO AMOUNT
@ 6,30 SAY AMOUNT
```

This stores 1200.57 in the AMOUNT variable and then displays the value at row 6, column 30.

HINT: When calculating screen locations, figure the possible length of an expression to be sure it will fit.

Keep in mind when you use the @ command and SAY option to design screen displays that the coordinates for the edges of the screen may or may not actually be displayed at your screen's edges. Some monitors cut off the edges, so to be safe you may want to stay away from the outer edges of the screen.

You can erase any part of the screen with the @ command and CLEAR option. The format is

@ row,column CLEAR

The screen beginning at *row,column* will be erased to the lower-right corner. You use the @ command and CLEAR option in a manner similar to the @ command and SAY option, but don't enter any prompts or variables after the word "CLEAR." For example, the command

```
@ 9,7 CLEAR
```

erases the screen beginning at 9,7 to the lower-right corner.

Using GET and READ with @ and SAY

Now that you know how to display information at selected places on the screen, you need a way to store responses to screen prompts. This is done with the GET and READ options, which in combination display existing variables or field names and the field length of the record being referenced by the pointer, and store the typed replies to screen messages and prompts. There are two formats:

> @ *row,column* SAY "*prompt*" GET *varname*... READ
> @ *row,column* SAY "*prompt*" GET *fieldname*... READ

The GET option tells FoxPro to get ready to accept information. The information displayed with GET can be either an existing memory variable or any field in the database in use. The READ option then tells FoxPro to enter Edit mode, which, much like Append mode, allows the user to move the cursor around the screen, to accept responses from the keyboard for any of the preceding GET options, and to store the responses in memory. In addition, the READ option lets you edit the displayed information. A READ command applies to all GET statements between the READ option and any previous use of the READ option, or the start of the program, whichever is closest.

A GET option does not have to be immediately followed by a READ option; it can be the last command in a series of GET statements. But if you use GET without READ, you cannot enter any responses from the keyboard. READ options are only used following GET options.

You could, for example, create a command file like this one:

```
@ 5,10 SAY "Enter name." GET LASTNAME
@ 7,10 SAY "Enter address." GET ADDRESS
@ 9,10 SAY "Enter city." GET CITY
@ 11,10 SAY "Enter state." GET STATE
READ
```

If you were to use the database containing the field names and run this command file, FoxPro would provide a screen display that prompts you for the desired information. The prompts would appear at the screen locations identified by the @ command and SAY option. Once the READ option was encountered, full-screen Edit mode would be entered, and the cursor would be placed at the start of the first area identified by a GET option. As data is entered, FoxPro stores all of the entries in memory under the field names or variable names used. The name would be stored in Lastname, the address in Address, the city in City, and so on. Once a READ occurs, data entered under the field names is written to the database file itself.

You could also use the INPUT command along with a prompt to place information on the screen and store a response, but with INPUT, it is not easy to specify where on the screen the information appears. The example that follows combines the use of the @ command and the SAY, GET, and READ options along with the PROMPT and MENU TO commands to produce a clear, well-designed menu screen.

Working with Memo Fields

Although you can use the name of a memo field along with the @-SAY-GET commands like those just shown, you will probably want to take advantage of better ways to enter and edit data in memo fields. If you include a memo field in a command file, as in

```
@ 12, 5 SAY "Preferences? " GET PREFERENCE
```

the field appears in a small box containing the word "memo," and you will have to use the same editing techniques discussed earlier to enter and exit the memo field. If you instead make use of the MODIFY MEMO command, you can automatically open a window for the editing of a memo field. The syntax for the command is

Use MODIFY MEMO to edit a memo field within a window.

MODIFY MEMO *field1* [,*field2*...] [NOWAIT]

When processed in a program, the command automatically opens a window for each of the named memo fields. The contents of the memo field for the current record appear in the window, and the window(s) remain open until closed with the usual methods for closing windows.

The MODIFY MEMO command can be entered from the command level or within a program to modify the contents of a memo field; the

NOWAIT option is used only within programs. Normally, a program halts while the window is open and continues when the window is closed. You can add the NOWAIT option to tell FoxPro to open the window and continue execution of the program.

In the case of the MEMBERS database, a program specifically designed to edit the contents of the Preference field might resemble the following:

```
*EditMemo.PRG edits memo field.
USE MEMBERS
INPUT "Which record number? " TO FINDIT
GOTO FINDIT
CLEAR
@ 22, 5 SAY "Member: " + TRIM(FIRSTNAME) + " " + LASTNAME
MODIFY MEMO PREFERENCE
RETURN
```

Your programs will probably use a more detailed method to search for the desired record, but this simple example demonstrates the use of the MODIFY MEMO command. Once the desired record number has been entered, the member name appears near the bottom of the screen and the memo field opens within a window. Editing of the memo field can be performed, and the window can be moved or resized as desired. When the window is closed, the RETURN statement in the program exits this routine.

Customizing a Data Entry Screen

One area of the system that could stand improvement is in the adding of data. Currently, the system relies on the APPEND command. With the @ command and the SAY, GET, and READ options, you can display the prompts more neatly than you can with the APPEND command, and you can store the data in the fields of the database.

Let's create a new command file called ADDER that will be used whenever you want to add a record to the database. Enter **MODIFY COMMAND ADDER**, and enter the following as the command file:

```
USE MEMBERS
CLEAR
@ 0,5,14,60 BOX
APPEND BLANK
```

```
@ 1,10 SAY "      Social Sec." GET SOCIAL
@ 2,10 SAY "        Lastname:" GET LASTNAME
@ 3,10 SAY "       Firstname:" GET FIRSTNAME
@ 4,10 SAY "         Address:" GET ADDRESS
@ 5,10 SAY "            City:" GET CITY
@ 6,10 SAY "           State:" GET STATE
@ 7,10 SAY "       ZIP Code:" GET ZIPCODE
@ 8,10 SAY "       Telephone:" GET PHONE
@ 9,10 SAY "      Birth date:" GET BIRTHDAY
@ 10,10 SAY " Expiration Date:" GET EXPIREDATE
@ 11,10 SAY "      Tape limit:" GET TAPELIMIT
@ 12,10 SAY "           Beta?:" GET BETA
READ
MODIFY MEMO PREFERENCE
RETURN
```

Examine this command file before saving it. After opening the file with USE, clearing the screen, and using the @...BOX command to draw a box, you then use the BLANK option of the APPEND command. Whenever FoxPro sees APPEND BLANK as a command, it adds a blank record to the end of the database, and the record pointer is positioned at the last record. Each @ command and SAY option prints a query, such as "Birth Date:". The GET option not only displays the contents of each field listed, but it displays them in reverse video in the dimensions of the field width. Since the record pointer is referencing the last record, which is empty, only the reverse video is displayed. The READ command toward the bottom of the file activates the full-screen entry and editing specified by the GET options. When data entry or editing has been completed for the last field, you return to the main menu section of the program.

Press Ctrl-W to save the command file. Now you'll need to make one change in the main menu command file to integrate the new ADDER command file into the system. Enter **MODIFY COMMAND MENU1** to change the program. Delete the USE MEMBERS line directly underneath CASE CHOICE = 1, and change APPEND in the command file to **DO ADDER**. Then, press Ctrl-W to save the file.

Try out the new command file by entering **DO MENU1**. Choose the first option on the menu, and try entering a new member of your own choosing.

Using PICTURE

Use PICTURE to restrict data entry.

The PICTURE option is used with the @ command to format data. Using PICTURE, you can display dollar amounts with both commas and decimal places, or you can display dates in American or European date formats. PICTURE restricts the way data can be entered into the system. You can accept numbers only, for dollar amounts, or a date only, rejecting any other characters.

The PICTURE option is divided into function and template symbols (see Table 15-1). The format is

@ *row,column* SAY *expression* PICTURE "*clause*"

You use the PICTURE option by adding the word PICTURE and then the letters or symbols that specify the function or template. The functions or templates in the clause are surrounded by quotes. An @ symbol must appear as the first character in a function.

Two examples of the PICTURE option are shown here:

```
@ 12,40 SAY "Enter effective date-" GET PICTURE "@E"
@ 14,20 SAY "Customer name is: "LASTNAME PIC-
TURE"!!!!!!!!!!!!!!!!!!"
```

In the first example, the @ symbol after the word PICTURE defines the clause as a function. The letter E defines the function as European date format. A template is used in the second example. The exclamation points in the template will result in a display of uppercase letters, regardless of how the letters were stored in the database.

Some of the functions used with PICTURE apply only to certain kinds of data. The C, X, B, (, and Z functions apply only to numeric data. The @ and ! functions apply to character data only, but the D and E functions apply to date, character, and numeric data.

You can combine function symbols for multiple functions. For example, the function symbols BZ align numeric data at the left side of the field and display any zero values as blanks.

You can get a better idea of how the PICTURE option is used if you try a few examples. First let's try the X and C functions. The X function will display DB, for debit, after a negative number, and the C function will

Symbol	Meaning
	FUNCTIONS
A	Displays alphabetic characters only
B	Left-justifies numeric data
C	Displays CR for credit, after a positive number
D	Displays American date format
E	Displays European date format
X	Displays DB for debit, after a negative number
Z	Displays any zeros as blanks
!	Displays capital letters only
(	Surrounds negative numbers with parentheses
.	*TEMPLATES*
9	Allows only digits for character data, or digits and signs for numeric data
#	Allows only digits, blanks, and signs
A	Allows only letters
L	Allows only logical data (.T. or .F.; .Y. or .N.)
N	Allows only letters and digits
X	Allows any characters
!	Converts letters to uppercase
$	Displays dollar signs in place of leading zeros
*	Displays asterisks in place of leading zeros
.	Specifies a decimal position
,	Displays a comma if there are any numbers to the left of the comma

Functions and Templates Used with PICTURE

Table 15-1.

display CR, for credit, after a positive number. Try the following commands to illustrate these functions:

15

```
CLEAR
STORE -1650.32 TO A
STORE 795 TO B
@5,0 SAY A PICTURE "@X"
@10,0 SAY B PICTURE "@C"
```

The results are as follows:

```
1650.32 DB
```

```
795 CR
```

This is useful in accounting.

The ! template is useful when you want character displays to appear in all uppercase letters. Try this:

```
CLEAR
STORE "small words" TO WORDS
@10,10 SAY WORDS PICTURE "@!"
```

Use # to force spaces within templates.

The # template reserves space for digits, blanks, or signs, and the comma template specifies where the comma should appear in numeric data. Try these templates with the following example:

```
STORE 1234.56 TO A
@16,0 SAY A PICTURE "#,###.##"
```

```
1,234.56
```

When you are using templates, you must use a symbol for each character that is to be displayed with SAY or GET. To display a character field that is ten characters wide in uppercase, for example, you would need ten exclamation points in the template. The template would look like this:

```
@20,10 SAY "Name is—+"NAME PICTURE "!!!!!!!!!!"
```

Let's try a PICTURE option in the command file for adding a record. Enter **MODIFY COMMAND ADDER**. Change the line of the program that reads

```
@ 1,10 SAY "Social Sec.: " GET SOCIAL
```

to this:

```
@ 1,10 SAY "Social Sec.: " GET SOCIAL PICTURE "999-99-9999"
```

Note the use of the hyphens in this example. Any characters that are not valid template symbols are displayed as literal data; hence, they are called *literals*. In this picture template, the hyphens are literals, while the 9s are valid template symbols.

Save the program with Ctrl-W, and then run the system with **DO MENU1**. Choose the Add New Entries option and enter another record. You'll see the new format caused by the PICTURE specification as you enter the social security number; the hyphens will automatically be added. You can get out of the system without making changes to the database by pressing the Esc key and then choosing the Exit System option to return to the command level.

Note that when you use functions and templates along with a GET command, as you did in this example, the data is stored in the specified format, and is not just displayed that way (as with the SAY command). The use of functions and templates along with GET commands can be very useful for forcing data entries into uppercase.

Using Format Files

Let's say that you wanted to enter only last names, first names, and membership expiration dates without being required to step through all of the other fields that normally appear on the screen—addresses, phone numbers, birth dates, and so on. You can limit the amount of information shown on a screen in either Append mode or Change mode by using a format file. A *format file* is a special file with the extension .FMT that contains an @ command and SAY and GET options; it displays messages and prompts according to your arrangements. Once you have created the format file, you can implement it with the SET FORMAT TO command. For an example, create a format file with the Editor by entering

```
MODIFY COMMAND QUICKIE.FMT
```

This creates a file called QUICKIE with the format extension .FMT. Now enter the following commands:

```
@ 10,10 SAY "The last name is: " GET LASTNAME
@ 12,10 SAY "The first name is: " GET FIRSTNAME
@ 14,10 SAY "The expiration date is: " GET EXPIREDATE
```

Press Ctrl-W to save the format file. When the prompt reappears, enter

```
USE MEMBERS
GO TOP
CHANGE
```

Notice that what you see is the normal editing screen with all of its fields. Press Esc to get back to the command level.

To use the format file, you must use the SET FORMAT TO filename command (you don't have to supply the .FMT extension). Enter

```
SET FORMAT TO QUICKIE
```

Now enter **APPEND**. With the new format file in effect, only the specified fields are shown. Press Esc to leave APPEND without making changes.

Now enter **GOTO 5**. This moves the pointer to record 5. Enter **CHANGE**. Instead of the normal editing screen, you get just those fields specified in the format file that apply to record 5. Press Esc to get out of Edit mode without making any changes. To disable a format file when you finish using it, simply enter **CLOSE FORMAT** without specifying a file name (because only one format file may be opened at a time). Enter **CLOSE FORMAT** now, before proceeding.

REMEMBER: The PICTURE and FUNCTION templates discussed earlier can be used in format files.

Format files can come in handy when you want to use the same screen format many times in different parts of a program. You can include SET FORMAT TO *filename* anywhere in a FoxPro command file, and the resulting format file will take effect for any appending or editing until you use CLOSE FORMAT.

Using Windows

One of FoxPro's greatest assets, which you should not ignore when designing programs, is its ability to display information within windows. From the prior use of commands like BROWSE and EDIT, it is obvious that FoxPro lets you add and edit data within windows, and it should also be clear by now that you can open multiple windows at the same time and place them at various locations on the screen. What may not be obvious is that you can use certain window-related commands within programs to display or edit data inside of windows.

There are three often-used commands that relate to window management within FoxPro.

✦ DEFINE WINDOW *windowname* is used to define the screen coordinates (location) and the display attributes for a window.

✦ ACTIVATE WINDOW *windowname* [ALL] is used to activate a window that has been defined. Once activated, all screen output appears in the window until another window is activated or until the current window is deactivated. The ALL option, when used, activates all previously defined windows, and current screen output appears in the last window to be defined.

✦ DEACTIVATE WINDOW *windowname* [ALL] is used to deactivate, or turn off, an active window. The ALL option, when used, deactivates all active windows.

To use windows in your program, you first use the DEFINE WINDOW command to define as many windows as will be needed (one DEFINE WINDOW command is used for each window). Window names can be up to ten characters in length. Then, as you need to display data in a window, you use the ACTIVATE WINDOW command to make the window active. When you are done with the window, you use the DEACTIVATE WINDOW command to deactivate the window.

Defining the Window

A number of options can be used with the DEFINE WINDOW command to control the appearance and colors of the window. All of the options are covered in detail in Appendix A; for now, some of them are detailed along with this command:

15

DEFINE WINDOW *windowname* FROM *row1,col1* TO *row2,col2*
[TITLE *character-expression*][DOUBLE/PANEL/NONE]
[SHADOW/NOSHADOW] [COLOR *standard/enhanced*[,*border*]]
[COLOR SCHEME *n*]

The *row1,col1* coordinates indicate the row and column number for the upper-left corner of the window. The *row2,col2* coordinates indicate the row and column number of the lower-right corner of the window. The TITLE option, followed by a character expression, defines an optional title. If it is used, the expression appears as a title at the top of the window.

Use PANEL to make your windows resemble standard FoxPro windows.

The DOUBLE, PANEL, and NONE options can be used to define a different border for the window. The default border, if no option is specified, is a single-line box. DOUBLE causes the window to have a double-line box. PANEL gives the window a panel border like that used by FoxPro for editing and browsing. NONE specifies no border.

The SHADOW and NOSHADOW options specify whether or not a shadow appears beneath the window. You must have used a SET SHADOWS ON command earlier in the program before any shadows that you define take effect.

The COLOR option lets you define color attributes for the window. The appropriate letters separated by a slash indicate standard and enhanced colors; separate the standard color pair from the enhanced color pair with a comma. The first letter in the pair is the foreground, and the second letter is the background. The color codes are as follows:

Black N	Yellow GR+
Cyan BG	Blue B
White W	Magenta RB
Blank X	Brown GR
Green G	Red R

For example, you could define the window as having the standard colors of a black-on-white background, and the enhanced colors of a blue-on-red background, by adding an option like this one to the DEFINE WINDOW command:

```
COLOR N/W, B/R
```

You can also use the COLOR SCHEME option to define the window colors. Use COLOR SCHEME followed by a number from 1 to 11 to set the window to one of the standard FoxPro color schemes. (See SET COLOR in Appendix A for more details on the color schemes.) For example, the standard user menus in FoxPro use color scheme 2, while the default Browse window uses color scheme 10. Hence, if you were to add the optional clause

```
COLOR SCHEME 10
```

to a DEFINE WINDOW command, the window would use the same default colors as the FoxPro Browse window. (Note that if you don't like the colors in a color scheme, you can use the Colors option of the Window menu to change them.)

You can use as many optional clauses as you need with the exception of both SET COLOR and COLOR SCHEME (it would make sense to use either SET COLOR or COLOR SCHEME to define the colors, but not both options at the same time). Here is an example of a window definition:

```
DEFINE WINDOW members1 FROM 8,8 TO 22,75 PANEL SHADOW
COLOR SCHEME 2
```

This defines a window with a panel border and a shadow underneath, with its upper-left corner at row 8, column 8 of the screen. The window's lower-right corner is at row 22, column 75 of the screen. The window colors are the same as those of color scheme 2, which is used by the FoxPro user menus.

Activating and Using the Window

Once you have defined the window with the DEFINE WINDOW command, use the ACTIVATE WINDOW *windowname* command to activate, or turn on, the window. When you activate a window, all screen output appears inside that window. When you use @-SAY commands to place data inside a window, it is important to realize that the coordinates are now *relative* to the window. This means that row 0, column 0 is no longer the upper-left corner of the screen; it is now the upper-left corner of the window. It remains that way until you stop using the window with a DEACTIVATE WINDOW command. It is important to grasp this point to avoid errors in your program. If, for example, you activate a window that is only 5 rows deep and you then try to display data at row 15, your program will halt with a "Position is off the screen" error message because the window you are using has no row 15.

You can use the LIST or DISPLAY command to display data without worrying about screen locations, and the data will be contained completely within the window. If the data wraps around lines in an unattractive fashion, you can either change the size of the window to fit more data or include fewer fields in the LIST or DISPLAY command. And you can activate a window and then use a BROWSE, CHANGE, or EDIT command to allow changes inside the window (although this is not generally necessary, since BROWSE, CHANGE, and EDIT cause windows to open on their own). You might find such a technique useful if for some reason you wanted a Browse or Edit window of a specific size to appear at a specific screen location.

Deactivating the Window

Once you are done with the window, use the DEACTIVATE WINDOW *windowname* command to turn off the window. Screen output is then restored to the normal screen. If you have activated a number of windows, you can use the ALL clause in place of a window name with the command, and all the windows will be deactivated.

An Example of Window Use

Assuming you've created the MEMBERS and RENTALS files in earlier chapters, you can try the following program to see how multiple windows can be used to visually highlight your application. Perhaps Generic Videos would like a program that asks for a user's name, displays the corresponding tape limit and membership expiration date, and then displays all tapes rented by that member. The program shown here presents the information inside of multiple windows, using shadows and different colors.

```
*windows.prg shows off window use.
STORE SPACE(15) TO MLAST
SET SHADOWS ON
```

```
DEFINE WINDOW members1 FROM 5,5 TO 9,50 PANEL SHADOW COLOR;
SCHEME 1
DEFINE WINDOW rentals1 FROM 8,8 TO 22,75 PANEL SHADOW COLOR;
SCHEME 2
DEFINE WINDOW askthem FROM 3,15 TO 6,45 PANEL SHADOW COLOR;
SCHEME 3
USE MEMBERS INDEX NAME
ACTIVATE WINDOW askthem
@ 1,1 SAY "Last name? " GET MLAST
READ
SEEK MLAST
IF .NOT. FOUND()
    @ 1,1 SAY "NAME NOT FOUND IN DATABASE!"
    WAIT
    DEACTIVATE WINDOW askthem
    CLOSE DATABASES
    RETURN
ENDIF
STORE SOCIAL TO FINDER
ACTIVATE WINDOW members1
@ 1,2 SAY "Name: " + TRIM(FIRSTNAME) + " " + LASTNAME
@ 2,2 SAY "Exp. date:"
@ 2,15 SAY EXPIREDATE
@ 2,25 SAY "Tape limit:"
@ 2,38 SAY TAPELIMIT
WAIT "Press a key to see rentals..."
SET ESCAPE OFF
ACTIVATE WINDOW rentals1
SELECT 2
USE RENTALS
DISPLAY ALL OFF FOR SOCIAL = FINDER
WAIT "Press a key when done viewing..."
DEACTIVATE WINDOW ALL
CLOSE DATABASES
SET ESCAPE ON
RETURN
```

Early in the program, the SET SHADOWS ON command permits the
display of shadows when called for by a SHADOW clause along with
the DEFINE WINDOW command. Next, three DEFINE WINDOW
commands are used to define three different windows for later use.
After opening a database and index file, the program activates the
window called Askthem and displays a prompt for a last name within
that window.

Once the user responds with a last name, a SEEK command finds the name in the index, and the window called Members1 is activated. The tape limit and expiration date, along with the member's full name, are displayed in this window, and the user is asked to press a key to see the tape rentals. Once the user presses a key, the window called Rentals1 is activated, and all tapes rented by that member are shown in it. At the end of the program, all of the windows are deactivated and the files are closed.

You may have noticed the addition of the SET ESCAPE OFF command just before the final window is opened. This is used to prevent a user from halting the program in midstream by pressing the [Esc] key. You may prefer to use the SET ESCAPE OFF command early on in most of your programs so users cannot interrupt a program by pressing [Esc].

Designing Light-bar Menus with @-PROMPT and MENU TO

You now have a main menu system for the Generic Videos database, but it uses ? and INPUT commands that do not provide much flexibility when it comes to placing the information on the screen. You can replace these commands with the @-PROMPT and MENU TO commands. Using @-PROMPT and MENU TO, you can create light-bar menus similar to those used by FoxPro.

A series of @-PROMPT commands is first used to display the desired menu options at specific positions on the screen. The format for this command is

> @ *row,column* PROMPT "*expression*" [MESSAGE "*expression*"]

where the character expression that follows the PROMPT clause appears in a bar at the specified row and column position. The MESSAGE clause is optional. If it is used, the character expression that follows MESSAGE will appear in the message area of the screen whenever that particular menu option is highlighted.

A series of @-PROMPT commands are followed by a MENU TO command. The format of this command is

> MENU TO *memory-variable*

It activates the menu choices defined with the PROMPT commands and waits for a user response. The user can highlight the desired menu option and press Enter, at which time a numeric value representing the chosen menu option gets passed on to the memory variable specified in the MENU TO command. For example, if the user highlights the first menu option and presses Enter, 1 gets stored to the variable. If the user highlights the fourth menu option and presses Enter, 4 gets stored to the variable.

To use these commands in the Generic Videos menu, you must get into the FoxPro Editor and edit the command file used to display the menu. Enter this:

```
MODIFY COMMAND MENU1
```

When the FoxPro Editor appears, the menu command file you developed in Chapter 13 will appear along with it. Change the file so it looks like the one shown next.

NOTE: You can delete a series of lines at once by placing the cursor at the start of the first unwanted line, holding down the Shift key, and moving the cursor down to the last unwanted line. With all the unwanted lines highlighted, press the Del key to remove the lines. You can use Enter to add new blank lines between existing lines.

```
USE MEMBERS
SET TALK OFF
STORE 0 TO CHOICE
DO WHILE CHOICE < 5
   CLEAR
   *Display main menu.
   @  5, 5 SAY "Generic Videos Database System Menu"
   @  6, 4 SAY "Highlight selection, and press Enter:"
   @  8,10 PROMPT "Add Members    "
   @  9,10 PROMPT "Edit Members   "
   @ 10,10 PROMPT "Print Report   "
   @ 11,10 PROMPT "Display Member"
   @ 12,10 PROMPT "Exit System    "
   @  7, 8 TO 13,25 DOUBLE
```

```
* above line draws double line box around menu.
MENU TO CHOICE
DO CASE
    CASE CHOICE = 1
        DO ADDER
    CASE CHOICE = 2
        DO EDITMEMB
    CASE CHOICE = 3
        REPORT FORM SAMPLE
    CASE CHOICE = 4
        DO SHOWMEMB
    CASE CHOICE = 5
        CLOSE DATABASES
        SET TALK ON
        CASE RETURN
    ENDCASE
ENDDO
```

When you are finished changing the command file, press Ctrl-W to save it. You then might want to try using the system; start it by entering **DO MENU1**. Choose the menu choice for adding a record, and while you are watching the system's operation, you might want to think about ways to improve further on the system design. Perhaps you can modify the command files used by your system so that other choices from the menu provide easy-to-understand screen displays. When you are finished using the system, Ctrl-W gets you out of any of the Edit or Append functions and back to the system menu.

Editing Records Under Program Control

You know that you can edit records with the CHANGE or EDIT command or by using @-SAY-GET and READ commands, but you must get to the record before you can change it. Let's use macro substitution for the editing functions of the Generic Videos database system. If you remember where you left that section of the system, the Editor program (EDITMEMB.PRG) displays all records in the database. The system then asks you for the record number to be edited, and the EDIT command is used to edit that record. If the database has grown beyond a screenful of members, however, you won't be able to see all of the records on the screen at once. Obviously, a better method of editing is needed.

The employees of Generic Videos have agreed that it would be best if they could enter the last name of a member to have FoxPro search for the record. When you first think about what must be done, you might draw up this list:

1. Ask for the last name of the member whose record is to be edited.
2. Store the name to a variable.
3. Using the macro function, find the name in the database.
4. Edit the record whose number corresponds to that name.

Let's change the EDITOR command file so that it does this task. Enter

```
MODIFY COMMAND EDITMEMB
```

Change the program so it looks like this:

```
CLEAR
STORE SPACE(15) TO TEST
USE MEMBERS
SET INDEX TO NAME
@ 5,10 SAY "Editing a record."
@ 7,10 SAY "Enter the last name of the member."
@ 10,10 SAY "Last name: " GET TEST
READ
IF TEST = " "
     RETURN
ENDIF
FIND &TEST
IF .NOT. FOUND()
     CLEAR
     @5,10 SAY "There is no such name in the database."
     WAIT
     *wait command causes a pause.
     RETURN
ENDIF
CHANGE
RETURN
```

Press Ctrl-W to save the file. Try the system again by entering **DO MENU1**, and choose the Edit menu selection. Try entering the name **Miller**. If all went well, the selected record will appear on the screen.

FIND &TEST is the key to the solution; whatever name is entered with the ACCEPT command is substituted for the macro when the FIND command is executed. The SEEK command, which accepts a memory variable directly, could be used in place of FIND and a macro. In this example, FIND was used instead to demonstrate the use of the macro (&) function.

One obvious flaw in this program's design is that the search routine is based on the last name only. If two persons have the same last name, such a design may not find the name you want. However, you can apply the same logic to combinations of fields if you use an index file built on that same combination of fields to perform the search. You could, for example, build the NAME index file on a combination of Lastname and Firstname with commands like

```
USE MEMBERS
INDEX ON LASTNAME + TRIM(FIRSTNAME) TO NAME
```

and then the search routine could be rewritten to prompt for both the last and the first names. The responses could be combined with the plus symbol, which combines (concatenates) text strings. The combined expression could then be used as the search term. As an example, the modified search routine shown here would work if the index was built on a combination of last and first names:

```
CLEAR
STORE SPACE(15) TO TESTLAST
STORE SPACE(15) TO TESTFIRST
USE MEMBERS
SET INDEX TO NAME
@ 5,10 SAY "Editing a record."
@ 7,10 SAY "Enter the last name of the member."
@ 8,10 SAY "Last name: " GET TESTLAST
@ 10,10 SAY "Enter the first name of the member."
@ 11,10 SAY "First name: " GET TESTFIRST
READ
STORE TESTLAST + TRIM(TESTFIRST) TO TEST
IF TEST = " "
     RETURN
ENDIF
FIND &TEST
IF .NOT. FOUND()
     CLEAR
```

```
        @5,10 SAY "There is no such name in the database."
        WAIT
        *wait command causes a pause.
        RETURN
ENDIF
CHANGE
RETURN
```

Data Entry and Editing with Memory Variables

Another common method of writing programs for data entry and editing makes use of memory variables for the temporary storage of data. This method has not been used for any of the examples in this book up to this point. However, it is popular with many programmers, and you may want to consider it in designing your own programs. This programming approach moves data from memory variables to fields. The program resembles the following:

```
*create memory variables.
CLEAR
MLAST = SPACE(15)
MFIRST = SPACE(15)
MADDRESS = SPACE(25)
MCITY  = SPACE(15)
MSTATE = SPACE(2)
MZIP = SPACE(10)
*display prompts, store data to variables.
@ 3,5 SAY "LAST NAME:" GET MLAST
@ 4,5 SAY "FIRST NAME:" GET MFIRST
@ 8,5 SAY "ADDRESS:" GET MADDRESS
@ 10,5 SAY "CITY:" GET MCITY
@ 10,35 SAY "STATE:" GET MSTATE
@ 10,45 SAY "ZIP CODE:" GET MZIP
READ
*open database, make new record, store variables.
USE NAMES INDEX NAMES
APPEND BLANK
REPLACE LASTNAME WITH MLAST, FIRSTNAME WITH MFIRST;
ADDRESS WITH MADDRESS, CITY WITH MCITY;
STATE WITH MSTATE, ZIP WITH MZIP
RETURN
```

Such a command file has three main parts. The first consists of a series of commands that create memory variables; the memory variables precisely match the field types and field lengths. The second portion of the file uses @-SAY-GET commands to display prompts at the desired screen locations, along with data entry fields for the desired data. The final portion of the file opens the database, uses an APPEND BLANK command to add one blank record to the end of the database, and uses the REPLACE command to move the data from the variables into the database fields. Once all of the required records have been added, the database can be closed. The code just described is often enclosed within a DO WHILE .T. loop, with a conditional prompt added just before the ENDDO that matches the DO WHILE command, as in the following example:

```
WAIT "Add another record? Y/N:" TO ANSWER
IF UPPER(ANSWER) = "N"
     CLOSE DATABASES
     EXIT
ENDIF
```

If the data entry person presses N in response to the prompt, the program ends.

For this method to be as popular as it is with programmers, it clearly has advantages. One significant one is *database integrity;* the database is open only during the append process and not necessarily throughout the entire application, minimizing chances of damage. Another is ease of validation; since the data is stored in memory variables and later moved to the fields of the actual database, you can add other lines to the program to see if the data is valid before moving it to the database. And you can make it easier on the data entry operators by storing default values in the memory variables. As an example, if 80% of the addresses that get stored in an order database are in San Diego, you could store the text string "San Diego", along with the required number of spaces following the string to fill the field, to the memory variable for the City field. It will then appear by default in the entry screen, and the users can overtype the entry to enter something else.

Now, the disadvantages: This approach involves a lot of programming, like it or not. Anyone who has written an entry routine like this one for a 60-field database will tell you that it is no fun typing all the lines of program code; you'll spend two pages just creating the variables! The effort involved in writing such a program is enough to make you wonder whether database integrity is all that important, or whether you can get by with a format file and a CHANGE or EDIT command.

Deleting Records Under Program Control

If you're going to be writing your own applications, you should add a routine for deleting unwanted records. This is too often left out of a system's design, as if users want to add but never want to delete records from a database. The logic is very similar to a search-and-edit program, because for both the editing and deleting you have to find the record first.

For deleting a record, your program-design pseudocode might look like this:

```
open database, index files
prompt user for variables to search by
FIND variable in index file
IF NOT FOUND
    show error message, exit routine
ELSE
    show record to user with @-SAY commands
    ask user for confirmation to delete record
    IF confirmation is given
        DELETE the record
    ELSE
        move to next record to see if it is same name
        ask user for confirmation to delete record
    ENDIF
ENDIF
```

The fastest way to build such a routine is probably to copy your "edit" routine, remove the lines of code that allow for changing the fields, add lines of code that ask for confirmation, and proceed to delete the record. Here is an example that uses a modified version of the program shown earlier for editing records based on a last and first name:

```
CLEAR
STORE SPACE(15) TO TESTLAST
STORE SPACE(15) TO TESTFIRST
USE MEMBERS
SET INDEX TO NAME
*name.idx is indexed on lastname + firstname.
@ 5,10 SAY "DELETING a record."
@ 7,10 SAY "Enter the last name of the member."
@ 8,10 SAY "Last name: " GET TESTLAST
@ 10,10 SAY "Enter the first name of the member."
@ 11,10 SAY "First name: " GET TESTFIRST
READ
STORE TESTLAST + TESTFIRST TO TEST
FIND &TEST
IF .NOT. FOUND()
      CLEAR
      @5,10 SAY "There is no such name in the database."
      WAIT
      *wait command causes a pause.
      RETURN
ENDIF
DO WHILE .NOT. EOF()
      STORE "N" TO DOIT
      @ 5,5 SAY " Lastname:"
      @ 5,15 SAY LASTNAME
      @ 6,5 SAY "Firstname:"
      @ 6,15 SAY FIRSTNAME
      @ 7,5 SAY "  Address:"
      @ 7,15 SAY ADDRESS
      @ 8,15 SAY TRIM(CITY) + " " + STATE + " " + ZIPCODE
      @ 12,20 SAY "DELETE THIS MEMBER? Y/N or C to CANCEL: "
      @ 12,62 GET DOIT
      READ
      DO CASE
          CASE UPPER(DOIT) = "Y"
          DELETE
          RETURN
          CASE UPPER(DOIT) = "N"
          SKIP
          CASE UPPER(DOIT) = "C"
          RETURN
      ENDCASE
ENDDO
RETURN
```

The advantage of placing the portion of the program that displays the member and asks for confirmation in a DO-WHILE loop is that if two members have the same last and first names, the user can press N for No to automatically view the next member. Once the user views the desired member to delete and presses Y for Yes, the record is deleted. Note also that this routine does not perform a PACK, because packing a database can be time consuming (particularly with larger databases). Most systems provide the user with an option to pack the file at some point in time. It probably isn't wise to do this all too often, nor is it necessary, since you can place a SET DELETED ON statement near the start of the program to hide the deleted records. Given that a PACK is going to be time consuming with all but the smallest of databases, this should be an option that is performed at the users' discretion.

Many systems provide a PACK option in the form of a question that the user sees just before exiting the system. This can be done with a program like the one shown here:

```
CLEAR
ACCEPT "  ==PACK database now? Y/N: " TO PACKANS
IF UPPER(PACKANS) = "Y"
     CLEAR
     @ 5,5 SAY "Please wait... do NOT interrupt!"
     SET TALK ON
     USE MEMBERS INDEX NAME
     PACK
     SET TALK OFF
ENDIF
QUIT
```

The user of your application, who may not want to spend the time at that particular instant, now has the option of performing or not performing the PACK.

Helpful Hints on Screen Design

Think about these aspects of screen design when you are designing a FoxPro system:

✦ Use menus as often as necessary. They should clearly say what choices are available to the person using the system.

✦ Avoid overly cluttered menus or data entry screens. It may be better to break the entry screen in half, input half of the information, clear the screen with CLEAR, and then input the other half of the information rather than trying to fit a large number of fields on one data entry screen. You can apply the same tactic to a menu by grouping a number of choices in a second menu—a reports menu, for example—that can be reached by a single choice on the main menu.

✦ Give users a way out—that is, a way of changing their minds after making a choice from a menu or selecting a particular entry screen. Many application designers handle this need by making the last option on any menu serve as an "exit" back to the previous menu with a RETURN statement.

✦ Finally, never leave the screen blank for any noticeable period of time. Few things are as unnerving to a computer user as a blank screen. A simple message that states that the computer is doing something (sorting, indexing, or whatever) is reassuring to the user.

CHAPTER

FOXPRO

16

PROGRAMMING FOR DATA RETRIEVAL

This chapter covers ways to retrieve data, in the form of reports, from within your programs. You should already be familiar with the use of the Report Generator, as detailed in Chapters 7 and 10, for designing reports. The stored reports created by the Report Generator can be called from within a program to produce a variety of reports. You can also write programs that produce reports, although the flexibility of the Report Generator makes this task necessary only on the rarest of occasions.

Generating Reports from Stored Report Forms

If you have designed your reports using the Report Generator, all that is needed to generate a report is to place the REPORT FORM command (detailed in Chapter 7) at the appropriate place in your program. You may also want to build selective indexes or set some sort of filter before generating the report, and it is a good idea to give users a way to cancel the report just before it starts.

In programs, include an option to cancel a report's printing.

A simple report-producing program called from one of the options in the main menu might resemble the following:

```
*REPORTER.PRG produces the membership report.
CLEAR
TEXT
************************************************************
This menu option prints the membership report.
Make sure that the printer is turned on, and that
paper is loaded.

Press C to CANCEL, any other key to start printing.
************************************************************
ENDTEXT
WAIT TO DOIT
IF UPPER(DOIT) = "C"
     *user canceled option, so...
     RETURN
ENDIF
REPORT FORM MEMBERS TO PRINT
RETURN
```

Using stored reports like the one used by this program is by far the easiest way to generate reports within a program. You can add more lines to the program to limit the records that are printed with an INDEX ON-FOR command, by placing a query into effect, or with a SET FILTER command. You can construct a query using the RQBE window (detailed in Chapter 6) and set up the query to print the stored report (see Chapter 7 for details). To place that query in effect from within your program and to generate the report, use the command

DO *queryname*.QPR

where queryname is the name that you saved the query under. Hence, if you stored a query that prints a report under the name SAMPLE1, you could use the following line of code within your program:

```
DO SAMPLE1.QPR
```

Upon execution of this line, the query would be placed into effect and the report printed. As an alternative, you can accomplish similar results with the SET FILTER command. With SET FILTER, for example, you could offer various menu options that select different filter conditions and then print the same stored report. As an example, one user might want to see the members in the video database restricted by a specific ZIP code, while another user might want to see all members who lived in a specific state. You could provide menu options in a simple reporting program like the one shown here to handle this task:

```
*REPORTER.PRG produces the membership report.
CLEAR
@ 5,5 PROMPT "All members      "
@ 6,5 PROMPT "By State       "
@ 7,5 PROMPT "By ZIP code range"
@ 4,4 TO 8,23 DOUBLE
MENU TO CHOICE
DO CASE
     CASE CHOICE = 1
     WAIT "All members chosen. Press a key."
     CASE CHOICE = 2
     STORE SPACE(2) TO MSTATE
     @ 12,10 SAY "For which state? " GET MSTATE
     READ
     SET FILTER TO UPPER(STATE) = UPPER(MSTATE)
     GO TOP
     CASE CHOICE = 3
     STORE SPACE(10) TO STARTZIP
     STORE SPACE(10) TO ENDZIP
     @ 12,10 SAY "Starting ZIP code? " GET STARTZIP
     @ 13,10 SAY "  Ending ZIP code? " GET ENDZIP
     @ 15,10 SAY "(enter same ZIP code for a single ZIP.)"
     READ
     SET FILTER TO ZIPCODE >= STARTZIP .AND. ZIPCODE <= ENDZIP
     GO TOP
ENDCASE
```

```
CLEAR
TEXT
************************************************************
Ready to print the membership report. Make sure that
the printer is turned on, and that paper is loaded.
Press C to CANCEL, any other key to start printing.
************************************************************
ENDTEXT
WAIT TO DOIT
IF UPPER(DOIT) = "C"
     *user canceled option, so...
     SET FILTER TO
     *above line needed to clear effects of filter.
     RETURN
ENDIF
REPORT FORM MEMBERS TO PRINT
SET FILTER TO
*above line needed to clear effects of filter.
RETURN
```

In this example, depending on the menu choice selected, one of two
filters may be set to limit the records printed. Note the inclusion of the
SET FILTER TO statement near the end of the program to clear any
existing filter. If a filter is set and not cleared after the report is done, it
may cause havoc in other parts of your program when records suddenly
appear to be "missing" from the database.

Users' Choice: Reporting to the Screen or Printer

Often, a program may need to display a report on the screen and
optionally send the output to the printer. Anyone who has designed a
single report to try to meet the two different needs of a screen and a
printer has discovered that the two tasks are similar but not identical.
The screen limitation of 24 lines puts a severe constraint on the
amount of information you can display at once; the program must
prompt for each display, or the data scrolls by so fast as to be useless.
With a printer, however, there is no need to stop every 24 lines, but
page ejects must be taken into consideration.

One way to handle such a need is to use a program like the one shown here:

```
PRINANS = "S"
@ 5,5 SAY 'Screen (S) or Printer (P)?" GET PRINANS
READ
IF UPPER(PRINANS) = "P"
    REPORT FORM MEMBERS TO PRINT
ELSE
    GO TOP
    CLEAR
    WAIT "Press C to CANCEL, any other key to view members."
    CLEAR
    DO WHILE .NOT. EOF( )
        REPORT FORM MEMBERS NEXT 20
        WAIT TO KEEPGOING
        IF UPPER(KEEPGOING) = "C"
            RETURN
        ENDIF
    ENDDO
ENDIF
RETURN
```

This lets the same stored report form work for both the screen and the printer. If the user answers the prompt with S for screen, the DO WHILE loop causes the REPORT FORM MEMBERS NEXT 20 statement to repeat over and over until the end of the file is reached. The scope of NEXT 20 limits the report to 20 records, which fit on a screen, and the WAIT command pauses the screen, allowing the user to view the records. In your application, you could change NEXT 20 to whatever number of records fit on your screen at one time.

Writing Reports with Program Code

Before proceeding with this topic, you should know that producing stored reports with the Report Generator is far easier than using the following methods of writing reports manually with program code. The methods are described here primarily because you may run into FoxPro applications written by other programmers who chose to use these methods. This was often due to the limitations in earlier versions of FoxBase. The Report Generator in FoxBase did not let you create form-oriented reports with ease, so many programmers wrote report programs to accomplish the task. It may help to be familiar with these methods of programming in case you ever want to modify another programmer's work, but if at all possible, you should avoid these techniques in favor of writing your reporting programs with stored reports created by the Report Generator.

Where possible, use stored reports in place of reports written through programming.

There are about as many ways to design a reporting program as there are to build data entry screens. About the only thing such programs have in common is one or more repetitive (DO WHILE) loops, which print selected contents of a record for each record within a group of records. Beyond this, the commands you need will vary with the complexity of the reports, the levels of grouping, whether or not the report is relational, and numerous other factors. However, many reports written in program code do follow a common methodology, which is something like this:

```
OPEN Database and Index files
FIND first record in desired group, or SET FILTER and go top
Initialize any memory variables for page and line counters
Route output to the printer
Print report headings
DO WHILE not at the end of the file or the desired data group
    Print the desired fields or expressions for one record
    Update counter for page position
    IF form feed counter exceeds max lines per page
        Print footers, if any
        EJECT the paper
        Print headers, if any
    ENDIF
    SKIP to the next record in logical sequence
ENDDO
```

There are two ways to route the data to the printer: by using SET PRINT ON and a series of ? statements or by using SET DEVICE TO PRINT followed by a series of @-SAY statements. As an example, the two simple programs shown here use both approaches within the design framework just shown:

```
*MEMLIST.PRG prints membership roster.
CLEAR
STORE 1 TO LINES
STORE 1 TO PAGES
USE MEMBERS INDEX NAMES
SET PRINT ON
```

```
? "*****************************************"
? " Membership Address and Phone Roster"
? "*****************************************"
DO WHILE .NOT. EOF( )
    ? "Name: " + TRIM(FIRSTNAME) + " " + LASTNAME
    ? "Phone: " + PHONE
    ?? "Expiration Date: " + DTOC(EXPIREDATE)
    ? "Home address: " + ADDRESS
    ? SPACE(15) + TRIM(CITY) + " " + STATE + " " + ZIPCODE
    ? "*******************************"
    STORE LINES+ 5 TO LINES
    IF LINES > 55
        ?
        ? SPACE(40) + "Page" + LTRIM(STR(PAGES))
        EJECT
        STORE 1 + PAGES TO PAGES
        STORE 1 TO LINES
        ? "*****************************************"
        ? " Membership Address and Phone Roster"
        ? "*****************************************"
    ENDIF
    SKIP
ENDDO
IF LINES > 1
    EJECT
ENDIF
SET PRINT OFF
RETURN
```

SET PRINT ON and the ? statements get the job done, but they don't offer precise control over where the data appears in the report. For more precision, you can use the other method of printing in a program, which is to use SET DEVICE TO PRINT to reroute screen output to the printer, combined with @-SAY commands to position the data on the printed page. The following example of a printing program creates a simple tabular report with custom headers and footers using this approach:

```
CLEAR
STORE 5 TO LINES
STORE 1 TO PAGES
USE MEMBERS INDEX NAMES
SET DEVICE TO PRINT
```

```
@ 2,15 SAY "MEMBERSHIP EXPIRATION DATES REPORT"
@ 3,10 SAY "****************************"
@ 4,10 SAY "Name         City"
@ 4,50 SAY "Tape Limit     Exp.Date"
DO WHILE .NOT. EOF( )
    @ LINES, 5 SAY TRIM(FIRSTNAME) + " " + LASTNAME
    @ LINES, 30 SAY CITY
    @ LINES, 50 SAY TAPELIMIT
    @ LINES, 60 SAY EXPIREDATE
    STORE LINES + 1 TO LINES
    IF LINES > 50
        @ LINES + 2,40 SAY "PAGE " + TRIM(STR(PAGES))
        EJECT
        STORE PAGES + 1 TO PAGES
        STORE 5 TO LINES
        @ 2,15 SAY "MEMBERSHIP EXPIRATION DATES REPORT"
        @ 3,10 SAY "****************************"
        @ 4,10 SAY "Name         City"
        @ 4,50 SAY "Tape Limit     Exp.Date"
    ENDIF
    SKIP
ENDDO
IF LINES > 5
    EJECT
ENDIF
SET DEVICE TO SCREEN
RETURN
```

Whichever approach best suits you can be modified to handle any complex reporting need. It is simple to implement multiple file reporting, for example, by selecting appropriate work areas and including file names and pointers, as discussed in Chapter 11, to find the related data. In one-to-many relationships, where one record in the controlling database may have dozens or hundreds of records in a related file, you can add program code to monitor the page count and line count and to eject pages and print new headings when appropriate.

Note that both of these examples of report code use memory variables incremented by the program to keep track of page numbers and the line counts. This approach was also common in FoxBase+ and other earlier dBASE-compatible languages. In FoxPro, however, system memory variables (discussed shortly in "Controlling Your Printer") can be used to keep track of page numbers and line postions. These system

16

memory variables work with the stored reports, and you may want to consider using them if you need reports that begin with a specific page number other than 1.

Creating Columnar Listings

Sometimes what you need is a report with data in a two-across or three-across format. You can spend an inordinate amount of time writing a program to handle this need, or you can use the LABEL FORM command as a part of your report. This works well when the data you need follows a format like this one:

```
                                                  Page 1
                                                  10/06/93


          Employee Address Roster
              ABC Company



    Marcia Morse            Carol Levy             David Jackson
    4260 Park Avenue        1207 5th Street        4102 Valley Lane
    Chevy Chase, MD         Washington, DC         Falls Church, VA
```

This use of the LABEL FORM command is similar to earlier described uses of the REPORT FORM command within a program. Create a label form by using the CREATE LABEL command, and choose 3-across or 2-across as desired from the Label menu. Decide how many records you want to appear on each page, and use the command

LABEL FORM *filename* NEXT *no.- of-recs-per-page* TO PRINT

within your program. The following program shows how this can be handled:

```
SET TALK OFF
USE MEMBERS INDEX NAMES
STORE 1 TO PAGES
SET DEVICE TO PRINT
DO WHILE .NOT. EOF( )
   @ 3,50 SAY "Page: " + LTRIM(STR(PAGES))
```

```
    @ 4,50 SAY DATE( )
    @ 5,20 SAY "Generic Videos Membership Address Roster"
    @ 7,0
    LABEL FORM MEMBERS NEXT 20 TO PRINT
    STORE PAGES + 1 TO PAGES
    EJECT
ENDDO
SET DEVICE TO SCREEN
```

This gives you a report fashioned after the example previously shown, with a minimum of programming. You will need to decide how many records can appear on each page, based on the size of the paper and the position of your headers and footers, and adjust the number that you use along with the NEXT scope in the LABEL FORM command accordingly.

Controlling Your Printer

By changing the printer memory variables, you can control the various print settings that are used when stored report forms are generated with the REPORT FORM command. Printer memory variables are special memory variables that FoxPro uses to control the output produced when a REPORT FORM command is directed to the printer. They affect settings like page length, page offset from the left margin, the number of pages printed within a report, and line spacing. You can change the values of these memory variables by storing different values to the variables before running the report with the REPORT FORM command.

If you perform a LIST MEMORY command, you see the printer memory variables, similar to the example shown here. The names of printer memory variables start with _P.

```
LIST MEMORY

    0 variables defined,    0 bytes used
  256 variables available

Print System Memory Variables

_ALIGNMENT    Pub    C    "LEFT"
_BEAUTIFY     Pub    C    " "
_BOX          Pub    L    .T.
_CALCMEM      Pub    N         0.00  (          0.00000000)
```

```
_CALCVALUE   Pub   N        0.00  (            0.00000000)
_CUROBJ      Pub   N          -1  (           -1.00000000)
_DBLCLICK    Pub   N        0.49  (            0.49432944)
_DIARYDATE   Pub   D   12/04/92
_DOS         Pub   L   .T.
_FOXDOC      Pub   C   "C:\FOXDOS\FOXDOC.EXE"
_FOXGRAPH    Pub   C   ""
_GENGRAPH    Pub   C   "C:\FOXDOS\GENGRAPH.PRG"
_GENMENU     Pub   C   "C:\FOXDOS\GENMENU.PRG"
_GENPD       Pub   C   "C:\FOXDOS\GENPD.APP"
_GENSCRN     Pub   C   "C:\FOXDOS\GENSCRN.PRG"
_GENXTAB     Pub   C   "C:\FOXDOS\GENXTAB.PRG"
_INDENT      Pub   N           0  (            0.00000000)
_LMARGIN     Pub   N           0  (            0.00000000)
_MAC         Pub   L   .F.
_MLINE       Pub   N           0  (            0.00000000)
_NETWARE     Pub   C   ""
_PADVANCE    Pub   C   "FORMFEED"
_PAGENO      Pub   N           3  (            3.00000000)
_PBPAGE      Pub   N           1  (            1.00000000)
_PCOLNO      Pub   N          55  (           55.00000000)
_PCOPIES     Pub   N           1  (            1.00000000)
_PDRIVER     Pub   C   ""
_PDSETUP     Pub   C   ""
_PECODE      Pub   C   ""
_PEJECT      Pub   C   "BEFORE"
_PEPAGE      Pub   N       32767  (        32767.00000000)
_PLENGTH     Pub   N          66  (           66.00000000)
_PLINENO     Pub   N          47  (           47.00000000)
_PLOFFSET    Pub   N           0  (            0.00000000)
_PPITCH      Pub   C   "DEFAULT"
_PQUALITY    Pub   L   .F.
_PRETEXT     Pub   C   ""
_PSCODE      Pub   C   ""
_PSPACING    Pub   N           1  (            1.00000000)
_PWAIT       Pub   L   .F.
_RMARGIN     Pub   N          80  (           80.00000000)
_STARTUP     Pub   C   "C:\FOXDOS\FOXSTART.APP"
_TABS        Pub   C   ""
_TALLY       Pub   N          24  (           24.00000000)
_TEXT        Pub   N          -1  (           -1.00000000)
_THROTTLE    Pub   N        0.00  (            0.00000000)
_TRANSPORT   Pub   C   "C:\FOXDOS\TRANSPRT.PRG"
_UNIX        Pub   L   .F.
```

```
_WINDOWS      Pub     L   .F.
_WRAP         Pub     L   .F.
```

The variables have the following meanings:

_PADVANCE contains a character expression of either LINEFEED or FORMFEED. Depending on the value of the expression, new pages are generated either with multiple linefeeds or with form feeds.

Use the _PAGENO variable to code page numbers into your reports.

_PAGENO indicates the page number to use on the first page of a report. The default is 1, but you can enter any value from 1 to 32,767.

_PBPAGE indicates the beginning page of a report when you don't want to print the entire report.

_PCOLNO indicates a new starting column position. This repositions the printer at the specified cursor location before the report begins.

_PCOPIES indicates the number of copies of a report desired; the default is 1.

_PDRIVER contains a character expression that is the name of the printer driver in use, such as EPSONFX (for Epson FX series) or HPLAS1 (for Hewlett-Packard LaserJet 1). If no printer has been chosen with the Printer Setup option, the default is a null string ("").

_PECODE contains any ending escape codes you want to send to the printer after the report is completed.

_PDSETUP loads a printer driver setup, or clears the current printer driver setup.

_PEJECT contains the character expression NONE, BEFORE, AFTER, or BOTH. NONE indicates no form feed is needed (other than those that naturally occur inside the report); BEFORE indicates a form feed should occur at the start of printing; AFTER indicates a form feed should occur at the end of printing; and BOTH indicates a form feed is needed both before and after printing.

PEPAGE indicates the ending page of a report when you don't want to print the entire report.

PLENGTH indicates the page length for the printed page. The default of 66 matches standard 11-inch (U.S.) paper; you can store 84 to this value if you are using 14-inch (U.S. legal-size) paper.

PLINENO indicates a new starting line number. This repositions the printer at the specifed row location before the report begins.

PLOFFSET indicates the left offset (distance from left edge) where printing will begin. Enter a desired numeric value, such as 15 for a left offset of 15 spaces.

PPITCH contains a character expression that selects the printing type style. Valid choices are PICA, ELITE, COMPRESSED, and DEFAULT. Note that a printer driver must be installed, and your printer must support the option, for the desired type style to be used successfully.

PQUALITY indicates whether quality printing mode will be used. A logical false stored to this variable turns off quality printing, and a logical true turns on quality printing. Note that a printer driver must be installed, and your printer must support quality printing for this variable to have an effect.

PSCODE contains any starting escape codes you want to send to the printer before the report begins printing.

PSPACING contains a numeric value of 1, 2, or 3, indicating the line spacing to be used within a report. The default value for this is 1.

PWAIT indicates whether the printer should pause between pages. A logical value of false indicates no pause, and a logical value of true indicates a pause.

Most of these parameters can be controlled in other ways, such as through the various selections you make when designing or printing a report or when you enter other commands such as SET MARGIN TO (the command equivalent of the left offset variable). However, these variables are quite useful if you want to offer your users multiple options for report printing while under program control. Depending on the user's response to various menu options, you could store certain values to different printer variables and then print the report with the REPORT FORM command.

Sending Escape Codes to the Printer

In its default mode, FoxPro treats the printer as a simple device capable of receiving ASCII and sends that ASCII information. This saves you the worry of trying to get a particular printer to match the output of FoxPro, but it also means that FoxPro will not by default use any special effects that your printer has to offer. You can take advantage of your printer's special effects by sending escape codes to the printer, using the CHR function to send the applicable code. As an example, the code for compressed print for Epson-compatible dot-matrix printers is the ASCII value of 27 (the escape code) followed by the ASCII value of 15. You can, therefore, switch an Epson-compatible printer into Compressed mode with commands like

```
SET PRINT ON
??? CHR(27) + CHR(15)
SET PRINT OFF
```

The printer remains in this mode until you send another escape code that clears the prior one or selects a different font, or until you manually reset the printer. (Note the use of the ??? command, which is ideal for sending data to the printer. Unlike the ? command, the ??? does not add a carriage return or linefeed code.)

Consult your printer manual for a listing of your escape codes. The popular escape codes for Epson-compatible dot-matrix printers are listed in Table 16-1.

If you use the escape codes to select different print styles often, consider storing them as memory variables and then saving those variables as part of a configuration file. When escape codes are stored as variables, you can use them wherever they are appropriate in your various printer routines by using a SET PRINT ON statement followed by a ? *varname* command, where *varname* is the memory variable that contains the escape code. As an example, you can store an escape code to a variable with a command like

```
BOLD = CHR(27) + CHR(47)
```

Code	Meaning
CHR(27)+CHR(4)	Italics On
CHR(27)+CHR(5)	Italics Off
CHR(27)+CHR(15)	Compressed On
CHR(27)+CHR(18)	Compressed Off
CHR(27)+CHR(45)	Emphasized On
CHR(27)+CHR(46)	Emphasized Off
CHR(27)+CHR(47)	Bold On
CHR(27)+CHR(48)	Bold Off

Epson Printer
Codes
Table 16-1.

Within your printer routines, you can start printing with commands like

```
WAIT "Press a key to begin printing report..."
SET PRINT ON
? BOLD
<more commands to print report...>
```

If you are using the Hewlett-Packard LaserJet or another laser printer compatible with the HP description language, you can use similar escape codes to select fonts, assuming they are available with your particular printer. The following simple menu program uses the approach of storing the escape codes for the HP LaserJet to a series of memory variables; then, depending on the chosen selection, the escape codes are routed to the printer to select the desired fonts.

```
*Fonts.PRG for HP Laserjet and compatibles.
STORE CHR(27)+"(0U"+CHR(27)+"(s 1p 10v 1s 0b 5T" to TmsRoman
STORE CHR(27)+"(0U"+CHR(27)+"(s 1p 10v 0s 3b 5T" to TmsRomanB
STORE CHR(27)+"(0U"+CHR(27)+"(sSY -1p 10v 0s 0b 5T" to;
TmsRomanC
STORE CHR(27)+"(0U"+CHR(27)+"(s 1p 10v 1s 0b 5T" to TmsRomanI
STORE CHR(27)+"(8U"+CHR(27)+"(s 0p 10h 12v 1s 0b 3T" to;
CourierI
STORE CHR(27)+"(8U"+CHR(27)+"(s 0p 10h 12v 1s 3b 3T" to;
CourierB
STORE CHR(27)+"(0U"+CHR(27)+"(s 1p 10h 14.4v 0s 3b 4T" to;
HelvBold
```

```
CLEAR
@ 3,25 SAY [SELECT A PRINTER FONT]
@ 5,15 SAY [ 1. Times Roman]
@ 7,15 SAY [ 2. Times Roman Italic]
@ 9,15 SAY [ 3. Times Roman Bold]
@ 11,15 SAY [ 4. Times Roman Compressed]
@ 13,15 SAY [ 5. Courier Italic]
@ 14,15 SAY [ 5. Courier Bold]
@ 15,15 SAY [ 6. Helvetica Bold]
@ 17,28 SAY [0. EXIT]
STORE 0 TO SELECTNUM
@ 19,10 SAY " YOUR CHOICE?" GET SELECTNUM PICTURE '9'
READ
SET PRINT ON
DO CASE
     CASE SELECTNUM = 1
     ??? TmsRoman
     CASE SELECTNUM = 2
     ??? TmsRomanI
     CASE SELECTNUM = 3
     ??? TmsRomanB
     CASE SELECTNUM = 4
     ??? TmsRomanC
     CASE SELECTNUM = 5
     ??? CourierI
     CASE SELECTNUM = 6
     ??? CourierB
     CASE SELECTNUM = 7
     ??? HelvBold
ENDCASE
SET PRINT OFF
RETURN
```

If you are using an HP-compatible laser, you may want to experiment with the various fonts before using them in an application. Because FoxPro assumes a standard character width for each printed character, the proportionally spaced fonts generated by a laser printer may or may not appear where you would like to see them. Figure 16-1 shows the results of a LIST command using the Courier Italic font of the HP

J. E. Jones Associates	Reston	VA	22094
The Software Bar, Inc.	Herndon	VA	22070
Computers R Us	Pasadena	CA	90556
Chapel Hill Life & Casualty	Carrboro	NC	27805
Sun City Transit Corporation	El Paso	TX	78809
Osborne McGraw Hill	Berkeley	CA	94710

Results of list
with Courier
Italic font
Figure 16-1.

LaserJet, and Figure 16-2 shows the results of the same LIST command
with the HP LaserJet set to the Helvetica Bold font. Without the ability
to incrementally space characters on the printed page, it becomes
impossible to maintain proper character spacing with the laser's
proportional fonts. This limits the use of the proportional fonts to
items like headings and cover pages.

J. E. Jones Associates	**Reston**	**VA**	**22094**
The Software Bar, Inc.	**Herndon**	**VA**	**22070**
Computers R Us	**Pasadena**	**CA**	**90556**
Chapel Hill Life & Casualty	**Carrboro**	**NC**	**27805**
Sun City Transit Corporation	**El Paso**	**TX**	**78809**
Osborne McGraw Hill	**Berkeley**	**CA**	**94710**

Results of list
with Helvetica
Bold font
Figure 16-2.

CHAPTER

FOXPRO

17

ADVANCED PROGRAMMING TOPICS

This chapter describes additional commands and programming techniques for creating more intricate command files to automate your work with FoxPro.

439

Hiding and Showing Variables

FoxPro offers two commands, PRIVATE and PUBLIC, that are used to classify memory variables. The terms *private* and *public* refer to how the individual programs within a large FoxPro program treat variables. Private variables are available only to the program in which they are created and to all programs called by that program. Variables that you create in one program are considered private by default; if you do not use the PUBLIC command, FoxPro assumes that all the variables you create are private variables. This means that if you create a variable in a program that is called by another program and then transfer control back to the calling program with the RETURN command, the contents of that memory variable are lost. You may or may not want those contents to be discarded, so you can use the PRIVATE and PUBLIC commands to specifically tell FoxPro how to handle your variables.

By default, variables created within programs are private variables.

The PUBLIC command tells FoxPro that a memory variable is to be made available to all programs, regardless of where the memory variable is created. The PRIVATE command tells FoxPro that the variable will be available only to the program that created the variable and all programs that are called by that specific program. Declaring a variable public requires two steps: using the PUBLIC command in the format PUBLIC *variablename* and declaring the actual variable with the STORE command or with an assignment symbol (=). Here is an example:

```
STORE 0 to YearsRents
PUBLIC YearsRents
STORE rentamt * 12 to YearsRents
```

In this example, the variable YearsRents will be available to all parts of the program, even if program control returns from the part of the program containing these commands to a higher level (calling) program.

There is normally little need to declare a memory variable private, since FoxPro sets all memory variables to private by default. However, there may be times when you want to declare a variable that was previously declared public as private. To do this, you can use the PRIVATE command in the format PRIVATE *variablename* in a similar manner to the way you use the PUBLIC command. An example is

```
PRIVATE Staffer
STORE LASTNAME + FIRSTNAME to Staffer
```

As an example of the problems that can occur if variables are not declared private or public, consider the following programs. The first program, FIRST.PRG, passes control to the second program, SECOND.PRG. The second program declares a variable (NAME) and then passes control back to the calling program, FIRST.PRG. The calling program then tries to display the contents of the memory variable NAME.

```
*FIRST.PRG is first program
CLEAR
? "This program will call the second program."
WAIT
DO SECOND
CLEAR
? "Control has returned to first program."
? "The name is: " + NAME
? "End of first program."
```

Declare variables public if you want to use them throughout a program.

```
*SECOND.PRG is second program
CLEAR
STORE "Smith" to name
? "The name is: " + NAME
WAIT "Press any key to return to first program."
RETURN
```

When the program is run with DO FIRST, an error message results after program control returns from the second program. FoxPro reports an error because the NAME variable was private to the second program. When control was passed back to the first program, the contents of the variable were lost. This problem can be solved by declaring the variable public, as shown in the following example:

```
*SECOND.PRG is second program
CLEAR
PUBLIC NAME
STORE "Smith" to name
? "The name is: " + NAME
WAIT "Press any key to return to first program."
RETURN
```

When the FIRST program is run after the change is made, the program completes successfully without an error.

You can use the ALL, LIKE, and EXCEPT options with PRIVATE to cover more than one variable at a time. Here are some examples of the use of these options with PRIVATE:

```
PRIVATE ALL EXCEPT ???names
PRIVATE ALL LIKE *rent
PRIVATE ALL EXCEPT YearsRents
```

You can use the accepted DOS wildcards, the asterisk (*), and question mark (?), as a part of the variable names. The asterisk represents any sequence of characters, and the question mark represents any single character.

Debugging Techniques

Debugging is the process of finding out why a program does not operate the way it was designed. Debugging can range from correcting a spelling error to rewriting the entire program. Some program bugs are relatively easy to find and solve, such as a misspelled command, which results in a "Syntax error" message displayed on the screen when the command is executed. Other program bugs may cause problems that don't surface until you reach a different part of the program, and these can be far more difficult to solve. But remember that it is truly a rare experience for a program of any complexity, written for the first time, to operate without any bugs.

FoxPro helps you find bugs by placing you at or near the source of the problem. When an error in a program causes the program to halt, the Editor automatically opens in a window, and the highlighted line is where the program halted. This line often (but not always) contains the cause of the error.

The bugs that you are likely to see most often in FoxPro are as follows:

✦ *Misspelled variable names and commands* The message "Syntax error" is usually displayed for misspelled commands. The message "Variable not found" is usually displayed for misspelled variables.

✦ *Missing ENDIF, ENDDO, ENDCASE, or ENDSCAN commands* Every DO WHILE loop must end with an ENDDO statement, every IF statement must be matched by an ENDIF statement, DO CASE statements must have matching ENDCASE statements, and SCAN statements must have matching ENDSCAN statements. FoxPro will wander off in the wrong direction if you leave out an ending statement.

✦ *Errors in loops* To avoid this major cause of program bugs, verify on paper that your program loops are properly designed to begin with. An example of an improperly designed DO WHILE loop is

17

```
STORE 0 TO CHOICE
DO WHILE CHOICE < 3
        INPUT "Enter selection:" TO CHOICE
        IF CHOICE = 1
                IF .NOT. EOF( )
                    SKIP
                ENDIF
                DELETE
        ELSE
                IF .NOT. EOF( )
                    SKIP
                ENDIF
                ? NAME, CITY, STATE
ENDDO
STORE RECNO( ) TO LOCATION
ENDIF
(rest of program...)
```

The flaw in this example is that the IF statement begins within the DO WHILE loop but ends outside of it. Whenever an IF-ENDIF statement is used inside a DO WHILE loop, the IF statement must terminate within the DO WHILE loop. The same is true for the other programming structures with matching statements—ENDSCAN, ENDDO, and ENDCASE. In this example, the properly designed loop looks like this:

```
STORE 0 TO CHOICE
DO WHILE CHOICE < 3
        INPUT "Enter selection:" TO CHOICE
        IF CHOICE = 1
                SKIP
                DELETE
        ELSE
                IF .NOT. EOF( )
                        SKIP
                ENDIF
```

```
                    ? NAME, CITY, STATE
          ENDIF
ENDDO
STORE RECNO( ) TO LOCATION
(rest of program...)
```

+ *Improper mixing of data types, such as character strings mixed with numeric variables or date strings mixed with logical expressions* If you tell FoxPro to store the value 3 to a variable and to store the character string "3" to another variable, the two items are interpreted in entirely different ways. FoxPro recognizes the first entry as a numeric value of 3. The second entry is stored as a string of characters—in this case, the character 3. If you apply a string option to the numeric variable or try to use the string variable in a calculation, you will get all sorts of errors in your program. Different types of variables cannot be used interchangeably unless you use functions (like ASC, DTOC, and VAL) to convert the type.

FoxPro provides you with debugging tools to help you track down hard-to-find bugs in your programs. These tools take the form of several SET commands: SET TALK, SET ECHO, SET STEP, and SET ALTERNATE.

Using SET TALK

You have routinely used the SET TALK command in previous examples. If SET TALK is activated (which it is by default), FoxPro displays responses to its commands that perform calculations or display record numbers (like LOCATE). This extra information isn't all that necessary during daily operation of the program, but in debugging it is useful to display results as the command file is being executed. To see this "talk" on the screen, tack on the SET TALK ON command at the beginning of the command file. You can then watch the screen as the program is run for hints that will help you find the errors in the program. Using SET TALK OFF turns off the screen display of processing results. Note that turning on either SET TALK or SET ECHO (detailed next) slows down program execution.

Using SET ECHO

SET ECHO is similar to SET TALK. The SET ECHO command causes each command line to be printed on the screen as it is executed. This lets you follow the flow of the program. Since SET ECHO is normally deactivated, enter a SET ECHO ON command before running the program. Entering a SET ECHO OFF command disables the display.

17

Using SET STEP

FoxPro programs often execute with such speed that it is difficult to pace the flow of the program. If you use the SET STEP ON command, FoxPro pauses after the execution of each command line and displays the program inside a Trace window. Two options that appear at the bottom of the window are Cancel and Resume. Choose Resume to continue stepping through the program, or choose Cancel to halt program execution.

Using SET ALTERNATE

For problems that occur only when you are not around and some one else is using the program, you can use the SET ALTERNATE commands to save a record of operations to a disk file. SET ALTERNATE TO *filename* creates a file that stores any keyboard entries and most screen displays. The file has the extension .TXT. When the SET ALTERNATE ON command is used, everything that appears on your screen, with the exception of full-screen editing operations, is stored in the text file in ASCII format. When you no longer want the information to be stored in the file, you use the SET ALTERNATE OFF command. You can continue to use SET ALTERNATE ON and SET ALTERNATE OFF as many times as desired to add more text to the file. When you are finished with the process altogether, you can close the file with the CLOSE ALTERNATE command.

You can later examine the contents of the text file to see what replies to the program were typed and what program responses occurred as a result. Obviously, using these commands may quickly consume disk space, so consider available disk space before using the SET ALTERNATE commands for an extended period of time.

HINT: SET ALTERNATE can also generate text files for use with word processors. See Chapter 18 for details.

Customizing FoxPro with Set Commands

Other SET commands can be used to customize your program and take advantage of various FoxPro features. The list presented here is not complete, but it does include the most commonly used SET commands.

SET BELL

The SET BELL ON command activates the beep that sounds during data entry. The beep is normally on and sounds when you fill a field with data or enter incorrect data into a field (such as character data into a numeric field). SET BELL OFF deactivates the beep.

SET CARRY

When you use APPEND, the record that appears on the screen is normally blank. Entering a SET CARRY ON command causes FoxPro to copy the entries in the fields of the previous record to the new record when you issue an APPEND command. SET CARRY OFF disables this feature.

SET COLOR

The SET COLOR command sets color for screen display for a color monitor and sets screen highlighting for a monochrome monitor. The normal format of the command is

   SET COLOR TO *standard, enhanced, border*

where *standard, enhanced,* and *border* are pairs of letters, separated by a slash, that represent the desired foreground and background colors or screen highlighting. The values are shown in Table 17-1. If you have a color monitor, try the following:

```
SET COLOR TO B/W, R/GR, BR
CLEAR
LIST STATUS
```

This results in a standard display of blue letters on a white background, an enhanced (reverse-video) display of red letters on a brown background, and a border color of magenta. On monochrome monitors, acceptable values are white, black, and the letter U (for underline), which causes all characters on the screen to be underlined.

SET CONSOLE

The SET CONSOLE command turns screen displays on or off. SET CONSOLE is normally on, but once a SET CONSOLE OFF command is encountered, no information is displayed on the screen, although commands will still be executed. Not until a SET CONSOLE ON is executed will information again be displayed. Using SET CONSOLE is like turning the monitor screen on or off.

SET DATE

The SET DATE command sets the desired format for date values and expressions. FoxPro offers any one of ten date formats: American

Color Code for
SET COLOR
Table 17-1.

Color	Code
Black	N
Blue	B
Green	G
Cyan	BG
Red	R
Magenta	BR
Brown	GR
White	W
Blank (secure)	X

(*MM/DD/YY*), ANSI (*YY.MM.DD*), British/French (*DD/MM/YY*), Italian (*DD-MM-YY*), Japan (*YY/MM/DD*), USA (*MM-DD-YY*), German (*DD.MM.YY*), MDY (*MM/DD/YY*), DMY (*DD/MM/YY*), and YMD (*YY/MM/DD*). Unless told otherwise, FoxPro sets the default value of the date format to American. The format of the command is SET DATE *format,* where *format* is American, ANSI, British, Italian, French, German, Japan, USA, MDY, DMY, or YMD.

SET DECIMALS

SET DECIMALS may be useful when dealing with foreign currencies.

This command sets the number of decimal places that are displayed during calculations. The format of the command is SET DECIMALS to *expression,* where *expression* is an integer value limiting the decimal places. Thus, if SET DECIMALS is assigned to 4, then 4 decimal places are displayed until another SET DECIMAL command is executed. The default is 2 digits. Numbers are rounded off as necessary to match the settings of SET DECIMALS.

SET ESCAPE

The SET ESCAPE command disables the ability of the Esc key to interrupt a program. To disable the Esc key, you enter the SET ESCAPE OFF command. SET ESCAPE ON turns the Esc key back on. In most cases, the use of SET ESCAPE OFF within a program is recommended. You probably do not want novice users pressing the Esc key and seeing the dialog box with the Cancel, Ignore, and Suspend choices appearing. Most novice users would have no idea what to do at such a point. Simply add a SET ESCAPE OFF statement near the start of your program to disable the use of the Esc key.

SET EXACT

The SET EXACT command tells FoxPro to perform (or not to perform) exact comparisons between character strings. The format of the command is SET EXACT ON/OFF. The default for SET EXACT is off. For example, assuming that SET EXACT is off, the commands

```
USE MEMBERS
LIST FOR LASTNAME = "Rob"
```

finds all records with Robinson in the Lastname field, because FoxPro will only compare as many characters as are contained in the string to the right of the operator (in this case, three characters). When SET EXACT is off, FoxPro will only compare as many characters as there are in the shorter string, so in the previous example FoxPro only looks at the first three characters because there are only three characters in "Rob". By comparison, the commands

```
SET EXACT ON
USE MEMBERS
LIST FOR LASTNAME = "Rob"
```

will not find any records in the MEMBERS database that apply, because Rob is not an exact match of Robinson.

HINT: Use SET EXACT to add precision to your searches.

SET NEAR

The SET NEAR command tells FoxPro to position the record pointer at the nearest record if a FIND or SEEK operation is unsuccessful. If SET NEAR is off (which is the default) and you perform a FIND or SEEK command that is not successful, the record pointer is placed at the end of the database, and the EOF function returns a logical true. You can use the SET NEAR ON command to tell FoxPro to get as close as possible if a search of the index is not successful. This can be useful when you are searching for the beginning of a range of data.

SET FUNCTION

The SET FUNCTION command changes the performance of the function keys. Each function key is assigned to a FoxPro command. When pressed, the keys execute the commands shown in Table 17-2

Function Key	FoxPro Command
F1	HELP;
F2	SET;
F3	LIST;
F4	DIR;
F5	DISPLAY STRUCTURE;
F6	DISPLAY STATUS;
F7	DISPLAY MEMORY;
F8	DISPLAY;
F9	APPEND;

Function Key
Assignments
Table 17-2.

(the semicolons following the commands produce carriage returns). You can change the function keys, with the exception of F1 and F10, to any character expression of 79 characters or fewer by entering

SET FUNCTION *integer-expression* TO "*character-string*"

The F1 key is reserved for the Help key, and the F10 key is reserved for the FoxPro menus.

The character string must be enclosed in quotes. For example, to change F7 from DISPLAY MEMORY to BROWSE, enter

```
SET FUNCTION "7" TO "BROWSE;"
```

Remember to include the semicolon to produce a return.

The SET FUNCTION command can be quite useful for reducing the number of repetitive steps during the data entry process. As an example, if you include the following SET FUNCTION commands within the MENU.PRG program for Generic Videos, the function keys are redefined to enter the names of various cities and states:

```
SET FUNCTION "2" TO "Silver Spring"
SET FUNCTION "3" TO "Rockville"
SET FUNCTION "4" TO "Columbia"
SET FUNCTION "5" TO "Washington"
```

```
SET FUNCTION "6" TO "Alexandria"
SET FUNCTION "7" TO "Falls Church"
SET FUNCTION "8" TO "Arlington"
SET FUNCTION "9" TO "Springfield"
```

When the commands shown in this example have been executed, users can press the respective function keys during the APPEND or CHANGE process to enter the names without typing the actual keystrokes. You can also assign a sequence of commands to a function key, providing you separate commands with a semicolon and do not exceed the 79-character limit. During large data entry jobs, reassigning the function keys in this manner can save hours of time in entering records.

SET INTENSITY

This command turns on or off the reverse-video display of fields during full-screen operations such as APPEND. To activate reverse video, use SET INTENSITY ON; to deactivate reverse video, use SET INTENSITY OFF. In general, you use SET INTENSITY OFF only if you use the SET DELIMITERS command to change the default delimiters. Otherwise, you won't be able to gauge the limits of the data entry areas. SET INTENSITY is normally on, but you can find out the current state of SET INTENSITY or the status of any SET command by entering

```
LIST STATUS
```

The status of the SET commands and the function key designations is then displayed, along with other status information regarding FoxPro. Here is an example:

```
Processor is INTEL 80386
Currently Selected Database:
Select area: 1, Database in Use: C:\FOXDOS\DATA\MEMBERS.DBF  Alias: MEMBERS
 Structural CDX file:   C:\FOXDOS\DATA\MEMBERS.CDX
            Index tag:   LASTNAME    Key: LASTNAME
            Index tag:   ALLNAMES    Key: LASTNAME+FIRSTNAME
            Index tag:   NEWNAMES    Key: LASTNAME+FIRSTNAME
            Index tag:   DAYS    Key: EXPIREDATE
            Memo file:   C:\FOXDOS\DATA\MEMBERS.FPT
         Lock(s): Exclusive USE
```

```
File search path: C:\FOXDOS\DATA
Default disk drive: C:
Print file/device:  PRN:
Work area =    1
Margin    =    0
Decimals  =    2
Memowidth = 50
Typeahead = 20
Blocksize = 64
Reprocess =         0
Refresh   =    0 SECONDS
DOS memory available = 300k
DOS memory utilized = 0k


Date format: American
Macro Hot Key = SHIFT+F10
UDF parameters are passed by: VALUE
Textmerge Options
          Delimiters:  Left = <<  Right = >>
          Show
```

Alternate	- off	Console	- on	Fixed	- off	Safety	- on
ANSI	- off	Cursor	- on	Heading	- on	Space	- on
Bell	- on	Debug	- on	Help	- on	Status	- off
Blink	- on	Deleted	- off	Intensity	- on	Sticky	- on
Brstatus	- off	Device	- scrn	Lock	- off	Sysmenus	- on
Carry	- off	Dosmem	- off	Logerrors	- on	Talk	- on
Century	- off	Echo	- off	Mouse	- on	Textmerge	- off
Clear	- on	Escape	- on	Multilocks	- off	Title	- off
Color	- on	Exact	- off	Near	- off	Unique	- off
Compatible	- off	Exclusive	- on	Optimize	- on		
Confirm	- off	Fields	- off	Ptrint	- off		

SET MEMOWIDTH TO

The SET MEMOWIDTH TO command controls the width of a memo
field when it is displayed with a LIST or DISPLAY command. The
default value is 50 characters wide. Using SET MEMOWIDTH TO to
narrow the default width of a memo field can result in a more pleasing
display of information. As an example, the commands

```
USE MEMBERS
LIST LASTNAME, FIRSTNAME, PREFERENCE
```

result in this display:

```
Record#        LASTNAME        FIRSTNAME       PREFERENCE
    1      Miller          Karen           Prefers science fiction,
horror movies. Fan of Star Trek films.

    2      Martin          William         Enjoys Clint Eastwood, John
Wayne films.

    3      Robinson        Carol           Likes comedy, drama
films.

    4      Kramer          Harry           Big fan of Eddie Murphy.
Also enjoys westerns.
```

The display is an unattractive one because the words in the memo field wrap around the screen at the right-hand margin. The commands

```
SET MEMOWIDTH TO 20
USE MEMBERS
LIST LASTNAME, FIRSTNAME, PREFERENCE
```

provide a much more attractive format for the display of the memo field, as shown here:

```
Record#        LASTNAME        FIRSTNAME       PREFERENCE
    1      Miller          Karen           Prefers science
                                           fiction, horror
                                           movies. Fan of Star
                                           Trek films.

    2      Martin          William         Enjoys Clint
                                           Eastwood, John Wayne
                                           films.

    3      Robinson        Carol           Likes comedy, drama
                                           films.

    4      Kramer          Harry           Big fan of Eddie
                                           Murphy. Also enjoys
                                           westerns.
```

SET MESSAGE TO

The SET MESSAGE TO command displays an optional message at a specific line, and it is used to determine which line the message will appear on. For messages to appear, SET STATUS must also be on. First you enter SET MESSAGE TO *n,* where *n* is a number representing the line on the screen where the message should appear. Next, you use the command SET MESSAGE TO *character-string,* where *character-string* is the text you want included in the message. The message will appear whenever menus are displayed using the MENU TO command. The commands

```
SET MESSAGE TO 24
SET MESSAGE TO "Generic Videos Database System - F1 for HELP"
```

cause the message to be displayed at the bottom of the screen if SET STATUS is on and a menu is being displayed.

SET SAFETY

If your programs exit to FoxPro and not to DOS, be sure to SET SAFETY back on.

The SET SAFETY command lets you specify whether a prompt will warn you when FoxPro is about to overwrite an existing file. When SET SAFETY is on and any command will result in the overwriting of an existing file (such as rebuilding an index or sorting to a file with the same name as an existing file), FoxPro displays a warning message within a pop-up menu, and you must confirm the desire to overwrite the file by choosing Overwrite from the menu. SET SAFETY is normally on with FoxPro. This can result in unwanted messages and interruptions within your programs when you intentionally want to overwrite a file. In such cases, you can include a SET SAFETY OFF command in your program, and FoxPro will not stop to ask for confirmation before overwriting a file. If you use SET SAFETY OFF in a program, it is a good idea to turn it on again before returning the user to the command level.

Using User-defined Functions

User-defined functions (UDFs) are functions that you design, and like the standard functions in FoxPro, they can be provided with values and they return values. You can use UDFs to accomplish specialized tasks that are outside the range of the standard functions provided with FoxPro.

You can place functions at the end of your program file, along with any other procedures your program may be using. All UDFs start with the FUNCTION command, and they contain the commands and parameters needed to return the desired values. The names given to UDFs must be eight characters or less. The syntax of a UDF is shown here:

17

> FUNCTION *UDFname*
> PARAMETERS *list-of-parameters*
> *commands....*
> RETURN *value-or-variable*

where *list-of-parameters* is a list of one or more memory variable names representing the values you will supply to the function. As an example, perhaps you often need to convert temperature readings in centigrade stored in a scientific database to Fahrenheit. You could define the following function for this purpose:

```
FUNCTION FARENHT
PARAMETERS ctemp
ftemp = 9/5 * (ctemp+32)
RETURN ftemp
```

Then, at any location in the program, you call the function just as you would any other function. If the database field containing the temperature readings were named TEMP, you could use a statement like

```
? FARENHT(TEMP)
```

and the FARENHT function would return the value contained in the Temp field, converted to Fahrenheit.

You can also specify that UDFs return a true or false value, depending on how the commands within your UDF evaluate a particular condition. An example of this technique appears in the sample UDF shown here, which checks to see if a two-letter code for a state entered by a user is actually a valid state:

```
FUNCTION ValState
PARAMETERS State
IF UPPER(state) $ "AK AL AR AZ CA CO CT DC DE FL GA + ;
HI IA ID IL IN KA KY LA MA MD ME MI MN MO MS MT NB + ;
NC ND NH NJ NM NY OH OK OR PA RI SC SD TN TX UT VA + ;
VT WA WI WV WY"
        RETURN .T.
ENDIF
RETURN .F.
```

A portion of a data entry program could use the function to verify for proper entries, as shown here:

```
@ 7, 5 SAY "State: " GET MSTATE
READ
IF .NOT. ValState(MSTATE)
        WAIT "Error in State code."
        LOOP
ENDIF
<...rest of program...>
```

If the user's response did not match one of the two-letter codes defined in the function, the function would return a value of false, causing the error message to appear.

Drawing Bar Graphs

Bar graphs can be drawn by using the CHR and REPLICATE functions to plot representative columns on the screen. If your printer supports the extended character set, you can route the output to the printer and achieve similar results. Given a database containing the data shown here:

```
Record#         SALESREP        REPNUMB         AMTSOLD
        1       Jones, C.       1003            350.00
        2       Artis, K.       1008            110.00
        3       Johnson, L.     1002            675.00
        4       Walker, B.      1006           1167.00
        5       Keemis, M.      1007             47.00
        6       Williams, E     1010            256.00
        7       Smith, A.M.     1009            220.00
        8       Allen, L.       1005            312.00
        9       Smith, A.       1001            788.50
```

```
10        Jones, J.     1011        875.00
11        Shepard, F.   1004       1850.00
12        Robertson, C. 1013        985.50
```

plotting the data with the following program results in the display shown in Figure 17-1.

```
*Bars.PRG is bar graph program.
SET TALK OFF
Divisor = 30
*See note in text on calculating Divisor.
*AmtSold is field in database to be graphed.
CLEAR
USE SALES
@ 2,1
*above line positions cursor at row 2, col 1.
DO WHILE .NOT. EOF( )
        BarLength = INT(AMTSOLD/DIVISOR)
        @ ROW( ), 2 SAY REPLICATE(CHR(177),BarLength)
        @ ROW( )+1,2 SAY "Name: " + SALESREP
        @ ROW( ) + 2,0
        IF ROW( ) > 18
                @ 20,2 SAY "-------—300-------600------900--" +;
                "----1200------1500------1800"
                @ 1,0 TO 21,79 DOUBLE
                @ 23,5
                WAIT "Press a key for next screen..."
                CLEAR
                @ 2,1
        ENDIF
        SKIP
ENDDO
IF ROW( ) > 2
        @ 20,2 SAY "-------—300-------600-------900--" +;
        "----1200------1500------.1800"
        @ 1,0 TO 21,79 DOUBLE
        @ 23,5
        WAIT
ENDIF
RETURN
```

The program takes the contents of a field that is to be graphed (in this case, Amtsold), divides it by a set amount (Divisor), and uses the INT

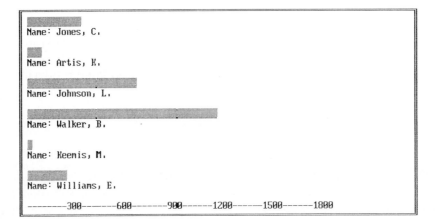

Bar graph

Figure 17-1.

function to return an integer based on that figure. This number, stored to the memory variable BarLength, is then used as an argument in the REPLICATE function to determine the length of the bar. The ROW function, which returns the current row in which the cursor is located, is used at various locations in the program to place data on the screen.

The calculation of the best value for Divisor is a simple matter. Assuming you want to use nearly a complete screen width for the longest bar, the value of Divisor must be no less than the value of the highest amount to be graphed, divided by the available screen width. In this example, the highest sales amount ($1850) divided by a screen width of 76 (which leaves room for the starting position and the borders) suggests a value of no less than 24. The example used a value of 30, partly to make the scale simple to construct and partly to leave room for increased sales performance. You will need to adjust the scope of your scale accordingly.

Using Modular Programming

Don't get the impression that this section is going to take you through a textbook discussion of the benefits of system analysis and modular design. You can find that kind of a discussion in many basic programming textbooks. What this section does demonstrate are ways to design FoxPro applications in modular form so you can easily utilize the same code repeatedly.

Assuming you write programs in FoxPro (and if you didn't, you probably would not be reading this chapter), chances are you're spending time on the development of more than one program. If all your FoxPro work centers around a single application (like that monster of a sales-tracking system that keeps tabs on things at your office), then writing very modular programs may not help you much except as an aid in debugging and providing a warm feeling for having developed efficient code. But if you have to develop or maintain a number of different applications at your work location or for others, you will save a lot of time by writing programs in modules and reusing the modules (with appropriate modifications) for different tasks.

The first step in adopting a system of modular FoxPro coding is to recognize that tasks in most FoxPro applications fall into the same common groups. Applications provide a main menu, leading to other choices stored in individual programs or as procedures. Among those other tasks handled within the submodules, or individual procedures of the FoxPro application, are the tasks of adding records, editing records, and deleting unwanted records. You can further break many of the subtasks down into common parts.

As an example, consider the task of editing records in a database. Well-written routines for editing records are faced with at least six tasks within the editing module:

1. Find the desired record to edit.
2. Store the contents of the fields into memory variables.
3. Display the prompts and memory variables on the screen.
4. Allow editing of the memory variables with GET statements.

5. Perform any data validation desired, and allow corrections when necessary.

6. Move the validated data into the database.

Most programs written to perform a task like this one are written as one complete submodule that handles all these steps. But if you are going to use and reuse your code for multiple applications, strict adherence to the concepts behind modular programming suggests that you take it a step further and create individual modules for the individual steps. This may seem like a lot of work, but the first time you need to use the existing code in another application, you'll be glad that you chose this method of design.

A general approach you can consider following in designing highly modular code for a FoxPro application is to write the following routines for each database file and then enclose the routines within a procedure file that can be accessed through the SET PROCEDURE TO *filename* command. For more information on procedures, see SET PROCEDURE in Appendix A. Such a procedure file might contain the following:

✦ A "display" procedure for adding borders and graphic designs in a consistent format

✦ A "makevars" procedure for creating memory variables

✦ A "fillvars" routine for moving the contents of a field into a memory variable

✦ A "sayer" routine to display the prompts and memory variables

✦ A "getter" routine for getting memory variables

✦ A "validate" routine for performing any desired data validation

✦ A "movevars" routine to move the contents of the memory variables into the database fields

✦ A "finder" routine to locate records based on FIND or SEEK commands using available index files

As an example, consider the procedures that are described within a procedure file:

```
*Procedrs.PRG
Procedure Border
@ 0,0 TO 19,79 DOUBLE
@ 0,1 TO 4,78 DOUBLE
Draw = 1
Do While Draw < 4
        @ Draw, 2 SAY REPLICATE(chr(176),76)
        Draw = Draw + 1
Enddo
Return
*************************
Procedure Finder
DO MAKEVARS
@ 3,5 SAY "Enter BLANKS to EXIT."
@ 5,5 SAY "Last name? " GET M_LAST
@ 6,5 SAY "First name? " GET M_FIRST
READ
STORE M_LAST + M_FIRST TO FINDIT
SEEK FINDIT
RETURN
*************************
Procedure Sayer
@ 5,10 SAY "Last Name:"
@ 5,22 SAY M_LAST
@ 6,10 SAY "First name:"
@ 6,22 SAY M_FIRST
@ 7,10 SAY "Address:"
@ 7,22 SAY M_ADDRESS
@ 8,15 SAY "City:"
@ 8,22 SAY M_CITY
@ 9,15 SAY "State:"
@ 9,22 SAY M_STATE
@ 10,15 SAY "Zip:"
@ 10,22 SAY M_ZIP
RETURN
*************************
Procedure Getter
@ 5,22 GET M_LAST
@ 6,22 GET M_FIRST
@ 7,22 GET M_ADDRESS
@ 8,22 GET M_CITY
@ 9,22 GET M_STATE
@ 10,22 GET M_ZIP
RETURN
```

```
*************************
Procedure MakeVars
PUBLIC M_LAST, M_FIRST, M_ADDRESS, M_CITY,;
M_STATE, M_ZIP
M_LAST = space(15)
M_FIRST = space(15)
M_ADDRESS = space(25)
M_CITY = space(15)
M_STATE = space(2)
M_ZIP = space(10)
RETURN
*************************
Procedure FillVars
M_LAST = LASTNAME
M_FIRST = FIRSTNAME
M_ADDRESS = ADDRESS
M_CITY = CITY
M_STATE = STATE
M_ZIP = ZIPCODE
RETURN
*************************
Procedure MoveVars
REPLACE LASTNAME WITH M_LAST, FIRSTNAME WITH M_FIRST,;
ADDRESS WITH M_ADDRESS, CITY WITH M_CITY,;
STATE WITH M_STATE, ZIPCODE WITH M_ZIP
RETURN
*************************
Procedure Validate
IF M_LAST = SPACE(15)
   WAIT " Name required!"
   VALID = .F.
ENDIF
RETURN
```

By putting all of these tasks in a procedure file and using DO
commands to call the procedures from your add, edit, and delete
subroutines, you can repeatedly use the same procedures in all of the
routines. A program for adding records utilizing these procedures can

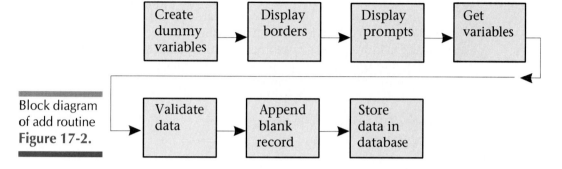

Block diagram
of add routine
Figure 17-2.

17

be visually laid out in a block diagram, as shown in Figure 17-2. The
resultant code that might be used is as follows:

```
*Adder.PRG adds records
VALID = .T.
DO WHILE .T.
     DO MAKEVARS
     CLEAR
     DO BORDER
     @ 3,10 SAY "DATA ENTRY SCREEN ADD NEW RECORDS"
     DO SAYER
     DO GETTER
     READ
     DO VALIDATE
     IF .NOT. VALID
          LOOP
     ENDIF
     APPEND BLANK
     DO MOVEVARS
     ACCEPT "Add another record? Y/N:" TO ANS
     IF UPPER(ANS) = "N"
          EXIT
     ENDIF
ENDDO
```

The beauty of taking program modularization down to this level is that you can get away with the same code that is already in the procedures for the edit and delete routines. An editing routine, assuming the database is indexed on a combination of last and first names, is illustrated in the block diagram shown in Figure 17-3. The resultant code that might be used is shown here:

```
*Editor.PRG edits records
SET INDEX TO NAMES
DO WHILE .T.
        CLEAR
        DO MAKEVARS
        DO FINDER
        VALID = .T.
        IF FOUND( )
            CLEAR
            DO BORDER
            DO FILLVARS
            DO SAYER
            DO GETTER
            READ
            DO VALIDATE
            IF .NOT. VALID
                EXIT
            ENDIF
            DO MOVEVARS
            CLEAR
            ACCEPT "Edit another? Y/N " TO ANS
            IF UPPER(ANS) = "N"
                    EXIT
            ENDIF
        ELSE
            CLEAR
            @ 5,5 SAY "No record by that name!"
            WAIT
            EXIT
        ENDIF
    ENDDO
```

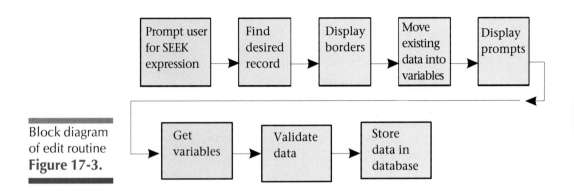

Block diagram
of edit routine
Figure 17-3.

Your routine for deleting records would use much of the same code, as illustrated in Figure 17-4 and shown in this code:

```
*Eraser.PRG deletes records
SET INDEX TO NAMES
DO WHILE .T.
     CLEAR
     STORE "Y" TO ANS
     DO MAKEVARS
     DO FINDER
     IF FOUND( )
          CLEAR
          DO BORDER
          DO FILLVARS
          DO SAYER
          @ 20,5 SAY "Delete record, are you SURE? Y/N:"
          @ 20,40 GET ANS
          READ
          IF UPPER(ANS) = "Y"
               DELETE
          ENDIF
     ELSE
          CLEAR
          @ 5,5 SAY "No record by that name!"
```

```
            WAIT
            EXIT
        ENDIF
ENDDO
```

Since the routines that perform the adding, editing, and deleting of records are generic routines (containing few or no specifics to that particular application), when you need to rewrite an application for a different database design, you'll need to make most changes only in the procedure file.

When do you modularize? It's easy to get carried away and modularize virtually every task in an application, but this probably won't buy you visible benefits in every case. A major objective of this approach is to save you the time it takes to duplicate program code in more than one location, so a general rule to follow is obvious: If the task is likely to be repeated at more than one place in your application, code that task as a procedure and call it from the procedure file. If the task will only be performed once, you may want to leave it as program code integral to that particular program, since calling it as a procedure won't provide you with any visible benefits.

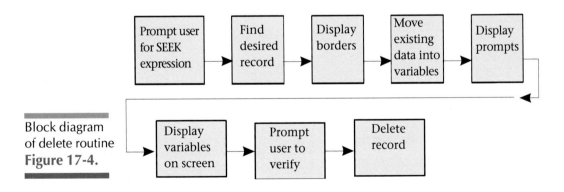

Block diagram of delete routine
Figure 17-4.

CHAPTER

FOXPRO

18

USING FOXPRO WITH OTHER SOFTWARE

The ability to exchange information with other programs enhances the power of FoxPro. FoxPro allows you to transfer files between it and most popular software available for the PC. There is just one condition to FoxPro's ability to transfer information: the other programs must be able to transfer information in a format acceptable to FoxPro.

If your work with FoxPro will include a considerable amount of data sharing between FoxPro and other popular software, consider upgrading to version 2.5 or above if you are not already using it. Version 2.5 of FoxPro significantly enhances the program's ability to share data easily with other programs by adding the capability to load and save data files in popular file formats, and it provides full file and program compatibility with its cousin, FoxPro for Windows. The formats in which FoxPro can transfer information include Lotus 1-2-3, Lotus Symphony, Microsoft Excel, Borland's Paradox, and Ashton-Tate's Framework II. By comparison, version 1.*x* of FoxPro can load and save files only in certain types of ASCII formats and in FoxBase Plus/dBASE III PLUS formats.

File Formats

You can transfer information between FoxPro and another program in various formats. Version 1.*x* of FoxPro includes Delimited format (ASCII text in a predefined format, with fields separated by characters or blanks), System Data format (SDF), and DBMEMO3/FOXPLUS format (files with memo fields in dBASE III/III PLUS and FoxBase Plus format). As described shortly, delimited and SDF files are composed of ASCII text in a special format.

In version 2 or above, you can transfer information by using any of the formats just described. Additionally, you can transfer files by using any one of five Lotus 1-2-3 or Symphony formats (WK1, WK3, WKS, WR1, and WRK) or in Microsoft Excel worksheet format (XLS). You can also transfer files by using the common Data Interchange Format (DIF), Paradox format, Microsoft Symbolic Link format (SYLK), or Microsoft Multiplan 4.0 format. And you can read Framework or RapidFile databases into FoxPro. While you cannot write files in Framework or RapidFile formats, you can write files in dBASE III PLUS format, which can be used easily by Framework or RapidFile.

ASCII Format

The term *ASCII format* refers to files that are composed of characters and spaces not necessarily arranged in any particular order. ASCII stands for the American Standard Code for Information Interchange, an international method of representing information in computers. Text files created by most word processors can be stored as ASCII text. You use ASCII files if you need to merge the contents of a database with a document created by a word processor. If, for example, your database contains a list of names, you can save those names to a text file in ASCII format. You can then use your word processor to call up the text file and use it as part of a document.

Delimited Format

Delimited-format ASCII files are composed of records in which the fields are *delimited,* or separated by a specific character or a space. If the character fields are surrounded by a certain character (such as a quotation mark) and fields are separated by a comma, the format is called Character-Delimited. If the fields are separated by a single space, the format is called Blank-Delimited.

Character-delimited files can use any character as the delimiter, but the most commonly used format surrounds the data in each character field with quotation marks and separates each field from other fields by a comma. Each record ends in a carriage return, so each record occupies a separate line. The following example shows a character-delimited file using this common format:

```
"Miller","Karen","4260 Park Avenue","Chevy Chase","MD","20815-0988"
"Martin","William","4807 East Avenue","Silver Spring","MD","20910-0124"
"Robinson","Carol","4102 Valley Lane","Falls Church","VA","22043-1234"
"Kramer","Harry","617 North Oakland Street","Arlington","VA","22203"
"Moore","Ellen","270 Browning Ave #2A","Takoma Park","MD","20912"
"Zachman","David","1617 Arlington Blvd","Falls Church","VA","22043"
"Robinson","Benjamin","1607 21st Street, NW","Washington","DC","20009"
"Hart","Wendy","6200 Germantown Road","Fairfax","VA","22025"
```

SDF Format

Like delimited files, files in SDF format store each record as an individual line, so the records are separated from each other by carriage returns. However, the fields in an SDF file are a preset width, regardless of the data stored in a particular record. All records are therefore identical in length. (The term SDF was popularized by Ashton-Tate, the original inventors of dBASE; many other vendors call the same type of file flat files, fixed-length files, or DOS text files.) FoxPro has the ability to store files in SDF format for use by other programs. Many

18

spreadsheets can store data on a disk in SDF. FoxPro can then read those files, using an SDF option of the APPEND command (which is discussed shortly).

The following example shows a file in SDF format created by FoxPro using the Lastname, City, Expiredate, and Tapelimit fields of the Generic Videos database. Note that dates are stored in a year-month-day format in the file.

Mainframe data is often stored in SDF format.

```
Miller       Chevy Chase      19940725   6
Martin       Silver Spring    19940704   4
Robinson     Falls Church     19950905   6
Kramer       Arlington        19941222   4
Moore        Takoma Park      19961117   6
Zachman      Falls Church     19940919   4
Robinson     Washington       19950917   6
Hart         Fairfax          19941019   2
```

The SDF format uses a fixed number of spaces for each field, regardless of the actual size of the information in the field. Information that is too long to fit in an SDF file is truncated.

DBMEMO3 or FOXPLUS Format

The DBMEMO3 and FOXPLUS formats create files in dBASE III/III PLUS and FoxPlus file format. Using either FOXPLUS or DBMEMO3 results in the creation of the same type of file. FoxPro provides these options to aid in the transferring of database files containing memo fields. FoxPro stores memo field data in a manner that is more efficient than, but not compatible with, most other dBASE-language products. As a result, trying to open a FoxPro database file containing memo fields causes error messages with products that normally accept dBASE files, such as Lotus 1-2-3, Excel, FoxBase and Foxbase Plus, dBASE III PLUS, and dBASE IV. To get around this problem, you can use the DBMEMO3 or FOXPLUS format when working with files with memo fields. Either format results in the creation of a file in the older FoxBase Plus/dBASE III PLUS format. That file can then be read by other products that have the ability to read dBASE files. You need the DBMEMO3/FOXPLUS format even when transferring data to dBASE IV, because FoxPro and dBASE IV use different methods of storing memo-field data.

Most database programs can use data in DBMEMO3/ FOXPROPLUS format.

Note that the DBMEMO3/FOXPLUS format is not needed if your database has no memo fields. (Using it won't hurt, but it won't provide any benefits, either.) Database files without memo fields can be used "as is" in any other product that can read a file in dBASE format.

Lotus File Formats

Programs made by Lotus Development (such as the popular Lotus 1-2-3 spreadsheet) use various Lotus file formats. Versions 2 or above of FoxPro provide the capability to write files in any one of four Lotus formats and to read files in any one of five Lotus formats. You can write files using the WK1, WKS, WR1, and WRS type formats. You can read files in any of these formats and in the WK3 format. Lotus 1-2-3 version 2.*x* uses the WK1 format, Lotus 1-2-3 version 3.*x* uses the WK3 format, Lotus 1-2-3 version 1A uses the WKS format, Lotus Symphony version 1.0 uses the WRK format, and Lotus Symphony versions 1.1 and 1.2 use the WR1 format. When data is read from any of these spreadsheet files into a FoxPro database, the columns of the spreadsheet become fields in the database, and the rows of the spreadsheet become records in the database file. Note that Lotus 1-2-3 version 3.*x* reads all Lotus file formats, so you can copy from FoxPro into any of the available Lotus formats if you are using Lotus version 3.*x*.

18

Microsoft File Formats

Version 2 or above of FoxPro reads and writes files using the MOD, SYLK, or XLS TYPE options. MOD files are compatible with Microsoft's Multiplan, version 4.01. SYLK is an acronym for Symbolic Link, a file format used by some Microsoft programs (including Microsoft Chart and earlier versions of Microsoft Multiplan). The XLS TYPE option is used with Microsoft Excel, a popular spreadsheet running under Windows and on the Macintosh.

Ashton-Tate File Formats

All versions of FoxPro can use the DBMEMO3 or FOXPLUS TYPE options to create database files in the popular dBASE III PLUS file format; these can be used by most Ashton-Tate products. In addition, version 2 or above of FoxPro can read files from Framework databases or RapidFile databases, using the FW2 and RPD type options.

Paradox and DIF File Formats

Version 2 or above of FoxPro reads and writes files by using the DIF type option and reads Paradox 3.5 files by using the PDOX type option. The DIF format (an abbreviation for Document Interchange Format) can be used by a wide assortment of programs, including VisiCalc (a spreadsheet), older versions of R:Base, and PC-File III (a database manager). Internally, the DIF format bears a resemblance to character-delimited format files.

When transferring data out of FoxPro, you must decide what format you wish to use. A list of some of the better known programs and the types of data they can exchange is shown in Table 18-1. As a general rule, most word processors transfer in ASCII, Delimited, or SDF format. You generally use the Delimited format for mailmerge files. Many spreadsheets transfer data in SDF format, and most database managers transfer data in Delimited format. All but the earliest versions of Lotus 1-2-3 and all versions of Symphony can read and write files in the dBASE file format. If it isn't obvious which format your software package uses, check the owner's manual.

Brand	Type of Package	File Type
WordPerfect	word processor	delimited, SDF, or DIF
Microsoft Word	word processor	delimited or SDF
Lotus 1-2-3	spreadsheet	WK1, WK3, or WKS
Excel	spreadsheet	XLS
Quattro Pro	spreadsheet	WK1, WK3, or WKS
dBASE III/IV	database manager	FOXPLUS/DBMEMO3
Paradox	database manager	FOXPLUS/DBMEMO3

File Formats for
Other Software
Table 18-1.

Data Sharing with the APPEND and COPY Commands

Many exchanges of data between FoxPro and other programs are accomplished with the aid of certain TYPE options within the COPY and APPEND commands. Using COPY, you can copy data from FoxPro to another program; using APPEND, you can append, or transfer, data from another program into a FoxPro database. The normal format for these commands, when used with a TYPE option, is as follows:

COPY TO *filename* [SCOPE] [FIELDS *fieldlist*]TYPE *type*

APPEND FROM *filename* [FIELDS *fieldlist*] TYPE *type*

18

In this case, *filename* is the name of the file to be transferred between FoxPro and the other program, and *type* is one of the acceptable types. The acceptable TYPE options in version 1.*x* are DELIMITED [WITH *character*], SDF, and DBMEMO3/FOXPLUS. Versions 2 and above add the TYPE options of DIF, MOD, PDOX, SYLX, WK1, WKS, WR1, WRK, and XLS. Also, the FW2 and RPD (Framework and RapidFile) TYPE options can be used with the APPEND FROM command but not with the COPY TO command. The WITH parameter of the DELIMITED option lets you specify a character to use as the field delimiter in place of the default quotation marks.

As a brief example, to copy the Generic Videos database into a dBASE III file that could be read by Lotus 1-2-3 version 3.0, you might use this command in version 2 or above:

```
COPY TO 123FILE TYPE WK3
```

and this command in version 1.*x*:

```
COPY TO 123FILE TYPE DBMEMO3
```

You might use the following command to transfer a file from SuperCalc 3 to FoxPro:

```
APPEND FROM SCFILE TYPE SDF
```

You can add other options, such as a scope (ALL, NEXT, or a record number) or a list of fields to the COPY command when transferring data to other programs. You can also use the FOR condition to specify records that will be transferred. Note that you can include a FOR clause when importing data from foreign files with APPEND, but a scope is not allowed when importing foreign files.

Examples of Transferring Files

The rest of this chapter provides working examples of transferring files. Since you may not be using the software packages described here, you may not be able to follow along with the examples. If you have the software package mentioned or a similar software package with the ability to use the file formats acceptable to FoxPro, try using the examples with your software.

Transferring from FoxPro to WordStar and Other Word Processors

Most word processors work with ASCII format, so let's try it first. Suppose you needed to pull names and salary amounts from the database to provide a memo to the company president containing all employees' salary amounts. You can use the TO FILE option of the LIST command to help you perform this task. When you enter the LIST command (along with any preferred fields) followed by TO FILE and a file name, the data displayed with LIST is also stored as ASCII text in the file you named within the command.

Try using the TO FILE option of the LIST command by entering the following:

```
USE MEMBERS
LIST LASTNAME, FIRSTNAME, EXPIREDATE TO FILE PEOPLE.TXT
```

Now exit FoxPro and load your word processor. Enter the command normally used by your word processor to read an ASCII file. When your word processor asks you for the file name to load, enter the drive and the path of your FoxPro data directory, followed by the file name PEOPLE.TXT. The file should then appear on your screen. Figure 18-1 shows an example of the file loaded into Write for Microsoft Windows.

File transfer
from FoxPro to
Windows Write
Figure 18-1.

You can also store the output of a report in a file by adding the TO FILE option at the end of a REPORT FORM command. As an example, the command

```
REPORT FORM SAMPLE TO FILE REPS.TXT
```

creates a file named REPS.TXT containing the data in the report format generated by the stored report SAMPLE.

At the bottom of the file that was transferred with FoxPro, there may be a left-pointing arrow or a similar graphics character (whether or not there is one depends on what word processor you are using). These characters represent an end-of-file marker that FoxPro produced when it was finished writing to the file. You can use the ⌈Backspace⌋ key or a DELETE command to erase these unwanted characters. Different word processors interpret this end-of-file marker in different ways, so you may see a character other than ^@ or a left-pointing arrow.

Get out of your word processor in the usual manner, and reload FoxPro now.

Transferring from FoxPro to MailMerge and Other Database Managers

Many word processors can use delimited files.

Delimited formats are used by the merge-print options of many word processors and by some other database managers. If you need to transfer data to another database manager, you should first check your documentation to see if the database manager will accept files in dBASE format. If it can, use the file directly (if no memo fields are present), or use the DBMEMO3/FOXPLUS format instead of the Delimited format. If you need data in Delimited format, use the DELIMITED option of the COPY command.

To create the delimited file, copy the fields from the active database to a separate file used by the other program. The format of the COPY command with the DELIMITED option is

COPY TO *filename* [SCOPE] [FIELDS *fieldlist*] TYPE DELIMITED

where *filename* is the name of the file that will contain the fields. You can limit which records to copy by including the scope, specified by ALL, NEXT, or RECORD. Fields can be limited by the FIELDS *fieldlist* option. When you specify the DELIMITED option, the .TXT extension is automatically appended to *filename*.

As an example, let's say that you need to transfer a list of the names, addresses, and cities from MEMBERS to a file named DATAFILE that will be used by another database manager. Enter the following commands:

```
USE MEMBERS
COPY TO DATAFILE FIELDS LASTNAME, FIRSTNAME, ADDRESS,
CITY, STATE, TYPE DELIMITED
```

The DATAFILE.TXT file created by COPY TO will contain one line for each record that was copied from MEMBERS. Each record includes the member's last name, first name, address, city, and state. Each field is enclosed by quotation marks, and fields are separated by commas. FoxPro automatically adds the .TXT extension unless you specify otherwise.

The TYPE command can be used to list on the screen the contents of any disk file. Let's examine DATAFILE with the TYPE command to see the Delimited file format. With the TYPE command you are required to supply the file extension (in this case, .TXT). Enter the command

```
TYPE DATAFILE.TXT
```

and your display will resemble the following:

```
"Miller","Karen","4260 Park Avenue","Chevy Chase","MD"
"Martin","William","4807 East Avenue","Silver Spring","MD"
"Robinson","Carol","4102 Valley Lane","Falls Church","VA"
"Kramer","Harry","617 North Oakland Street","Arlington","VA"
"Moore","Ellen","270 Browning Ave #3C","Takoma Park","MD"
"Zachman","David","1617 Arlington Blvd","Falls Church","VA"
"Robinson","Benjamin","1607 21st Street, NW","Washington","DC"
"Hart","Wendy","6200 Germantown Road","Fairfax","VA"
```

This file can be used by many other database managers, or it can be used by the merge-print options of many word processors to create a form letter. (More detailed explanations of using FoxPro data for a Microsoft Word or WordPerfect mailmerge appear in the next section.) In such cases, you must use the appropriate commands of the particular database manager or to import a file in the Delimited format.

Remember that when you import data into FoxPro with the APPEND command, the database structure must match the structure of the records within the file that contains the data. In other words, the fields must be in the same order, and the fields in the FoxPro database should be wide enough to accommodate the incoming data. As an example, if you had a file of names and addresses in your word processor laid out in this format:

Lastname	(longest name: 12 characters)
Firstname	(longest name: 10 characters)
Salary	(dollar amounts not larger than 999.99)
Hired	(a date)

and you wanted to transfer data in such a format to a FoxPro database, you would need to create a database structure like the following one:

18

Field Name	Field Type	Width	Decimal
Lastname	Character	12	
Firstname	Character	10	
Salary	Numeric	6	2
Hired	Date	8	

In such a case, the field names would not matter. What is important is that the fields in the matching database structure are in the same order as in the structure of the records in the incoming file.

Creating Files for Use with Mailmerge Options

If your word processor supports some type of mailmerge or merge-print operation, you may prefer to create a foreign file and use that file with your word processor to generate form letters. The precise approach differs from word processor to word processor, so some of the more popular approaches are covered in detail here.

Microsoft Word

With Microsoft Word, you can create a delimited file with the default delimiters of commas and quotation marks. Microsoft Word expects the names of the fields to appear as the very first line of text in the foreign file, with the fields separated by commas (under Word for DOS) or separated by tabs or commas (under Word for Windows). Using the prior example again, the foreign file that Microsoft Word needs to use would resemble this:

```
last,first,address,city,state,zip
"Miller","Karen","4260 Park Avenue","Chevy Chase","MD","20815-0988"
"Martin","William","4807 East Avenue","Silver Spring","MD","20910-0124"
"Robinson","Carol","4102 Valley Lane","Falls Church","VA","22043-1234"
```

18

```
"Kramer","Harry","617 North Oakland Street","Arlington","VA","22203"
"Moore","Ellen","270 Browning Ave #2A","Takoma Park","MD","20912"
```

A quick and painless way to do this is to build a file that contains the heading and then use the DOS COPY command to combine the heading file with the foreign file to produce a file ready for use by Microsoft Word. This could be done entirely within FoxPro with commands like these:

```
SET TALK OFF
SET ALTERNATE TO HEADS
SET ALTERNATE ON
? "Last,First,Address,City,State,Zip"
?
CLOSE ALTERNATE
COPY TO WFILE FIELDS LAST, FIRST, ADDRESS,;
CITY, STATE, ZIPCODE TYPE DELIMITED
RUN COPY HEADS.TXT + WFILE.TXT WORDFILE.TXT
```

See your word processor documentation for details on duplicating delimited files.

Note that if you are using Word for Windows, the TYPE DELIMITED option should be TYPE DELIMITED WITH TAB. The resultant file, called WORDFILE.TXT in this case, would resemble the foreign file shown earlier, with the header containing the field names for use by Microsoft Word as the first line in the foreign file.

When designing a form letter from within Microsoft Word for DOS, use `Ctrl`-`[` to mark the start of each field and `Ctrl`-`]` to mark the end of each field. The `Ctrl`-`[` key combination actually produces a symbol that resembles a double less-than sign, and pressing `Ctrl`-`]` produces a symbol resembling a double greater-than sign. In Word for Windows, first create a main merge document by using the usual procedures (see your Word documentation for details). Then, while typing the document, use `Ctrl`-`F9` to produce a double- brace symbol, and type the name of the field between the double braces. Using these characters, you can create a form letter like the following example:

```
<<data wordfile.txt>>


                            Johnson, Johnson
                            Fennerson & Smith
                            303 Broadway South
                            Norfolk, VA 56008


<<first>> <<last>>
<<address>>
<<city>>, <<state>> <<zip>>

Dear <<first>> <<last>>:


      In response to your letter received, we are
pleased to enclose a catalog of our latest products. If
we can answer any questions, please do not hesitate to
call.


Sincerely,



Mike Rowe
Sales Manager
```

You could generate the form letters using the Print Merge command from within Microsoft Word. (See your Microsoft Word documentation for details, if needed.)

An Export Program for WordPerfect

If you wish to use the Mailing Merge feature of WordPerfect, then you must do things a little differently than with most other software. WordPerfect expects to see data on individual lines, all flush left, with the ends of fields marked by a ^ R followed by a carriage return. The end of a record is indicated by a ^ E followed by a return. A data file when loaded within WordPerfect would resemble the following:

```
Jerry^R
Sampson^R
1412 Wyldewood Way^R
Phoenix^R
AZ^R
78009^R
^E
Paris^R
Williamson^R
P.O. Box 1834^R
Herndon^R
VA^R
22070^R
^E
Mary^R
Smith^R
37 Mill Way^R
Great Neck^R
NY^R
12134^R
```

Unfortunately, you cannot create a file like this with something as simple as a COPY command. You can, however, write a short program to accomplish this task. To generate such a file, simply write each desired field out to a line of a file, and end that line with a ^R (ASCII 18). After the last field of the record, write a line containing only ^E (ASCII 5). You can use the SET ALTERNATE TO and SET ALTERNATE ON commands to turn on the output to a foreign text file, and write each desired line until done; then close the foreign file with the CLOSE ALTERNATE command.

As an example, the following program would perform such a task. You could enter the command MODIFY COMMAND *filename* (where *filename* is the name you want to give the program) and enter the program as shown, saving it with Ctrl-W. Substitute your field names and database file name for the ones used in the following example.

```
*CREATES Word Perfect MAIL MERGE FILES.
USE MEMBERS
SET TALK OFF
STORE CHR(18) TO ENDFIELD
STORE CHR(5) TO ENDREC
SET ALTERNATE TO PERFECT
SET ALTERNATE ON
GO TOP
DO WHILE .NOT. EOF( )
  ? TRIM(FIRSTNAME) + ENDFIELD
  ? TRIM(LASTNAME) + ENDFIELD
  ? TRIM(ADDRESS) + ENDFIELD
  ? TRIM(CITY) + ENDFIELD
  ? STATE + ENDFIELD
  ? ZIPCODE + ENDFIELD
  ? ENDREC
  SKIP
ENDDO
CLOSE ALTERNATE
RETURN
```

When you run the program with the DO command, the result would be a foreign file similar to the one just shown, with each field on a separate line terminated by the ASCII character ^ R, with ^ E on lines between the records. To use the files in a WordPerfect form letter document, first make note of the order of the fields as output by your program (the first field after an end-of-record indicator is field 1, the next is field 2, and so on). In WordPerfect, when creating the form letter, use the Alt - F9 key combination to define the field numbers desired. For example, when you press Alt - F9 and enter **F** followed by **3** (to indicate field #3) and then press the Enter key, WordPerfect enters a symbol (^F3^) that indicates that the contents of the third field in the sequence will appear in that position when the form letters are generated. Our WordPerfect form letter might resemble the following:

```
                    Johnson, Johnson
                    Fennerson & Smith
                    303 Broadway South
                    Norfolk, VA 56008


   ^F1^ ^F2^
   ^F3^
   ^F4^, ^F5^ ^F6^


   Dear ^F1^ ^F2^:


        In response to your letter received, we are
   pleased to enclose a catalog of our latest products. If
   we can answer any questions, please do not hesitate to
   call.


   Sincerely,



   Mike Rowe
   Sales Manager
```

Save the letter by using the usual save commands for WordPerfect. To generate the form letters in WordPerfect, first use [Ctrl]-[F5] to import the FoxPro file, select 1 from the menu (DOS Text File), and then select 2 (Retrieve). Eliminate any blank lines at the top of the document, and save the file with [F10] under a new name. Use [F7] to exit the document and get to a blank screen. Then press [Ctrl]-[F9], choose Merge, enter the name of the form letter, and then enter the name of the file containing the data. WordPerfect will proceed to create the letters, which can then be printed in the usual manner.

Transferring Between FoxPro and Lotus 1-2-3 or Symphony

Exchanging data between Lotus 1-2-3 or Symphony and FoxPro is a simple matter. Version 1.*x* of FoxPro has the ability to read and write files in dBASE III format. Versions 2 and above of FoxPro can read and write files in most Lotus formats. And all but the earliest versions of Lotus and Symphony can read and write data in dBASE III file format.

If you want to transfer data to Lotus 1-2-3 or Symphony, use the COPY command with the various Lotus type options, or with the DBMEMO3/FOXPLUS file type where memo fields exist, as shown here in version 2 or above:

```
COPY TO LOTUSFIL TYPE WKS
```

and as shown here in version 1.*x:*

```
COPY TO LOTUSFIL TYPE DBMEMO3
```

The COPY TO command copies the contents of an existing database to a file that can be read by Lotus 1-2-3 or Symphony. If you created the file in dBASE III PLUS format, you must use the Translate option of Lotus 1-2-3 to convert the file into 1-2-3 file format (see your Lotus documentation for details on the Translate option).

To transfer spreadsheet data from Lotus 1-2-3 or Symphony to FoxPro version 1.*x,* use the Translate option in 1-2-3 or Symphony to save the file in dBASE format. Then you can load the file directly in FoxPro; since the file is in dBASE format, no APPEND command is needed. No translation is needed if you are using FoxPro version 2 or above; simply use the appropriate TYPE option of the APPEND command to append the contents of the Lotus worksheet to an existing FoxPro database.

If you have Lotus 1-2-3, try the following commands to create a file for conversion to a 1-2-3 spreadsheet:

```
USE RENTALS
COPY TO 123FILE
```

if you are using version 1.*x,* or

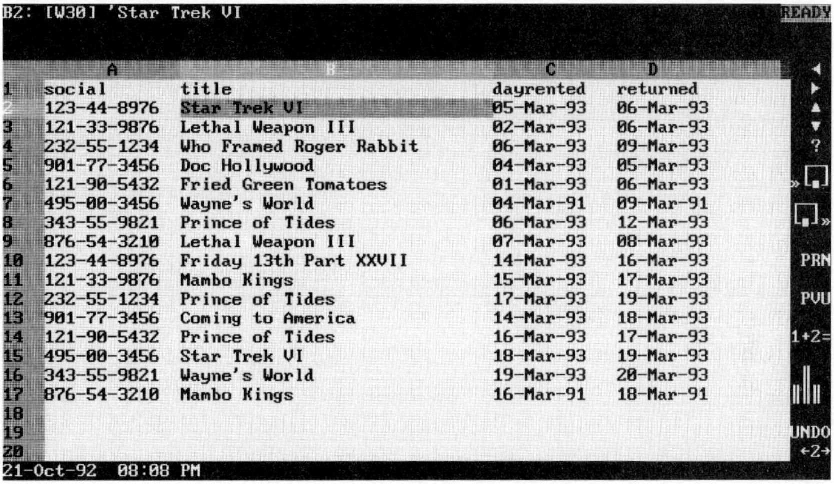
B2: [W30] 'Star Trek VI READY

	A	B	C	D
1	social	title	dayrented	returned
2	123-44-8976	Star Trek VI	05-Mar-93	06-Mar-93
3	121-33-9876	Lethal Weapon III	02-Mar-93	06-Mar-93
4	232-55-1234	Who Framed Roger Rabbit	06-Mar-93	09-Mar-93
5	901-77-3456	Doc Hollywood	04-Mar-93	05-Mar-93
6	121-90-5432	Fried Green Tomatoes	01-Mar-93	06-Mar-93
7	495-00-3456	Wayne's World	04-Mar-91	09-Mar-91
8	343-55-9821	Prince of Tides	06-Mar-93	12-Mar-93
9	876-54-3210	Lethal Weapon III	07-Mar-93	08-Mar-93
10	123-44-8976	Friday 13th Part XXVII	14-Mar-93	16-Mar-93
11	121-33-9876	Mambo Kings	15-Mar-93	17-Mar-93
12	232-55-1234	Prince of Tides	17-Mar-93	19-Mar-93
13	901-77-3456	Coming to America	14-Mar-93	18-Mar-93
14	121-90-5432	Prince of Tides	16-Mar-93	17-Mar-93
15	495-00-3456	Star Trek VI	18-Mar-93	19-Mar-93
16	343-55-9821	Wayne's World	19-Mar-93	20-Mar-93
17	876-54-3210	Mambo Kings	16-Mar-91	18-Mar-91
18				
19				
20				

21-Oct-92 08:08 PM

FoxPro table in spreadsheet
Figure 18-2.

```
COPY TO 123FILE TYPE WKS
```

if you are using version 2 or above. Enter **QUIT** to leave FoxPro and return to the DOS prompt. If your copy of 1-2-3 is in a different subdirectory of a hard disk, then use the DOS COPY command to copy the file, 123FILE.DBF or 123FILE.WKS, to that directory.

Some spreadsheets will not recognise memo fields from a FoxPro file.

Load Lotus 1-2-3 in your usual manner. If you created the file in dBASE format, when the Lotus Access menu appears, choose Translate to get into the Translate utility. (Note that you can also get into the Translate utility directly from DOS by entering **TRANS** at the DOS prompt.) You are first asked which format you wish to translate from; choose dBASE III. The next screen asks which format you wish to translate to; select your version of 1-2-3 or Symphony as appropriate. A screen with some notes regarding dBASE files appears, and you can press Esc to continue.

Enter the file name of the incoming file, 123FILE.DBF (or select it from the list of files), and accept the default name for the converted file (123FILE.WKS or 123FILE.WK1, depending on your version of 1-2-3). Select Yes to proceed with the translation.

Once the file has been translated (or if you created the file using FoxPro 2 or above), you can use the usual file load commands in 1-2-3 or

Symphony to load the spreadsheet. In the example in Figure 18-2, the Set Column-Width command in Lotus 1-2-3 was used to widen the columns, to allow for a full display of the Social, Title, Dayrented, and Returned fields.

Spreadsheet users should keep in mind that nearly all spreadsheets are limited in size by the available memory of the computer, while FoxPro files are limited in practice by available disk space. It is possible to export a file so large that it cannot be loaded into your spreadsheet. When creating files for spreadsheets from large databases, you may find it necessary to export small portions of the file. You can use the FOR condition with the commands, or you can set a filter with the SET FILTER command before exporting the data to the spreadsheet file. Also, when transferring spreadsheet data to FoxPro, you should only export the database section of the spreadsheet (excluding any titles, macro references, or explanatory text).

NOTE: When you translate logical fields from a dBASE file, Lotus 1-2-3 recognizes only T (true) and F (false). It does not recognize Y (yes) and N (no), even though these are acceptable logical values in FoxPro.

Transferring from FoxPro to Non-dBASE-compatible Spreadsheets

If you need to save a file in SDF format, you use the SDF option of the COPY command. The SDF format is used for transferring data from FoxPro to spreadsheets that cannot read dBASE files. (This format is also useful for exchanging data with mainframe computers.) Try this variation of the COPY command to create an SDF file:

```
USE MEMBERS
COPY TO CALCFILE FIELDS LASTNAME, CITY, EXPIREDATE TYPE SDF
```

The CALCFILE file created by this command will contain one line for each record, with each record containing Lastname, City, and Expiredate fields. Instead of being surrounded by quotes and separated

18

by commas, each field is allotted space according to its width. To see the file in SDF format, enter

```
TYPE CALCFILE.TXT
```

and the following is displayed on your screen:

```
Miller      Chevy Chase      19940725
Martin      Silver Spring    19940704
Robinson    Falls Church     19950905
Kramer      Arlington        19941222
Moore       Takoma Park      19961117
Zachman     Falls Church     19940919
Robinson    Washington       19950917
Hart        Fairfax          19941019
```

How you load the file into your spreadsheet depends on what spreadsheet you are using. It would be impossible to explain the file loading commands for all spreadsheets, but in most cases you need to use an appropriate load command that lets your spreadsheet receive files in the SDF format. Your spreadsheet documentation should contain details on how you can do this.

Transferring from Other Spreadsheets to FoxPro

Assuming the use of FoxPro version 2 or above, your first choice when transferring data from a spreadsheet to FoxPro should be either one of the Lotus file types or the XLS file type (in the case of Microsoft Excel). Many spreadsheets (even those made by companies other than Lotus) can read and write files in one of the Lotus file formats. When appending from a Lotus or Excel spreadsheet, you need to use the APPEND FROM command, which means you need a database file with the same structure as the spreadsheet. If your intended database already exists, it is usually easiest to copy the range of desired data in the spreadsheet to a blank area of the spreadsheet and move the columns around until the structure of the spreadsheet matches the structure of the database. Then, save that range of the spreadsheet to a separate file (see your spreadsheet manual for details) and load the spreadsheet file into FoxPro with the appropriate TYPE option of the APPEND FROM command.

With version 1.*x* of FoxPro, note that an increasing number of spreadsheets (including Microsoft Excel, Twin, and VP-Planner) can work with the popular dBASE III file format. Check your spreadsheet owner's manual to see if your spreadsheet can save files in dBASE III file format. Most spreadsheets that cannot write dBASE-compatible files do provide an option for printing a file to disk, and the resulting disk file matches the SDF format. Different spreadsheets use different commands to create such files, so check your spreadsheet manual for instructions. In most cases, the way to get a spreadsheet into SDF format is to use the "print to disk" option of the particular spreadsheet.

Before transferring an SDF file into a database, be sure that the database field types and field widths match the SDF format precisely. You can use the APPEND FROM command with the SDF option to transfer the data into FoxPro. The format of APPEND FROM with the SDF option is

APPEND FROM *filename* TYPE SDF

(Note that you can't use a scope with APPEND when appending from non-FoxPro files.) The APPEND FROM with TYPE SDF operates exactly like APPEND FROM with TYPE DELIMITED. The file name is the name of the file that will be transferred and appended to the active database file.

The fields in the database must be exactly as wide as the fields in the SDF file. An alternative method for transferring data from a spreadsheet is to convert the SDF file to a delimited file. This is done by using your word processor to edit the file, removing extra spaces between fields, and adding commas and quotation marks to separate the fields. You can then transfer the data with the DELIMITED option of the APPEND FROM command, but this time you need not be concerned that the field widths precisely match the width of the SDF files. If the database fields are narrower, the incoming data is truncated to fit the field.

Transferring from Other Word Processors to FoxPro

Transferring data from other programs into a FoxPro database may take just a little more work than the process of sending FoxPro data to other programs (particularly to word processors). This is because files brought into a FoxPro database must follow a precise format, such as an SDF or Delimited format. Thus, when you send data from your word processor to a FoxPro database, you must edit the file from your word processor until it matches the format of a delimited or an SDF file.

WordPerfect users should note that it is possible to create a delimited file in WordPerfect, which can then be read easily into FoxPro. To do so, you must merge a secondary file (a file containing data) with a primary file (a merge document containing only quotes, commas, and field markers). See your WordPerfect manual for additional details.

After your word processor creates a file in Delimited or SDF format, you can use the APPEND command of FoxPro to load the file. At first glance it may seem easier to use the SDF format instead of the Delimited format because you don't have to type all the quotes and commas. But if you choose the SDF format, you must keep track of the size of each field; each field must have the same width as the database field in which you will be transferring data. For this reason, it is sometimes easier to use the Delimited format.

When transferring files created by your word processor (or any other program) to FoxPro, you must also create or use a FoxPro database with a structure that matches the design of the files you wish to transfer. For purposes of simplicity, the following examples assume that the files created by other software match the structure of the Generic Videos database.

Let's try a transfer using a delimited file. Suppose you have created a mailing list with a word processor and you now want to use that mailing list with FoxPro. If you have a word processor that can create files in ASCII text, follow along.

Use your word processor to create the following delimited file and give it the name MAIL2.TXT. If you are using Microsoft Word, WordPerfect, or IBM DisplayWrite, save the file as ASCII text.)

```
"123-80-7654","Johnson","Larry","4209 Vienna Way","Asheville","NC","27995"
"191-23-5566","Mills","Jeanette","13 Shannon Manor","Phoenix","AZ","87506"
"909-88-7654","Simpson","Charles","421 Park Avenue","New York","NY","10023"
```

Save the file as ASCII text with your word processor's save commands. Now load FoxPro. You use the DELIMITED option of the APPEND

FROM command to append the file to MEMBERS. The format of the APPEND command when used to import a delimited file is

APPEND FROM *filename* DELIMITED

To transfer MAIL2.TXT to FoxPro, enter the following commands:

```
USE MEMBERS
APPEND FROM MAIL2.TXT TYPE DELIMITED
```

FoxPro responds with the message "3 records added." To examine the database, enter **GO TOP** and then **LIST**, and at the bottom of the database you will see that the names and addresses from the mailing list have been added to the database.

In this example, fields are in order of social security number, last name, first name, address, city, state, and ZIP code. Fortunately, this is the same order as the fields in MEMBERS. In real life, though, things may not be as simple. When the fields in the database used by the other program do not match the database used by FoxPro, you will need to perform whatever work is necessary to make them match. You can do this in one of two ways: either change the order of the data in the other file or design a new database in FoxPro that matches the order of the data in the other file. In most cases, it is easiest to first create a matching file structure in FoxPro and then append the data from the other file. After the data has been appended to FoxPro, either modify the structure of the file or copy the data into a second file that has the fields in the desired order (in which case, FoxPro will match fields by the field names).

Notes About FoxPro and Other dBASE Compatibles

Files from FoxBase and FoxBase Plus can be used in FoxPro without your having to perform any changes. If you are using FoxPro 2.5 or above, you can work with files from FoxPro for Windows. You can also use FoxPro database files within FoxBase and FoxBase Plus. However, because of differences in the way memo-field text is stored, FoxBase or FoxBase Plus will not open a FoxPro database that contains memo fields. You must convert the database by using the COPY TO *filename* command with the TYPE DBMEMO3 or TYPE FOXPLUS option. The copied file can then be opened by FoxBase or FoxBase Plus.

You should use the same DBMEMO3/FOXPLUS TYPE option if exporting a file containing memo fields for use with other dBASE compatibles. This includes dBASE III PLUS, dBASE IV, PC-File DB, and Clipper. FoxPro files without memo fields can be used with no changes in these products.

18

A P P E N D I X

FOXPRO

GLOSSARY OF FOXPRO COMMANDS

This appendix contains a listing of FoxPro commands. Each command name is followed by the syntax of the command and a description of how the command works. Examples of applications are provided for some commands. You will recognize most commands from the tutorial section; others will be introduced here.

Because this book offers a beginning-to-intermediate-level text, some commands and options relating to advanced programming are not covered in detail here. Refer to your FoxPro documentation or to a more advanced text such as *FoxPro 2.5 for DOS: The Complete Reference* (Berkeley, CA: Osborne McGraw-Hill, 1993) for additional information about these commands.

Glossary Symbols and Conventions

1. All commands are printed in UPPERCASE, although you can enter them in either upper- or lowercase letters.

2. All parameters of the command are listed in *italics*.

3. Any part of a command or parameter that is enclosed in left and right [ ] brackets is optional.

4. When a slash separates two choices in a command, as in ON/OFF, you specify one choice but not both.

5. Ellipses (. . .) following a parameter or command mean that the parameter or command can be repeated "infinitely"—that is, until you exhaust the memory of the computer.

6. The *scope* parameter, which is always an option, can have four different meanings, depending on the command: ALL for all records; NEXT *n* for *n* number of records beginning at the current position of the record pointer; REST for all records from the pointer position to the end of the file; and RECORD *n* for record number *n*.

7. The term *expC* indicates a character expression, *expN* indicates a numeric expression, and *expL* indicates a logical expression. Where data type does not matter, the term *expression* is used.

List of Commands

\ or \\

Syntax

```
\ <<text line>>
\\ <<text line>>
```

The \ and \\ commands are used in implementing the text-merge capability of FoxPro. The \ and \\ commands send a line of text to the current output device. If the \ command is used, a carriage return and linefeed are sent before the contents of the text line are evaluated. If the \\ command is used, a carriage return and linefeed are not sent.

Expressions (including field names), variables, and functions placed within delimiters in the text line will be evaluated if SET TEXTMERGE is ON (see SET TEXTMERGE). If SET TEXTMERGE is OFF, the expressions, variables, or functions appear as literal characters. For example, if SET TEXTMERGE were ON, the following command

```
\ <<LASTNAME>>
```

which consists of the command followed by a field called Lastname, would output the contents of that field for the current record of the active database. If SET TEXTMERGE were OFF, the same command would output the name of the field enclosed by the double angle brackets (in this case, Lastname).

? or ??

Syntax

```
? / ??[expression][PICTURE "clause"][FUNCTION "functionlist"]
[AT expN]
```

A

The ? command displays the value of a FoxPro expression. If a single question mark (?) is used, the cursor executes a carriage return and linefeed, and then the value of the expression is displayed. If the double question mark (??) is used, the cursor is not moved before the value of the expression is displayed. The PICTURE and FUNCTION options may be used to customize the appearance of the displayed information. The AT option may be used to place the expression at a specific column location.

???

Syntax

```
??? expC
```

The ??? command sends characters to the printer without changing the current row and column positions. Use this command to send control codes or escape sequences to the printer. To specify control codes, enclose the ASCII code in curly braces.

##

Syntax

```
@ row,col[SAY expression][PICTURE expression][FUNCTION list]
[GET variable][PICTURE expression][FUNCTION list][RANGE low,
high][VALID condition][ERROR expC][COLOR std/enhanced]
[COLOR SCHEME expN][WHEN expC][DEFAULT expC][OPEN WINDOW none]
[ENABLE/DISABLE][SIZE n rows by n cols]
```

The @ command places the cursor at a specific screen location, which is identified by *row,col*. The @ command can be used with one or more of the named options. The SAY option displays the value of the expression following the word "SAY." The GET option allows editing of the variable (which can be a field). The PICTURE option allows the use of templates, which specify the way data will be displayed or accepted in response to the GET option. The RANGE option is used with the GET option to specify a range of acceptable entries. The VALID option specifies acceptable entries for GET by using a condition. ERROR displays a custom error message if VALID is not met. COLOR defines new color settings for the @-SAY-GET command. COLOR SCHEME is a numeric value from 1 to 11, denoting colors based on the corresponding color scheme (see SET COLOR OF SCHEME). Note that a READ command must follow the use of GET commands to achieve full-screen editing. WHEN is a logical expression that permits or prevents editing in the GET. DEFAULT provides a default value for the GET. OPEN WINDOW is used with memo fields, to open a predefined window for the field.

DISABLE is used to disable editing in a GET field; the cursor skips the field. SIZE *rows x cols* can be used to define a size for the field other than the default.

Example

To place the message "Enter shareholder name:" at screen location 12,2 and to allow full-screen editing of the value contained in the variable SHN, enter

```
@ 12,2 SAY "Enter shareholder name:" GET SHN
```

Note that there are some additional options of the @ . . . GET command that are not covered here, due to their advanced nature. These options create check boxes, radio buttons, list boxes, pop-ups, and push buttons within programs. Refer to your FoxPro documentation for further information on these options of the @ . . . GET command.

@-BOX

Syntax

```
@ row1,col1,row2,col2 BOX expC
```

This command draws a box between the specified coordinates. (Note that this command is compatible with FoxBase Plus. If compatibility with dBASE IV is desired, use the @ *row,col* TO *row,col* variation of the command.) An optional character expression containing up to nine different characters may be specified, in which case those characters are used to construct the box. The first four characters define the four corners, starting from the upper-left corner and moving clockwise. The next four characters define the four sides, starting from the top and moving clockwise. The last character, if specified, is used as the background. If no character expression is provided, a single-line box is drawn.

Example

To draw a single-line box with the upper-left corner at row 4, column 1, and the lower-right corner at row 18, column 70, enter

```
@ 4,1,18,70 BOX
```

@-CLEAR TO
Syntax

```
@ row,col CLEAR / CLEAR TO row,col
```

This variation of the @ command clears a portion of the screen. If @ *row,col* CLEAR is used, the screen is cleared to the right of and below the coordinates provided. If @ *row,col* CLEAR TO *row,col* is used, the screen is cleared within a rectangular area, with the first coordinate indicating the upper-left corner and the second coordinate indicating the lower-right corner.

Example

To erase a rectangular area from row 4, column 5, to row 12, column 70, while leaving the remainder of the screen unchanged, enter

```
@ 4,5 CLEAR TO 12,70
```

@ . . . EDIT
Syntax

```
@ row,col EDIT variable-name[FUNCTION expC2][DEFAULT expr]
SIZE expN1, expN2[,expN3][ENABLE / DISABLE][MESSAGE expC3]
[VALID expL1 [ERROR expC4]][WHEN expL2][NOMODIFY][SCROLL]
[TAB / NOTAB][COLOR SCHEME expN4 / COLOR color-pairs-list]
```

The @ . . . EDIT command allows editing of text in a rectangular area. The text to be edited can be a field (referenced by the field name), a memo field, a variable, or an array element. All standard FoxPro editing features are available, wordwrap occurs normally, and text can be scrolled vertically. This command is used in advanced programming; for further details on this subject, refer to a more advanced programmer's text or to your FoxPro programmer's documentation.

@-FILL TO
Syntax

```
@ row1,col1 FILL TO row2,col2 [COLOR std/enhanced ] [COLOR
SCHEME expN]
```

A

The @-FILL TO command changes the color of the screen within the defined area. The *std/enhanced* is *x/y*, where *x* is the code for the standard color and *y* is the code for the enhanced color. If the COLOR option is omitted, the screen is cleared within the defined area. COLOR SCHEME is a numeric value from 1 to 11, denoting a color based on the corresponding color scheme (see SET COLOR OF SCHEME).

Example

```
@ 5,5 FILL TO 10,40 COLOR B/R
```

@-MENU
Syntax

```
@ row,col MENU array,expN1[,expN2][TITLE expC]
```

This command creates a pop-up menu. Note that the DEFINE BAR and DEFINE POPUP commands can accomplish the same result; DEFINE BAR and DEFINE POPUP are compatible with dBASE IV programs, while @ *row,col* MENU is compatible with FoxBase Plus programs. The row and column locations specify the left corner location of the menu; *array* contains a one-dimensional array that contains the menu items; *expN1* is the number of items in the menu; and *expN2* is an optional number of menu items to be displayed on the screen at one time, to a maximum of 17. TITLE is an optional menu title that appears at the top of the menu window.

@-PROMPT

Syntax

```
@ row,col PROMPT expC [MESSAGE expC]
```

This command, along with the MENU TO command, is used to create light-bar menus. (These commands for menu design are compatible with FoxBase Plus and Clipper; if compatibility with dBASE IV is desired, use the DEFINE POPUP and DEFINE BAR commands instead.) A series of PROMPT commands is used to display the options on the screen at the positions indicated by the *row,col* coordinates. The MENU TO command invokes the light-bar menu, and the user response is controlled by the cursor keys. A maximum of 128 prompts can be displayed on the screen at a time. If an optional message is included, the message appears at the row defined with the SET MESSAGE TO command when that particular option is highlighted in the menu.

Example

```
@ 5,5 PROMPT "1. Add records    "
@ 6,5 PROMPT "2. Edit records   "
@ 7,5 PROMPT "3. Delete records"
@ 8,5 PROMPT "4. Print records  "
@ 9,5 PROMPT "5. Quit System    "
MENU TO Mychoice
DO CASE
     CASE Mychoice = 1
          DO ADDER
     CASE Mychoice = 2
          DO EDITOR
     CASE Mychoice = 3
          DO ERASER
     CASE Mychoice = 4
          DO REPORTER
     CASE Mychoice = 5
          QUIT
ENDCASE
```

@-TO
Syntax

```
@ row,col TO row,col[DOUBLE / PANEL / border-string]
[COLOR standard [,enhanced ]][COLOR SCHEME expN]
```

This variation of the @ command draws a line or a rectangular border (box) on the screen. The first value represents the upper-left screen coordinate, and the second value represents the lower-right screen coordinate. If both coordinates share a horizontal or vertical coordinate, a line is drawn; otherwise, a rectangular border is drawn. When used with the DOUBLE options, the @ command draws double lines or borders (or a combination) on the screen. COLOR *standard* [,*enhanced*] denotes a color-pair combination for the foreground and background colors for the line or box. COLOR SCHEME is a numeric value from 1 to 11, denoting colors based on the corresponding color scheme (see SET COLOR OF SCHEME).

Example
To draw a single line from row 3, column 5, to row 3, column 50, enter the following:

```
@ 3,5 TO 3,50
```

To draw a double-line box with the upper-left corner at row 4, column 1, and the lower-right corner at row 18, column 70, enter

```
@ 4,1 TO 18,70 DOUBLE
```

ACCEPT
Syntax

```
ACCEPT [expC] TO memvar
```

The ACCEPT command stores a character string to the memory variable *memvar*. ACCEPT can be followed by an optional character expression.

A

If this expression is included, its contents will appear on the screen when the ACCEPT command is executed.

Example

To display the prompt "Enter owner name:" and store to the memory variable OWNER the character string that the user enters in response to the prompt, enter

```
ACCEPT "Enter owner name:" TO OWNER
```

ACTIVATE MENU

Syntax

```
ACTIVATE MENU menuname [PAD padname] [NOWAIT]
```

The ACTIVATE MENU command activates a predefined menu and displays that menu on the screen. If the PAD option is specified, the highlight bar appears at the named pad; otherwise, the first pad in the menu is highlighted.

The NOWAIT clause forces program execution to continue after the menu is displayed.

Example

```
ACTIVATE MENU MainMenu PAD Add A Record
```

ACTIVATE POPUP

Syntax

```
ACTIVATE POPUP popup-name
[AT row,col] [BAR expN] [NOWAIT]
```

The ACTIVATE POPUP command activates a predefined pop-up menu and displays it on the screen. The AT clause defines the menu's location. BAR *expN* defines which bar of the menu is highlighted by default. The NOWAIT clause forces program execution to continue after the pop up is displayed.

Example

```
ACTIVATE POPUP Printer
```

ACTIVATE SCREEN
Syntax

```
ACTIVATE SCREEN
```

The ACTIVATE SCREEN command redirects output to the screen instead of to a predefined window.

Example

```
ACTIVATE SCREEN
```

ACTIVATE WINDOW
Syntax

```
ACTIVATE WINDOW windowname-list / ALL [BOTTOM / TOP / SAME] [NOSHOW]
```

The ACTIVATE WINDOW command activates a predefined window from memory. After the ACTIVATE WINDOW command is used, all screen output is directed to that window. If the ALL option is used, all defined windows in memory are displayed in the order in which they were defined. Use BOTTOM or TOP to place a window at the bottom or top of a stack of existing windows. The SAME option applies only to windows previously hidden with DEACTIVATE WINDOW or HIDE WINDOW. Use SAME to put the previously hidden window back in the same position it occupied earlier. Use the NOSHOW option to send output to a window without changing the window's status (for example, if it was hidden, output goes to the window but it remains hidden).

Example

```
ACTIVATE WINDOW MyWindow
```

APPEND

Syntax

```
APPEND [BLANK]
```

The APPEND command appends records to a database. When the APPEND command is executed, a blank record is displayed, and FoxPro enters full-screen editing mode. If the BLANK option is used, a blank record is added to the end of the database, but full-screen editing mode is not entered.

APPEND FROM

Syntax

```
APPEND FROM filename[FIELDS fieldlist][FOR condition][TYPE
filetype][DELIMITED[WITH delimiter / BLANK / TAB]]
```

APPEND FROM copies records from *filename* and appends them to the active database. The FOR/WHILE option specifies a condition that must be met before any records will be copied. If the file name containing the data to be copied is not a FoxPro database, an acceptable type option must be used. Valid type options are DELIMITED, DELIMITED WITH BLANK, DELIMITED WITH TAB, DELIMITED WITH "*specified-character*," SDF, and the following: DIF, FW2, MOD, PDOX, RPD, SYLK, WK1, WK3, WKS, WR1, WRK, and XLS.

APPEND FROM ARRAY

Syntax

```
APPEND FROM ARRAY arrayname FOR condition
```

The APPEND FROM ARRAY command appends records to a database file from a named array. (Note that APPEND FROM ARRAY is compatible with dBASE IV; if you need compatibility with FoxBase Plus, use the GATHER FROM command instead.) The contents of each row in the array are transferred to a new record in the database file. The first column in the array becomes the first field, the second column in the array becomes the second field, and so on. If there are more elements in the array than fields in the database, the extra elements are ignored. If there are more fields in the database than there are elements in the array, the extra fields remain empty. The FOR clause, which is optional, lets you define a condition that must be met before data in the array will be added to a new record. An array must exist (defined with DECLARE and filled with data using STORE) before you can successfully use the APPEND FROM ARRAY command.

Example

```
APPEND FROM ARRAY TempData FOR Dues = "paid"
```

APPEND MEMO
Syntax

```
APPEND MEMO memofield-name FROM filename [OVERWRITE]
```

The APPEND MEMO command imports a file into a memo field. The contents of the file are normally added to the end of any existing text in the memo field. If the OVERWRITE option is used, the contents of the file overwrites any existing text in the memo field. FoxPro assumes that the file has an extension of .TXT. If this is not the case, the extension must be specified along with the file name. If the file has no extension, include a period at the end of the file name.

Example

```
APPEND MEMO comments FROM letter.doc
```

AVERAGE
Syntax

```
AVERAGE fieldlist [scope] [FOR condition] [WHILE condition]
[TO memvarlist / TO ARRAY arrayname] [NOOPTIMIZE]
```

The AVERAGE command computes an average of the specified numeric field listed in *fieldlist*. If the TO option is not used, the average is displayed on screen. If TO is used, the average of the first field is assigned to the first memory variable, the average of the second field to the second memory variable, and so on down the list; and the average is stored as the memory variable specified. If the *scope* option is not used, the quantifier of ALL is assumed, meaning all records in the database will be averaged unless you use the FOR or WHILE option. The FOR option can be used to specify a condition that must be met for the fields to be averaged. If you use the WHILE option, records will be averaged until the condition is no longer true. The NOOPTIMIZE clause turns off FoxPro's internal optimization techniques (also known as Rushmore).

BROWSE
Syntax

```
BROWSE FIELDS[fieldlist] [FOR for-clause] [FORMAT] [FREEZE
field] [LAST][NOAPPEND] [NOCLEAR][NODELETE][NOEDIT / NOMODIFY]
[NOMENU] [NOFOLLOW] [NORMAL] [NOWAIT] [SAVE] [WIDTH expN]
[WINDOW windowname] [PREFERENCE expC] [COLOR[standard]
[,enhanced][,border]] / [COLOR SCHEME expN] [NOOPTIMIZE]
[NOLINK] [NOLGRID] [NORGRID] [LEDIT] [LPARTITION] [PARTITION n]
[REDIT] [TIMEOUT n]
```

The BROWSE command displays up to 20 records from a database on screen. If the database contains too many fields to fit on the screen, BROWSE displays only the fields that fit. You can view more fields by scrolling to the left or right with the mouse or the [Tab] key. The contents of any field can be edited while in Browse mode. To save changes made during Browse, press [Ctrl]-[W]; to exit Browse, press [Esc]. The FIELDS option displays only the fields listed in *fieldlist*. FORMAT tells the Browse window to assume any settings of an active format file. FREEZE *field* freezes the cursor within the named field. LAST tells FoxPro to use the most recent configuration (window size, column sizes) of Browse, as stored in the FoxUser configuration file. NORMAL causes the Browse window to assume normal color attributes rather than those of a previously defined window.

If NOFOLLOW is included, changes to a field that is part of an index expression will not cause the Browse display to follow the record to its new location in the database. The NOWAIT option is used within programs; when included, program control continues immediately after the Browse window is opened, rather than waiting for the user to exit Browse mode. The SAVE option is also used only in programs; it keeps both the Browse window and any memo field window that is active open after editing is completed.

The NOAPPEND, NOEDIT, and NODELETE options restrict the use of appending, editing, or deleting when in Browse mode. The WIDTH option lets you adjust the width of columns. The WINDOW option causes the Browse display to appear in a previously defined window. PREFERENCE, when used initially, states the Browse settings under the name provided to the FoxUser file. When used with a previously stored name, PREFERENCE causes the Browse settings stored with that name to take effect. NOMENU prevents user access to the Browse menu. NOCLEAR leaves the Browse window visible on the screen after Browse mode is exited. The COLOR or COLOR SCHEME option may be used to specify colors for the Browse window.

If the FOR clause is included, only records matching the logical expression specified in the FOR clause will be included in the Browse window. The LEDIT and REDIT clauses cause the Browse window to be split, with one side in the Change (or Edit) mode. Use LEDIT to place the left half of the window in Edit mode; use REDIT to place the right half of the window in Edit mode. The PARTITION *n* clause forces the Browse window to split into partitions; the numeric value *n* specifies the column where the window is split. Use LPARTITION along with the PARTITION clause; when LPARTITION is included, the cursor is placed in the first field of the left partition.

The NOLGRID and NORGRID clauses remove the field lines from the left or right partition of a split Browse window. Use NOLGRID to remove the field lines from the left partition, and use NORGRID to remove the field lines from the right partition. The NOLINK clause breaks the normal link between the two sides of a split Browse window, allowing independent movement in each side. The NOOPTIMIZE clause turns off FoxPro's internal optimization techniques (also known as Rushmore). The TIMEOUT *n* clause lets you specify how long a Browse

A

window will wait for input; the value of *n* (in seconds) controls the
length of time the window remains on the screen without any user
input before the window closes. Note that the TIMEOUT clause can
only be used in programs; it has no effect when used from the
Command Window.

BUILD APP
Syntax

```
BUILD APP .fxp file FROM projectname
```

The BUILD APP command converts information stored in a project file
into a complete application. This command is typically used by
advanced programmers in building applications for mass distribution;
for further details on this subject, refer to a more advanced
programmer's text or to your FoxPro programmer's documentation.

BUILD PROJECT
Syntax

```
BUILD PROJECT project-file FROM
[program/menu/report/label/screen/library]
```

The BUILD PROJECT command creates a project database by opening
and processing one or more database, program, screen, report, label, or
library files. The project database can then be used along with the
BUILD APP command to build a complete application. This command
is typically used by advanced programmers in building applications for
mass distribution; for further details on this subject, refer to a more
advanced programmer's text or to your FoxPro programmer's
documentation.

CALCULATE
Syntax

```
CALCULATE [scope]options[FOR condition][WHILE condition]
[TO memvarlist/TO ARRAY arrayname] [NOOPTIMIZE]
```

The CALCULATE command calculates amounts, using standard financial and statistical functions. The functions are defined as part of the options list shown here. All records are processed until the scope is completed or the condition is no longer true. When used, the NOOPTIMIZE clause turns off FoxPro's internal optimization techniques (also known as Rushmore). The following financial and statistical functions can be used within the options list:

AVG(*expN*) calculates the numerical average of value *expN*.
CNT( ) counts the records in a database file. If a condition has been specified with the FOR clause, the condition must be met before the record will be counted.
MAX(*exp*) determines the maximum value in a field; *exp* is usually a field name or an expression that translates to a field name.
MIN(*exp*) determines the minimum value in a field; *exp* is usually a field name or an expression that translates to a field name.
NPV(*rate, flows,initial*) calculates the net present value where *rate* is the discount rate, *flows* is a series of signed periodic cash-flow values, and *initial* is the initial investment.
STD(*exp*) determines the standard deviation of values stored in a database field; *exp* is usually a field name or an expression that translates to a field name.
SUM(*exp*) determines the sum of the values in a database field; *exp* is usually a field name or an expression that translates to a field name.
VAR(*exp*) determines the variance of the values in a database field; *exp* is usually a field name or an expression that translates to a field name. The value supplied by VAR(*exp*) is a floating-point number.

A

Example

```
USE PERSONNL
SET TALK ON
CALCULATE MAX(SALARY), MIN(SALARY), AVG(SALARY)
```

CALL
Syntax

```
CALL module name [WITH expC / memvar]
```

The CALL command executes a binary (assembly language) program that was previously loaded into memory with the LOAD command (see LOAD). The WITH option is used to pass the value of the expression or memory variable to the binary program. The CALL command should be used only with external programs designed as binary modules. Normal executable programs should be accessed with the RUN / ! command.

CANCEL
Syntax

```
CANCEL
```

The CANCEL command halts execution of a command file and returns FoxPro to the Command window.

CHANGE
Syntax

```
CHANGE [scope] [FIELDS fieldlist] [FOR condition] [WHILE condition]
[NOAPPEND] [NOCLEAR] [NOEDIT] [NODELETE] [NOMENU]
```

The CHANGE command permits editing of fields listed in *fieldlist.* If the *scope* option is absent, the quantifier ALL is assumed. The FOR/WHILE option allows editing to only those records satisfying the condition. The NOAPPEND, NOEDIT, and NODELETE options restrict the appending, editing, or deleting of records. The NOCLEAR option leaves the display on the screen after the user exits the CHANGE process. NOMENU prevents the menu display.

Example
To edit the Tapelimit and Expiredate fields in the MEMBERS database, enter

```
CHANGE FIELDS TAPELIMIT, EXPIREDATE
```

CLEAR
Syntax

```
CLEAR
```

The CLEAR command erases the screen. CLEAR can also be used as an option of the @ command to clear the screen below and to the right of the location specified by the @ command.

Examples
To erase the entire screen, enter

```
CLEAR
```

To erase the screen below and to the right of the cursor at 12,20, enter

```
@ 12,20 CLEAR
```

CLEAR ALL
Syntax

```
CLEAR ALL
```

The CLEAR ALL command closes all open database, memo, index, and format files and resets the current work area to 1.

CLEAR FIELDS
Syntax

```
CLEAR FIELDS
```

The CLEAR FIELDS command clears the list of fields specified by the SET FIELDS command. The CLEAR FIELDS command has no effect if SET FIELDS was not previously used to specify fields (see SET FIELDS).

A

CLEAR GETS
Syntax

```
CLEAR GETS
```

The CLEAR GETS command clears all pending GET statements, or all GET statements that have not yet been accessed by a READ command. Use CLEAR GETS to prevent the next READ command in the program from invoking full-screen editing of the fields or variables named in the previous GET.

Example

```
ACCEPT "Enter Y to store entries, N to delete" TO ANS
IF ANS = "N"
  CLEAR GETS
ELSE
  READ
ENDIF
```

CLEAR MEMORY
Syntax

```
CLEAR MEMORY
```

The CLEAR MEMORY command erases all current memory variables.

CLEAR MENUS
Syntax

```
CLEAR MENUS
```

The CLEAR MENUS command clears all menus from the screen and erases all menus from memory.

CLEAR POPUPS
Syntax

CLEAR POPUPS

The CLEAR POPUPS command clears all pop-up menus from the screen and erases all pop-up menus from memory.

CLEAR PROGRAM
Syntax

CLEAR PROGRAM

The CLEAR PROGRAM command clears the buffer of any compiled program.

CLEAR PROMPTS
Syntax

CLEAR PROMPTS

The CLEAR PROMPTS command releases all menu prompts created with the @-PROMPT command from a screen or window.

CLEAR READ
Syntax

CLEAR READ [ALL]

The CLEAR READ command terminates the current READ. When CLEAR READ is used, program control returns to the previous READ command (if any). The ALL clause, when used, terminates all READS on all levels. The CLEAR READ command may be useful when multiple data entry screens are displayed by using nested levels of @ . . . SAY . . . GET commands followed by multiple READ statements.

CLEAR TYPEAHEAD
Syntax

```
CLEAR TYPEAHEAD
```

The CLEAR TYPEAHEAD command clears the contents of the typeahead buffer (see SET TYPEAHEAD).

CLEAR WINDOWS
Syntax

```
CLEAR WINDOWS
```

The CLEAR WINDOWS command clears all active windows from the screen and erases all windows from memory (see DEFINE WINDOW).

CLOSE [ALL]
Syntax

```
CLOSE filetype / [ALL]
```

The CLOSE command closes all file types listed in *filetype,* which can be ALTERNATE, DATABASES, FORMAT, INDEX, or PROCEDURE. If the ALL option is used, all open files are closed, including any that may have been opened by using low-level file functions of FoxPro.

CLOSE MEMO
Syntax

```
CLOSE MEMO memo-field [ALL]
```

The CLOSE MEMO command closes an open memo-field window. The ALL option closes all open memo windows.

COMPILE
Syntax

```
COMPILE filename / skeleton
```

The COMPILE command reads a FoxPro program or command file and creates an object (.DBO) file, which is an execute-only FoxPro program file. A skeleton composed of wildcards can be used in place of the file name; for example, COMPILE M*.PRG would compile all .PRG files beginning with the letter M.

Example

```
COMPILE mailer.prg
```

CONTINUE
Syntax

```
CONTINUE
```

The CONTINUE command resumes a search started by LOCATE. After LOCATE finds the record matching the criteria specified in the command, you can find additional records that meet the same criteria by entering CONTINUE (see LOCATE).

COPY
Syntax

```
COPY TO filename[scope][FIELDS fieldlist][FOR condition][WHILE
condition][[WITH] CDX | PRODUCTION][NOOPTIMIZE][TYPE][DBMEMO3/
FOXPLUS/DIF/MOD/SDF/SYLK/WK1/WKS/WR1/WRK/XLS/DELIMITED [WITH
delimiter /WITH BLANK/WITH TAB]]
```

The COPY command copies all or part of the active database to *filename*. If *scope* is not listed, ALL is assumed. The FIELDS option pinpoints the fields to be copied. The FOR option copies only those records meeting the condition. The WHILE option copies records as long as the condition is true. Specifying SDF will copy the file in SDF format; specifying DELIMITED will copy the file in Delimited format. The DBMEMO3 or FOXPLUS type is used when databases with memo fields must be copied out to dBASE III/III PLUS or FoxBase file format.

Note that additional TYPE options can be used to copy to foreign files. The additional type options, detailed in Chapter 18, are DIF, MOD, SYLK, WK1, WKS, WR1, WRK, and XLS.

Use the WITH CDX or WITH PRODUCTION clause to specify whether a new structural compound index file should be created along with the new database. (Both options perform the same task; include WITH CDX or WITH PRODUCTION if you want the .CDX file created with the database file.) The NOOPTIMIZE clause disables the normal internal optimization technology (also known as Rushmore).

Example
To copy Lastname, Firstname, and City fields from the active database MEMBERS to TOWNS, enter

```
COPY TO TOWNS LASTNAME, FIRSTNAME, CITY
```

COPY FILE
Syntax

```
COPY FILE source-file TO destination-file
```

The COPY FILE command creates an identical copy of a file. You must supply the extension in both *source-file* and *destination-file*. Note that you can include a drive and path designation along with the destination if desired.

Example

To copy a file named REPORTER.FRX to a new file named TESTER.FRX, enter

```
COPY FILE REPORTER.FRX TO TESTER.FRX
```

COPY INDEXES

Syntax

```
COPY INDEXES index-file-list / ALL [TO .cdx filename]
```

The COPY INDEXES command converts single-entry index files (.IDX files) into index tags within a compound index file (.CDX file). If you omit the TO clause, the .IDX index file information is added as tags to the structural compound index file. If you omit the TO clause and no structural compound index file exists, a new one is created with the same name as the database, and the tags are added to that file.

If you include the TO clause, the .IDX file index information is added as tags to the .CDX file specified as part of the option.

Example

To copy to the structural compound index file three .IDX files called NAMES, STATES, and ZIPS, you could use the following command:

```
COPY INDEXES names, states, zips
```

COPY MEMO

Syntax

```
COPY MEMO memofield-name TO filename [ADDITIVE]
```

The COPY MEMO command copies the contents of a memo field to a text file. A drive name and path can be included as a part of the file

A

name. If the ADDITIVE option is used, the text of the memo field will be added to the end of an existing file name; if the ADDITIVE option is omitted, any existing file with the same name will be overwritten.

Example

```
USE MEMBERS
GO 4
COPY MEMO preference TO A:COMMENTS.TXT
```

COPY STRUCTURE
Syntax

```
COPY STRUCTURE TO filename [FIELDS fieldlist]
[WITH CDX/PRODUCTION]
```

The COPY STRUCTURE command copies the structure of an active database to *filename,* creating a new, empty database file. Specifying FIELDS with *fieldlist* will copy only those fields to the new structure.

Use the WITH CDX or WITH PRODUCTION clause to specify whether a new structural compound index file should be created along with the new database. (Both options perform the same task; include WITH CDX or WITH PRODUCTION if you want the .CDX file created with the database file.)

COPY STRUCTURE EXTENDED
Syntax

```
COPY TO filename STRUCTURE EXTENDED
```

The COPY STRUCTURE EXTENDED command creates a new database with records that contain information about the fields of the old database. The new database contains the fields Fieldname, Fieldtype, Fieldlen, and Fielddec. One record in the new database is added for each field in the old database.

COPY TAG
Syntax

```
COPY TAG tagname [OF .cdx filename] TO index-file
```

The COPY TAG command converts a compound index (.CDX) file's tag information into a single index style (.IDX) index file. If you omit the OF clause, the index information is copied from the tag of the structural compound index file.

Example

To copy the index tag named NAMES from the structural compound index file to an .IDX-style index file called LASTNAME.IDX, you could use the following command:

```
COPY TAG names TO lastname.idx
```

COPY TO ARRAY
Syntax

```
COPY TO ARRAY arrayname [FIELDS fieldlist ][SCOPE][FOR
condition][WHILE condition][NOOPTIMIZE]
```

The COPY TO ARRAY command copies data from the fields of a database into an array. (Note that the COPY TO ARRAY command is compatible with dBASE IV; if you need compatibility with FoxBase Plus, use the SCATTER TO command instead.) For each record in the database, the first field is stored in the first element of the array, the second field in the second element, and so on. (You must first declare the array with the DECLARE command.) If the database has more fields than the array has elements, the contents of extra fields are not stored to the array. If the array has more elements than the database has fields, the extra elements in the array are not changed. Note that memo fields are not copied into the array. When used, the NOOPTIMIZE clause turns off FoxPro's internal optimization techniques (also known as Rushmore).

A

Example

```
USE HOURS
DECLARE ThisWeek [6,5]
COPY TO ARRAY ThisWeek NEXT 5
```

COUNT
Syntax

```
COUNT [scope][FOR condition][WHILE condition][TO memvar][NOOPTIMIZE]
```

The COUNT command counts the number of records in the active database that meet a specific condition. The *scope* option quantifies the records to be counted. The FOR option can be used to specify a condition that must be met before a record will be counted. If you use the WHILE option, counting will take place until the condition is no longer true. The TO option can be used to store the count to the memory variable *memvar*. When used, the NOOPTIMIZE clause turns off FoxPro's internal optimization techniques (also known as Rushmore).

Example
To count the number of records containing the letters MD in the State field and to store that count as the memory variable MTEMP, enter

```
COUNT FOR STATE = "MD" TO MTEMP
```

CREATE
Syntax

```
CREATE filename
```

The CREATE command creates a new database file and defines its structure. If CREATE is entered without a file name, FoxPro prompts you for one when the structure is saved. If CREATE is followed by a file name, a database with that file name will be created. The file name extension .DBF is added automatically to the file name unless you specify otherwise.

CREATE COLOR SET
Syntax

```
CREATE COLOR SET color set name
```

The CREATE COLOR SET command creates a new color set from the current color settings. When you use this command, all color pairs in every color scheme are saved in the newly created color set. A color set name can be up to ten characters long, and can contain numbers and underscores, but cannot start with a number. After creating the color set, you can load the color set with the SET COLOR SET command.

CREATE FROM
Syntax

```
CREATE file1 FROM file2
```

The CREATE FROM command creates a new database, with its structure based on a file created earlier with the COPY STRUCTURE EXTENDED command (see COPY STRUCTURE EXTENDED).

CREATE LABEL
Syntax

```
CREATE LABEL [filename]
```

The CREATE LABEL command creates a label form file. This file can be used with the LABEL FORM command to produce mailing labels.

CREATE MENU
Syntax

A

```
CREATE MENU [filename / ?][[WINDOW windowname1][IN [WINDOW]
windowname2 / IN SCREEN]
```

The CREATE MENU command activates the FoxPro menu creation
utility. After the desired menu is created, information about the menu
is stored in a special database with an .MNX extension. For details on
this subject, refer to a more advanced programmer's text, or to your
FoxPro programmer's documentation.

CREATE PROJECT
Syntax

```
CREATE PROJECT [file / ?][WINDOW windowname1][IN [WINDOW]
windowname2 / IN SCREEN]
```

The CREATE PROJECT command opens a project window, used for the
creation of a project database. A *project database* is a special database
used to keep track of all parts of a FoxPro project. This command is
typically used by programmers when building complete applications.
For details on this subject, refer to a more advanced programmer's text,
or to your FoxPro programmer's documentation.

CREATE QUERY
Syntax

```
CREATE QUERY [filename / ?]
```

The CREATE QUERY command displays the RQBE window, allowing
the creation of a query. The command is equivalent to choosing New
from the File menu and selecting Query in the dialog box. More details
about designing and saving queries can be found in Chapter 6.

CREATE REPORT
Syntax

```
CREATE REPORT [filename]
```

The CREATE REPORT (or, as an alternative, MODIFY REPORT) command creates or allows the user to modify a report form file for producing reports. Once the report has been outlined with the CREATE REPORT command, the report can be displayed or printed with the REPORT FORM command. As with CREATE LABEL, if you omit a file name, FoxPro will ask for one when you save the report.

CREATE SCREEN
Syntax

```
CREATE SCREEN [file | ?] [WINDOW windowname1] [IN [WINDOW]
windowname2 / IN SCREEN]
```

The CREATE SCREEN command activates the FoxPro Screen Creation utility, used to design custom screen forms. The WINDOW and IN WINDOW clauses may be used to place the screen within a window or within the child window of a parent window. The IN SCREEN command places the screen within the full screen (this is also the default). For more details on the Screen Creation utility, see Chapter 12.

CREATE VIEW [FROM ENVIRONMENT]
Syntax

```
CREATE VIEW [FROM ENVIRONMENT]
```

The CREATE VIEW command saves the current environment to a view file. The command operates in the same manner, whether or not the FROM ENVIRONMENT clause is specified. The optional clause is supported for compatibility with dBASE.

DEACTIVATE MENU
Syntax

```
DEACTIVATE MENU [ALL]
```

The DEACTIVATE MENU command deactivates the active menu and clears the menu from the screen. The menu remains in memory and can be recalled with the ACTIVATE MENU command. If the ALL clause is included, all menus currently on the screen are removed from the screen.

Example

```
DEACTIVATE MENU
```

DEACTIVATE POPUP
Syntax

```
DEACTIVATE POPUP [ALL]
```

The DEACTIVATE POPUP command deactivates the active pop-up menu and erases it from the screen. The pop-up menu remains in memory and can be recalled to the screen with the ACTIVATE POPUP command. If the ALL option is included, all pop-up menus currently on the screen are removed from the screen.

Example

```
DEACTIVATE POPUP
```

DEACTIVATE WINDOW
Syntax

```
DEACTIVATE WINDOW windowname / ALL
```

The DEACTIVATE WINDOW command deactivates the window or windows named within the command and erases them from the screen. The windows remain in memory and can be restored to the screen with the ACTIVATE WINDOW command. If the ALL option is not used, the most recently activated window is deactivated. If a window is under-lying the most recent window, it becomes the active window. If the ALL option is included, all active windows are deactivated.

Example

```
DEACTIVATE WINDOW output
```

DECLARE
Syntax

```
DECLARE arrayname 1 [no.-of-rows, no.-of-cols][arrayname2]
[no.-of-rows, no.-of-cols]
```

A

The DECLARE command creates an array. (Note that the DECLARE command is compatible with dBASE IV. If you desire compatibility with FoxBase Plus, use the DIMENSION command instead.) In the definition list, you enter the array name and the dimensions of the array. Array names may be up to ten characters in length. Array dimensions consist of the row and column numbers. If a column number is omitted, FoxPro creates a one-dimensional array. If row and column numbers are used, they must be separated by a comma, and FoxPro creates a two-dimensional array. Arrays declared within programs are private unless declared public with the PUBLIC command.

Examples
To declare a private array, enter

```
DECLARE ARRAY Finance[10,4]
```

To declare an array as public within a program, enter

```
PUBLIC ARRAY Finance[10,4]
```

Note that these examples both declare an array and make it public. You can make a previously declared array public with the syntax PUBLIC *arrayname.*

DEFINE BAR
Syntax

```
DEFINE BAR line-number / system-option-name OF popupname
PROMPT expC [BEFORE expN / AFTER expN] [KEY key-label]
[MARK expC] [MESSAGE expC] [SKIP [FOR expL]] [COLOR color:
pairs-list / COLOR SCHEME expN]
```

The DEFINE BAR command defines one bar option within a pop-up menu. The *popupname* must have been previously defined with the DEFINE POPUP command. The line number specifies the line number within the pop-up menu; line 1 appears on the first line of the pop-up, line 2 on the second line of the pop-up, and so on. The text specified with PROMPT appears as text in the bar of the menu. The MESSAGE option can be used to specify text that will appear at the bottom of the screen when the specified menu bar is highlighted. The SKIP option causes the bar to appear, but the bar will not be selectable within the menu.

The system-option-name clause can be used to place items that are available from the System menu in your pop-ups. The BEFORE and AFTER clauses determine the physical location of an option, relative to the option number specified by *expN*. The KEY clause assigns another key to a pop-up option. The MARK clause, when used along with the SET MARK command, allows the placement of a check mark besides the pop-up option. Use the COLOR or COLOR SCHEME option to change the colors of the pop-up.

Example

```
DEFINE BAR MainMenu FROM 3,10 TO 10,30
DEFINE BAR 1 OF MainMenu PROMPT "Add records"
DEFINE BAR 2 OF MainMenu PROMPT "Edit records"
DEFINE BAR 3 OF MainMenu PROMPT "Delete records"
DEFINE BAR 4 OF MainMenu PROMPT "Print reports"
DEFINE BAR 5 OF MainMenu PROMPT "Exit system"
```

DEFINE BOX
Syntax

```
DEFINE BOX FROM print-column TO print-column HEIGHT expression
[AT LINE print-line][SINGLE / DOUBLE / border-definition-string]
```

The DEFINE BOX command lets you define a box that appears around printed text. Use the specified options in the command to define the starting column on the left, the ending column on the right, the height of the box, and the starting line for the top of the box. The *border-definition-string* option lets you specify a character that will be used as the box border; the default, if this option is omitted, is a single line.

Example

```
DEFINE BOX FROM 4 TO 76 HEIGHT 45 AT LINE 5
```

DEFINE MENU
Syntax

```
DEFINE MENU menuname [BAR [AT LINE expN]] [IN [WINDOW]
windowname / IN SCREEN] [KEY key-label] [MARK expC]
[MESSAGE expC] [NOMARGIN] [COLOR color-pairs-list / COLOR
SCHEME expN]
```

The DEFINE MENU command defines a bar menu. If the MESSAGE option is added, the text of the message appears at the bottom of the screen when the menu is displayed (see ACTIVATE MENU).

The BAR clause creates a bar-style menu that imitates the style of the FoxPro System menus. Use the IN WINDOW or IN SCREEN clause to define whether the defined menu is in a window or in the full screen. (If the clause is omitted, the window appears in the full screen.) The KEY clause assigns another key to a pop-up option. The MARK clause, when used along with the SET MARK command, allows the placement of a check mark beside the pop-up option. The NOMARGIN clause, when used, omits the extra space that normally appears to the left of each menu pad. Use the COLOR or COLOR SCHEME option to change the colors of the pop-up.

Example

```
DEFINE MENU MainMenu
```

DEFINE PAD
Syntax

```
DEFINE PAD padname OF menuname PROMPT expC [AT row,
col] [BEFORE padname / AFTER padname] [KEY key-label
[MARK expC] [MESSAGE expC] [SKIP [FOR expL]] [COLOR color-
pairs-list / COLOR SCHEME expN]
```

The DEFINE PAD command defines one pad of a bar menu. Use a separate statement containing this command for each desired pad within the menu. The text specified with PROMPT appears inside the menu pad. If the AT *row,col* option is omitted, the first pad appears at the far left, and each successive pad appears one space to the right of the previous pad. Any text that accompanies the MESSAGE option appears on the message line (see SET MESSAGE TO) when that pad is highlighted within the menu.

The KEY clause assigns another key to a pop-up option. The BEFORE and AFTER clauses determine the physical location of a pad, relative to the pad number specified by *expN*. The MARK clause, when used along with the SET MARK command, allows the placement of a check mark beside the pop-up option. The SKIP clause, when used, causes a pad to be skipped if the logical expression evaluates as true. Use the COLOR or COLOR SCHEME option to change the colors of the menu pad.

Example

```
DEFINE MENU MainMenu
DEFINE PAD Adder OF MainMenu PROMPT "Add" MESSAGE "Add new records"
DEFINE PAD Editor OF MainMenu PROMPT "Edit" MESSAGE "Edit records"
DEFINE PAD Eraser OF MainMenu PROMPT "Delete" MESSAGE "Delete records"
```

```
DEFINE PAD Printer OF MainMenu PROMPT "Print" MESSAGE "Print reports"
DEFINE PAD Quit OF MainMenu PROMPT "Exit" MESSAGE "leave application"
```

DEFINE POPUP
Syntax

```
DEFINE POPUP popupname [FROM row1,col1 [TO row2,
col2] [IN WINDOW windowname / IN SCREEN] [FOOTER expC]
[KEY key:label] [MARGIN] [MARK expC] [MESSAGE expC] [MOVER]
[MULTI] [PROMPT FIELD field / PROMPT FILES [LIKE skel]
PROMPT STRUCTURE] [RELATIVE] [SCROLL] [SHADOW] [TITLE expC]
[COLOR color-pairs-list / COLOR SCHEME expN]
```

Use the DEFINE POPUP command to define a pop-up menu. The FROM
and TO row and column coordinates define the upper-left and
lower-right corners of the pop-up. If the TO coordinate is omitted,
FoxPro will make the menu as large as needed to contain the prompts
within the menu. The PROMPT FIELD, PROMPT FILE, and PROMPT
STRUCTURE clauses are optional. These allow you to display selection
lists of field contents, file names, or field names from a database
structure. The COLOR or COLOR SCHEME option may be used to
specify colors for the pop-up. By default, pop-ups take on the colors of
color scheme 2. If the optional SHADOW clause is included, a shadow
appears beneath the pop-up.

The IN WINDOW and IN SCREEN clauses can be used to define
whether the pop-up appears in a window or in the full screen. (If the
clause is omitted, the default is the full screen.) The FOOTER clause
assigns a text footer, centered in the bottom border of the pop-up. The
KEY clause assigns another key as a hot key for the pop-up. The
MARGIN clause causes an extra space to appear to the left and the right
of each pop-up option. The MARK clause, when used along with the
SET MARK command, allows the placement of a check mark beside the
pop-up option. The MESSAGE clause displays the specified message, in
the position specified by the SET MESSAGE command.

A

The MOVER clause, when included, allows the movement of pop-up options, using the double-headed arrow that appears at the left edge of the pop-up. The MULTI option allows multiple choices from a single pop-up option. The RELATIVE clause lets you change the order in which items appear in the pop-up. If a menu pop-up is created by using the RELATIVE clause, menu options appear in the order that they were defined. The SCROLL clause, when included, adds a scroll bar at the right edge of the pop-up; mouse users can use the scroll bar to scroll through the menu options. The TITLE clause adds a title to the border of the pop-up. Use the COLOR or COLOR SCHEME option to change the colors of the pop-up.

Example

```
DEFINE POPUP MainMenu FROM 5,5 TO 14,40
DEFINE POPUP PrintMen FROM 15,12 TO 30,17
```

DEFINE WINDOW
Syntax

```
DEFINE WINDOW windowname FROM row1,col1 TO row2,col2
[DOUBLE/PANEL/NONE/border-definition-string][TITLE expC]
[CLOSE/NOCLOSE][SHADOW][GROW/NOGROW]
[FLOAT/NOFLOAT][ZOOM/NOZOOM][COLOR[standard]
[,enhanced][,border]] / [COLOR SCHEME expN]
[FOOTER expC][MINIMIZE][FILL]
```

The DEFINE WINDOW command defines display attributes and screen coordinates for a window. The FROM and TO coordinates define the upper-left and lower-right corners of the window. The default border is a single-line box; you can use the DOUBLE, PANEL, NONE, or *border-definition-character* option to specify a different border for the window. (Use ASCII codes for the border definition option.) By default, windows take on the colors of color scheme 1. The expression named with TITLE appears at the top of the window.

The CLOSE/NOCLOSE option specifies whether the window may be closed with the System menu or by clicking the close box. If the option is omitted or NOCLOSE is specified, the window may not be closed (other than by deactivating it). The SHADOW option causes a shadow to appear beneath the window. By default, windows do not have shadows. The FLOAT/NOFLOAT and ZOOM/NOZOOM options determine whether the window can be moved (in the case of FLOAT) or zoomed (in the case of ZOOM). If the options are omitted or if the NOFLOAT or NOZOOM option is specified, the window may not be moved or zoomed. The options GROW/NOGROW specify whether the user will be permitted to resize the window. If GROW is included, the user can resize the window; if NOGROW is included, the user cannot.

The FOOTER clause lets you add text in the form of a footer. The text appears centered in the border at the bottom of the window. The MINIMIZE clause causes the window to appear minimized in size. The FILL clause lets you fill the background of a window with the character specified in the character expression.

A

Example

```
DEFINE WINDOW MyWindow FROM 5,5 TO 7,52 DOUBLE COLOR B/W
ACTIVATE WINDOW MyWindow
@ 1,6 SAY "Are you SURE you want to do this?"
```

DELETE

Syntax

```
DELETE [scope][FOR condition][WHILE condition][NOOPTIMIZE]
```

The DELETE command marks specific records for deletion. If DELETE is used without a record number, the current record is marked for deletion. The *scope* option is used to identify the records to be deleted. The FOR option can be used to specify a condition that must be met before a record will be deleted. If you use the WHILE option, records will be deleted until the condition is no longer true. DELETE marks a record for deletion; the PACK command actually removes the record. When used, the NOOPTIMIZE clause turns off FoxPro's internal optimization techniques (also known as Rushmore).

Example

To mark records within the next 24 records for deletion, beginning
with the current record and specifying that they have an entry of VA in
the State field in order to be deleted, enter

```
DELETE NEXT 24 FOR STATE = "VA"
```

DELETE FILE
Syntax

```
DELETE FILE filename.ext / [?]
```

The DELETE FILE command deletes a file from the disk. If an extension
is present, it must be specified. If the optional question mark is used in
place of a file name, a list box of all files in the current directory
appears. The user can then select the file to be deleted from the list box.

DELETE TAG
Syntax

```
DELETE TAG tagname1 [OF .cdx file1][, tagname2 [OF .cdx
file2]].../ ALL
```

The DELETE TAG command removes the named tag from a compound
index file. If the OF clause is omitted, FoxPro looks in the structural
compound index file for the tags to be deleted. The ALL clause causes
all tags to be deleted from the compound index file, and the file itself is
also deleted.

Example

To delete an index tag named ZIPS stored in a compound index file
named ABCSTAFF.CDX, you could use the command

```
DELETE TAG zips OF abcstaff
```

DIMENSION
Syntax

```
DIMENSION arrayname 1 [no.-of-rows,no.-of-cols][arrayname2]
[no.-of-rows,no.-of-cols]...[arraynamex] [no.-of-rows,no.-of-cols]
```

The DIMENSION command creates an array. (Note that the DIMENSION command is compatible with FoxBase Plus. If you desire compatibility with dBASE IV, use the DECLARE command instead.) In the definition list, you enter the array name and the dimensions of the array. Array names may be up to ten characters in length. Array dimensions consist of the row and column numbers. If a column number is omitted, FoxPro creates a one-dimensional array. If row and column numbers are used, they must be separated by a comma, and FoxPro creates a two-dimensional array.

Example

```
DIMENSION ARRAY Finance[10,4]
```

DIR
Syntax

```
DIR [drive:][filename][skeleton][TO PRINT[PROMPT]/TO FILE filename]
```

The DIR command displays the directory of all database files or files of a specific type if a file extension is specified. *Drive* is the drive designator, and *filename* is the name of a file with or without an extension. Skeletons composed of wildcards, which are asterisks or question marks, can be used as part of or as a replacement for *filename*. In the case of database files, the display produced by DIR includes the number of records contained in the database, the date of the last update, and the size of the file in bytes. The TO PRINT and TO FILE options may be used to route the directory display to the printer or to a file name. If the PROMPT clause is included with TO PRINT, a dialog box is displayed before printing starts.

A

Example

To display all index files from the current default drive, enter

```
DIR *.IDX
```

DISPLAY

Syntax

```
DISPLAY [scope][fieldlist][FOR condition][WHILE condition][OFF]
[TO PRINT[PROMPT] / TO FILE filename]
```

The DISPLAY command displays a record from the active database. You can display more records by including the *scope* option. The FOR option limits the display of records to those satisfying the condition. If you use the WHILE option, records will be displayed until the condition is no longer true. Only the fields listed in *fieldlist* will be displayed; if *fieldlist* is absent, all fields will be displayed. The OFF option will prevent the record number from being displayed. The TO PRINT and TO FILE options may be used to route the display to the printer or to a file called *filename*. Note that when the TO FILE option is used, the default extension for the file is .TXT. If the PROMPT clause is included with TO PRINT, a dialog box is displayed before printing starts.

Example

To display the Lastname, Firstname, City, and State fields for ten records beginning with the current record, enter

```
DISPLAY NEXT 10 LASTNAME, FIRSTNAME, CITY, STATE
```

DISPLAY MEMORY

Syntax

```
DISPLAY MEMORY[LIKE skeleton][TO PRINT/TO FILE filename]
```

The DISPLAY MEMORY command displays all active memory variables, their sizes, and their contents. The numbers of active variables and available variables are listed along with the numbers of bytes consumed and bytes available. Wildcards may be used as skeletons; for example, DISPLAY MEMORY LIKE MEM* would display all variables beginning with the letters MEM. The TO PRINT and TO FILE options may be used to route the display to the printer or to a file name. Note that when the TO FILE option is used, the default extension for the file is .TXT.

DISPLAY STATUS
Syntax

```
DISPLAY STATUS[TO PRINT[PROMPT]/TO FILE filename]
```

The DISPLAY STATUS command displays, for every active work area, the name and alias of the currently open database, any filter condition currently in effect, and the expressions used in any open index files. The current drive designator, function key settings, and settings of SET commands are also displayed. The TO PRINT and TO FILE options may be used to route the display to the printer or to a file name. Note that when the TO FILE option is used, the default extension for the file is .TXT. If the PROMPT option is included with the TO PRINT clause, a dialog box is displayed before printing starts.

DISPLAY STRUCTURE
Syntax

```
DISPLAY STRUCTURE [IN alias] [TO PRINT[PROMPT] / TO FILE filename]
```

The DISPLAY STRUCTURE command displays the structure of the active database, unless the IN *alias* option is used. The complete file name, along with the current drive designator, number of records, date of last update, and name of fields, including their statistics (type, length, and decimal places), is listed. If you have established a fields list with SET FIELDS, a > symbol appears to the left of the selected fields in the structure list. The IN alias option causes the structure of a file open in another work area (as specified by the alias) to be displayed. The TO PRINT and TO FILE options may be used to route the display to the printer or to a file name. Note that when the TO FILE option is used, the default extension for the file is .TXT. If the PROMPT option is included with the TO PRINT clause, a dialog box is displayed before printing starts.

DO
Syntax

```
DO filename [WITH parameterlist][IN filename]
```

The DO command starts execution of a FoxPro command file. The file name extension of .PRG or .DBO is assumed unless otherwise specified. If the WITH option is specified and followed by a list of parameters in *parameterlist,* those parameters are transferred to the command file.

The IN *filename* clause can be used to do a procedure that is stored in a different program file.

DO CASE
Syntax

```
DO CASE
 CASE condition
   commands...
 [CASE condition]
  [commands...]
 [OTHERWISE]
  [commands...]
ENDCASE
```

The DO CASE command selects one course of action from a number of choices. The conditions following the CASE statements are evaluated until one of the conditions is found to be true. When a condition is true, the commands between the CASE statement and the next CASE, or OTHERWISE and ENDCASE, will be executed. FoxPro then executes the command following the END-CASE statement. If none of the conditions in the CASE statements are found to be true, any commands following the optional OTHERWISE statement will be executed. If the OTHERWISE statement is not used and no conditions are found to be true, FoxPro proceeds to the command following the ENDCASE statement.

Example

In the following DO CASE commands, FoxPro chooses from among three possible alternatives: (1) executing a command file named MENU, (2) appending records to the database, or (3) exiting from FoxPro.

```
DO CASE
  CASE SELECT = 1
  DO MENU
  CASE SELECT = 2
  APPEND
  CASE SELECT = 3
  QUIT
ENDCASE
```

A

DO WHILE

Syntax

```
DO WHILE condition
   commands...
ENDDO
```

The DO WHILE command repeatedly executes commands between DO WHILE and ENDDO as long as *condition* is true. When FoxPro encounters a DO WHILE command, the condition in that command statement is evaluated: if the condition is false, FoxPro proceeds to the command following the ENDDO command; but if it is true, FoxPro executes the commands following the DO WHILE command until the ENDDO command is reached. When the ENDDO command is reached, the condition in the DO WHILE statement is again evaluated. If it is still true, the commands between DO WHILE and ENDDO are again executed. If the condition is false, FoxPro proceeds to the command below the ENDDO command.

Example

To display Lastname, Firstname, City, and State fields for each record until the end of the database, you could use the following program:

```
DO WHILE .NOT. EOF()
   ? LASTNAME, FIRSTNAME, CITY, STATE
```

```
        SKIP
ENDDO
```

EDIT
Syntax

```
EDIT [scope][NOAPPEND][NOCLEAR][NOEDIT][NODELETE]
[NOMENU][FIELDS list][FOR condition][WHILE condition]
```

The EDIT command invokes the FoxPro full-screen Editor. If no record
number is specified in the scope, the current record, which is identified by
the current position of the record pointer, will be displayed for editing.

The FIELDS option will display only the fields listed in field list. The
NOCLEAR option causes the edit display to remain on the screen after
the changes are completed. The NOAPPEND, NOEDIT, and NODELETE
options restrict the use of appending, editing, or deleting when in Edit
mode. The NOMENU option prevents access to the Edit menu. The FOR
and WHILE options let you specify conditions that must be met before
a record will appear in the edit screen.

EJECT
Syntax

```
EJECT
```

The EJECT command causes the printer to perform a formfeed.

EJECT PAGE
Syntax

```
EJECT PAGE
```

The EJECT PAGE command causes the printer to perform a formfeed.
Use the EJECT PAGE command along with the ON PAGE command to
handle page ejects for printed reports. The EJECT PAGE command

invokes any end-of-page routines you have established with the ON PAGE command, and it increments _PAGENO and resets _PLINENO to 0. Note that the output of the EJECT PAGE command is made available to a disk file or screen if output is being sent to a disk file or screen instead of to the printer.

ERASE
Syntax

```
ERASE filename.ext / [?]
```

The ERASE command erases the named file from the directory. The name must include the file extension. You can also use the command DELETE FILE *filename.ext* to erase a file. If the file is on a disk that is not in the default drive, you must include the drive designator. If the optional question mark is used in place of a file name, a list box appears. The user can select the file to be deleted from the list box.

A

EXIT
Syntax

```
EXIT
```

The EXIT command exits a DO WHILE, FOR, or SCAN loop and proceeds to the first command following the end of the loop (that is, the command after the ENDDO, ENDFOR, or ENDSCAN command).

Example
The following command-file portion uses EXIT to exit the DO WHILE loop if a part number of 9999 is entered:

```
DO WHILE .T.
    ? "Enter part number to add to inventory."
    ? "Enter 9999 to exit."
    INPUT TO PARTNO
    IF PARTNO = 9999
        EXIT
    ENDIF
```

```
    APPEND BLANK
    REPLACE PARTNUMB WITH PARTNO
    EDIT
ENDDO
```

EXPORT
Syntax

```
EXPORT TO file [FIELDS fieldlist [scope] [FOR condition]
[WHILE condition] [NOOPTIMIZE] [TYPE] DIF / MOD / SYLK / WK1 /
WKS / WR1 / WRK / XLS
```

The EXPORT command exports a database file to a foreign file of the type specified with the TYPE option. (See Chapter 18 for more details on the various type options.) Use the FIELDS clause to limit the fields that are copied to the foreign file. The FOR and WHILE clauses can be used to limit records that are copied to the other file. Use the NOOPTIMIZE clause to disable the normal optimization techniques (also known as Rushmore).

EXTERNAL
Syntax

```
EXTERNAL ARRAY / LABEL / LIBRARY / MENU / PROCEDURE / REPORT /
SCREEN filename / arrayname
```

The EXTERNAL command makes the FoxPro project manager aware of an undefined reference. This is an advanced command used in programming; for details on this subject, refer to a more advanced programmer's text or to your FoxPro programmer's documentation.

FILER
Syntax

```
FILER [LIKE skeleton][NOWAIT]
```

The FILER command displays the FoxPro file maintenance utility. Use the LIKE option with a skeleton to display a specific type of file. The NOWAIT option, when used, causes program execution to continue after the Filer utility appears.

FIND
Syntax

```
FIND character-string
```

The FIND command positions the record pointer at the first record containing an index key that matches *character-string*. If there are leading blanks in *character-string, character-string* must be enclosed by single or double quotes; otherwise, no quotes are necessary. If the specific character string cannot be found, the EOF value is set to true and a NO FIND message is displayed on the screen (if FoxPro is not executing a command file). An index file must be open before you use the FIND command.

FLUSH
Syntax

```
FLUSH
```

The FLUSH command flushes all active buffers to disk, without closing the files.

FOR
Syntax

```
FOR memvar = expN1 TO expN2 [STEP expN3]
    commands...
ENDFOR/NEXT
```

The FOR and accompanying ENDFOR or NEXT statements set up a repetitive loop that repeats a set number of times, as defined by the

A

numeric expressions. The value of *expN1* marks the starting point, and the value of *expN2* marks the ending point. The loop repeats the number of times specified between *expN1* and *expN2,* unless an incremental value other than 1 is specified with the optional STEP clause. Once the set number of repetitions has been accomplished, FoxPro proceeds to the command below the ENDFOR or NEXT command. If a STEP clause is used, *memvar* is incremented or, if the value of STEP is negative, decremented every time the ENDFOR or NEXT is encountered until *memvar* equals or exceeds *expN2.*

Example

To use the FOR-ENDFOR commands to print Lastname, Firstname, City, and State fields for a specified number of records, you could use the following program:

```
USE MEMBERS
INPUT "Print how many records? " TO COUNTERS
STORE 1 TO BEGIN
FOR BEGIN = 1 TO COUNTERS
    ? LASTNAME, FIRSTNAME, CITY, STATE
    SKIP
ENDFOR
```

FUNCTION

Syntax

```
FUNCTION procedurename
```

The FUNCTION command identifies a procedure that serves as a user-defined function.

Example

```
FUNCTION StateTax
PARAMETERS SaleCost, TaxRate
```

```
Gross = SaleCost + (SaleCost * TaxRate)
RETURN(Gross)
```

GATHER FROM
Syntax

```
GATHER memory variable FROM array[FIELDS fieldlist][MEMO]
```

The GATHER FROM command moves data from a set of variables or an array of memory variables into a database file. (Note that GATHER FROM is compatible with FoxBase Plus; if you need compatibility with dBASE IV, use APPEND FROM ARRAY instead.) The elements of the array are transferred, beginning with the first element of the array, into the corresponding records of the database file. If there are more elements in the array than fields in the database, the extra elements are ignored. If there are more fields in the database than there are elements in the array, the extra fields remain empty. The FOR clause, which is optional, lets you define a condition that must be met before data in the array will be added to a new record. Note that memo fields are ignored during the data transfer process unless the MEMO clause is included.

GETEXPR
Syntax

```
GETEXPR [expC] TO memvar
```

The GETEXPR command brings up the Expression Builder. The expression constructed by the user with the Expression Builder is then stored to the memory variable specified as part of the GETEXPR command. The GETEXPR command can be used within a program to allow the user to define selection criteria for printing a report or a set of labels.

GO or GOTO
Syntax

A

```
GO or GOTO BOTTOM/TOP/ExpN [IN alias]
```

The GO and GOTO commands position the record pointer at a record. GO
TOP moves the pointer to the beginning of a database, and GO BOTTOM
moves it to the end of a database. If a numeric value is provided, the
pointer moves to that record number. The IN *alias* clause can be used to
move the record pointer in a database that is open in another work area;
alias can be either the file alias or a work area number.

HELP
Syntax

```
HELP [commandname-or-functionname]
```

The HELP command provides instructions on using FoxPro commands
and functions, as well as other information. If you enter HELP without
specifying a command or function, a menu-driven system of help
screens allows you to request information on various subjects. If HELP
is followed by a command or function, information about that
command or function will be displayed.

HIDE MENU
Syntax

```
HIDE MENU [[name1][,name2...]]/[ALL] [SAVE]
```

The HIDE MENU command hides a current menu bar while retaining
the menu bar in memory. If the ALL option is used, all current menu
bars are hidden. Use the SAVE option to place an image of the menu
bar on the screen or in a window. This option can prove useful when
developing or testing programs.

HIDE POPUP
Syntax

```
HIDE POPUP [[name1][,name2...]/[ALL] [SAVE]
```

The HIDE POPUP command hides a current pop-up menu while retaining the pop-up in memory. If the ALL option is used, all current pop-ups are hidden. Use the SAVE option to place an image of the menu bar on the screen or in a window. This option can prove useful when developing or testing programs.

HIDE WINDOW
Syntax

```
HIDE WINDOW [[name1[,name2...]]/[ALL]
```

The HIDE WINDOW command hides a current window while retaining the window in memory. If the ALL option is used, all current windows are hidden.

IF
Syntax

```
IF condition
  commands...
[ELSE]
  commands...
ENDIF
```

IF is a decision-making command that will execute commands when certain conditions are true. If the condition for the IF statement is true, the commands between IF and ENDIF will be executed. Should the condition be false and there is an ELSE, the commands between ELSE and ENDIF will be executed. However, if the condition for IF is not true and there is no ELSE, FoxPro will drop to the ENDIF statement without executing any commands.

IMPORT
Syntax

```
IMPORT FROM filename [TYPE] DIF / FW2 / MOD / PDOX / RPD / SYLK
/ WK1 / WK3 / WKS / WR1 / WRK / XLS
```

The IMPORT command imports a foreign file of the type specified with the TYPE option and creates an equivalent database file. Use the TYPE option to specify the format of the foreign file. (See Chapter 18 for more details on the various type options.)

INDEX

Syntax

```
INDEX ON expC TO .idx filename / TAG tagname [OF .cdx filename]
[FOR expL] [COMPACT] [ASCENDING / DESCENDING] [UNIQUE]
[ADDITIVE]
```

The INDEX command creates an index file based on an expression (which is usually a field name or a combination of fields) from the active database. Depending on the field, the index file will be indexed alphabetically, numerically, chronologically, or logically. If the index based on the first field has duplicate entries, the duplicates are indexed according to additional fields in *fieldlist*, provided additional fields have been listed. When the UNIQUE option is used, duplicate entries are omitted from the index. The indexing occurs in ascending order unless you add the DESCENDING option. Use the FOR option to limit records included in the index.

The TAG *tagname* and OF *.cdx filename* options can be used to specify that the index should be a tag of a compound index file. If the OF clause is omitted and the TAG clause is included, the tag is added to the structural compound index file; if none exists, one with the same name as the database is created. The COMPACT clause forces the creation of an index file in the compact format. The ASCENDING clause specifies an index in ascending order; this is also the default if no ASCENDING or DESCENDING clause is used.

Example

To create an index file called TOWNS based on the values in a field named City, enter

```
INDEX ON CITY TO TOWNS
```

INPUT

Syntax

```
INPUT[expC][TO memvar]
```

The INPUT command stores an entry that is entered by the user to a memory variable. An optional character expression can display a message to the user during keyboard entry. The expression can be a memory variable or a character string.

Example

To display the prompt "Enter name to search for:" and store the response to the memory variable NEWNAME, enter

```
INPUT "Enter name to search for:" TO NEWNAME
```

INSERT

Syntax

```
INSERT[BLANK][BEFORE]
```

The INSERT command adds a new record below the record pointer's position and renumbers the records below the insertion. Specifying BEFORE causes the record to be inserted at the record pointer; thus, if the pointer is at record 3, the new record will be 3 and the records below it renumbered. If the BLANK option is omitted, FoxPro allows immediate editing of the new record; otherwise, the record will be blank, but Edit mode will not be entered.

Example

To insert a new record at position 10 in the active database, enter

```
GO 10
INSERT BEFORE
```

A

JOIN
Syntax

```
JOIN WITH alias TO filename FOR condition [FIELDS fieldlist]
[FOR condition] [NOOPTIMIZE]
```

The JOIN command creates a new database by combining specific records and fields from the active database and the database listed as *alias*. The combined database is stored in *filename*. You can limit the choice of records from the active database by specifying a FOR condition. All fields from both files will be copied if you do not include a field list; but if you do, only those fields specified in the field list will be copied. Specify fields from the nonactive database by supplying *filename -> fieldname*. When used, the NOOPTIMIZE clause turns off FoxPro's internal optimization techniques (also known as Rushmore).

KEYBOARD
Syntax

```
KEYBOARD expC
```

The KEYBOARD command stuffs the keyboard buffer with the character expression supplied as *expC*. The data stays in the keyboard buffer until FoxPro looks for input, at which time the buffer is read.

LABEL FORM
Syntax

```
LABEL FORM label-filename / ? [scope][SAMPLE][FOR condition]
[WHILE condition][TO PRINT][TO FILE filename][ENVIRONMENT][OFF]
[PREVIEW][NOOPTIMIZE]
```

The LABEL FORM command prints mailing labels from a label form file (extension .LBX). The SAMPLE option allows a sample label to be printed. The FOR option can be used to specify a condition that must be met before a label for a record will be printed. If you use the WHILE option, records will be printed until the condition is no longer true. The TO PRINT option sends output to the printer, and the TO FILE option sends output to a named disk file. The ENVIRONMENT option causes a view file with the same name as the label file to be used before printing begins. If the question mark is substituted in place of a file name, a box containing a list of all label files appears. The user may then select the label file to print from the list. The OFF option causes the display of labels on the screen to be suppressed while the labels are printed or sent to a file.

The PREVIEW option causes an on-screen preview display of the labels to appear. Use the NOOPTIMIZE clause to disable the normal optimization techniques (also know as Rushmore).

A

Example

To print mailing labels by using a label form named MAILERS for records with State fields containing NM and to restrict printing to the next 25 records beginning at the current record-pointer position, enter

```
LABEL FORM MAILERS NEXT 25 FOR STATE = "NM" TO PRINT
```

LIST

Syntax

```
LIST [OFF][scope][fieldlist][FOR condition ][WHILE condition ][TO
PRINT / TO FILE filename]
```

The LIST command provides a list of database contents. The *scope* option quantifies the records to be listed. If *scope* is absent, ALL is assumed. The FOR option specifies a condition that must be met before a record will be listed. If you use the WHILE option, records will be listed until the condition is no longer true. The OFF option prevents the record number from being listed. If the TO PRINT option is used, the listing will be printed on the printer. TO FILE directs the list to a disk file.

LIST FILES
Syntax

```
LIST FILES [ON drive/dir [LIKE skeleton][TO PRINT/TO FILE filename]
```

The LIST FILES command displays a list of disk files. Use the ON option to specify a drive and/or directory. Wildcards may be used as skeletons; for example, LIST FILES LIKE *.IDX would display all files with the extension of .IDX. The TO PRINT and TO FILE options may be used to route the list to the printer or to the named disk file.

LIST MEMORY
Syntax

```
LIST MEMORY [LIKE skeleton][TO PRINT / TO FILE filename]
```

The LIST MEMORY command lists the names, sizes, and types of memory variables. Wildcards may be used to define file name skeletons; for example, LIST MEMORY LIKE MEM* would display all variables beginning with the letters MEM. If the TO PRINT option is used, the listing will be printed on the printer. If the TO FILE option is used, the listing will be directed to the named disk file.

LIST STATUS
Syntax

```
LIST STATUS [TO PRINT / TO FILE filename]
```

The LIST STATUS command lists information on currently open work areas, the active file, and system settings. All open files and open index file names are displayed, along with work area numbers, any expressions used in index files, the default disk drive, function key settings, and settings of the SET commands. If the TO PRINT option is used, the listing will be printed on the printer. LIST STATUS does not pause during the listing, which is the only difference between LIST STATUS and DISPLAY STATUS.

LIST STRUCTURE
Syntax

```
LIST STRUCTURE [TO PRINT / TO FILE filename] [IN ALIAS alias]
```

The LIST STRUCTURE command lists the structure of the database in use, including the name, the number of records, all names of fields, and the date of the last update. If the TO PRINT option is used, the listing will be printed on the printer. The TO FILE option may be specified to redirect the output to a file. LIST STRUCTURE does not pause during the listing, which is the only difference between LIST STRUCTURE and DISPLAY STRUCTURE. The IN ALIAS option may be used to list the structure of a file in another work area; *alias* may be either an alias name or a work area number.

LOAD
Syntax

```
LOAD binary-filename
```

The LOAD command is used to load binary (assembly language) programs into memory for future use. An extension is optional; if omitted, it is assumed to be .BIN.

LOCATE
Syntax

```
LOCATE [scope] [FOR condition] [WHILE condition] [NOOPTIMIZE]
```

The LOCATE command finds the first record that matches *condition*. The *scope* option can be used to limit the number of records that will be searched, but if *scope* is omitted, ALL is assumed. The LOCATE command ends when a record-matching condition is found, after which FoxPro displays the location of the record but not the record itself. Use the CONTINUE command after a LOCATE command to locate additional records meeting the same condition (see CONTINUE).

The FOR option specifies a condition that must be met before a record will be located. If you use the WHILE option, a record will be located until the condition is no longer true. When used, the NOOPTIMIZE clause turns off FoxPro's internal optimization techniques (also known as Rushmore).

Example

To locate a record containing the character string Smith in the Lastname field, enter

```
LOCATE FOR LASTNAME = "Smith"
```

LOOP

Syntax

```
LOOP
```

The LOOP command causes a jump back to the start of a DO WHILE loop. The LOOP command is normally executed conditionally within an IF statement.

MENU

Syntax

```
MENU BAR array1,expN1
MENU expN2,array2,expN3[,expN4]
READ MENU BAR TO var1,var2[SAVE]
```

The MENU BAR, MENU, and READ MENU BAR TO commands create a menu bar system, where the menu bar appears in a horizontal format across the top of the screen and each option of the menu when chosen displays a list of associated choices in a pop-up menu. (Before creating a menu bar, you must use the DIMENSION command to initialize an array for each list of menu options.) Use the MENU BAR command to insert the character expressions contained in *array1* into the menu bar; *array1* is a two-dimensional array of character strings. *Array1*(i,1) becomes the menu pad that is displayed on the menu bar at position i.

Array1(i,2) can be used to define an optional message that will appear at the SET MESSAGE TO location when the pad is selected. *ExpN1* defines the number of pads that appear on the menu bar.

Use the MENU command to insert menu pop-ups into a menu bar. *ExpN2* defines the position on the menu bar where the pop-up being defined will appear; *expN3* defines the number of options on the pop-up menu. *ExpN4*, which is optional, limits the number of menu options shown on the screen at any time. If there are more options in the menu than this limit, the options scroll within the pop-up menu. *Array2* is a one-dimensional array containing the character strings that are used as menu options. Use a backslash (\) as the first character to make an option nonselectable. Use a backslash followed by a hyphen (\-) to draw a graphics bar in place of a menu item.

Use the READ MENU BAR TO command to activate the menu bar defined by the prior commands. Use *var1* and *var2* to control which menu bar pad and menu options are selected by default when the menu is initially displayed. Once a selection has been made by the user, *var1* and *var2* will contain values that correspond to the menu selection. These values may then be acted on by the program. Use the optional SAVE clause to cause the menu bar to remain on the screen after a menu option has been chosen.

Example

```
*Mainmenu.PRG displays main menu.
SET TALK OFF
SET MESSAGE TO 24 CENTER
*Initialize arrays used for menu bar.
DIMENSION TOPBAR(3,2)
TOPBAR(1,1) = '  ADD  '
TOPBAR(2,1) = ' EDIT  '
TOPBAR(3,1) = ' PRINT '
TOPBAR(1,2) = 'Add data to file'
TOPBAR(2,2) = 'Edit data in file'
TOPBAR(3,2) = 'Print data in file'
*Initialize array used for Add pop-up.
DIMENSION Adder(4)
Adder(1) = 'Add Members   '
Adder(2) = 'Add Rentals   '
Adder(3) = 'Add Purchases '
```

A

```
Adder(4) = 'Exit this menu'
*Initialize array used for Edit pop-up.
DIMENSION Edits(4)
Edits(1) = 'Edit Members    '
Edits(2) = 'Edit Rentals    '
Edits(3) = 'Edit Purchases '
Edits(4) = 'Exit this menu'
*Initialize array used for Print pop-up.
DIMENSION Print(4)
Print(1) = 'Print Members    '
Print(2) = 'Print Rentals    '
Print(3) = 'Print Purchases '
Print(4) = 'Exit this menu'
*Insert the pop-ups into the menu bar.
MENU BAR TOPBAR,3
MENU 1,Adder,4
MENU 2,Edits,4
MENU 3,Print,4
*Activate the menu system.
READ MENU BAR TO 1,1
```

MENU TO
Syntax

```
MENU TO memvar
```

The MENU TO command is used along with the @-PROMPT command to implement light-bar menus. See @-PROMPT for a complete explanation of the use of the MENU TO command.

MODIFY COMMAND / MODIFY FILE
Syntax

```
MODIFY COMMAND/FILE filename [skeleton][NOEDIT][NOWAIT]
[RANGE expN1[,expN2][WINDOW windowname][SAVE]
```

MODIFY COMMAND or MODIFY FILE starts the FoxPro Editor, which can be used for editing command files or ASCII text files. If MODIFY

COMMAND is used, the file name will be given the extension .PRG unless a different extension is named. If MODIFY FILE is used, no extension is added unless one is specified in the file name. The WINDOW option may be used to open the file in a previously defined window. The *skeleton* option may be used to open windows for all files that match the file skeleton supplied. The NOEDIT option causes the text to be displayed, but editing is not allowed. The NOWAIT option causes program execution to continue as soon as the window is opened. The RANGE option may be used to open an editing window with a range of characters selected for editing. The characters selected begin with the position specified in *expN1* and continue for *expN2* characters. If *expN2* is omitted, editing begins at the character position specifed by *expN1*. The SAVE option causes the window to remain visible after editing is completed.

MODIFY LABEL

Syntax

```
MODIFY LABEL filename / ? [[WINDOW windowname1] [IN [WINDOW]
windowname2 | IN SCREEN]] [NOENVIRONMENT] [NOWAIT] [SAVE]
```

The MODIFY LABEL command creates or allows editing of a label form file. This file can be used with the LABEL FORM command to produce mailing labels. The file name will be given the extension .LBX. If the question mark is used in place of a file name, FoxPro displays a list of all label files in the current directory. The user may then select a label file for editing from the list. The SAVE option causes the label design window to remain visible after changes to the label are completed.

The WINDOW and IN WINDOW clauses can be used to specify that the label design should take place in a window or in the child window of a parent window. The IN SCREEN clause forces label design to use the full screen; this is also the default if no WINDOW clause is used. The NOENVIRONMENT clause is used when you do not want to restore the environment that was in place when you originally created the labels. The NOWAIT clause, used within programs, causes program execution to continue after the label design screen or window has appeared.

MODIFY MEMO
Syntax

```
MODIFY MEMO memofield1[,memofield 2...][NOEDIT][NOWAIT]
[RANGE expN1[,expN2]][WINDOW windowname][SAVE]
```

MODIFY MEMO places the contents of a memo field in the FoxPro Editor. The WINDOW option may be used to open the memo field in a previously defined window. The NOEDIT option causes the text to be displayed, but editing is not allowed. The NOWAIT option causes program execution to continue as soon as the window is opened. The RANGE option may be used to edit a memo field with a range of characters selected for editing. The characters selected begin with the position specified in *expN1* and continue for *expN2* characters. If *expN2* is omitted, editing begins at the character position specified by *expN1*. The SAVE option causes the memo window to remain visible after editing is completed.

MODIFY MENU
Syntax

```
MODIFY MENU [filename / ?] [[WINDOW windowname] [IN
[WINDOW] windowname2 | SCREEN]] [NOWAIT] [SAVE]
```

The MODIFY MENU command modifies an existing menu. The command brings up the FoxPro menu-creation utility. See CREATE MENU for additional details.

MODIFY PROJECT
Syntax

```
MODIFY PROJECT [filename / ?] [[WINDOW windowname] [IN [WINDOW]
windowname2 / SCREEN]] [SAVE]
```

The MODIFY PROJECT command modifies an existing project. The command opens the Project window. See CREATE MENU for additional details.

MODIFY QUERY
Syntax

```
MODIFY QUERY [file / ?] [NOWAIT]
```

The MODIFY QUERY command modifies an existing query. The command causes the RQBE window to be displayed, containing the previously stored query. For more details on designing and saving queries, see Chapter 6.

MODIFY REPORT
Syntax

```
MODIFY REPORT filename / ? [[WINDOW windowname1][IN [WINDOW]
windowname2 | IN SCREEN]][NOENVIRONMENT][NOWAIT][SAVE]
```

The MODIFY REPORT command allows you to use the Report Generator to create or modify a report form file for producing reports. The file names produced will be given the extension .FRX. If the question mark is used in place of a file name, FoxPro displays a list of all report form files in the current directory. The user may then select a report file for editing from the list. The SAVE option causes the report design to remain visible after changes to the report are completed.

The WINDOW and IN WINDOW clauses can be used to specify that the report design should take place in a window or in the child window of a parent window. The IN SCREEN clause forces report design to use the full screen; this is also the default if no WINDOW clause is used. The NOENVIRONMENT clause is used when you do not want to restore the environment that was in place when you originally created the report.

A

The NOWAIT clause, used within programs, causes program execution to continue after the report design screen or window has appeared.

MODIFY SCREEN
Syntax

```
MODIFY SCREEN [filename / ?] [[WINDOW windowname1] [IN
[WINDOW] windowname2 / IN SCREEN]] [NOENVIRONMENT] [NOWAIT]
[SAVE]
```

The MODIFY SCREEN command modifies an existing screen form, created with the CREATE SCREEN command. See CREATE SCREEN for additional details.

MODIFY STRUCTURE
Syntax

```
MODIFY STRUCTURE
```

The MODIFY STRUCTURE command allows you to alter the structure of the active database. After the structure has been modified, a backup copy containing the original data remains on disk with the same file name but with a different extension, .BAK.

MODIFY WINDOW
Syntax

```
MODIFY WINDOW window name / SCREEN FROM row1, column1
TO row2, column2 / AT row3, column3 SIZE row4, column4
[TITLE expC1] [HALFHEIGHT] [DOUBLE / PANEL / NONE / SYSTEM]
[CLOSE / NOCLOSE] [FLOAT / NOFLOAT] [GROW / NOGROW]
[MINIMIZE] [ZOOM / NOZOOM] [COLOR SCHEME expN2 / COLOR color pair list /
COLOR RGB (color value list)]
```

The MODIFY WINDOW command changes the attributes of an existing user-defined window or the main FoxPro window. (Use the DEFINE

WINDOW command to create user-defined windows.) Note that you cannot use MODIFY WINDOW to change the attributes of FoxPro system windows (such as the Command window, Browse windows, and the Filer). Use MODIFY WINDOW to change the location, default font, title, border, controls, and color of a user-defined window or the main FoxPro window. You can change any of these attributes by including the options shown above. As an example, include the TO and FROM or AT and SIZE clauses to specify a new location or size for a user-defined window. To prevent a user-defined window from being moved, include the NOFLOAT option. Use *window name* to specify the user-defined window you wish to modify. (The specified window must first be created with the DEFINE WINDOW command.) Use SCREEN instead of a window name to modify the attributes of the main FoxPro window. (To later return the main FoxPro window to its startup configuration, use the MODIFY WINDOW SCREEN command, without including any additional options. For additional information about the MODIFY WINDOW options, see DEFINE WINDOW in this appendix.

A

MOVE POPUP
Syntax

```
MOVE POPUP popupname TO row,col / BY delta-row, delta-column
```

The MOVE POPUP command moves a pop-up to a different screen location.

Examples

To move a pop-up to the starting position of row 14, column 18, you could use the command

```
MOVE POPUP MyPop TO 14,18
```

To move the pop-up six lines down and four lines to the right, you could use the command

```
MOVE POPUP MyPop BY 6,4
```

MOVE WINDOW
Syntax

```
MOVE WINDOW windowname TO row,col /BY delta-row,delta-col
```

The MOVE WINDOW command moves a predefined window to a new location on the screen.

Examples
To move the window to the starting position of row 15, column 20, enter

```
MOVE WINDOW MyWindow TO 15,20
```

To move the window six lines down and four lines to the right, enter

```
MOVE WINDOW MyWindow BY 6,4
```

NOTE or * or &&
Syntax

```
NOTE or * or &&
```

The NOTE or * or && command is used to insert comments in a command file. Use && to add a comment at the end of an existing statement. Use NOTE or * at the beginning of a line when the entire line is to be a comment. Text after the * or the && or the word NOTE in a command file will be ignored by FoxPro.

ON
Syntax

```
ON ERROR command
ON ESCAPE command
ON KEY command
```

This command causes a branch within a command file, specified by *command,* to be carried out when the condition identified by ON (an error, pressing the Esc key, or pressing any key) is met. If more than one ON condition is specified, the order of precedence is ON ERROR, ON ESCAPE, and then ON KEY. All ON conditions remain in effect until another ON condition is specified to clear the previous condition. To clear an ON condition without specifying another condition, enter ON ERROR, ON ESCAPE, or ON KEY without adding a command.

Examples

To cause program control to transfer to another program called ERRTRAP if an error occurs, enter

```
ON ERROR DO ERRTRAP
```

To cause the program to display a customized error message if an error occurs, use the following form:

```
ON ERROR ? "A serious error has occurred. Call J.E.J.A. Tech
Support for instructions."
```

To cause the program to call another program named HELPER.PRG containing customized help screens if the Esc key is pressed, enter

```
ON ESCAPE DO HELPER
```

To halt processing within a program and transfer program control to a program named HALTED.PRG if any key is pressed, enter

```
ON KEY DO HALTED
```

Use of the ON KEY syntax of the command will result in the key that is pressed being stored in the keyboard buffer. The routine that is called by the ON KEY command should use a READ command or INKEY function to clear the buffer.

A

ON BAR
Syntax

```
ON BAR expN OF popupname1 [ACTIVATE POPUP popupname2 /
ACTIVATE MENU menuname]
```

The ON BAR command activates a pop-up or a bar menu when a particular bar of a pop-up is selected. Use *expN* to specify the desired bar that, when chosen, will activate the other pop-up or menu. The corresponding ACTIVATE POPUP or ACTIVATE MENU clause specifies the pop-up or the menu that is activated as the result of the choice.

ON KEY =
Syntax

```
ON KEY = expN [command]
```

The ON KEY = *expN* command branches to a subroutine when the user presses the key that has the ASCII code indicated by the expression.

ON KEY-LABEL
Syntax

```
ON KEY [LABEL key-label] [command]
```

The ON KEY-LABEL command branches to a subroutine based on the pressing of a specific key as identified by the key label.

ON PAD
Syntax

```
ON PAD padname OF menuname
[ACTIVATE POPUP popupname]
[ACTIVATE MENU menuname]
```

The ON PAD command ties a given pad within a bar menu to a specific pop-up menu. When the named pad is selected from the menu, the associated pop-up menu appears. Use the ACTIVATE MENU clause to activate a bar menu.

Example

```
ON PAD Add OF MainMenu ACTIVATE POPUP AddRecs
ON PAD Edit OF MainMenu ACTIVATE POPUP EditRecs
ON PAD Print OF MainMenu ACTIVATE POPUP PrintRec
```

ON PAGE
Syntax

```
ON PAGE [AT LINE expN command]
```

The ON PAGE command executes the command named after the ON PAGE command whenever FoxPro reaches the designated line number or encounters an EJECT PAGE command. The ON PAGE command is generally used to call a procedure that prints a footer, ejects a page, and prints a header. Using ON PAGE without any clauses cancels the effects of the previous ON PAGE command.

Example

```
ON PAGE AT LINE 58 DO FOOTERS
SET PRINT ON
LIST LASTNAME, FIRSTNAME, SALARY, HIREDATE
(...more commands...)

PROCEDURE FOOTERS
?
? " Salary listing- for personnel use only."
EJECT PAGE
? " SALARY LISTING "
?
? DATE()
RETURN
```

A

ON READERROR

Syntax

```
ON READERROR [command]
```

The ON READERROR command runs a program or executes a named command or procedure after testing for an error in input. The ON READ-ERROR command is called in response to invalid dates, improper responses to a VALID clause, or improper entries when a RANGE clause is in effect. ON READERROR without the *command* clause cancels the previous ON READERROR command.

ON SELECTION BAR

Syntax

```
ON SELECTION BAR expN OF popupname [command]
```

The ON SELECTION BAR command links a program, a procedure, or a command to a specific bar of a bar menu. When the bar identified by the value of *ExpN* is chosen from the menu, the command, procedure, or program named is executed.

ON SELECTION BAR without the rest of the expression cancels the effects of the previous ON SELECTION BAR command.

Example

```
ON SELECTION BAR 2 OF MyPop DO REPORTER
```

ON SELECTION MENU

Syntax

```
ON SELECTION MENU menuname / ALL [command]
```

The ON SELECTION MENU command links a program, a procedure, or a command to any pad of a bar menu. When any pad is chosen from the menu, the command, procedure, or program named is executed.

ON SELECTION MENU without the rest of the expression cancels the effects of the previous ON SELECTION MENU command.

Example

```
ON SELECTION MENU OF MyPop DO SUBMENU2
```

ON SELECTION PAD
Syntax

```
ON SELECTION PAD padname OF menuname [command]
```

The ON SELECTION PAD command links a program, procedure, or command to a specific pad of a bar menu. When the named pad is chosen from the menu, the command, procedure, or program named within the ON SELECTION statement is executed. ON SELECTION PAD without the *padname* clause cancels the previous ON SELECTION PAD command.

Example

```
ON SELECTION PAD Print OF MainMenu DO REPORTER
```

ON SELECTION POPUP
Syntax

```
ON SELECTION POPUP popupname /ALL [command]
```

The ON SELECTION POPUP command names a program, procedure, or command that executes when a selection is made from a pop-up menu. If no command or procedure is named, the active pop-up is deactivated. If the ALL option is used, the command or procedure applies to all pop-ups. ON SELECTION POPUP without the *popupname* clause cancels the previous ON SELECTION POPUP command.

Example

```
ON SELECTION POPUP Print DO Reporter
```

PACK
Syntax

```
PACK [MEMO] [DBF]
```

The PACK command removes records that have been marked for deletion by the DELETE command and rebuilds any open index files. Because the command involves recopying much of the active database, it can be time consuming with large files.

You can add the MEMO or DBF clause to specifically pack just the database file without packing the memo fields or to pack just the memo field file without packing the database. The MEMO clause causes a pack of the memo field file, but the database file is not packed. The DBF clause causes a pack of just the database file, but the memo field file is not packed. If you omit both clauses under FoxPro 2, both the database file and the memo field file are packed.

PARAMETERS
Syntax

```
PARAMETERS parameter-list
```

The PARAMETERS command is used within a command file to assign variable names to data items that are received from another command file with the DO command. The PARAMETERS command must be the first command in a command file. The number, order, and data types of the items in the parameter list must match the list of parameters included with the WITH option of the DO command that called the command file.

Example

The following portion of a command file shows the use of the
PARAMETERS command to receive a location for displaying an error
message, along with the contents of the message:

```
PROCEDURE ErrMessage
PARAMETERS Row, Message
@ Row, 36-(LEN(TEXT)/2) SAY Text
RETURN
```

PLAY MACRO
Syntax

```
PLAY MACRO macroname [TIME n seconds]
```

The PLAY MACRO command plays a previously stored macro. Use the
optional TIME clause to specify a time interval, in seconds, between
macro keystrokes.

PRINTJOB/ENDPRINTJOB
Syntax

```
PRINTJOB
commands
ENDPRINTJOB
```

The PRINTJOB command places stored print-related settings into effect
for the duration of a printing job. Desired values must be stored to
print-system memory variables before the PRINTJOB command is
encountered. When PRINTJOB is executed, starting codes stored to
_pscodes are sent to the printer; a formfeed is sent if _peject contains
BEFORE or BOTH; _pcolno is initialized to zero; and _plineno and ON
PAGE are activated. When the printing process is complete and the
ENDPRINTJOB command is encountered, any ending print codes stored

to _pecodes are sent to the printer; a formfeed is sent if _peject contains AFTER or BOTH; FoxPro returns to the PRINTJOB command if the _pcopies variable contains more than 1 (set to more than one copy of the report); and _plineno and ON PAGE are deactivated.

Example

```
*sets compressed print on for Epson with ESC code 018.
*does page eject after end of each report.
*spools two copies of report to printer.
STORE 018 to _pecodes
STORE "AFTER" to _peject
STORE 2 to _pcopies
PRINTJOB
REPORT FORM Payroll TO PRINT
END PRINTJOB
```

PRIVATE
Syntax

```
PRIVATE ALL [LIKE/EXCEPT skeleton] /
memvarlist / ARRAY array-definition-list]
```

This command sets specified variables to private, hiding values of those variables from all higher level parts of a program. Skeletons are file name patterns that include the acceptable DOS wildcards of asterisk (*) and question mark (?). Memory variables are private by default.

Examples
To hide all variables, excluding BILLPAY, from higher level parts of the program, enter

```
PRIVATE ALL EXCEPT BILLPAY
```

To hide all variables with eight-character names that end in TEST from higher level parts of the program, enter

```
PRIVATE ALL LIKE ????TEST
```

To hide only the variable named PAYOUT from higher level parts of the program, enter

```
PRIVATE PAYOUT
```

PROCEDURE
Syntax

```
PROCEDURE procedure-name
```

The PROCEDURE command identifies the start of each separate procedure within a procedure file.

Although using a one-line procedure is inefficient (procedures should be at least two lines long), the following example demonstrates a simple procedure.

Example

```
PROCEDURE ERROR1
@ 2,10 SAY "That is not a valid answer. Try again."
RETURN
```

PUBLIC
Syntax

```
PUBLIC memvarlist / ARRAY array-definition-list
```

This command sets named variables or arrays to public, making the values of those variables or arrays available to all levels of a program.

Example
To make the variables named BILLPAY, DUEDATE, and AMOUNT available to all modules of a program, enter

```
PUBLIC BILLPAY, DUEDATE, AMOUNT
```

A

QUIT
Syntax

```
QUIT
```

The QUIT command closes all open files, leaves FoxPro, and returns you to the operating system prompt.

READ
Syntax

```
READ [CYCLE] [ACTIVATE expL1] [DEACTIVATE expL2] [MODAL]
[WITH window-title-list] [SHOW expL3] [VALID expL4 / expN1]
[WHEN expL5] [OBJECT expN2] [TIMEOUT expN3] [SAVE]
[NOMOUSE] [LOCK / NOLOCK] [COLOR [color-pairs-list] / COLOR
SCHEME expN4]
```

The READ command allows entry from an @ command with a GET option. Normally, a READ command clears all GETs when all data entry or editing is completed. The SAVE option is used to avoid clearing all GETs after completion of data entry or editing.

The CYCLE clause is used to leave the READ active when moving past the last or first GET. The ACTIVATE clause is executed when READ is issued and whenever the current READ window changes. (ACTIVATE can be considered to be a window-level WHEN clause.) The DEACTIVATE clause is executed if you bring another window forward (or whenever the value of WONTOP( ) changes). DEACTIVATE can be considered to be a window-level VALID clause. The SHOW clause is used along with the SHOW GETS command (see SHOW GETS). The SHOW clause is executed whenever the SHOW GETS command is issued.

The optional VALID clause is evaluated when you exit from the READ. The WHEN clause can be used to determine whether the READ will take place, depending on the value of the logical expression. The OBJECT specifies which object is initially selected within the READ. Use the TIMEOUT clause to specify how long (in seconds) a READ will be in effect if no key is pressed. Normally, all GETs are cleared following a

READ; use the SAVE statement to reissue a READ without reissuing the GETS. The NOMOUSE option prevents objects from being selected with the mouse, and the COLOR and COLOR SCHEME options can be used to specify colors for the READ.

READ MENU
Syntax

```
READ MENU TO memory-variable [SAVE]
```

The READ MENU TO command activates a pop-up menu defined with the @-MENU command (see @-MENU). The SAVE option causes the menu to remain visible after a menu selection has been made.

A

RECALL
Syntax

```
RECALL [scope] [FOR condition] [WHILE condition] [NOOPTIMIZE]
```

The RECALL command unmarks records that have been marked for deletion. If *scope* is not listed, ALL is assumed. The FOR option can be used to specify a condition that must be met before a record will be recalled. If you use the WHILE option, deleted records will be recalled until the condition is no longer true. When used, the NOOPTIMIZE clause turns off FoxPro's internal optimization techniques (also known as Rushmore).

REINDEX
Syntax

```
REINDEX [COMPACT]
```

The REINDEX command rebuilds all open index files in the current work area. If any changes have been made to the database while its index file was closed, you can update the index file with REINDEX.

All tags in all open compound index files are updated. Also, the COMPACT option can be used to cause the reindexed files to use the compact file format.

RELEASE
Syntax

```
RELEASE memvarlist / ALL [LIKE / EXCEPT wildcards]
RELEASE MODULE modulename / MENUS menuname-list / POPUP
popupname-list / WINDOW windowname-list
RELEASE BAR barlist/RELEASE PAD padname OF menuname
```

The RELEASE command removes all or specified memory variables from memory. Wildcards, which are asterisks or question marks, are used with the LIKE and EXCEPT options. The asterisk can represent one or more characters, the question mark one character. The RELEASE MENUS, RELEASE POPUP, RELEASE WINDOW, and the RELEASE BAR and RELEASE PAD variations of the command release the named objects from active memory. The RELEASE MODULE command releases any binary files loaded with the LOAD command from memory.

Example
To release all memory variables except those ending with the characters TAX, enter

```
RELEASE ALL EXCEPT ???TAX
```

RENAME
Syntax

```
RENAME filename.ext TO new-filename.ext
```

The RENAME command changes the name of a file. The name must include the file extension. If the file is on a disk that is not in the default drive, the drive designator must be included in *filename.ext.*

REPLACE
Syntax

```
REPLACE [scope] field WITH expression [...field2 WITH
expression2...] [FOR condition] [WHILE condition] [ADDITIVE] [NOOPTIMIZE]
```

The REPLACE command replaces the contents of a specified field with
new values. You can replace values in more than one field by listing
more than one *field* WITH *expression;* be sure to separate each field
replacement with a comma. The FOR option can be used to specify a
condition that must be met before a field in a record will be replaced. If
you use the WHILE option, records will be replaced until the condition
is no longer true. If the *scope,* FOR, or WHILE option is not used, the
current record (at the current record-pointer location) will be the only
record replaced. The ADDITIVE option can be used when replacing a
memo field to add the expression to the existing text in the field.
FoxPro will automatically insert a carriage return between the old text
and the new. When used, the NOOPTIMIZE clause turns off FoxPro's
internal optimization techniques (also known as Rushmore).

Example

To replace the contents of a field called Salary at the current record
with a new amount equal to the old amount multiplied by 1.05, enter

```
REPLACE SALARY WITH SALARY * 1.05
```

REPORT FORM
Syntax

```
REPORT FORM filename / ? [scope] [FOR condition] [WHILE
condition] [PLAIN] [HEADING character-string] [SUMMARY]
[NOEJECT] [TO PRINT / TO FILE filename] [OFF]
[PREVIEW] [NOCONSOLE] [NOOPTIMIZE]
```

The REPORT FORM command uses a report form file (previously
created with the CREATE REPORT command) to produce a report. A file

name with the extension .FRX is assumed unless otherwise specified. The FOR option can be used to specify a condition to be met before a record will be printed. If you use the WHILE option, records will be printed until the condition is no longer true. If *scope* is not included, ALL is assumed. The PLAIN option omits page headings. The HEADING option (followed by a character string) provides a header in addition to any header that was specified when the report was created with CREATE REPORT. The NOEJECT option cancels the initial formfeed. The SUMMARY option causes a summary report to be printed. TO PRINT directs output to the screen and the printer, while TO FILE directs output to a disk file. If the question mark is substituted for a file name, a list of all report files appears. The user may then select the report to print from the list. The optional OFF clause, when used, turns off the normal screen output while the report is being printed.

The PREVIEW option causes an on-screen preview display of the labels to appear. The NOCONSOLE option disables the output that is normally sent to the screen. Use the NOOPTIMIZE clause to disable the normal optimization techniques (also known as Rushmore) used by FoxPro 2.

RESTORE
Syntax

```
RESTORE FROM filename / MEMO memofield [ADDITIVE]
```

The RESTORE command reads memory variables into memory from a memory variable file or from a memo field. When used with files, RESTORE FROM assumes that *filename* ends with .MEM; if it does not, you should include the extension. If the ADDITIVE option is used, current memory variables will not be deleted.

RESTORE MACROS
Syntax

```
RESTORE MACROS FROM macro-filename / MEMO memofield
```

The RESTORE MACROS command restores macros that were saved in a macro file or in a memo field to memory. If the MEMO clause is used, the macros are restored from a memo field. Any macros existing in memory that are assigned to the same keys when you use this command will be overwritten.

RESTORE SCREEN
Syntax

```
RESTORE SCREEN [FROM memvar]
```

The RESTORE SCREEN command restores a screen from the buffer or from the named memory variable (see SAVE SCREEN).

A

RESTORE WINDOW
Syntax

```
RESTORE WINDOW windowname-list / ALL FROM filename /
MEMO memofield
```

The RESTORE WINDOW command restores window definitions that were saved in a file or in a memo field with the SAVE WINDOW command. If the MEMO clause is used, the windows are restored from a memo field.

RESUME
Syntax

```
RESUME
```

The RESUME command is a companion to the SUSPEND command. RESUME causes program execution to continue at the line following the line at which program operation was suspended (see also SUSPEND).

RETRY

Syntax

RETRY

The RETRY command returns control to a calling program and executes the same line that called the program containing the RETRY command. The function of RETRY is similar to the function of the RETURN command; however, where RETURN executes the next successive line of the calling program, RETRY executes the same line of the calling program. RETRY can be useful in error-recovery situations, where an action can be taken to clear the cause of an error and repeat the command.

Example

```
*printing program includes error recovery.
WAIT "Press a key to start the report."
ON ERROR DO PROBLEMS
REPORT FORM MyFile TO PRINT
ON ERROR
RETURN

*...more commands...

*PROBLEMS.PRG
*error trapping for printer program.
CLEAR
? "Printer is NOT READY."
? "Take corrective action, then press any key."
WAIT
RETRY
RETURN
```

RETURN

Syntax

RETURN [TO MASTER / *expression* / TO *procedurename*]

The RETURN command ends execution of a command file or procedure. If the command file was called by another command file, program control returns to the other command file. If the command file was not called by another command file, control returns to the *command level*. If the TO MASTER option is used, control returns to the highest level command file. If the TO *procedurename* option is used, control returns to the named procedure. The *expression* option is used to return the value in a user-defined function to another procedure or command file.

RUN or !
Syntax

```
RUN [/N] filename
! [/N] filename
```

The RUN command executes a non-FoxPro program from within the FoxPro environment, provided there is enough available memory. The program must be an executable file (having an extension of .COM, .EXE, or .BAT). When the program completes its execution, control is passed back to FoxPro. You can also execute DOS commands with RUN. The exclamation point (!) can be substituted for the word RUN. The /N option can be used to specify an amount of memory to be freed, where N is a numeric value. If N is omitted, RUN frees a standard amount of memory (which varies, depending on your system). If N is 0, RUN frees as much memory as possible, swapping large portions of FoxPro out to disk. Any value other than 0 is interpreted as memory needed in kilobytes, and as much of FoxPro as necessary is swapped out to disk to provide the memory.

SAVE
Syntax

```
SAVE TO filename / MEMO memofield-name [ALL LIKE / EXCEPT skeleton]
```

The SAVE command copies memory variables to a disk file or to the contents of a memo field. Wildcards, which are asterisks or question marks, are used with parts of file names as skeletons along with the LIKE and EXCEPT options. The asterisk can represent one or more characters, the question mark one character.

Example

To save all existing six-letter memory variables ending in the letters TAX to a disk file named FIGURES, enter

```
SAVE TO FIGURES ALL LIKE ???TAX
```

SAVE MACROS
Syntax

```
SAVE MACROS TO macro-filename / MEMO memofield
```

The SAVE MACROS command saves macros currently in memory to a macro file. If the MEMO option is used, the macros are saved to the named memo field of the current record.

SAVE SCREEN
Syntax

```
SAVE SCREEN [TO memvar]
```

The SAVE SCREEN command saves the current screen image to the buffer. If the TO clause is included along with a variable name, the screen image is saved to the named memory variable. You can later use RESTORE SCREEN to redisplay the screen.

SAVE WINDOW
Syntax

```
SAVE WINDOW windowname-list / ALL TO window-filename /
MEMO memofield
```

The SAVE WINDOW command saves the windows named in the list to a disk file. If the ALL option is used, all windows in memory are saved to a file. If the MEMO option is used, the windows are saved to the named memo field of the current record. The windows can be restored to memory by using the RESTORE WINDOW command.

SCAN
Syntax

```
SCAN [scope] [FOR condition] [WHILE condition]
 + [commands...]
    [LOOP]
    [commands]
    [EXIT]
ENDSCAN
```

The SCAN and ENDSCAN commands are simplified alternatives to the DO WHILE and ENDDO commands. The SCAN-ENDSCAN commands cause the file in use to be scanned, processing all records that meet the specified conditions.

Example

```
USE MEMBERS
SCAN FOR EXPIREDATE <= DATE()+60
    SET PRINT ON
    ? "Dear: "
    ?? trim(FIRSTNAME) + " " + LASTNAME
    ?
    ? "Your membership expires within the next 60 days."
    ? "Please call 555-1212 to renew your membership."
    EJECT
    SET PRINT OFF
ENDSCAN
```

SCATTER TO
Syntax

```
SCATTER memory variable [FIELDS fieldlist ] TO array
```

The SCATTER TO command moves data from the current record of a database file or from memory variables into an array. (Note that SCATTER TO is compatible with FoxBase Plus; if you need compatibility with dBASE IV, use COPY TO ARRAY instead.) The fields of the current record are transferred, beginning with the first field of the record, into the corresponding elements of the array. If the database has more fields than the array has elements, the contents of extra fields are not stored to the array. If the array has more elements than the database has fields, the extra elements in the array are not changed. Note that memo fields are ignored during the data-transfer process.

SCROLL

Syntax

```
SCROLL row1,col1,row2,col2,expN1,expN2
```

The SCROLL command causes a rectangular portion of the screen to scroll. The upper-left corner of the portion is designated by *row1,col1* and the lower-right corner is designated by *row2,col2*. The numeric expression indicates the number of lines of the area to scroll. A negative number forces a scroll downwards, and a positive number forces a scroll upwards.

Use *expN2* to scroll horizontally. A positive value scrolls to the right by *N2* columns. A negative value scrolls to the left by *N2* columns.

SEEK

Syntax

```
SEEK expression
```

The SEEK command searches for the first record in an indexed file whose field matches a specific expression. If *expression* is a character string, it must be enclosed by single or double quotes. If *expression* cannot be found and FoxPro is not executing a command file, the EOF value is set to true and a "No find" message is displayed on the screen. An index file must be open before you can use the SEEK command. Also note the use of two related commands, SET EXACT and SET NEAR.

Use SET EXACT to tell FoxPro to find a precise match. Use SET NEAR to tell FoxPro that if a match cannot be found, the record pointer should be positioned at the closest record rather than the end of the file.

SELECT

Syntax

```
SELECT n or SELECT alias
```

This variation of the SELECT command chooses from among ten possible work areas for database files. When FoxPro is first loaded into the computer, it defaults to work area 1. To use multiple files at once, you can select other work areas with the SELECT command; other files can then be opened in those areas. Acceptable work areas are the numbers 1 through 10.

Example

To open a file named TAXES in work area 5, enter

```
SELECT 5
USE TAXES
```

SELECT - SQL

Syntax

```
SELECT [ALL / DISTINCT][alias.]select_item[AS
column_name][, [alias.]select_item[AS column_name]...]
FROM database [local_alias][database[local_alias]...]
[[INTO destination] / [TO FILE filename [ADDITIVE] / TO
PRINTER]] [NOCONSOLE][PLAIN][NOWAIT][WHERE joincondition [AND
joincondition ...][AND / OR filtercondition][AND / OR
filtercondition...]]][GROUP BY groupcolumn[, groupcolumn
[ORDER BY order_item[ASC / DESC][, order_item[ASC / DESC]...]]
```

This variation of the SELECT command retrieves data from a table (made up of fields from one or more FoxPro database files). SELECT commands can be entered manually in the Command window, or you can create them by designing a query in the RQBE window. The use of

A

the SELECT-SQL statement is an advanced topic, beyond the scope of this text; for more information, refer to your FoxPro documentation or to a text on the SQL Data Retrieval language.

SET
Syntax

```
SET
```

This command causes the View window to be displayed. The View window options (at the left edge of the window) can then be used to view and modify most available SET parameters within FoxPro.

SET ALTERNATE
Syntax

```
SET ALTERNATE ON/OFF
SET ALTERNATE TO filename [ADDITIVE]
```

The SET ALTERNATE TO command creates a text file with the extension .TXT, and when activated by SET ALTERNATE ON, stores all keyboard entries and screen displays to the file. The SET ALTERNATE OFF command halts the process, after which CLOSE ALTERNATE is used to close the file. (You can SET ALTERNATE OFF temporarily, and turn it on again later before using CLOSE ALTERNATE, to resume sending output to the file.) If the ADDITIVE option is used, SET ALTERNATE appends to the end of any existing file.

Example
To store the actions of the LIST command to a text file, enter

```
SET ALTERNATE TO CAPTURE
SET ALTERNATE ON
LIST LASTNAME, FIRSTNAME
SET ALTERNATE OFF
CLOSE ALTERNATE
```

SET ANSI
Syntax

```
SET ANSI ON/OFF
```

The SET ANSI command determines how comparisons of strings of different lengths are made with FoxPro's SQL commands. When SET ANSI is ON, character strings are compared for the full length of the string. Hence, "Derek" and "Derek" do not match if SET ANSI is ON. When SET ANSI is OFF, strings are compared character by character only until the shorter string ends. Hence, "Derek " and "Derek" match if SET ANSI is OFF.

A

SET AUTOSAVE
Syntax

```
SET AUTOSAVE ON/OFF
```

The SET AUTOSAVE command, when turned on, causes FoxPro to save changes to disk after each I/O operation. This reduces the chances of data loss due to power or hardware failure. The default for SET AUTOSAVE is OFF.

SET BELL
Syntax

```
SET BELL ON/OFF
```

The SET BELL command controls whether audible warnings will be issued during certain operations. SET BELL ON enables the bell, and SET BELL OFF disables the bell.

SET BELL TO
Syntax

```
SET BELL TO frequency/duration
```

The SET BELL TO command controls the frequency and duration of the bell. The frequency is the desired tone in hertz, and each unit of duration is approximately .0549 seconds. Available frequency is from 19 to 10,000 and available duration is from 1 to 19.

SET BLINK
Syntax

```
SET BLINK ON/OFF
```

The SET BLINK command determines whether screen elements (borders, shadows, text) can be made to blink on EGA or VGA monitors. SET BLINK ON enables blinking of selected elements. Use the Color option of the Window menu or the SET COLOR OF command to change the actual elements to blinking.

SET BLOCKSIZE
Syntax

```
SET BLOCKSIZE TO expN
```

The SET BLOCKSIZE command defines the size of blocks used to store memo fields on disk. Each block is 512 bytes, and *expN* can be a value from 1 to 32. If e*xpN* is greater than 32, disk space for memo fields is allocated in bytes rather than in 512-byte blocks. The default value for SET BLOCKSIZE is 64.

SET BORDER
Syntax

```
SET BORDER TO [SINGLE/DOUBLE/PANEL/NONE/
border-definition-string1] [,border-definition-string2]
```

The SET BORDER command redefines the border, which is a single line. The SINGLE option defines a single line; the DOUBLE option defines a double line; the PANEL option defines a panel built with the ASCII 219 character; and NONE defines no border. The *border-definition-string* option may contain up to 8 ASCII values separated by commas. Value 1 defines the top of the border; value 2 the bottom; values 3 and 4 the left and right edges; and values 5, 6, 7, and 8 the upper-left, upper-right, lower-left, and lower-right corners, respectively. By default, *border-definition-string1* is also used for the active window. The optional *border-definition-string2* defines the appearance of the border if the window is not active.

SET CARRY
Syntax

```
SET CARRY ON/OFF
```

The SET CARRY command controls whether data will be copied from the prior record into a new record when APPEND or INSERT is used. By default, SET CARRY is OFF.

SET CENTURY
Syntax

```
SET CENTURY ON/OFF
```

This command causes or does not cause the century to be visible in the display of dates. For example, a date that appears as 12/30/86 will appear as 12/30/1986 after the SET CENTURY ON command is used.

SET CLEAR
Syntax

```
SET CLEAR ON/OFF
```

The SET CLEAR command determines whether the screen will be cleared after a SET FORMAT TO or a QUIT command. If SET CLEAR is OFF, the screen will not be cleared upon execution of SET FORMAT TO or QUIT. The default for SET CLEAR is ON.

SET CLOCK
Syntax

```
SET CLOCK ON/OFF
```

The SET CLOCK command defines whether the system clock will appear. SET CLOCK ON displays the clock, and SET CLOCK OFF hides the clock.

SET CLOCK TO
Syntax

```
SET CLOCK TO row,col
```

The SET CLOCK TO command defines the location of the system clock, as defined by the row and column coordinates provided.

SET COLOR OF
Syntax

```
SET COLOR OF NORMAL / MESSAGES / TITLES / BOX /
HIGHLIGHT / INFORMATION / FIELDS TO [color-pairs-list]
```

The SET COLOR OF command can be used to define colors for standard items, such as messages, titles, boxes, and highlights. *Color-pairs-list* is one to ten color pairs, with foreground and background values separated by a slash and each color pair separated by a comma.

SET COLOR OF SCHEME
Syntax

```
SET COLOR OF SCHEME expN TO [color-pairs-list ]
```

The SET COLOR OF SCHEME command sets the colors of the numbered scheme to the colors list identified in *color-pairs-list. The expN* is a numeric expression from 1 to 11 or from 17 to 24. (Schemes 12 through 16 are reserved by FoxPro.) Schemes 17 through 24 can be user defined. Schemes 1 through 11 apply to the following objects:

Scheme 1	User windows
Scheme 2	User menus
Scheme 3	Menu bar
Scheme 4	Pop-up menus
Scheme 5	Dialog boxes
Scheme 6	Dialog pop-ups
Scheme 7	Alert boxes
Scheme 8	Windows
Scheme 9	Window pop-ups
Scheme 10	Browse window
Scheme 11	Report Layout window

The color pairs list is one to ten color pairs, with foreground and background values separated by a slash and each color pair separated by a comma.

SET COLOR OF SCHEME TO
Syntax

```
SET COLOR OF SCHEME expN1 TO [SCHEME expN2]
```

The SET COLOR OF SCHEME TO command copies the colors of the first color scheme to the second color scheme. The *expN* is a numeric expression from 1 to 11 or from 17 to 24. (Schemes 12 through 16 are reserved by FoxPro.) Schemes 17 through 24 can be user defined. If SCHEME *expN2* is omitted, colors will be copied from the last named color set.

SET COLOR ON/OFF
Syntax

```
SET COLOR ON/OFF
```

The SET COLOR ON/OFF command is used to change between color and monochrome monitors. SET COLOR ON turns on color mode, and SET COLOR OFF turns on monochrome mode.

SET COLOR SET TO
Syntax

```
SET COLOR SET TO [colorset-name]
```

The SET COLOR SET TO command loads a color set that was defined and saved previously. Use the Color option of the Window menu to define and save a color set.

SET COLOR TO
Syntax

```
SET COLOR TO color-pairs-list
```

The SET COLOR command is used to select screen colors and display attributes. *Color-pairs-list* is one to ten color pairs, with foreground and background values separated by a slash and each color pair separated by a comma.

SET COMPATIBLE
Syntax

```
SET COMPATIBLE ON/OFF
```

The SET COMPATIBLE command turns on or off compatibility with FoxBase Plus. When SET COMPATIBLE is OFF, FoxBase Plus programs run in FoxPro without modification.

SET CONFIRM
Syntax

```
SET CONFIRM ON/OFF
```

The SET CONFIRM command controls the behavior of the cursor during editing. When SET CONFIRM is ON, the (Enter) key must be pressed to move from one field to another when editing in a highlighted field, even if you completely fill the field. When CONFIRM is OFF, the cursor automatically advances when you fill a field.

SET CONSOLE
Syntax

```
SET CONSOLE ON/OFF
```

A

The SET CONSOLE command turns output to the screen on or off. SET CONSOLE does not control output to the printer. Use SET CONSOLE within a program when you want to hide any screen display while leaving the keyboard active (during the typing of a user's password, for example).

SET CURRENCY
Syntax

```
SET CURRENCY TO [expC]
```

The SET CURRENCY command changes the symbol used for currency. A character expression containing up to nine characters may be used as the currency symbol.

SET CURRENCY LEFT/RIGHT
Syntax

```
SET CURRENCY LEFT/RIGHT
```

The SET CURRENCY LEFT/RIGHT command changes the placement of the currency symbol, allowing the symbol to appear to the left or the right of the value.

SET DATE
Syntax

```
SET DATE AMERICAN/ANSI/BRITISH/ITALIAN/FRENCH/GERMAN
/JAPAN/USA/MDY/DMY/YMD
```

This command sets the display format for the appearance of dates. American displays as MM/DD/YY; ANSI displays as YY.MM.DD; British displays as DD/MM/YY; Italian displays as DD-MM-YY; French displays as DD/MM/YY; German displays as DD.MM.YY; Japan displays as YY/MM/DD; USA displays as MM-DD-YY; MDY displays as MM/DD/YY; DMY displays as DD/MM/YY; and YMD displays as YY/MM/DD. The default value is American.

SET DECIMALS
Syntax

```
SET DECIMALS TO expN
```

The SET DECIMALS command changes the number of decimal places that are normally displayed during calculations.

SET DEFAULT
Syntax

```
SET DEFAULT TO drive: directory
```

This command changes the default drive and/or directory used in file operations.

SET DELETED
Syntax

```
SET DELETED ON/OFF
```

With SET DELETED set OFF (as it is by default), all records marked for deletion will be displayed when commands such as LIST and REPORT FORM are used. With SET DELETED set to ON, deleted records are omitted from the output of LIST, DISPLAY, LABEL FORM, and REPORT FORM commands. They are also omitted from the Edit and Browse displays, unless you explicitly move the record pointer to a deleted record with a GOTO command before issuing the EDIT or BROWSE command.

SET DEVELOPMENT
Syntax

```
SET DEVELOPMENT ON/OFF
```

The SET DEVELOPMENT command, when ON, tells FoxPro to compare creation dates of .PRG files and compiled .DBO files, so that when a program is run, an outdated .DBO file will not be used. The FoxPro Editor automatically deletes old .DBO files as programs are updated, so the SET DEVELOPMENT command is not needed if you use the FoxPro Editor. If you use another editor to create and modify program files, add a SET DEVELOPMENT ON statement at the start of your programs.

SET DEVICE
Syntax

```
SET DEVICE TO PRINTER/SCREEN/FILE filename
```

The SET DEVICE command controls whether @ commands are sent to the screen or the printer. SET DEVICE is normally set to SCREEN, but if PRINTER is specified, output will be directed to the printer. The FILE option directs output to the named disk file.

SET DISPLAY TO
Syntax

```
SET DISPLAY TO
MONO/COLOR/CGA/EGA25/EGA43/MONO43/VGA25/VGA43/VGA50
```

The SET DISPLAY TO command chooses a monitor type and sets the number of lines displayed. For the number of lines option to have effect, the graphics hardware must support the type chosen within the SET DISPLAY TO command.

SET DOHISTORY
Syntax

```
SET DOHISTORY ON/OFF
```

The SET DOHISTORY command turns on or off the storage of commands from command files in the Command window. When DOHISTORY is ON, program file commands are stored in the Command window as they are executed. You can later edit and reexecute those commands as if they had been entered at the command level.

SET ECHO
Syntax

```
SET ECHO ON/OFF
```

The SET ECHO command determines whether instructions from command files will be displayed or printed during program execution. Setting ECHO to ON can be useful when debugging programs. The default for SET ECHO is OFF.

SET ESCAPE
Syntax

```
SET ESCAPE ON/OFF
```

The SET ESCAPE command determines whether the [Esc] key will interrupt a program during execution. The default for SET ESCAPE is ON.

SET EXACT
Syntax

```
SET EXACT ON/OFF
```

A

The SET EXACT command determines how precisely two character strings will be compared. With SET EXACT OFF, which is the default case, comparison is not strict: a string on the left of the test is equal to its substring on the right if the substring acts as a prefix of the larger string. Thus, "turnbull" = "turn" is true even though it is clearly not. SET EXACT ON corrects for this lack of precision. Note that SET EXACT determines whether you can FIND or SEEK the first part of an index key. If SET EXACT is OFF, you can search for the first part of the key; if SET EXACT is ON, you must search for the entire key expression.

SET FIELDS
Syntax

```
SET FIELDS ON/OFF
```

This command respects or overrides a list of fields specified by the SET FIELDS TO command.

SET FIELDS TO
Syntax

```
SET FIELDS TO [fieldlist / ALL [LIKE/EXCEPT skeleton]] ADDITIVE]
```

This command sets a specified list of fields that will be available for use. The ALL option causes all fields present in the active database to be made available. The LIKE/EXCEPT *skeleton* options select fields that match or do not match the skeleton. The ADDITIVE option adds the fields to a prior list of fields.

SET FILTER
Syntax

```
SET FILTER TO [condition]
```

The SET FILTER command displays only those records in a database that meet a specific condition.

Example
To display only those records in a database that contain the name "Main St." in the Address field during a DISPLAY or LIST command, enter

```
SET FILTER TO "Main St." $ ADDRESS
```

SET FIXED
Syntax

```
SET FIXED ON/OFF
```

The SET FIXED command sets the number of decimal places used within a numeric display.

SET FORMAT TO
Syntax

```
SET FORMAT TO filename / ?
```

The SET FORMAT TO command lets you activate a format file called *filename* to control the format of the screen display used during EDIT,

CHANGE, and APPEND operations. If *filename* has the extension .FMT, you need not supply the extension. The SET FORMAT command without a specified file name cancels the effects of the previous SET FORMAT command. The question mark, if used, causes a list of format files to appear.

SET FULLPATH
Syntax

```
SET FULLPATH ON/OFF
```

The SET FULLPATH command specifies whether full path names appear with file names returned by the DBF and NDX functions. If SET FULLPATH is OFF, only the drive designator and file name are returned by the functions. If SET FULLPATH is ON, the drive designator, path name, and file name are returned by the functions.

A

SET FUNCTION
Syntax

```
SET FUNCTION expN / key-label TO character-string
```

The SET FUNCTION command resets a function key to a command or sequence of commands of your choice. The maximum width of a command sequence is 75 characters. You can view the current settings with the DISPLAY STATUS command.

Example
To change the function of the F5 key to open a file named MEMBERS and enter Append mode, enter

```
SET FUNCTION "5" TO "USE MEMBERS;APPEND;"
```

The semicolon (;) represents a carriage return.

SET HEADING
Syntax

```
SET HEADING ON/OFF
```

The SET HEADING command determines whether column headings appear when the LIST, DISPLAY, CALCULATE, AVERAGE, or SUM command is used.

SET HELP
Syntax

```
SET HELP ON/OFF or SET HELP TO filename
```

The SET HELP command turns on or off the FoxPro on-line help facility. When SET HELP is ON, pressing F1 or entering HELP as a command displays the Help window. When SET HELP is OFF, the Help window is not available.

All help commands are stored in a database file named FOXHELP.DBF. You can use the SET HELP TO *filename* command to specify a different database file. This can be useful if you are designing your own custom help system for an application.

SET HELPFILTER
Syntax

```
SET HELPFILTER [AUTOMATIC] TO expL
```

The SET HELPFILTER command permits the display of a subset of help topics in the Help window. Only those records in the help database that meet the logical condition specified by the expression will be available in the Help window. The AUTOMATIC clause causes the filtering effect to be canceled after the Help window is closed. (You can also cancel the effects of SET HELPFILTER by issuing another SET HELPFILTER TO command, without specifying an expression.)

SET HOURS
Syntax

```
SET HOURS TO [12/24]
```

The SET HOURS command changes the time display to the desired format, 12 or 24 hours. If you choose the 12-hour clock, AM or PM is displayed along with the time.

SET INDEX
Syntax

```
SET INDEX TO [index-file-list / ? [ORDER expN / .idx index-file
/ [TAG] tagname [OF .cdx file]] [ASCENDING
/ DESCENDING][ADDITIVE]
```

The SET INDEX command opens the index file *filename*. If your file has the .IDX extension, you do not need to include the extension in the command. If a question mark is substituted in place of a file name, a list of all index files appears. The user may then select the index file to activate from the list.

You can use the ORDER, TAG, and ASCENDING/DESCENDING clauses. Use ORDER and TAG to specify a master index file or a master tag in a compound index file. Use ASCENDING or DESCENDING to specify whether the records should be accessed in ascending or descending order. For example, if an index file was originally created in ascending order, you use the DESCENDING option to force the records to be displayed or retrieved in descending order.

SET INTENSITY
Syntax

```
SET INTENSITY ON/OFF
```

The SET INTENSITY command determines whether reverse video is on or off during full-screen operations. SET INTENSITY is ON when you begin a session with FoxPro. If you SET INTENSITY to OFF, you should generally turn on the delimiters to mark the boundaries of the data entry area for each field.

SET LIBRARY
Syntax

```
SET LIBRARY TO filename [ADDITIVE]
```

The SET LIBRARY command opens external API (Application Program Interface) libraries. The use of API Libraries is an advanced topic that is beyond the scope of this book; for details on this subject, refer to a more advanced programmer's text or to your FoxPro programmer's documentation.

SET LOGERRORS
Syntax

```
SET LOGERRORS ON/OFF
```

The SET LOGERRORS command determines whether FoxPro stores compilation errors in a file.

SET MARGIN
Syntax

```
SET MARGIN TO expN
```

The SET MARGIN command resets the left printer margin from the default of 0.

SET MARK
Syntax

```
SET MARK TO expC
```

The SET MARK command specifies the delimiter used to separate the month, day, and year of a date. The character expression must be a single character, enclosed by quotes.

Example

```
SET MARK TO "#"
```

A

SET MARK OF
Syntax

```
SET MARK OF MENU menuname
    TO expC1 / expL1

SET MARK OF PAD padname
    OF menuname
    TO expC2 / expL2

SET MARK OF POPUP popupname
    TO expC3 / expL3

SET MARK OF BAR expN
    OF popupname
    TO expC4 / expL4
```

The SET MARK OF command places a check mark character before each pad or option in user-defined menus. The character used for the check mark is specified by the character expression. The value of the logical expression may be used in the program to toggle the check mark on and off.

SET MEMOWIDTH
Syntax

```
SET MEMOWIDTH TO expN
```

SET MEMOWIDTH controls the width of columns containing the display or printed listings of contents of memo fields. The default value provided if this command is not used is 50.

SET MESSAGE
Syntax

```
SET MESSAGE TO expC
```

This variation of the SET MESSAGE command identifies a user-definable message that appears at the position specified earlier with SET MESSAGE TO (see the next command).

Example

To display the message "Press F1 for assistance." on the message line, enter

```
SET MESSAGE TO "Press F1 for assistance."
```

SET MESSAGE TO
Syntax

```
SET MESSAGE TO [expN / LEFT / CENTER / RIGHT]
```

This variation of the SET MESSAGE command specifies the screen or window line and the optional left, center, or right placement for screen messages when the MENU TO command is used.

SET MOUSE
Syntax

```
SET MOUSE TO expN
```

The SET MOUSE command will adjust the sensitivity of the mouse. Permissible values are from 1 to 10, with 1 being the least sensitive and 10 being the most sensitive. The default for the SET MOUSE command is 5.

SET NEAR
Syntax

```
SET NEAR ON / OFF
```

The SET NEAR command can be used to position the record pointer at the nearest record when a FIND or a SEEK is unsuccessful. If SET NEAR is ON, the record pointer is placed at the next record after the expression that could not be located. If SET NEAR is OFF, the record pointer is placed at the end of the file when the expression is not found.

SET ODOMETER
Syntax

```
SET ODOMETER TO [expN]
```

The SET ODOMETER command tells FoxPro how often commands that display a record count (such as APPEND and COPY) should update the screen display. The default value is 100, and the maximum value is 32,767. Setting ODOMETER to a higher value can speed up command execution slightly.

SET OPTIMIZE
Syntax

```
SET OPTIMIZE ON / OFF
```

A

The SET OPTIMIZE command allows you to enable or disable the query-optimization techniques (also called Rushmore). FoxPro uses Rushmore along with commands that support FOR clauses, to enhance performance. In rare cases where Rushmore should be disabled, use the SET OPTIMIZE OFF command. Note that some commands also support a NOOPTIMIZE option; this option disables Rushmore for the specific command.

SET ORDER

Syntax

```
SET ORDER TO [expN SY| .idx index-file / [TAG] tagname [OF
.cdx file][IN work area SY| alias][ASCENDING  SY| DESCENDING]]
[ADDITIVE]
```

This command makes the specified index file the active index without changing the open or closed status of other index files.

You can use the TAG, IN and ASCENDING/DESCENDING clauses. Use TAG to specify a master tag in a compound index file. Use ASCENDING or DESCENDING to specify whether the records should be accessed in ascending or descending order. For example, if an index file was originally created in ascending order, you can use the DESCENDING option to force the records to be displayed or retrieved in descending order. Use the IN clause to designate the master index file or tag for a database that is open in another work area.

Example

If three index files, NAME, CITY, and STATE, have been opened in that order, and STATE is the active index, to change the active index to CITY, enter

```
SET ORDER TO 2
```

SET PATH

Syntax

```
SET PATH TO pathname
```

The PATH command identifies a search path that will be searched for files if a file is not found in the current directory. Note that the PATH command does not alter an existing DOS path; it merely specifies a search path for database and related FoxPro files.

Example

To change the path from the default path to a path named FoxPro on drive C, enter

```
SET PATH TO C: \FOXPRO
```

For more information on search paths, read your DOS manual (version 2.1 or later).

SET POINT
Syntax

```
SET POINT TO expC
```

The SET POINT command changes the character used as the decimal point. The specified expression can be any single character enclosed by quotes.

Example

```
SET POINT TO ","
```

SET PRINTER
Syntax

```
SET PRINTER ON/OFF
```

The SET PRINTER command directs output to the printer as well as to the screen. The default for SET PRINTER is OFF. (The SET PRINT ON/OFF command is identical to this command.)

A

SET PRINTER TO

Syntax

```
SET PRINTER TO LPT1/COM1/COM2/other-DOS-device/filename
```

SET PRINTER TO reroutes printer output to the device or disk file specified.

SET PROCEDURE

Syntax

```
SET PROCEDURE TO procedure-filename
```

The SET PROCEDURE command opens a procedure file. SET PROCEDURE is placed in the command file that will reference the procedures in a procedure file or in its calling program.

SET RELATION

Syntax

```
SET RELATION TO [expression1 INTO alias] [ADDITIVE]
[[,expression2 INTO alias] [ADDITIVE]...]
```

The SET RELATION command links the active database to an open database in another area. If the key-expression option is used, the active file must contain that key, and the other file must be indexed on that key. The ADDITIVE option may be used to specify multiple relations out of a single work area.

Example

To set a relation between the active database and a database named PARTS using a key field named CUSTNO, enter

```
SET RELATION TO CUSTNO INTO PARTS
```

SET RELATION OFF
Syntax

```
SET RELATION OFF INTO alias
```

The SET RELATION OFF command breaks an existing relation between two databases. The parent database must be the currently selected database, and *alias* indicates the related (child) database; *alias* may be the alias name or a work area number.

SET RESOURCE
Syntax

```
SET RESOURCE ON/OFF
```

The SET RESOURCE command tells FoxPro whether to save any changes made to the FoxPro environment when exiting the program. Changes are saved to the resource file (FOXUSER.DBF). If SET RESOURCE is OFF, changes will not be saved upon exiting FoxPro.

SET RESOURCE TO
Syntax

```
SET RESOURCE TO filename
```

The SET RESOURCE TO command tells FoxPro to use a different file as the resource file. By default, the resource file is a database named FOXUSER.DBF. You can provide another file name along with the SET RESOURCE TO command to cause that file to be used as the resource file.

SET SAFETY
Syntax

```
SET SAFETY ON/OFF
```

The SET SAFETY command determines whether a confirmation message will be provided before existing files are overwritten by commands such as SORT or COPY, or before a ZAP command is executed. SET SAFETY is normally set to ON.

SET SEPARATOR
Syntax

```
SET SEPARATOR TO expC
```

The SET SEPARATOR command specifies the symbol that should be used to separate hundreds in numeric amounts. The default is the comma, which is standard in U.S. currency. The expression may be any single character enclosed by quotes.

Example

```
SET SEPARATOR TO "."
```

SET SHADOWS
Syntax

```
SET SHADOWS ON/OFF
```

The SET SHADOWS command enables or disables shadows underneath windows.

SET SKIP
Syntax

```
SET SKIP TO alias1 [,alias2...]]
```

The SET SKIP command, which you use along with SET RELATION, lets you access all records within the linked file that match a particular index-key value in the parent file. Use SET SKIP to identify one-to-many relationships, where one record in the parent file is related to many records in the related, or child, file. When you use SET SKIP, subsequent LIST, DISPLAY, REPORT FORM, and LABEL FORM commands will process all records that match the expression used to define the relation, rather than just the first matching record.

SET SPACE
Syntax

```
SET SPACE ON/OFF
```

The SET SPACE command, when ON, tells FoxPro to add a space between expressions printed with the ? and ?? commands. The default for SET SPACE is ON.

Example

```
SET SPACE ON
USE ABCSTAFF
GO 1
? LASTNAME, FIRSTNAME
Morse Marcia
SET SPACE OFF
? LASTNAME, FIRSTNAME
MorseMarcia
```

SET STATUS
Syntax

```
SET STATUS ON/OFF
```

The SET STATUS command turns on or off the status display at the bottom of the screen.

SET STEP
Syntax

```
SET STEP ON/OFF
```

A

This is a debugging command that determines whether processing will stop each time a command in a command file is executed. The default of SET STEP is OFF.

SET STICKY
Syntax

```
SET STICKY ON/OFF
```

The SET STICKY command affects the operation of menu pads and menu pop-ups when the mouse is used. When SET STICKY is ON and a menu pad is selected with the mouse, the associated menu pop-up remains open on the screen until an option is selected (or Esc is pressed). When SET STICKY is OFF and a menu pad is selected with the mouse, the associated menu pop-up closes as soon as the mouse button is released.

SET SYSMENU
Syntax

```
SET SYSMENU ON / OFF / AUTOMATIC / TO [system-menu-popuplist /
padlist] / TO [DEFAULT]
```

The SET SYSMENU command controls access to the FoxPro System menus within a program. Use ON to enable menu access, and use OFF to disable menu access. The AUTOMATIC option makes the menus visible during program execution, and options are either enabled or disabled as appropriate, depending on the current command within your program. You can use the TO clause to specify that only certain menu pads or pop-ups are available from the FoxPro System menus.

SET TALK
Syntax

```
SET TALK ON/OFF/WINDOW
```

The SET TALK command determines whether results of FoxPro commands (such as the current record number after a SKIP or LOCATE, or the results of a SUM or AVERAGE command) are displayed on the screen. The default for SET TALK is ON.

The WINDOW option can be used to direct the output of SET TALK to a small window at the upper-right corner of the screen.

SET TEXTMERGE
Syntax

```
SET TEXTMERGE [ON / OFF] [TO [file] [ADDITIVE]] [WINDOW
windowname] [SHOW / NOSHOW]
```

The SET TEXTMERGE command enables or disables the evaluation of the database fields, variables, or the results of expressions using a text-merge operation. If SET TEXTMERGE is ON, the database fields, variables, and expressions enclosed by the text-merge delimiters are evaluated and output when placed after the \ or \\ command, or when placed between TEXT and ENDTEXT. If SET TEXTMERGE is OFF, the fields, variables, or expressions are not evaluated; instead, the actual names for the fields, variables, or expressions are output. Use the TO clause to direct the output of a text-merge operation to a file; use the ADDITIVE clause to add the output to an existing file. Use the WINDOW clause to direct output to the named window. To suppress visual output, use the NOSHOW clause; the SHOW clause may later be used to restore visual output.

SET TEXTMERGE DELIMITERS
Syntax

```
SET TEXTMERGE DELIMITERS [TO] [expC1 [,expC2]]
```

Use the SET TEXTMERGE DELIMITERS command to change the default text-merge delimiters. (The default delimiters are double sets of angle brackets.) If just *expC1* is specified, the specified character is used for both delimiters. If you specify *expC1* and *expC2*, then *expC1* becomes the left delimiter and *expC2* becomes the right delimiter.

SET TOPIC
Syntax

```
SET TOPIC TO [expC / expL]
```

The SET TOPIC command determines how help topics are displayed.
When help is selected, a list of available topics is normally displayed. If
you enter SET TOPIC TO *expC* where *expC* is the name of a help topic,
that particular topic will be displayed whenever help is selected. The
logical expression *expL* is used when creating a user-defined help system.

SET TYPEAHEAD
Syntax

```
SET TYPEAHEAD TO numeric-expression
```

This command sets the size, in number of keystrokes, of the typeahead
buffer. The default value is 20. The size of the typeahead buffer can be
increased to prevent fast typists from outrunning the keyboard. An
acceptable value is any number between 0 and 32,000.

SET UNIQUE
Syntax

```
SET UNIQUE ON/OFF
```

This command is used with the INDEX command to create lists of
items with no duplicates. The list may not be indexed adequately if
there are duplicates. When you build an index with UNIQUE set ON,
there is only one index entry for each unique index key. (Note that an
alternate way to achieve the same effect is to add the UNIQUE clause to
the INDEX ON command.) The default setting for SET UNIQUE is OFF.

SET VIEW
Syntax

```
SET VIEW ON/OFF
```

The SET VIEW command enables or disables the View window.

SET VIEW TO
Syntax

```
SET VIEW TO filename
```

The SET VIEW TO command activates the named view file, placing all settings in that view file (open databases, indexes, relations, and filters) into effect.

SET WINDOW OF MEMO
Syntax

```
SET WINDOW OF MEMO TO windowname
```

The SET WINDOW command sets a window for use when editing the contents of memo fields. The window listed as *windowname* must have been previously defined with the DEFINE WINDOW command.

SHOW GET
Syntax

```
SHOW GET variable[, expN [PROMPT expC]] [ENABLE /
DISABLE] [LEVEL expN] [COLOR color-pairs-list / COLOR SCHEME expN]
```

The SHOW GET command redisplays a single GET field or object. When the field or object is redisplayed, editing can be enabled or disabled with the ENABLE/DISABLE clauses. The PROMPT clause can be used to display a character expression as a prompt for the object. Use the LEVEL clause to display a field or object on a READ level other than the current one. Use the COLOR or COLOR SCHEME clause to set the colors for the object.

SHOW GETS
Syntax

```
SHOW GETS variable [ENABLE / DISABLE] [LEVEL expN] [WINDOW
windowname] [COLOR color-pairs-list / COLOR SCHEME expN]
```

The SHOW GETS command redisplays all GET fields or objects. When the fields or objects are redisplayed, editing can be enabled or disabled with the ENABLE/DISABLE clauses. The WINDOW clause can be used to display the fields or objects in a window. Use the LEVEL clause to display fields or objects on a READ level other than the current one. Use the COLOR or COLOR SCHEME clause to set the colors for the objects.

SHOW MENU
Syntax

```
SHOW MENU menuname / ALL [PAD padname] [SAVE]
```

The SHOW MENU command displays a menu without activating the menu. The command is primarily used in the program design process to check the visual appearance of a menu. The ALL option causes all menus to be shown. The SAVE option places images of menus on the screen. This option is normally used for testing and debugging programs.

SHOW OBJECT
Syntax

```
SHOW OBJECT expN [PROMPT expC] [ENABLE / DISABLE] [LEVEL
expN] [COLOR color-pairs-list / COLOR SCHEME expN]
```

The SHOW OBJECT command redisplays a single GET field or object. The SHOW OBJECT command differs from SHOW GET in that SHOW OBJECT refers to the field or object by the object number; SHOW GET refers to the field or object by name (field name, variable name, or array element name). When the field or object is redisplayed, editing can be enabled or disabled with the ENABLE/DISABLE clauses. The PROMPT clause can be used to display a character expression as a prompt for the object. Use the LEVEL clause to display a field or object on a READ level other than the current one. Use the COLOR or COLOR SCHEME clause to set the colors for the object.

SHOW POPUP
Syntax

```
SHOW POPUP popupname / ALL [SAVE]
```

The SHOW POPUP command displays a pop-up menu without activating the menu. The command is primarily used in the program design process to check the visual appearance of a menu. The ALL option causes all pop-ups to be shown. The SAVE option is used to place images of pop-ups on the screen. This option is normally used for testing and debugging programs.

SHOW WINDOW
Syntax

```
SHOW WINDOW windowname / ALL [SAVE] [TOP/BOTTOM/SAME]
```

The SHOW WINDOW command displays a window without activating the window. The command is primarily used in the program design process to check the visual appearance of a window. The ALL option causes all windows to be shown. Use BOTTOM or TOP to place a window at the bottom or top of a stack of existing windows. The SAME option applies only to windows previously hidden with DEACTIVATE WINDOW or HIDE WINDOW. Use SAME to put the previously hidden window back in the same position it occupied earlier. The SAVE option places images of the window on the screen. This option is normally used for testing and debugging programs.

A

SIZE POPUP
Syntax

```
SIZE POPUP popupname TO expN1, expN2 / BY expN3, expN4
```

The SIZE POPUP command resizes a pop-up menu. If the TO clause is used, the pop-up will be changed to the new size, where *expN1* is the new size in rows and *expN2* is the new size in columns. If the BY clause is used, the pop-up will be changed relative to its existing size, with *expN3* representing rows and *expN4* representing columns; for example, the command SIZE POPUP BY 4,3 would make an existing pop-up four rows larger and three columns wider.

SKIP
Syntax

```
SKIP expN [IN aliasname]
```

The SKIP command moves the record pointer. SKIP moves one record forward if no value is specified. Values can be expressed as memory variables or as constants. The IN *aliasname* option can be used to move the record pointer within a file in another work area.

Example
To skip two records back, enter

```
SKIP -2
```

SORT
Syntax

```
SORT TO filename ON field1 [/A][/C][/D] [,field2 [/A][/C][/D]...]
[ASCENDING/DESCENDING] [scope] [FOR condition] [WHILE
condition] [FIELDS fieldlist] [NOOPTIMIZE]
```

The SORT command creates a rearranged copy of a database. The order of the new database depends on the fields and options specified. The /C option creates a sorted file in dictionary order, where there is no differentiation between upper- and lowercase. Use /A for ascending order on a specific field, /D for descending order on a specific field. Use the ASCENDING or DESCENDING option to specify ascending or descending order for all fields. (The /A or /D option can be used with any field to override the effects of the ASCENDING or DESCENDING option.) The FIELDS option may be used to specify fields to be included in the sorted file; if omitted, all fields are included. You can sort up to 10 fields in a single sort; you cannot sort on memo fields or on logical fields. When used, the NOOPTIMIZE clause turns off FoxPro's internal optimization techniques (also known as Rushmore).

Example

To sort a database on the Lastname and then Firstname field, both in descending order, and output the sorted file to a file named NEWNAME, enter

```
SORT TO NEWNAME ON LASTNAME, FIRSTNAME DESCENDING
```

STORE

Syntax

```
STORE expression TO memvarlist / array-element-list
```

The STORE command creates a memory variable and stores a value to that variable or to the named array.

Example

To multiply a field called Salary for the current record by 1.05 and store it in the new memory variable named NEWAMT, enter

```
STORE SALARY * 1.05 TO NEWAMT
```

SUM

Syntax

```
SUM [scope] [fieldlist] [TO memvarlist] [TO ARRAY arrayname]
[FOR condition] [WHILE condition] [NOOPTIMIZE]
```

The SUM command provides a sum total of *fieldlist* involving numeric fields. If the TO option is not used, the sum is displayed (assuming SET TALK is ON) but not stored in memory. If the TO option is used, the sum is displayed (assuming SET TALK is ON) and is stored as the specified memory variable. If the *scope* option is not used, ALL is assumed by FoxPro. The FOR option can be used to specify a condition that must be met before an entry in a field can be summed. If you use the WHILE option, records will be summed until the condition is no longer true. The TO ARRAY option stores the values summed to the elements of the named array. When used, the NOOPTIMIZE clause turns off FoxPro's internal optimization techniques (also known as Rushmore).

Example

To total the contents of two specified fields (Salary and Taxes) and store those sums to the memory variables A and B, enter

```
SUM SALARY, TAXES TO A,B
```

SUSPEND

Syntax

```
SUSPEND
```

The SUSPEND command suspends execution of a command file or procedure and returns program control to the command level, while leaving current memory variables intact. Execution of the command file or procedure can be restarted where it was interrupted with the RESUME command.

TEXT
Syntax

```
TEXT
text to be displayed
ENDTEXT
```

The TEXT command displays blocks of text from a command file. If SET PRINT is ON, the text will be printed.

In FoxPro 2, note that expressions (including field names), memory variables, and functions placed between TEXT and ENDTEXT statements will be evaluated if SET TEXTMERGE is ON. If SET TEXTMERGE is OFF, expressions, variables, and functions are output as literal characters, including the text-merge delimiters. For example, a line between a TEXT and END-TEXT statement containing the expression <<TIME( )>> would appear as <<TIME( )>> if SET TEXTMERGE was OFF. The same expression would appear as the current time according to the computer's clock if SET TEXTMERGE was ON.

A

Example

```
TEXT
Press the RETURN key to run the payroll.
Or press the ESCAPE key to exit.
ENDTEXT
```

TOTAL
Syntax

```
TOTAL TO filename ON key [scope] [FIELDS fieldlist] [FOR
condition] [WHILE condition] [NOOPTIMIZE]
```

The TOTAL command adds the numeric fields in a database and creates a new database containing the results. The file to be totaled must be indexed or sorted on the key field. If the FIELDS *fieldlist* option is used, fields totaled will be limited to those fields named in the list. If the *scope* option is not used, the quantifier of ALL is assumed, meaning all records in the database will be totaled unless you use the FOR or WHILE option. The FOR option can be used to specify a condition that must be met for the fields to be totaled. If you use the WHILE option, records will be totaled until the condition is no longer true. When used, the NOOPTIMIZE clause turns off FoxPro's internal optimization techniques (also known as Rushmore).

Example

To total the Salary, Fedtax, Statetax, and Fica fields in a database named PAYROLL and store those totals to a second database named RECORDS, you could use commands like these:

```
USE PAYROLL
TOTAL TO NEWFIL ON FIELDS SALARY, FEDTAX, STATETAX, FICA
```

TYPE
Syntax

```
TYPE filename.ext [TO PRINT / TO FILE filename] [NUMBER]
```

The TYPE command displays the contents of a disk file on screen. If the TO PRINT option is used, the file will be printed. The TO FILE option directs the output of the TYPE command to a named disk file. The NUMBER option causes line numbers to be included.

UPDATE
Syntax

```
UPDATE [RANDOM] ON keyfield FROM alias REPLACE field WITH
expression [,field2 WITH expression2...]
```

The UPDATE command uses data from a specified database, *alias,* to make changes to the database in use. The value in the matching record in the file you are updating from is added to the value in the active file.

Example

To update the Rentamt field in a database named WORLDWIDE, based on the contents of the Rentamt field in a database named CURRENCY, enter

```
SELECT 2
USE CURRENCY
SELECT 1
USE WORLDWID INDEX LASTNAME
UPDATE ON LASTNAME FROM CURRENCY REPLACE RENTAMT
WITH CURRENCY->RENTAMT RANDOM
```

Both files must be sorted or indexed on the key field unless RANDOM is included, in which case only alias need be indexed.

A

USE

Syntax

```
USE [database-file / ?] [IN work area] [AGAIN] [INDEX
index-file-list / ? [ORDER [expN / .idx index-file / [TAG]
 tagname [OF .cdx file] [ASCENDING / DESCENDING]]]]
[ALIAS alias] [EXCLUSIVE] [NOUPDATE]
```

The USE command opens a database file and related index files in a work area. If the ? is used in place of the database file name, a list of available files appears. Use the INDEX option to specify index files that will be open or active. Use the ALIAS option to open the file in a different work area. Entering the USE command without specifying a file name will close the file that is currently open.

Use the AGAIN clause to open the same database simultaneously in a different work area. The ORDER and TAG clauses can be used to designate the master index file or the master tag of a compound index file. The ASCENDING and DESCENDING clauses may be used to determine whether records are displayed and retrieved in ascending or descending order. For example, if the index file opened with the database was originally created in descending order, the ASCENDING clause would cause the records to be accessed in ascending order.

The ALIAS clause may be used to assign an alternate name, or alias, to the database. Work areas may then be selected by referring to the work area number, the database name, or the alias. The EXCLUSIVE clause has an effect only under FoxPro/LAN; it causes the database to be opened for exclusive use, and other network users cannot use the database until it is closed. The NOUPDATE clause prevents changes to the database file.

WAIT
Syntax

```
WAIT [expC] [TO memvar]
```

The WAIT command halts operation of a command file until a key is pressed. If a character expression is included, it will be displayed on the screen. If the TO option is used, the key pressed will be stored as a memory variable.

ZAP
Syntax

```
ZAP
```

The ZAP command removes all records from the active database file. The ZAP command is equivalent to a DELETE ALL command followed by a PACK command.

ZOOM WINDOW
Syntax

```
ZOOM WINDOW windowname MIN / MAX / NORM [AT row1, col1 /
FROM row1, col1 [SIZE row2, col2 / TO row2, col2]]
```

The ZOOM WINDOW command changes the size of a window. Windows can be reduced to minimum size (minimized), enlarged to maximum size (maximized), or sized anywhere in between. The MIN clause minimizes the named window, and the MAX clause maximizes the named window. Note that if a window is a child window (a window within a window), the window can maximized only up to the size of the parent window. The NORM clause can be used to return a window to its original size, after it was minimized or maximized.

The AT and FROM clauses can be used to restore a minimized or maximized window to a different location. The *row1, col1* coordinates specify the upper-left corner of the window. The optional *row2, col2* coordinates specify the lower-right corner of the window. If the second set of coordinates is omitted, the window takes on the same size as it had before it was minimized or maximized.

A P P E N D I X

B

GLOSSARY OF FUNCTIONS

This appendix summarizes the FoxPro functions. Following the name of each function is the function's syntax and a description of its purpose. For a similar summary of FoxPro commands, see Appendix A.

Glossary Symbols and Conventions

1. All functions are printed in UPPERCASE, although you can enter them in either upper- or lowercase letters.

2. The term *expC* indicates a character expression, *expN* indicates a numeric expression, and *expL* indicates a logical expression. Where data type does not matter, the term *expr* is used.

3. Whenever a function calls for or permits an *alias* argument, you can use the alias name (in quotes), or you can use the work-area number or letter.

4. Any part of a parameter that is enclosed by [ ] (left and right brackets) is optional.

5. Ellipses (...) following a parameter means that the parameter can be repeated infinitely; that is, until you exhaust the memory of the computer or reach the limit of 1024 characters on a single program line.

Summary of Functions

ABS

Syntax

```
ABS(expN)
```

The ABS function returns the absolute (positive) value of the specified numeric expression.

ACOPY

Syntax

```
ACOPY(array1, array2 [, expN1 [, expN2 [, expN3]]])
```

The ACOPY function copies elements of the array named in *array1* to the elements of the array named in *array2*. The number of elements copied to the destination array is returned if the copy is successful; otherwise, a value of –1 is returned. *ExpN1*, which is optional, denotes the starting position in the source array. *ExpN2* is the number of elements to copy, beginning with *expN1*. If *expN2* is omitted, the copying begins at the first element of the array. *ExpN3*, which is also optional, denotes the starting element in the target array. If *expN3* is omitted, the copying begins at the first element in the target array.

ACOS
Syntax

```
ACOS(expN)
```

The ACOS function returns the arc cosine of *expN,* as measured in radians between 0 and +pi (3.14159). Allowable values for *expN* are from +1 to –1.

ADEL
Syntax

B

```
ADEL (array, expN [,2])
```

The ADEL function deletes a single element within an array, or it deletes a row or column from a two-dimensional array. If the deletion is successful, a value of 1 is returned; otherwise, –1 is returned. *Array* denotes the name of the array, and *expN* identifies the element to delete. For example, if *expN* is 3, the third element in the array is deleted. Also note that when an array element is deleted with ADEL, the element is not left blank; instead, the contents of all remaining elements after the deleted element are shifted forward by one element, leaving the last element unused and set to a logical false (.F.) value. The optional ,2 argument is used to specify that the deletion take place in a two-dimensional array rather than a one-dimensional array. When the option is used, a column is deleted rather than a single element.

ADIR
Syntax

```
ADIR(array [,expC1 [, expC2]])
```

The ADIR function fills array elements with information from a disk directory. *Array* is the name of the array where the file information is to be stored. *ExpC1* is any DOS file skeleton. The array will be filled with file names, sizes, creation dates and times, and DOS attributes for all files matching the skeleton. *ExpC2,* which is optional, specifies additional information that is to be returned—D for subdirectory information, H for hidden files, S for system files, and V for volume names.

AELEMENT
Syntax

```
AELEMENT(array, expN1 [, expN2])
```

The AELEMENT function returns the element number of an array element, based on the row and column location for that element. (Array elements can be referred to in one of two ways—by element number or by row-and-column location. Use AELEMENT to convert a row-and-column location to an element number.) *Array* is the name of the array, *expN1* is the row location, and *expN2,* which is used with two-dimensional arrays, is the column location.

AFIELDS
Syntax

```
AFIELDS(array)
```

The AFIELDS function fills array elements with field attributes from the current work area. The array elements are filled with field names, field types, field lengths, and field decimal places.

The array is filled with the contents of the four columns that normally appear as a result of the LIST STRUCTURE command. Field names are stored in the first column, and the contents of the column will be character elements. Field types are stored in the second column, and the contents of the column will be character elements containing a single letter—C for character, D for date, L for logical, M for memo, N for numeric, or F for floating. Field lengths are stored in the third column, and the contents of the column will be numeric elements. The number of decimal places for the fields is stored in the fourth column, and the contents of the column will be numeric elements.

AINS
Syntax

```
AINS(array, expN [,2])
```

The AINS function inserts a new element into an existing array. *Array* is the name of the array that receives the new element, and *expN* is an element number for one-dimensional arrays or a row number or column number for two-dimensional arrays. The optional ,2 argument specifies that the insertion takes place in a two-dimensional array rather than a one-dimensional array. When the option is used, a column is inserted rather than a single element.

Note that when the new element is inserted, the last element of the array is discarded, and all remaining elements following the new element are moved back by one position. If the insertion is successful, a value of 1 is returned; otherwise, a value of –1 is returned.

B

ALEN
Syntax

```
ALEN(array [, expN]
```

The ALEN function returns the number of elements, rows, or columns in an array. *Array* is the array name, and *expN* denotes whether the function should return the number of elements, rows, or columns. If *expN* is 0 (or if *expN* is omitted), the number of elements is returned. If *expN* is 1, the number of rows is returned. If *expN* is 2, the number of columns is returned.

ALIAS
Syntax

```
ALIAS([expN/expC])
```

The ALIAS function returns the alias of the database open in the work area specified by *expN*, or the work area number specified by *expC*. If *expN* or *expC* is omitted, ALIAS returns the alias of the current work area.

ALLTRIM
Syntax

```
ALLTRIM(expC)
```

ALLTRIM returns the character expression *expC* minus any leading and trailing blanks.

ASC
Syntax

```
ASC(expC)
```

The ASC function returns the decimal ASCII code for the leftmost character in *expC*.

ASCAN
Syntax

```
ASCAN(array, expression [, expN1 [, expN2]])
```

The ASCAN function scans an array, searching for a particular value. *Array* names the array to be scanned, and *expression* denotes the data to search for. The expression can be any data type. *ExpN1*, which is optional, denotes the starting element where the search will begin; if it is omitted, ASCAN begins with the first element. *ExpN2*, which is also optional, denotes the number of elements that should be searched; if it is omitted, ASCAN searches to the end of the array.

ASCAN returns a numeric value, indicating the position of the data in the array. If ASCAN cannot find the data, a value of 0 is returned.

Note that ASCAN does respect the status of SET EXACT. If SET EXACT is ON, the contents of the array element must precisely match the contents of *expression,* in length and in content. If SET EXACT is OFF, the contents of *expression* are tested from left to right until a match is found; any remaining characters in the array element are ignored.

ASIN
Syntax

```
ASIN(expN)
```

The ASIN function returns the arc sine of *expN,* as measured in radians between –pi/2 and +pi/2 (–1.57079 to 1.57079). Acceptable values for *expN* are from +1 to –1.

ASORT
Syntax

```
ASORT(array [, ExpN1 [, expN2 [, expN3]]])
```

The ASORT function sorts an array. The elements contained in the array are sorted in ascending order. *Array* denotes the name of the array. *ExpN1*, which is optional, is a numeric value that denotes the element at which to start the sort. If *expN1* is omitted, the sort begins with the first element. *ExpN2*, which is used along with *expN1*, is a numeric value that denotes the column where sorting starts; when *expN2* is used, *expN1* is then assumed to be the row where sorting starts. *ExpN3* denotes a sort order—0 for ascending or 1 for descending.

ASUBSCRIPT
Syntax

```
ASUBSCRIPT(array, expN1, expN2)
```

The ASUBSCRIPT function returns the row or column location of an array element, based on an element's number. (Array elements can be referred to in one of two ways—by element number or by row-and-column location. Use ASUBSCRIPT to convert an element number to a row-and-column location.) *Array* is the name of the array. *ExpN1* is the element number. *ExpN2,* which is used with two-dimensional arrays, must be 1 if the row location is desired, or 2 if the column location is desired.

AT
Syntax

```
AT(expC1, expC2[, expN])
```

The AT function finds *expC1* in *expC2*. (Note that *expC2* may be a memo field.) The function returns as an integer the starting position of *expC1*. If *expC1* is not found, the function returns a 0. If the optional *expN* is used, the *expN*th occurrence of *expC1* is searched for.

ATAN
Syntax

```
ATAN(expN)
```

The ATAN function returns the arctangent of *expN*, as measured in radians between –pi/2 and +pi/2 (–1.57079 to 1.57079). *ExpN* can be any value.

ATC
Syntax

```
ATC(expC1, expC2[,expN])
```

The ATC function searches a character string *expC1* for another character string *expC2*. If *expC1* is not found, the function returns a 0. If the optional *expN* is used, the *expN*th occurrence of *expC1* is searched for. The ATC function operates just like the AT function, but the ATC function is not case sensitive.

ATCLINE
Syntax

```
ATCLINE(expC1, expC2)
```

The ATCLINE function finds *expC1* within *expC2* and then returns the line number where it was found. *ExpC2* can be a memo field. If *expC1* is not found in *expC2*, the function returns a 0. ATCLINE is not case sensitive; the ATLINE function performs the same task but is case sensitive. ATCLINE is usually used to locate text within a memo field and return the line number containing the desired text.

ATLINE
Syntax

```
ATLINE(expC1, expC2)
```

The ATLINE function finds *expC2* within *expC1* and then returns (as an integer) the line number where it was found. If *expC1* is not found in *expC2*, the function returns a 0.

ATN2
Syntax

```
ATN2(expN1, expN2)
```

The ATN2 function returns the arc-tangent angle (as measured in radians) for all four quadrants. You specify the X and Y coordinates (or sine and cosine of the angle) instead of specifying the tangent value as with the ATAN function. *ExpN1* is the X coordinate or sine of the angle, and *expN2* is the Y coordinate, or cosine of the angle.

BAR
Syntax

```
BAR()
```

The BAR function returns the number of the option most recently selected from the active pop-up menu. Use the DEFINE BAR command to assign each menu item a number. If no pop-up menu is active, the BAR function returns a 0.

BETWEEN
Syntax

```
BETWEEN(expr1, expr2, expr3)
```

The BETWEEN function returns a logical true (.T.) if *expr1* is greater than or equal to *expr2* and less than or equal to *expr3;* otherwise, the function returns a logical false (.F.). The expressions used must be of the same type.

BOF
Syntax

```
BOF([alias])
```

The BOF function returns a logical true (.T.) if the record pointer is at the beginning of file (above the first record in the database file). Use the optional *alias* to test for the beginning of the file in a different work area.

CAPSLOCK
Syntax

CAPSLOCK([*expL*])

The CAPSLOCK function turns the `Caps Lock` keyboard mode on or off, or it returns the current state of `Caps Lock`. The CAPSLOCK(.T.) function turns the `Caps Lock` mode on, and CAPSLOCK(.F.) turns the `Caps Lock` mode off. If *expL* is omitted, the status of `Caps Lock` is returned without changing the state of the keyboard.

CDOW
Syntax

CDOW(*expD*)

The CDOW function returns the name of the day of the week for the given date expression.

CDX
Syntax

CDX(*expN* [, *alias*])

The CDX function returns the names of open compound index (.CDX) files. Note that the CDX function is identical in operation to the MDX function. *ExpN* is a numeric value that identifies the desired compound index file, according to the following possibilities. If the database has a structural compound index file and *expN1* is 1, the name of the structural compound index file is returned. If *expN1* is 2, the name of the first .CDX compound index file (as identified by the INDEX clause of the USE command, or the SET INDEX command) is returned. If *expN1* is 3, the second .CDX compound index file name is returned, and so forth. If *expN1* is greater than the number of open .CDX compound index files, the function returns a null string.

B

If the database does not have a structural compound index file and *expN1* is 1, the name of the first .CDX compound index file (as identified by the INDEX clause of the USE command, or by the SET INDEX command) is returned. If *expN1* is 2, the second .CDX compound index file name is returned, and so forth. If *expN1* is greater than the number of open .CDX compound index files, the function returns a null string.

Use the *alias* option to return the names of compound index files open in different work areas.

CEILING
Syntax

CEILING(*expN*)

The CEILING function returns the nearest integer greater than or equal to *expN*. Positive numbers with decimals are rounded up to the next-highest number, and negative numbers with decimals are rounded up to the number closest to 0.

CHR
Syntax

CHR(*expN*)

The CHR function returns the character whose decimal ASCII code is equivalent to *expN*.

CHRSAW
Syntax

CHRSAW([*expN*])

The CHRSAW function checks the keyboard buffer for the presence of a character and returns a logical true (.T.) if a character is found in the keyboard buffer. The optional *expN* specifies the number of seconds to wait for a keypress before returning the value.

CHRTRAN
Syntax

```
CHRTRAN(expC1, expC2, expC3)
```

The CHRTRAN function translates the characters of *expC1*. The strings in *expC2* and *expC3* are used as a translation table. Any occurrences of the first character in *expC2* are replaced by the first character in *expC3*, the second character in *expC2* by the second character in *expC3*, and so forth.

CMONTH
Syntax

```
CMONTH(expD)
```

The CMONTH function returns the name of the month that corresponds to the date expression.

B

CNTBAR
Syntax

```
CNTBAR(popupname)
```

The CNTBAR function returns the number of bars in the named pop-up menu.

CNTPAD
Syntax

```
CNTPAD(popupname)
```

The CNTPAD function returns the number of menu pads in the named menu bar.

COL
Syntax

COL()

The COL function returns the current column location of the cursor.

COS
Syntax

COS(*expN*)

The COS function returns the cosine of *expN* as measured in radians. To convert an angle from degrees to radians, use the DTOR function.

CTOD
Syntax

CTOD(*expC*)

The CTOD function returns the date value that corresponds to *expC* in the default date format (generally MM/DD/YY). Use the SET DATE and SET CENTURY commands to change the default format.

CURDIR
Syntax

CURDIR([*expC*])

The CURDIR function returns the current DOS directory on the drive identified by *expC*. If no such drive exists, CURDIR returns a null string. If *expC* is omitted, the default drive is assumed.

DATE
Syntax

```
DATE()
```

The DATE function returns the current system date.

DAY
Syntax

```
DAY(expD)
```

The DAY function returns the numeric day of the month that corresponds to the date expression.

DBF
Syntax

```
DBF([alias])
```

The DBF function returns the database file name for the file open in the specified work area. If no *alias* is specified, the DBF function returns the file name for the currently selected work area. If no file is open in the work area, the function returns a null string.

DELETED
Syntax

```
DELETED([alias])
```

B

The DELETED function returns a logical true (.T.) if the current record is marked for deletion; otherwise, it returns a logical false (.F.). Use the optional *alias* to test for deleted records in an unselected work area.

DIFFERENCE
Syntax

```
DIFFERENCE(expC1, expC2)
```

The DIFFERENCE function returns a numeric value between 0 and 4, representing the phonetic difference between two character strings, *expC1* and *expC2*. The DIFFERENCE function can be useful for searching databases when the precise spelling of an entry is not known.

DISKSPACE
Syntax

```
DISKSPACE()
```

The DISKSPACE function returns the number of bytes available on the default drive.

DMY
Syntax

```
DMY(expD)
```

The DMY function returns a date expression in European format (DD-Month-YY) for the given date expression.

DOW
Syntax

DOW(*expD*)

The DOW function returns the numeric day of the week corresponding to the date expression. The value returned ranges from 1 (for Sunday) to 7 (for Saturday).

DTOC
Syntax

DTOC(*expD* [,1])

B

The DTOC function returns a character string containing the date that corresponds to the date expression. Use the SET DATE and the SET CENTURY commands to change the format of the string. The optional ,1 argument causes DTOC to return the string in the YYYYMMDD format, similar to the DTOS function.

DTOR
Syntax

DTOR(*expN*)

The DTOR function converts the angle specified by *expN* from degrees to radians.

DTOS
Syntax

DTOS(*expD*)

The DTOS function returns a character string in the format YYYYMMDD for the given date expression. This function is useful when indexing on a date field.

EMPTY
Syntax

EMPTY(*expression*)

The EMPTY function returns a logical true (.T.) if the expression *expression* is blank. The function will also return a value of true if the expression is a numeric expression with a value of 0 or a logical expression with a value of false.

EOF
Syntax

EOF([*alias*])

The EOF function returns a logical true (.T.) if the end-of-file is reached (the record pointer passes the last record in the database, or a FIND, LOCATE, or SEEK command was unsuccessful). Use the optional *alias* to test for end-of-file in a different work area. Note that if you establish a relation with SET RELATION and the related file does not contain a record with the key matching the current record, the record pointer will be at the end-of-file in the related file.

ERROR
Syntax

ERROR()

The ERROR function returns the number of the error causing the ON ERROR condition. An ON ERROR routine must be in effect for the ERROR function to return a value other than 0.

EVALUATE
Syntax

EVALUATE(*expC*)

The EVALUATE function evaluates a character expression and returns the result. The expression must be a character string enclosed in quotes, and the character string may contain a character expression, variable, or database field name.

EXP
Syntax

EXP(*expN*)

The EXP function returns the value of e raised to the *n*th power. *ExpN* is the exponent, *N*, in the equation e ^ N. The value of e is roughly 2.71828 (the base of natural logarithms).

FCHSIZE
Syntax

FCHSIZE(*expN1*,*expN2*)

The FCHSIZE function changes the size of a file opened with a low-level file function. *ExpN1* is the file handle, returned by the FOPEN( ) function when you open a file for low-level use or by FCREATE( ) if you have just created the file. (If a file is opened with FOPEN( ), it must be opened with write or read/write privileges to change its size.) *ExpN2* is the size you want the file to be. If *expN2* is less than the original file size, the file will be truncated. If *expN2* is greater than the original file size, the file's size will be increased as needed.

The FCHSIZE function returns the final size of the file, in bytes. If FCHSIZE is unable to change the file size (usually due to insufficient disk space, or because an invalid file handle has been specified) the function returns a value of –1.

FCLOSE
Syntax

```
FCLOSE(expN)
```

The FCLOSE function flushes the buffers for the file with the numeric file handle as specified by *expN* to disk and closes the file. Use the FCREATE or FOPEN function to assign a file handle to the file.

FCOUNT
Syntax

```
FCOUNT([alias])
```

The FCOUNT function returns the number of fields in a database. Use the [*alias*] option to return the number of fields in a database that is open in an unselected work area.

FCREATE
Syntax

```
FCREATE(expC[, expN])
```

The FCREATE function creates a new file named *expC* and opens the file for use. If a file with the name *expC* already exists, the existing file is overwritten. FCREATE also assigns the file a numeric "handle" to identify the file when other low-level file functions are used. By default, the file will have a DOS read/write attribute assigned. The optional numeric expression can be used to specify the attribute of the file created, using one of the following values:

0	Read/write (default)
1	Read-only
2	Hidden
3	Read-only/hidden
4	System
5	Read-only/system
6	System/hidden
7	Read-only/system/hidden

FEOF
Syntax

FEOF (*expN*)

The FEOF function returns a logical true (.T.) if the file pointer is positioned at the end of the file (EOF). *ExpN* indicates the numeric handle of the file that you wish to test for the end-of-file.

FERROR
Syntax

FERROR ( )

The FERROR function tests whether a low-level file function has been successful. FERROR returns a 0 if the last low-level function was successfully performed. If the last function was not successful, a value not equal to 0 is returned.

FFLUSH
Syntax

FFLUSH (*expN*)

B

The FFLUSH function flushes the file whose handle is *expN*. If the file was written to, FFLUSH writes all data in the buffers to disk.

FGETS
Syntax

FGETS(*expN1*[, *expN2*])

The FGETS function returns a series of bytes from the file having the file handle specified by *expN1*. FGETS returns a series of bytes from a file until a carriage return is encountered. The optional numeric argument *expN2* can be used to specify the number of bytes that the function will return.

FIELD
Syntax

FIELD(*expN1*[, *alias*])

The FIELD function returns the name of the field in the active database that corresponds to the numeric position specified in the expression. If there is no corresponding field in the active database, FIELD returns a null string. Use the optional *alias* to return a field name from a database that is open in an unselected work area.

FILE
Syntax

FILE(*expC*)

The FILE function returns a logical true (.T.) if the character expression matches the name for an existing file in the default directory. If no such file can be found, the FILE function returns a logical false (.F.).

FILTER
Syntax

```
FILTER([alias])
```

The FILTER function returns the filter expression of the current work area. Use the optional *alias* to return a filter from an unselected work area. If no filter is in effect, a null string is returned.

FKLABEL
Syntax

```
FKLABEL(expN)
```

The FKLABEL function returns the name of the function key that corresponds to *expN*.

B

FKMAX
Syntax

```
FKMAX()
```

The FKMAX function returns the number of programmable function keys available on your keyboard.

FLOOR
Syntax

```
FLOOR(expN)
```

The FLOOR function returns the nearest integer value less than or equal to the numeric expression. All positive numbers with a decimal will be rounded down to the next-lowest number, and all negative numbers with a decimal will be rounded down to the next number farther from 0.

FOPEN
Syntax

```
FOPEN(expC[, expN])
```

The FOPEN function opens the file named by *expC* for use. *ExpC* may include a full path name for files on drives or in directories that are not in the current search path. The optional numeric expression can be used to specify an attribute of read-only, read/write, or write-only. Use 0 for read-only (the default), 1 for write-only, or 2 for read/write. If a file named by FOPEN is not found, the function returns a value of –1.

FOUND
Syntax

```
FOUND([alias])
```

The FOUND function returns a logical true (.T.) if the last CONTINUE, FIND, LOCATE, or SEEK command was successful. A logical false (.F.) is returned if the search command was unsuccessful. Note that if you have established a relation with SET RELATION and you specify the related file with *alias,* the function returns a logical true if the pointer is on a record with a key value matching that of the current record in the active database.

FPUTS
Syntax

```
FPUTS(expN1, expC[, expN2])
```

The FPUTS function writes the character string within *expC* to the file whose file handle is *expN1*. FPUTS is different from FWRITE in that FPUTS adds a carriage return and linefeed to the end of each line. The entire character string identified as *expC* is written, unless the optional numeric argument *expN2* is used; the value of *expN2* specifies the number of characters to write.

FREAD
Syntax

FREAD(*expN1*, *expN2*)

The FREAD function returns as a character string a specified number of bytes from a file whose file handle is *expN1*. The numeric value of *expN2* is the number of bytes to read, starting from the current position of the file pointer. (Use the FOPEN function to open the file.)

FSEEK
Syntax

FSEEK(*expN1*, *expN2*[, *expN3*])

The FSEEK function moves the file pointer within a file. *ExpN1* is the file's handle (returned from the FOPEN function), and *expN2* is the number of bytes the file pointer must be moved. If *expN2* is positive, the file pointer is moved toward the end of the file. If *expN2* is negative, the file pointer is moved toward the beginning of the file. The number of bytes moved is normally relative to the beginning of the file. The optional argument specified in *expN3* can be used to change this relative position. If *expN3* is 0, movement is relative to the start of the file (the default). If *expN3* is 1, movement is relative to the current position of the file pointer. If *expN3* is 2, movement is relative to the end of the file.

B

FSIZE
Syntax

FSIZE(*field*[, *alias*])

FSIZE returns the size of the specified *field* in bytes. Use the optional *alias* to select a field from a file in an unselected work area.

FULLPATH
Syntax

```
FULLPATH(file[,1/file2])
```

FULLPATH returns the full DOS path name for the given *file*. If the file is not found in the default directory, FULLPATH will search the FoxPro path for the file. If the optional argument ,1, is added, the search will use the DOS path.

A second file name can be used in place of the optional argument ,1, in which case the function returns the relative path between the two files.

FV
Syntax

```
FV(expN1, expN2, expN3)
```

The FV function returns the future value of an investment. FV calculates the future value of a series of equal payments earning a fixed interest rate. The future value is the total of all payments plus the interest. *ExpN1* is the payment amount, *expN2* is the interest rate, and *expN3* is the number of periods. If the payments are compounded monthly and the interest rate is compounded yearly, divide the interest rate by 12 to get the proper results.

FWRITE
Syntax

```
FWRITE(expN1, expC[, expN2])
```

The FWRITE function lets you write to a file whose handle is *expN1*. The numeric value of *expN2* is the number of bytes to write, starting from the current position of the file pointer. (Use the FOPEN function to open the file and assign a handle.)

GETBAR
Syntax

GETBAR(*expC*, *expN*)

The GETBAR function returns the number of a bar at a specific position in a pop-up menu. This function can be useful when pop-up options have been added, removed, or rearranged. *ExpC* denotes the pop-up name, and *expN* denotes a position within the pop-up.

GETDIR
Syntax

GETDIR([*expC1*, [,*expC2*]])

The GETDIR function displays the Select Directory dialog box. You can use this dialog box to choose a directory. The function returns the name of the directory you choose as a character string. If you do not choose a directory (by clicking Cancel or pressing Esc), the GETDIR function returns a null string.

Use *expC1* to define a prompt for the directory list that appears in the dialog box. Use *expC2* to specify the directory that is displayed by default in the dialog box.

GETENV
Syntax

GETENV(*expC*)

The GETENV function returns a character string that contains the contents of the DOS environmental variable named as the character expression.

B

GETFILE
Syntax

GETFILE([*expC1*][, *expC2*])

The GETFILE function causes the FoxPro Open File dialog box to be displayed. Using the dialog box, a file may be chosen. The function then returns the name of the chosen file. *ExpC1* is an optional extension; if used, only files with that extension will appear in the list box. *ExpC2* is an optional prompt that appears at the top of the Open File dialog box.

GETPAD
Syntax

GETPAD(*expC*, *expN*)

The GETPAD function returns the name of a menu pad at a specific position in a bar menu. This function can be useful when menu pads have been added, removed, or rearranged. *ExpC* denotes the menu name, and *expN* denotes a position within the menu.

GOMONTH
Syntax

GOMONTH(*expD*, *expN*)

The GOMONTH function returns a date that is *expN* months before or after *expD*. If *expN* is positive, the date returned is *expN* months after *expD*. If *expN* is negative, the date returned is *expN* months before *expD*.

HEADER
Syntax

HEADER([*alias*])

The HEADER function returns the number of bytes in the header of the database open in the current work area. If no database is open in the specified work area, 0 is returned. Use the optional *alias* to return the bytes in the header of a file open in an unselected work area.

IIF
Syntax

```
IIF(expL, expr1, expr2)
```

The IIF function (Immediate IF) returns the value of *expr1* if the logical expression is true and returns the value of *expr2* if the logical expression is false. *Expr1* and *expr2* must be of the same data type.

INKEY
Syntax

```
INKEY([expN][,expC])
```

The INKEY function returns an integer value between 0 and 255. This value corresponds to the decimal ASCII code for the key that was pressed. A 0 will be returned if no key has been pressed. Include the optional *expC* to show or hide the cursor, or to check for a mouse click. If *expC* is the letter S, the cursor is visible. If *expC* is the letter H, the cursor is hidden. If *expC* is the letter M, INKEY( ) returns a value of 151 for a mouse click.

INLIST
Syntax

```
INLIST(expr1, expr2[, expr3...])
```

The INLIST function determines if an expression is contained in a series of expressions. INLIST returns a logical true (.T.) if *exp1* is contained in the list of expressions *expr2, expr3,* and so on. The expressions must all be of the same data type.

B

INSMODE
Syntax

`INSMODE([expL])`

The INSMODE function changes the insert /overwrite mode based on *expL*. If *expL* is omitted, the function returns the insert mode setting.

INT
Syntax

`INT(expN)`

The INT function returns the integer portion of *expN*. No rounding occurs; any decimal values are simply dropped.

ISALPHA
Syntax

`ISALPHA(expC)`

The ISALPHA function returns a logical true (.T.) if the first character of *expC* is a-z or A-Z. A logical false (.F.) is returned if *expC* begins with a nonalphabetic or numeric character.

ISCOLOR
Syntax

`ISCOLOR()`

The ISCOLOR function returns a logical true (.T.) if the system has color capability (whether or not a color monitor is being used) and returns a logical false (.F.) if the system has monochrome capability.

SDIGIT

Syntax

`ISDIGIT(expC)`

The ISDIGIT function returns a logical true (.T.) if the first character of *expC* is a digit (0-9).

ISLOWER

Syntax

`ISLOWER(expC)`

The ISLOWER function returns a logical true (.T.) if the first character in *expC* is a lowercase letter or a logical false (.F.) if the first character is anything other than a lowercase letter.

ISUPPER

Syntax

`ISUPPER(expC)`

The ISUPPER function returns a logical true (.T.) if the first character in *expC* is an uppercase character and a logical false (.F.) if the first character is anything other than an uppercase character.

KEY

Syntax

`KEY([.cdx filename,] expN [, alias])`

The KEY function returns the index expression of the specified index file. The numeric expression identifies the index file, where 1 is the first

B

index file opened, 2 is the second index file opened, and so on. Use the *alias* option to return the key expression for an index file that is open in an unselected work area.

The *.cdx filename* option can be used to specify an index tag in a compound index file.

LASTKEY
Syntax

```
LASTKEY()
```

The LASTKEY function returns the decimal ASCII value for the last key pressed. (The LASTKEY function returns the same ASCII values as the INKEY function.)

LEFT
Syntax

```
LEFT(expC, expN)
```

The LEFT function returns the leftmost number of characters specified in *expN* from the character expression *expC,* starting with the first or leftmost character.

LEN
Syntax

```
LEN(expC)
```

The LEN function returns the length of a character string expression specified in *expC*. *ExpC* can be a memo field name, in which case the length of the text stored within the memo field is returned. Note that in the case of character fields, LEN returns the length of the field, not the length of the text within the field. With character fields, you must add a TRIM function to get the length of the text stored in the field.

LIKE
Syntax

```
LIKE(expC1, expC2)
```

The LIKE function compares two character expressions and returns a logical true (.T.) if the character string in *expC2* contains the characters in *expC1*. The pattern can include the wildcard characters * (representing any sequence of characters) and ? (representing any single character).

LINENO
Syntax

```
LINENO()
```

The LINENO function returns the line number of the next statement in the program that is currently running.

LOCFILE
Syntax

```
LOCFILE(expC1 [, expC2] [, expC3])
```

The LOCFILE function locates a disk file and returns the file name along with the complete search path. To be found, the file must be in the current directory, or somewhere in the FoxPro path. If the specified file cannot be found, the Open File dialog box appears so a manual search can be attempted. *ExpC1* indicates the file name. The optional *expC2* specifies extensions of files to be displayed in the Open File dialog box. The optional *expC3* is a prompt to be displayed at the top of the Open File dialog box.

LOG
Syntax

LOG(*expN*)

The LOG function returns the natural logarithm of a number specified by *expN*. *ExpN* must be greater than 0. Use the SET DECIMALS command to specify the number of decimal places returned.

LOG10
Syntax

LOG10(*expN*)

The LOG10 function returns the common (base 10) logarithm of a number specified by *expN*. *ExpN* must be greater than 0. Use the SET DECIMALS command to specify the number of decimal places returned.

LOOKUP
Syntax

LOOKUP(*field1*, *search expression*, *field2* [,*expC*])

The LOOKUP function searches a database for a record and returns a value from a specified field when the record is found. Field1 is the name of the field from which the value is to be returned. Search expression is the expression used as the basis for the search. *Field2* specifies the name of the field you want to search. The optional *expC* specifies the name of a compact index tag that can be used to speed up the search.

LOWER
Syntax

```
LOWER(expC)
```

The LOWER function converts all uppercase letters in *expC* to lowercase. The function will not affect nonalphabetic characters. The LOWER function does not change the way the data is stored unless you use it as part of a STORE or REPLACE command. The function is generally used for finding or comparing data, when you do not know what case the data was originally entered as.

LTRIM
Syntax

```
LTRIM(expC)
```

The LTRIM function trims all leading blanks from the character expression defined as *expC*.

LUPDATE
Syntax

```
LUPDATE(alias)
```

The LUPDATE function returns the last update of the active database. Use the optional *alias* to return the last update for a file open in an unselected work area.

MAX
Syntax

MAX(*expr1, expr2*[, *expr3*...])

The MAX function returns the maximum value from the list of expressions. The expressions must all be of the same data type.

MCOL
Syntax

MCOL([*expC*])

The MCOL function returns a value representing the column location of the mouse pointer, in the screen or within a window. The optional *expC* denotes the name of a window. If *expC* is omitted, the column coordinate of the mouse pointer relative to the entire screen is returned by the function. If the mouse pointer lies outside of a window and the window is named in expC, the function returns a value of –1.

MDOWN
Syntax

MDOWN()

The MDOWN function returns the state of the left mouse button. If the left mouse button is depressed when MDOWN() is executed, a logical true (.T.) is returned. Otherwise, a logical false (.F.) is returned.

MDX
Syntax

MDX(*expN* [, *alias*])

The MDX function returns the names of open compound index (.CDX) files. Note that the MDX function is identical in operation to the CDX function. *ExpN* is a numeric value that identifies the desired compound index file, according to the following possibilities. If the database has a structural compound index file and *expN1* is 1, the name of the structural compound index file is returned. If *expN1* is 2, the name of the first .CDX compound index file (as identified by the INDEX clause of the USE command or by the SET INDEX command) is returned. If *expN1* is 3, the second .CDX compound index file name is returned, and so forth. If *expN1* is greater than the number of open .CDX compound index files, the function returns a null string.

If the database does not have a structural compound index file and *expN1* is 1, the name of the first .CDX compound index file (as identified by the INDEX clause of the USE command or by the SET INDEX command) is returned. If *expN1* is 2, the second .CDX compound index file name is returned, and so forth. If *expN1* is greater than the number of open .CDX compound index files, the function returns a null string.

Use the *alias* option to return the names of compound index files open in different work areas.

MDY
Syntax

```
MDY(expD)
```

The MDY function returns a Month DD, YY (or Month DD, YYYY) character string for a given date expression. The month is always spelled out, and the day always takes the DD format. If SET CENTURY is OFF, the year takes the YY format; otherwise, the year takes the YYYY format.

MEMLINES
Syntax

```
MEMLINES(memofield)
```

The MEMLINES function returns the number of lines in the named memo field for the current record. Note that the number of lines in the memo field will be affected by the current value of SET MEMOWIDTH.

MEMORY
Syntax

```
MEMORY()
```

The MEMORY function returns the amount of free conventional memory as a numeric value in kilobytes.

MENU
Syntax

```
MENU()
```

The MENU function returns the name of the currently active menu. If a menu is not active, MENU returns a null string.

MESSAGE
Syntax

```
MESSAGE([1])
```

The MESSAGE function returns the current error message, which is useful for situations in which FoxPro detects an error within a program. The MESSAGE function can be used along with the ON ERROR command for error-trapping and recovery purposes. The optional argument of 1 tells FoxPro to return the actual program code for the last line that caused the ON ERROR condition.

MIN
Syntax

```
MIN(expr1, expr2[, expr3...])
```

The MIN function returns the minimum value expression from the list of expressions. The expressions must all be of the same data type.

MLINE
Syntax

```
MLINE(memofield, expN [, expN2])
```

The MLINE function returns the specified line *expN* from the named memo field in the current record. Note that the value of SET MEMOWIDTH will affect the number of lines in a memo field.

The optional argument *expN2* denotes any offset from the start of the memo field line.

MOD
Syntax

```
MOD(expN1, expN2)
```

The MOD function returns the remainder when *expN1* is divided by *expN2*. A positive number is returned if *expN2* is positive, and a negative number is returned if *expN2* is negative. If there is no remainder, a 0 is returned.

MONTH
Syntax

```
MONTH(expD)
```

The MONTH function returns the numeric month (1 to 12) that corresponds to the date expression. The numbers 1 through 12 correspond to January through December.

MRKBAR
Syntax

```
MRKBAR(ExpC, ExpN)
```

The MRKBAR function returns a logical value, indicating whether a specific bar of a pop-up menu is marked. (The SET MARK command can be used to mark or unmark a pop-up bar.) *ExpC* is the name of the pop-up menu. *ExpN* is the number that identifies the specific bar of the menu. If the bar is marked, the function returns a logical true (.T.); otherwise, the function returns a logical false (.F.).

MRKPAD
Syntax

```
MRKPAD(expC1, expC2)
```

The MRKPAD function returns a logical value, indicating whether a specific pad of a bar menu is marked. (The SET MARK command can be used to mark or unmark a menu pad.) *ExpC1* is the name of the menu bar. *ExpC2* is the pad name. If the pad is marked, the function returns a logical true (.T.); otherwise, the function returns a logical false (.F.).

MROW
Syntax

```
MROW([expC])
```

The MROW function returns a value representing the row location of the mouse pointer, in the screen or within a window. The optional *expC* denotes the name of a window. If *expC* is omitted, the row coordinate of the mouse pointer relative to the entire screen is returned by the function. If the mouse pointer lies outside of a window and the window is named in *expC*, the function returns a value of –1.

MWINDOW
Syntax

```
MWINDOW([window-name])
```

The MWINDOW function returns the name of the window that the mouse pointer is positioned over, or it returns a logical true if the mouse pointer is positioned over a window specified by *window-name*. If the MWINDOW function is used without an optional window name, the name of the window which the mouse pointer is positioned over is returned. If the mouse pointer is not positioned over any window, a null string is returned. If you include a window name in MWINDOW( ), a logical true (.T.) is returned if the mouse pointer is positioned over the specified window. If the mouse pointer is not positioned over the specified window, a logical false (.F.) is returned.

NDX
Syntax

```
NDX(expN[, alias])
```

The NDX function returns the name of an open index file in the current work area. The numeric expression specifies the order of the index file, 1 being the first index file opened, 2 the second index file opened, and so on. Use the optional *alias* to return the name of an open index file in an unselected work area.

NUMLOCK
Syntax

```
NUMLOCK([expL])
```

The NUMLOCK function changes the `Num Lock` keyboard mode or returns the status of the `Num Lock` mode. NUMLOCK(.T.) turns on `Num Lock`, and NUMLOCK(.F.) turns off `Num Lock`. If the logical expression is omitted, NUMLOCK returns the status of the `Num Lock` mode.

OBJNUM
Syntax

OBJNUM(*variable* [, *expN*])

The OBJNUM function returns the object number of a GET object. (GET objects such as fields, check boxes, push buttons, and radio buttons are assigned object numbers, in the order in which they are created.) *Variable* is the name of the variable used to create the GET object. When nested READs are used, the optional argument of *expN* can be used to specify an object at a different READ level.

OCCURS
Syntax

OCCURS(*expC1*, *expC2*)

The OCCURS function returns an integer that represents the number of times *expC1* occurs in *expC2*. If *expC1* is not found in *expC2*, the function returns a 0.

ORDER
Syntax

ORDER([*alias*])

ORDER returns the name of the master (or active) index file in the current work area. Use the optional *alias* to return the name of the active index in an unselected work area.

OS
Syntax

OS()

The OS function returns the name and version of the operating system.

PAD
Syntax

```
PAD()
```

The PAD function returns the name of the pad last chosen from the active menu bar. The function returns a null string if no menu is active.

PADC, PADL, PADR
Syntax

```
PADC(expression, expN[, expC])
PADL(expression, expN[, expC])
PADR(expression, expN[, expC])
```

B

These functions pad the expression supplied as *expression* with a designated character on the left side, the right side, or on both sides. *ExpN* specifies the total length of the resultant string. The expression is padded with blanks unless an optional character is supplied as *expC;* if provided, the optional character is used to pad the expression. Use PADC to pad an expression on both sides; use PADL to pad an expression on the left side; and use PADR to pad an expression on the right side. You can pad character, date, or numeric expressions with these functions.

PARAMETERS
Syntax

```
PARAMETERS()
```

The PARAMETERS function returns a numeric value indicating the number of parameters passed to the procedure most recently called.

PAYMENT
Syntax

```
PAYMENT(expN1, expN2, expN3)
```

The PAYMENT function returns the amount of a loan payment. PAYMENT assumes that the interest rate is constant and that payments are made at the end of each period. *ExpN1* is the principal amount, *expN2* is the interest rate, and *expN3* is the number of payments. If the payments are compounded monthly and the interest rate is compounded yearly, divide the interest rate by 12 to get the proper results.

PCOL

Syntax

```
PCOL()
```

The PCOL function returns the current column position of the printer.

PI

Syntax

```
PI()
```

The PI function returns the numeric constant pi (approximately 3.14159).

POPUP

Syntax

```
POPUP()
```

The POPUP function returns the name of the active pop-up menu.

PRINTSTATUS

Syntax

```
PRINTSTATUS()
```

The PRINTSTATUS function returns a logical true (.T.) if the printer is ready and a logical false (.F.) if it is not.

PRMBAR
Syntax

```
PRMBAR(expC, expN)
```

The PRMBAR function returns the prompt text for a specific option of a pop-up menu. *ExpC* denotes the pop-up name, and *expN* denotes the bar number of the pop-up menu.

PRMPAD
Syntax

```
PRMPAD(expC1, expC2)
```

The PRMPAD function returns the prompt text for a specific pad of a bar menu. *ExpC1* denotes the menu name, and *expC2* denotes the pad name in the bar menu.

B

PROGRAM
Syntax

```
PROGRAM([expN])
```

The PROGRAM function returns the name of the program currently running or the program that was running when an error occurred. The optional numeric expression can be used for nesting programs (calling a program from a program). When used, the value of *expN* indicates how many levels back FoxPro should go to get the program name.

PROMPT
Syntax

```
PROMPT()
```

The PROMPT function returns the prompt for the last option chosen from the active menu pad or pop-up menu. The function returns a null string if no pop-up menu is active.

PROPER
Syntax

PROPER (*expC*)

The PROPER function returns the character expression specified in *expC* with initial capitals. Each word in the character string has the first letter capitalized and the remaining letters in lowercase.

PROW
Syntax

PROW ( )

The PROW function returns the current row position of the printer. Note that when an EJECT command is issued, PROW is reset to 0.

PUTFILE
Syntax

PUTFILE([*expC1*][, *expC2*][, *expC3*])

The PUTFILE function displays the Save As dialog box. The user can enter or choose a file name, and the file name is returned as a character expression by the function. The optional *expC1* argument is a prompt string that, if used, appears above the text box. The optional *expC2* argument is a default file name that appears in the text box. The optional *expC3* argument is a default file extension.

PV
Syntax

```
PV(expN1, expN2, expN3)
```

The PV function returns the present value of an investment, or the amount that must be invested to earn a known future value. *ExpN1* is the payment made each period, *expN2* is the interest rate, and *expN3* is the number of periods. If the payments are compounded monthly and the interest rate is yearly, divide the interest rate by 12 to get the proper results.

RAND
Syntax

```
RAND([expN])
```

The RAND function returns a random number between 0 and 1. The optional numeric expression can be used to provide a seed different than the default for generating the random number. A given seed will always produce the same sequence of random numbers; you can vary the sequence of random numbers by varying the seed. If *expN* is negative, the seed is taken from the system clock.

To obtain a random number in a particular range, multiply the result of the RAND function by a chosen value. For example, you could get a random number between 50 and 100 by using (RAND*50)+50.

RAT
Syntax

```
RAT(expC1, expC2[, expN])
```

The RAT function (Reverse AT) searches *expC2*, starting from the right, for the *expN*th occurrence of the character string *expC1*. The function returns as an integer the position where *expC1* is found. If *expC1* is not found in *expC2* the specified number of times, the function returns a 0. If *expN* is omitted, the default is 1.

RATLINE
Syntax

```
RATLINE(expC1, expC2)
```

The RATLINE function (Reverse ATLINE) searches *expC2* for the last occurrence of *expC1*. The function returns the line number of the line where *expC1* was found. If *expC1* is not found in *expC2*, the function returns a 0. Note that *expC2* can be a memo field.

RDLEVEL
Syntax

```
RDLEVEL()
```

The RDLEVEL function returns a numeric value representing the level of the current READ. (READs can be nested up to four levels deep in FoxPro 2.)

READKEY
Syntax

```
READKEY()
```

The READKEY function returns an integer value that indicates the key pressed when exiting from the editing commands APPEND, BROWSE, CHANGE, CREATE, EDIT, INSERT, MODIFY, and READ. READKEY provides a value between 0 and 36 if no changes were made to the data, or a value between 256 and 292 if changes were made to the data.

RECCOUNT
Syntax

```
RECCOUNT([alias])
```

The RECCOUNT function returns the number of records in the database open in the current work area. If no database is open, RECCOUNT returns a 0. Use the optional *alias* to return the number of records in a database open in an unselected work area.

RECNO
Syntax

```
RECNO([alias])
```

The RECNO function returns the current record number. Use the optional *alias* to return the current record number in a database open in an unselected work area. Note that RECNO(0) can follow an unsuccessful SEEK to determine what record number to return. If a SEEK is unsuccessful, the use of RECNO(0) immediately after the SEEK returns the record number of the closest matching record.

RECSIZE
Syntax

```
RECSIZE([alias])
```

The RECSIZE function returns the size of the database record in the current work area. Use the optional *alias* to return the size of the database record for a database open in an unselected work area. If no database is open, RECSIZE returns a 0.

RELATION
Syntax

```
RELATION(expN[, alias])
```

The RELATION function returns the relational expression for the Nth relation of the work area identified by *alias*. Use the optional *alias* to specify an unselected work-area number, work-area letter, or *alias* name. If no relation exists, the function returns a null string.

REPLICATE
Syntax

```
REPLICATE(expC, expN)
```

The REPLICATE function returns a character string consisting of *expC* repeated *expN* times.

RIGHT
Syntax

```
RIGHT(expC/memvar, expN)
```

The RIGHT function returns the rightmost part of the character string *expC* or memory variable *memvar*. Use the numeric expression *expN* to specify the number of characters that will be returned.

ROUND
Syntax

```
ROUND(expN1, expN2)
```

The ROUND function rounds off the number supplied in *expN1*. Use *expN2* to specify the number of decimal places to round off to. If *expN2* is negative, the rounded number returned is a whole number.

ROW
Syntax

ROW()

The ROW function returns the current row location of the cursor.

RTOD
Syntax

RTOD(*expN*)

The RTOD function converts radians to degrees. The numeric expression is the value in radians, and the value returned by the function is the equivalent value in degrees.

RTRIM
Syntax

RTRIM(*expC*)

The RTRIM function strips the trailing spaces from the named character string. The RTRIM function is identical to the TRIM function.

SCHEME
Syntax

SCHEME(*expN1* [, *expN2*])

The SCHEME function returns a color-pair list or a color pair from a color scheme. To return the complete color-pair listing for a color scheme, provide the color scheme number as *expN1*. To return a single pair listing from a color scheme, provide the optional argument *expN2*, which is the position of the color pair in the color-pair list.

B

SCOLS
Syntax

SCOLS()

The SCOLS function returns the number of columns available on the display screen.

SECONDS
Syntax

SECONDS()

The SECONDS function returns the value of the system clock, using a seconds.thousandths format.

SEEK
Syntax

SEEK(*expr*[, *alias*])

The SEEK function returns a logical true (.T.) if the search expression can be found in the active index. If the search expression is not found, the function returns a logical false (.F.), and the record pointer is placed at the end of the file. Use the optional *alias* to search an open index in an unselected work area.

SELECT
Syntax

SELECT()

The SELECT function returns the number of the current work area (assuming SET COMPATIBLE is OFF). If SET COMPATIBLE is ON, the function returns the number of the highest unused work area.

SET
Syntax

```
SET(expC[,1])
```

The SET function returns the status of the various SET commands. The character expression contains the name of the desired SET command. Note that you need to use quotes around *expC* if it is a character string rather than a memory variable. Using SET without the optional argument returns the ON/OFF setting. Using SET with the optional argument (,1) returns the SET TO setting.

SIGN
Syntax

```
SIGN(expN)
```

SIGN returns a numeric value that represents the sign of the numeric expression. If *expN* is positive, SIGN returns a value of 1. If *expN* is negative, SIGN returns a value of –1. If *expN* is 0, SIGN returns a 0.

SIN
Syntax

```
SIN(expN)
```

The SIN function returns the sine of *expN*, where *expN* is an angle measured in radians. To convert degrees to radians, use the DTOR function.

SKPBAR
Syntax

```
SKPBAR(expC, expN)
```

The SKPBAR function returns a logical value that indicates if an option (bar) on a menu popup is enabled or disabled. If the specified pop-up option is disabled, true (.T.) is returned. If the pop-up option is enabled, false (.F.) is returned. Use *expC* to indicate the name of the menu popup that contains the option. Use *expN* to indicate the pop-up option number for which you want to test the enabled or disabled status.

SKPPAD
Syntax

```
SKPPAD(expC1, expC2)
```

The SKPPAD function returns a logical value that indicates if a menu pad on a menu bar is enabled or disabled. If the specified menu pad is disabled, true (.T.) is returned. If the menu pad is enabled, false (.F.) is returned. Use expC1 to indicate the name of the menu bar that contains the pad. Use *expC2* to indicate the name of the menu pad for which you want to test the enabled or disabled status.

SOUNDEX
Syntax

```
SOUNDEX(expC)
```

The SOUNDEX function returns a four-character string that represents the phonetic SOUNDEX code for the character expression *expC*. The four-character code returned by the SOUNDEX function can be useful for finding similar-sounding names or for building an index to perform lookups based on the sound of a word.

SPACE
Syntax

```
SPACE(expN)
```

The SPACE function returns a character string containing the specified number of blank spaces. The maximum number of spaces that can be specified by *expN* is 65,504.

SQRT
Syntax

SQRT(*expN*)

The SQRT function returns the square root of the numeric expression *expN*. The numeric expression must be a positive number.

SROWS
Syntax

SROWS()

SROWS returns the number of rows available on the screen.

STR
Syntax

STR(*expN1*[, *expN2*[, *expN3*]])

The STR function converts a numeric expression to a character expression, where *expN1* is the numeric expression to be converted to a character string. Use the optional *expN2* to specify a length (including the decimal point and decimal places), and use the optional *expN3* to specify a number of decimal places.

STRTRAN
Syntax

STRTRAN(*expC1*, *expC2*[, *expC3*][, *expN1*][, *expN2*])

The STRTRAN function performs a search-and-replace operation on a character string. The function returns the given expression *expC1*, with occurrences of *expC2* replaced with *expC3*. Replacements start at the *expN1*th occurrence and continue for a total of *expN2* replacements.

STUFF
Syntax

```
STUFF(expC1, expN1, expN2, expC2)
```

The STUFF function inserts or removes characters from any part of a character string. *ExpC1* is the existing character string, *expN1* is the starting position in the string, *expN2* is the number of characters to remove, and *expC2* is the character string to insert.

SUBSTR
Syntax

```
SUBSTR(expC, expN1[, expN2])
```

The SUBSTR function extracts a portion of a string from a character expression. *ExpC* is the character expression to extract the string from, *expN1* is the starting position in the expression, and *expN2* is the number of characters to extract from the expression.

SYS
Syntax

```
SYS(expN)
```

The SYS functions return character-string values that contain various system data. *ExpN* is a numeric value that corresponds to the appropriate system function. The more commonly used system functions are shown here; consult your FoxPro documentation for a complete listing.

SYS(1)	Returns the current system date
SYS(2)	Returns the number of seconds since midnight
SYS(3)	Returns a unique legal file name
SYS(5)	Returns the current default device
SYS(6)	Returns the current print device
SYS(7)	Returns the name of the current format file
SYS(9)	Returns your FoxPro serial number
SYS(12)	Returns the amount of free memory
SYS(13)	Returns the printer status
SYS(23)	Returns the amount of EMS memory used by FoxPro
SYS(24)	Returns the EMS limit specified in CONFIG.FP
SYS(2003)	Returns the current directory name
SYS(2006)	Returns the type of graphics hardware in use

B

TAG
Syntax

```
TAG([.cdx filename,] expN [, alias])
```

The TAG function returns tag names from compound index (.CDX) files, or it returns the names of open index (.IDX) files. The *.cdx filename* argument, when used, lets you return the tag names from a specific compound index file. *ExpN* denotes the order of the tag; if *expN* is 1, the name of the first tag in the compound index file is retrieved; if *expN* is 2, the name of the second tag in the compound index file is retrieved, and so on. Use the *alias* clause to return tag names from index files open in different work areas.

If the *.cdx filename* argument is omitted, the TAG function first returns names of the .IDX files (based on their order specified by the USE command or by the SET INDEX command). Next, the function returns tag names from the structural compound index file, if there is one. Finally, the function returns tag names from other compound index files, in the order that the tags were created and in the order the compound index files were identified with the USE and /or SET INDEX commands.

TAN
Syntax

TAN(*expN*)

The TAN function returns the tangent of *expN,* where *expN* is measured in radians. To convert degrees to radians, use the DTOR function.

TARGET
Syntax

TARGET(*expN*[, *expr*])

The TARGET function returns the alias of the work area that is the target of the *N*th relation from the work area specified by *expr.* Use the optional *expr* to specify another work area by alias, number, or letter. If *expr* is omitted, the current work area is used. If the relation specified by the function does not exist, a 0 is returned.

TIME
Syntax

TIME([*expN*])

The TIME function returns the current system time in the format of HH:MM:SS (if SET HOURS is set to 24) or in the format of HH:MM:SS am/pm (if SET HOURS is set to 12). If you include the numeric argument *expN,* the function's result includes hundredths of a second. (Note, however, that maximum accuracy of the clock is about 1/18th of a second.)

TRANSFORM
Syntax

TRANSFORM(*expression*, *expC*)

The TRANSFORM function formats character strings or numbers with PICTURE options without using the @-SAY command. *Expression* is the variable or field to format; *expC* is a character expression that contains the PICTURE clause.

TRIM
Syntax

TRIM(*expC*)

The TRIM function trims trailing spaces from a character string. If the character string is composed entirely of spaces, TRIM returns a null string. The TRIM function is identical to the RTRIM function.

TYPE
Syntax

TYPE(*expC*)

The TYPE function returns a single character indicating the data type of the expression named in *expC*. The character C denotes character type, L denotes logical type, N denotes numeric type, D denotes date type, M denotes memo type, and U denotes an undefined type.

UPDATED
Syntax

UPDATED()

The UPDATED function returns a logical true (.T.) if any data was changed in the associated GETs when the last READ command was processed.

UPPER
Syntax

UPPER(*expC*)

The UPPER function converts all alphabetic characters in *expC* to uppercase letters. The UPPER function does not change the way the data is stored unless you use the function as part of a STORE or REPLACE command. It is generally used for finding or comparing data when you do not know what case the data was originally entered as.

USED
Syntax

USED([*expression*])

The USED function returns a logical true (.T.) if a database is open in the current work area. Use the optional *expression* to identify a different work area by its alias, number, or letter. If no database is open in the specified work area, a logical false (.F.) is returned.

VAL
Syntax

VAL(*expC*)

The VAL function converts a character expression containing numbers into a numeric value. Starting at the leftmost character and ignoring leading blanks, VAL processes digits until a nonnumeric character is encountered. If the first character of *expC* is not a number, VAL returns a value of 0.

VARREAD
Syntax

VARREAD()

The VARREAD function returns the name of the field or variable currently being edited. The function can be useful when designing context-sensitive help systems, so that different help messages can appear for different fields.

VERSION
Syntax

VERSION()

The VERSION function returns a character string indicating the version number of FoxPro.

WBORDER
Syntax

WBORDER([*window-name*])

The WBORDER function returns a logical true (.T.) if the window specified by *window-name* has a border.

B

WCHILD
Syntax

WCHILD([*windowname* / *expN1*])

The WCHILD function returns the number of child windows in a parent window or the names of the child windows in a parent window. If the names are returned, they are returned in the order that they were stacked in the parent window. The *windowname* argument is the name of the desired window; if this argument is omitted, the function assumes the use of the current window. If a window name is specified, the optional numeric expression *expN1* can also be used. When *expN1* is used, the name of the child window is returned. The value of *expN1* corresponds to the desired child window, varying from 0 (denoting the child window at the bottom of the stack) up to the number of child windows in the stack.

WCOLS
Syntax

WCOLS([*expC*])

The WCOLS function returns the number of columns available in the active window. Use the optional *expC* to name a window other than the currently active window.

WEXIST
Syntax

WEXIST(*expC*)

The WEXIST function returns a logical true (.T.) if the window named in *expC* has been previously defined.

WLAST
Syntax

WLAST([*window-name*])

The WLAST function returns the name of the window that was active prior to the current window, or returns a logical true (.T.) if the named window was active prior to the current window.

WLCOL
Syntax

WLCOL([*window-name*]

The WLCOL function returns a numeric value representing the column location of the upper-left corner of a window. Use the optional *window-name* to identify the window by name. If *window-name* is omitted, the function returns the column location of the upper-left corner of the currently active window.

Because windows can be positioned partially off the screen, it is possible to retrieve negative values from WCOL(). If a window's upper-left corner is located to the left of the screen, negative values are returned by WCOL( ).

WLROW
Syntax

```
WLROW([window-name]
```

The WLROW function returns a numeric value representing the row location of the upper-left corner of a window. Use the optional *window-name* to identify the window by name. If *window-name* is omitted, the function returns the row location of the upper-left corner of the currently active window.

Because windows can be positioned partially off the screen, it is possible to retrieve negative values from WLROW( ). If a window's upper-left corner is located above the top of the screen, negative values are returned by WLROW( ).

WMAXIMUM
Syntax

```
WMAXIMUM[window-name]
```

The WMAXIMUM function returns a logical true (.T.) if the specified window is maximized. If the specified window is not maximized, a logical false (.F.) is returned. If the optional *window-name* is omitted, a logical value is returned indicating whether the currently active window is maximized.

B

WMINIMUM
Syntax

WMINIMUM[*window-name*]

The WMINIMUM function returns a logical true (.T.) if the specified window is minimized. If the specified window is not minimized, a logical false (.F.) is returned. If the optional *window-name* is omitted, a logical value is returned indicating whether the currently active window is minimized.

WONTOP
Syntax

WONTOP([*expC*])

The WONTOP function returns the name of the window that is frontmost on the screen. If the optional *expC* is used to name a window, the function returns a logical true (.T.) if the named window is frontmost.

WOUTPUT
Syntax

WOUTPUT([*expC*])

The WOUTPUT function returns the name of the window currently receiving output. If the optional *expC* is used to name a window, the function returns a logical true (.T.) if output is currently being directed to the window named in *expC*. If output is not being directed to a window, the function returns a null string.

WPARENT
Syntax

WPARENT([*windowname*])

The WPARENT function returns the name of a parent window for a specific child window. The *windowname* argument denotes the child window for which the name of the parent window is desired. If the argument is omitted, the function assumes the use of the current window. If the current window is not a child window, the function returns a null string.

WREAD
Syntax

```
WREAD([window-name])
```

The WREAD function returns a logical true (.T.) if the specified window is participating in the current READ. If the specified window is not involved in the current read, a logical false (.F.) is returned.

B

WROWS
Syntax

```
WROWS([expC])
```

The WROWS function returns the number of rows available in the active window. Use the optional *expC* to return the number of rows available in the window named in *expC*.

WTITLE
Syntax

```
WTITLE([window-name])
```

The WTITLE function returns the title of the specific window named in *window-name*. If the optional *window-name* clause is omitted, WTITLE returns the title of the topmost window.

WVISIBLE

Syntax

WVISIBLE(*expC*)

The WVISIBLE function returns a logical true (.T.) if the window named in *expC* has been activated and is not hidden. The function returns a logical false (.F.) if the window has not been activated, has been deactivated, or is hidden.

YEAR

Syntax

YEAR(*expD*)

The YEAR function returns the numeric year corresponding to the date expression.

CHAPTER

FOXPRO

DBASE COMMANDS NOT SUPPORTED BY FOXPRO

While FoxPro is compatible with dBase IV and dBase III Plus, some commands in the dBase language are specific to dBase IV, and hence are not supported by FoxPro.

The following dBASE IV commands are not supported by FoxPro 2.5 at the time of this writing.

ASSIST
BEGIN TRANSACTION
CONVERT
CREATE APPLICATION
DEBUG
DISPLAY HISTORY
DISPLAY USERS
END TRANSACTION
LOGOUT
MODIFY APPLICATION
MODIFY VIEW
PROTECT
RESET
ROLLBACK
SET CATALOG ON/OFF
SET CATALOG TO
SET DESIGN
SET ENCRYPTION
SET HISTORY
SET INSTRUCT
SET MENU
SET PRECISION
SET SQL
SET TITLE
SET TRAP

Note that FoxPro versions 1.*x* do not support the dBASE commands just listed and do not support the following additional dBASE commands.

COPY INDEXES
COPY TAG
CREATE QUERY
CREATE SCREEN
DELETE TAG
EXPORT TO
IMPORT FROM
MODIFY QUERY

MODIFY SCREEN
SET DEBUG
SET DELIMITERS
SET REFRESH
SET REPROCESS
SET SCOREBOARD
SET SKIP
UNLOCK

C

INDEX

D

F

M

N

Z